Kamisama Kiss ♥

Story & Art by
Julietta Suzuki

CHARACTERS

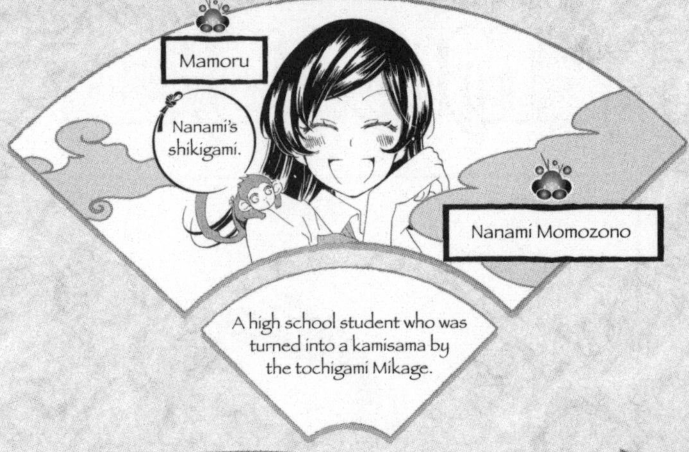
Mamoru
Nanami's shikigami.
Nanami Momozono
A high school student who was turned into a kamisama by the tochigami Mikage.

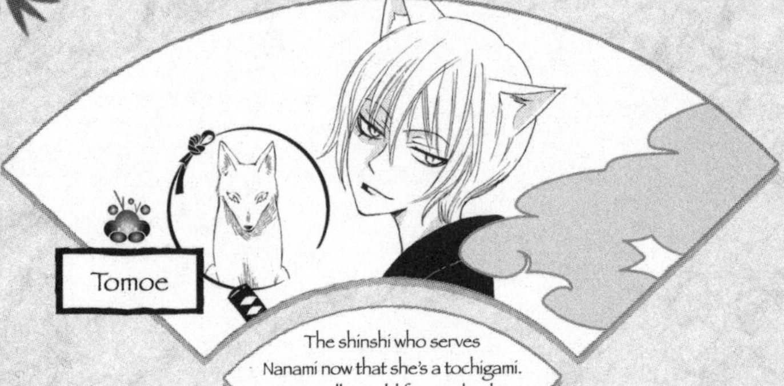
Tomoe
The shinshi who serves Nanami now that she's a tochigami. Originally a wild fox ayakashi. He was recently transformed into a fox...

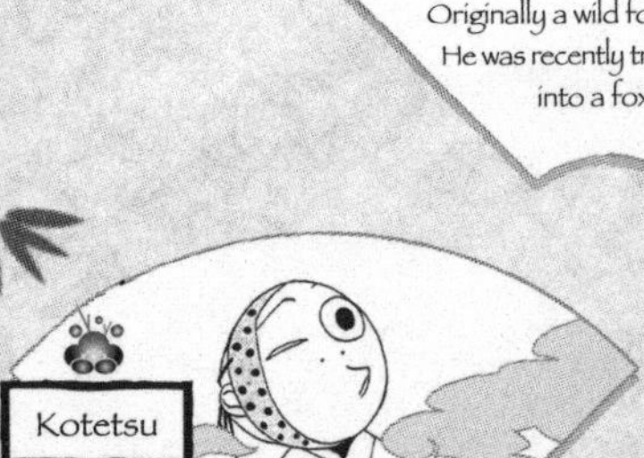
Kotetsu
Onibi-warashi, spirit of the Mikage shrine.

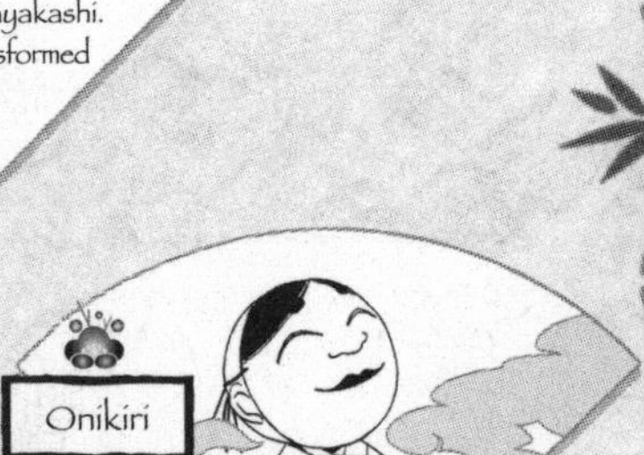
Onikiri
Onibi-warashi, spirit of the Mikage shrine.

This is the last page.

In keeping with the original Japanese comic format, this book reads from right to left—so action, sound effects, and word balloons are completely reversed. This preserves the orientation of the original artwork—plus, it's fun! Check out the diagram shown here to get the hang of things, and then turn to the other side of the book to get started!

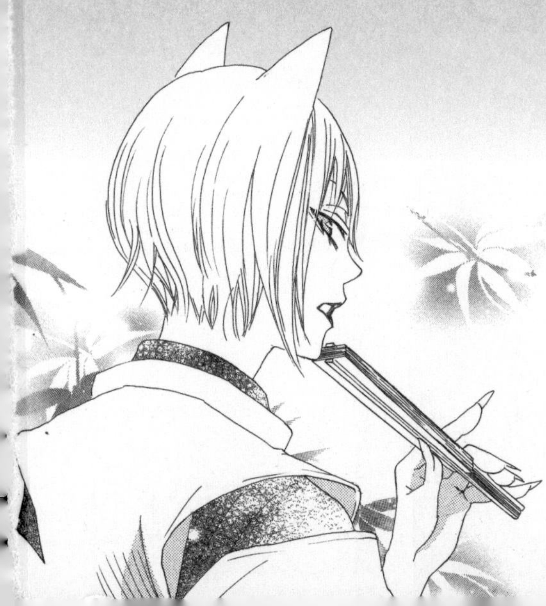

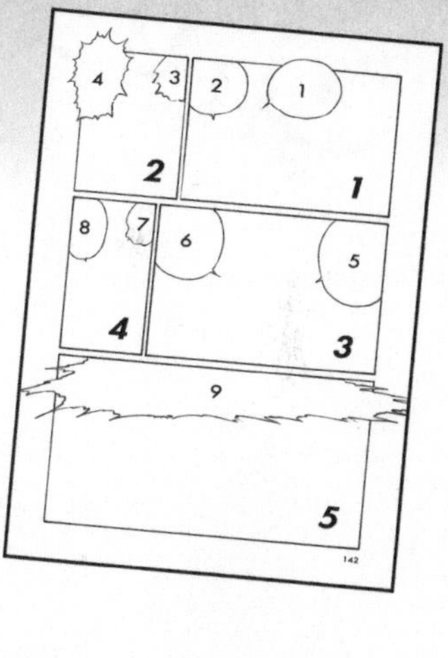
1
2
3
4
1
2
5
6
3
7
8
4
9
5
142

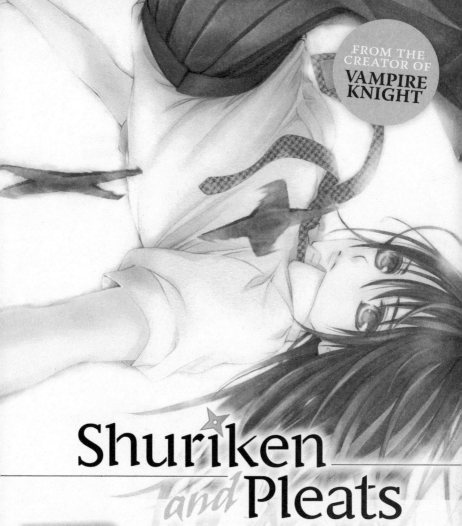

FROM THE
CREATOR OF
**VAMPIRE
KNIGHT**

Shuriken
and Pleats

When the master she has sworn to protect is killed, Mikage Kirio,
a skilled ninja, travels to Japan to start a new, peaceful life for
herself. But as soon as she arrives, she finds herself fighting to
protect the life of Mahito Wakashimatsu, a man who is under
attack by a band of ninja. From that time on, Mikage is drawn
deeper into the machinations of his powerful family.

www.viz.com

RATED
T
FOR
TEEN
ratings.viz.com

Shuriken to Pleats © Matsuri Hino 2015/HAKUSENSHA, Inc.

IDOL dreams

STORY & ART BY
ARINA TANEMURA

At age 31, office worker Chikage Deguchi feels she missed her chances at love and success. When word gets out that she's a virgin, Chikage is humiliated and wishes she could turn back time to when she was still young and popular. She takes an experimental drug that changes her appearance back to when she was 15. Now Chikage is determined to pursue everything she missed out on all those years ago—including becoming a star!

www.viz.com

Behind the Scenes!!

STORY AND ART BY **BISCO HATORI**

From the creator of
Ouran High School Host Club

Ranmaru Kurisu comes from a family of hardy, rough-and-tumble fisherfolk and he sticks out at home like a delicate, artistic sore thumb. It's given him a raging inferiority complex and a permanently pessimistic outlook. Now that he's in college, he's hoping to find a sense of belonging. But after a whole life of being left out, does he even know how to fit in?!

KAMISAMA KISS
VOL. 22
Shojo Beat Edition

STORY AND ART BY
Julietta Suzuki

English Translation & Adaptation/Tomo Kimura
Touch-up Art & Lettering/Joanna Estep
Design/Yukiko Whitley, Sarah Richardson
Editor/Pancha Diaz

KAMISAMA HAJIMEMASHITA by Julietta Suzuki
© Julietta Suzuki 2015
All rights reserved.
First published in Japan in 2015 by HAKUSENSHA, Inc., Tokyo.
English language translation rights arranged with
HAKUSENSHA, Inc., Tokyo.

The stories, characters and incidents mentioned
in this publication are entirely fictional.

Printed in the U.S.A.

Published by VIZ Media, LLC
P.O. Box 77010
San Francisco, CA 94107

10 9 8 7 6 5 4 3 2 1
First printing, October 2016

www.viz.com   www.shojobeat.com

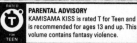

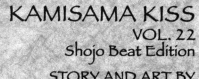
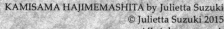
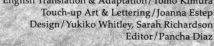

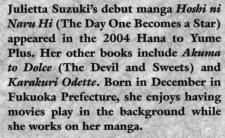

Julietta Suzuki's debut manga *Hoshi ni Naru Hi* (The Day One Becomes a Star) appeared in the 2004 Hana to Yume Plus. Her other books include *Akuma to Dolce* (The Devil and Sweets) and *Karakuri Odette*. Born in December in Fukuoka Prefecture, she enjoys having movies play in the background while she works on her manga.

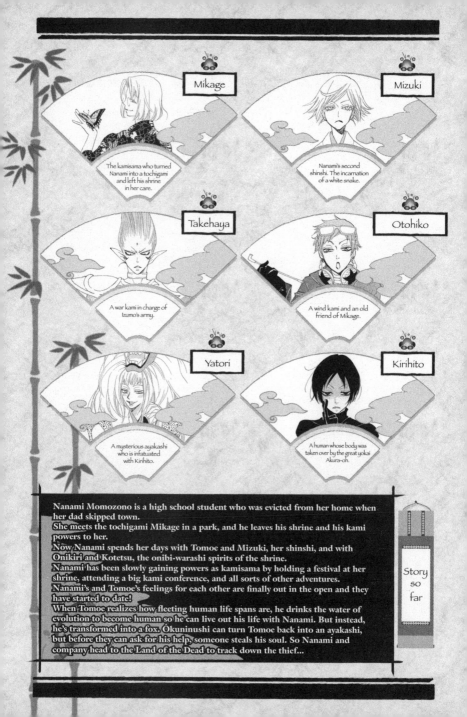

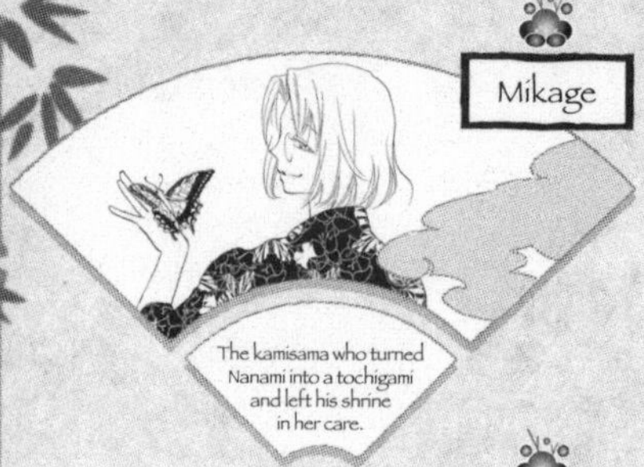
Mikage
The kamisama who turned Nanami into a tochigami and left his shrine in her care.

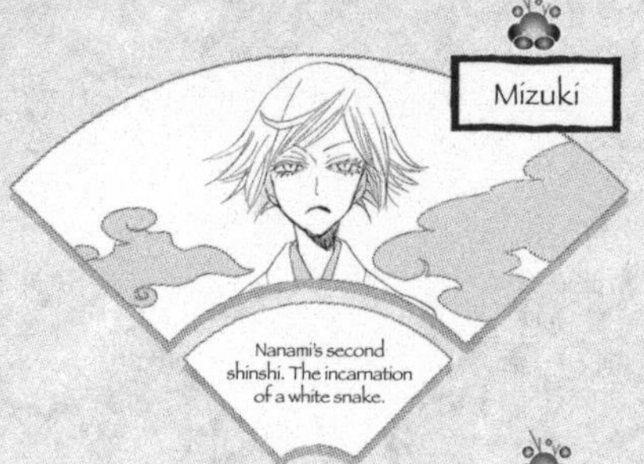
Mizuki
Nanami's second shinshi. The incarnation of a white snake.

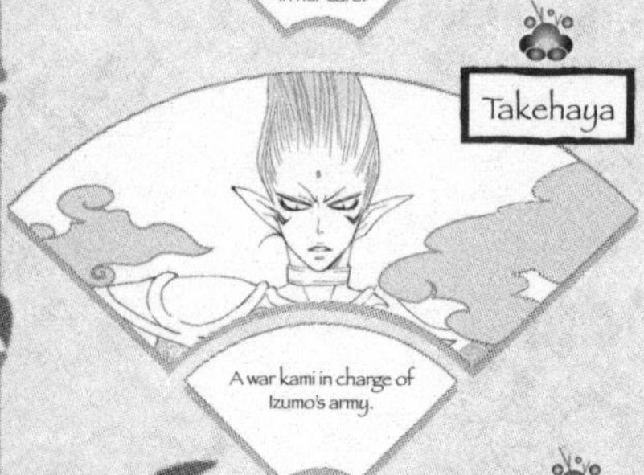
Takehaya
A war kami in charge of Izumo's army.

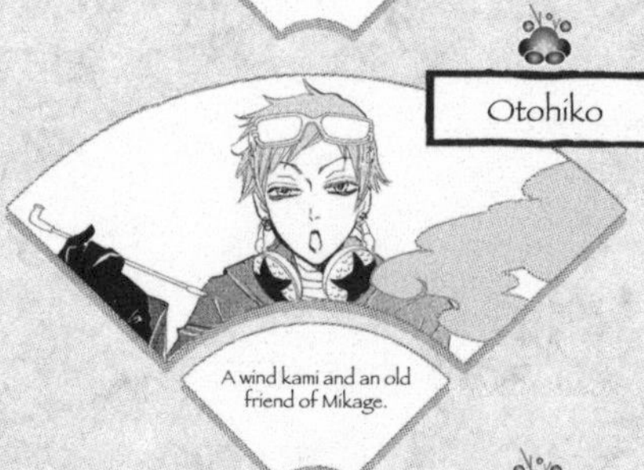
Otohiko
A wind kami and an old friend of Mikage.

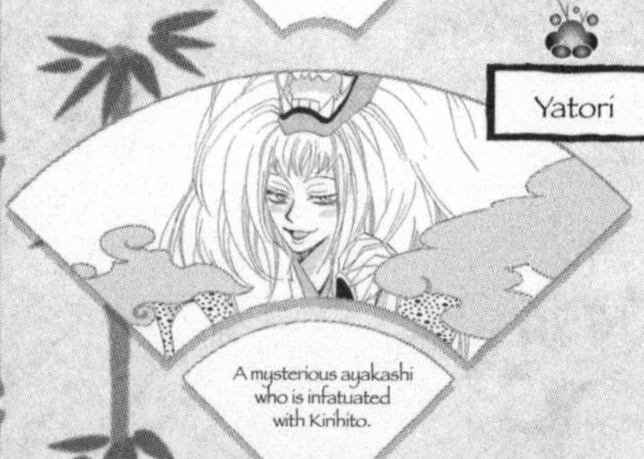
Yatori
A mysterious ayakashi who is infatuated with Kirihito.

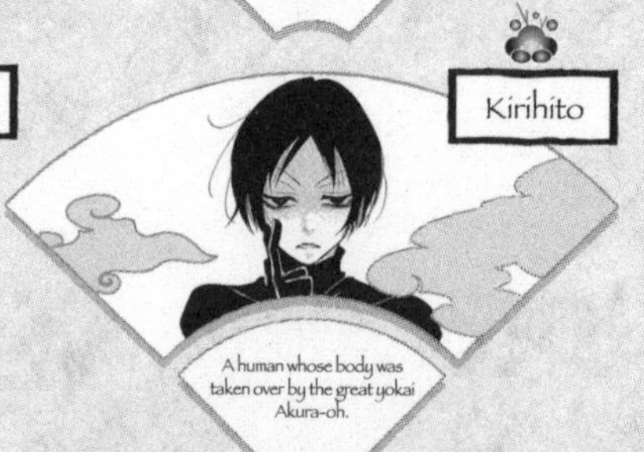
Kirihito
A human whose body was taken over by the great yokai Akura-oh.

Story so far

Nanami Momozono is a high school student who was evicted from her home when her dad skipped town.
She meets the tochigami Mikage in a park, and he leaves his shrine and his kami powers to her.
Now Nanami spends her days with Tomoe and Mizuki, her shinshi, and with Onikiri and Kotetsu, the onibi-warashi spirits of the shrine.
Nanami has been slowly gaining powers as kamisama by holding a festival at her shrine, attending a big kami conference, and all sorts of other adventures.
Nanami's and Tomoe's feelings for each other are finally out in the open and they have started to date!
When Tomoe realizes how fleeting human life spans are, he drinks the water of evolution to become human so he can live out his life with Nanami. But instead, he's transformed into a fox. Ôkuninushi can turn Tomoe back into an ayakashi, but before they can ask for his help, someone steals his soul. So Nanami and company head to the Land of the Dead to track down the thief...

Kamisama Kiss

Volume 22
CONTENTS

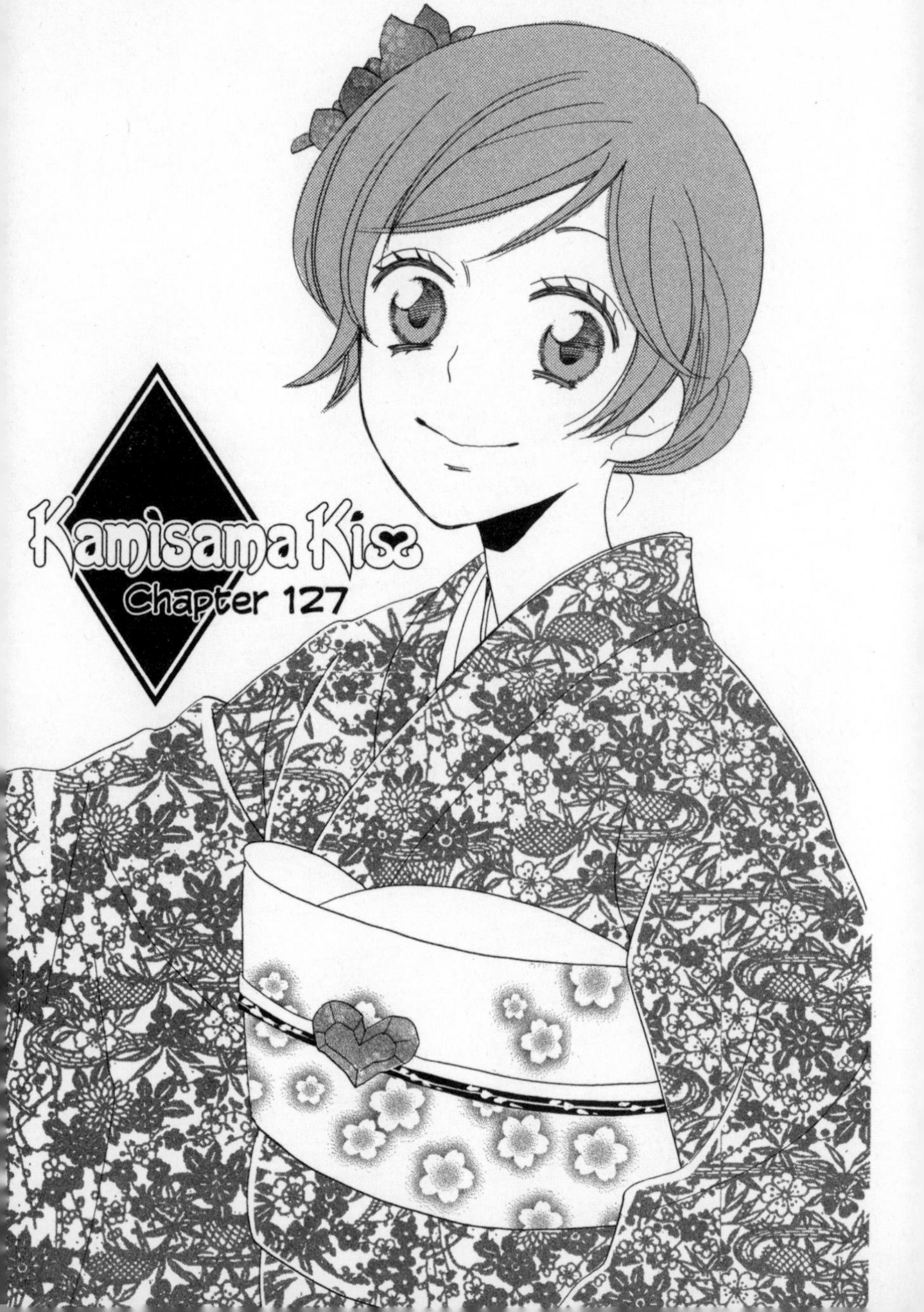
Kamisama Kiss
Chapter 127

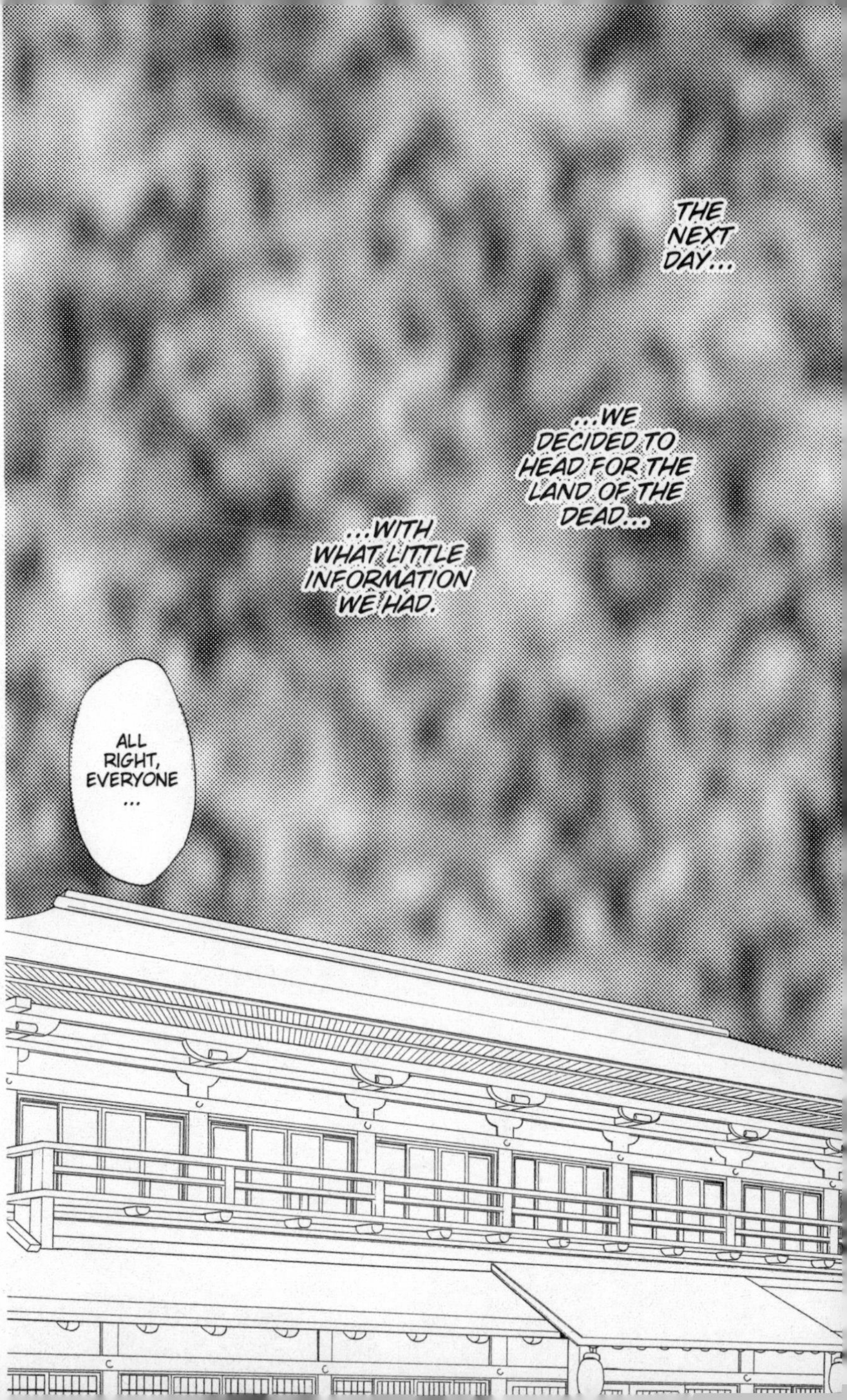
THE NEXT DAY...
...WE DECIDED TO HEAD FOR THE LAND OF THE DEAD...
...WITH WHAT LITTLE INFORMATION WE HAD.
ALL RIGHT, EVERYONE ...

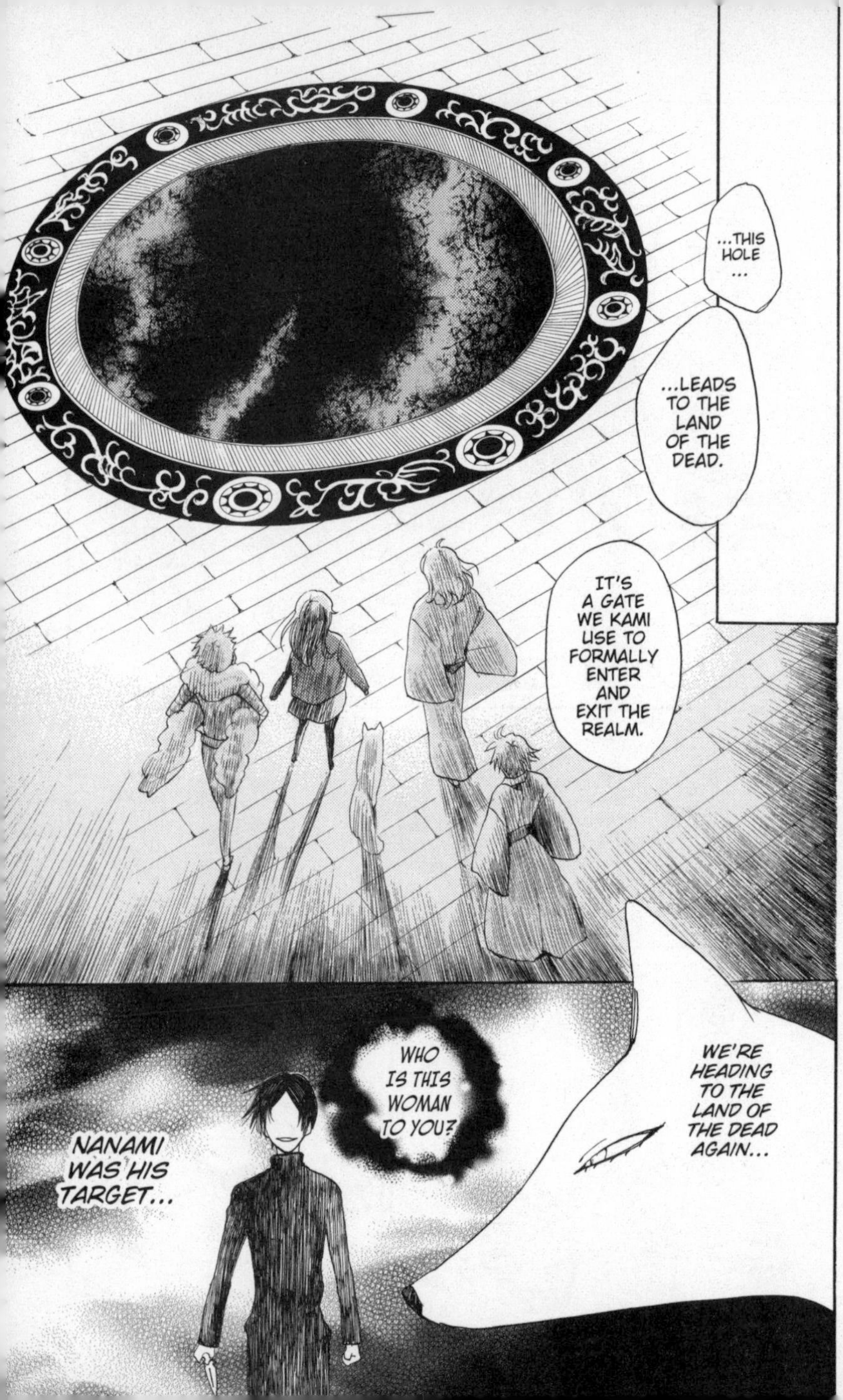
...THIS HOLE ...
...LEADS TO THE LAND OF THE DEAD.
IT'S A GATE WE KAMI USE TO FORMALLY ENTER AND EXIT THE REALM.
WE'RE HEADING TO THE LAND OF THE DEAD AGAIN...
WHO IS THIS WOMAN TO YOU?
NANAMI WAS HIS TARGET...

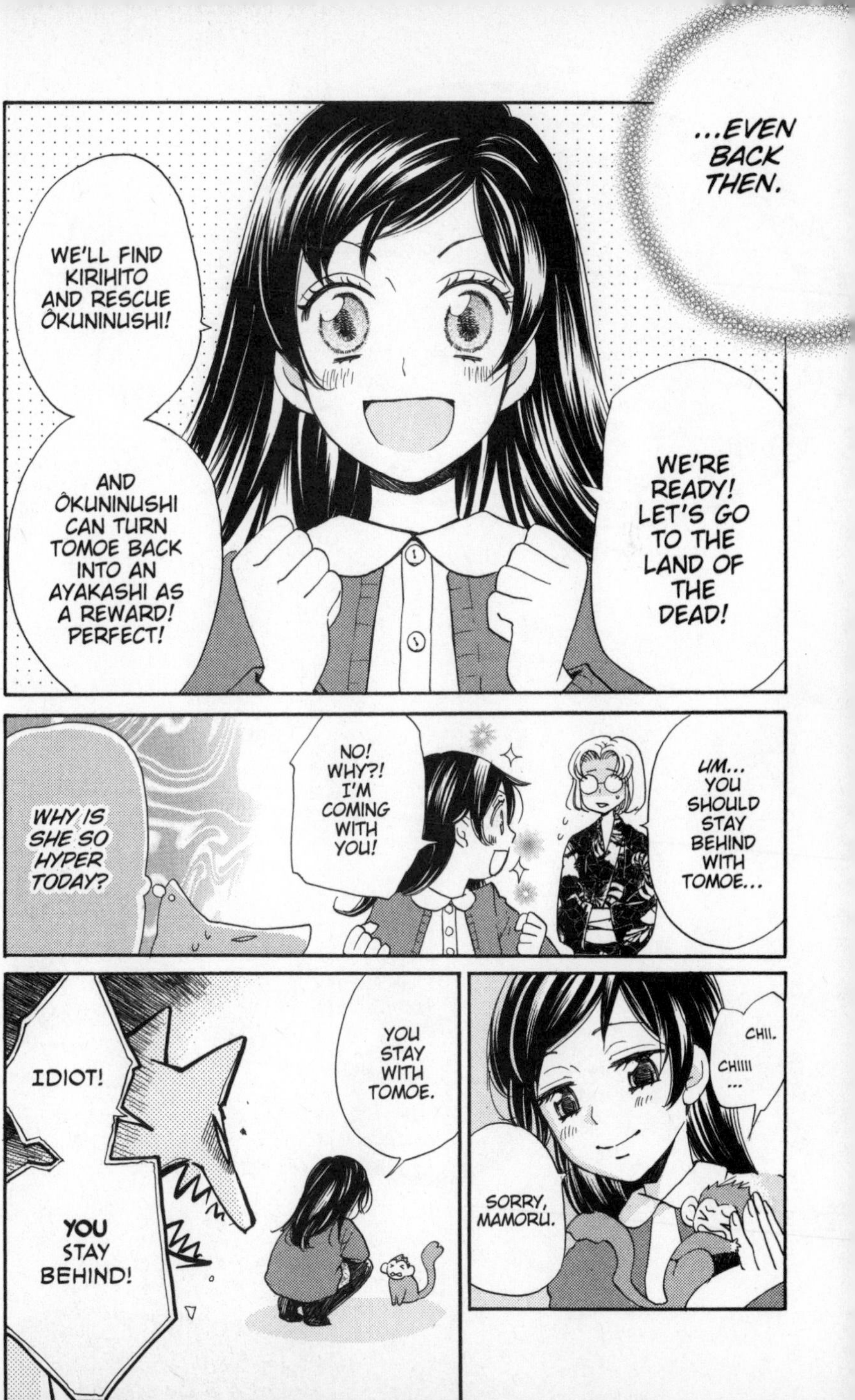
...EVEN BACK THEN.
WE'RE READY! LET'S GO TO THE LAND OF THE DEAD!
WE'LL FIND KIRIHITO AND RESCUE ÔKUNINUSHI!
AND ÔKUNINUSHI CAN TURN TOMOE BACK INTO AN AYAKASHI AS A REWARD! PERFECT!
UM... YOU SHOULD STAY BEHIND WITH TOMOE...
NO! WHY?! I'M COMING WITH YOU!
WHY IS SHE SO HYPER TODAY?
CHII.
CHIIII ...
SORRY, MAMORU.
YOU STAY WITH TOMOE.
IDIOT!
YOU STAY BEHIND!

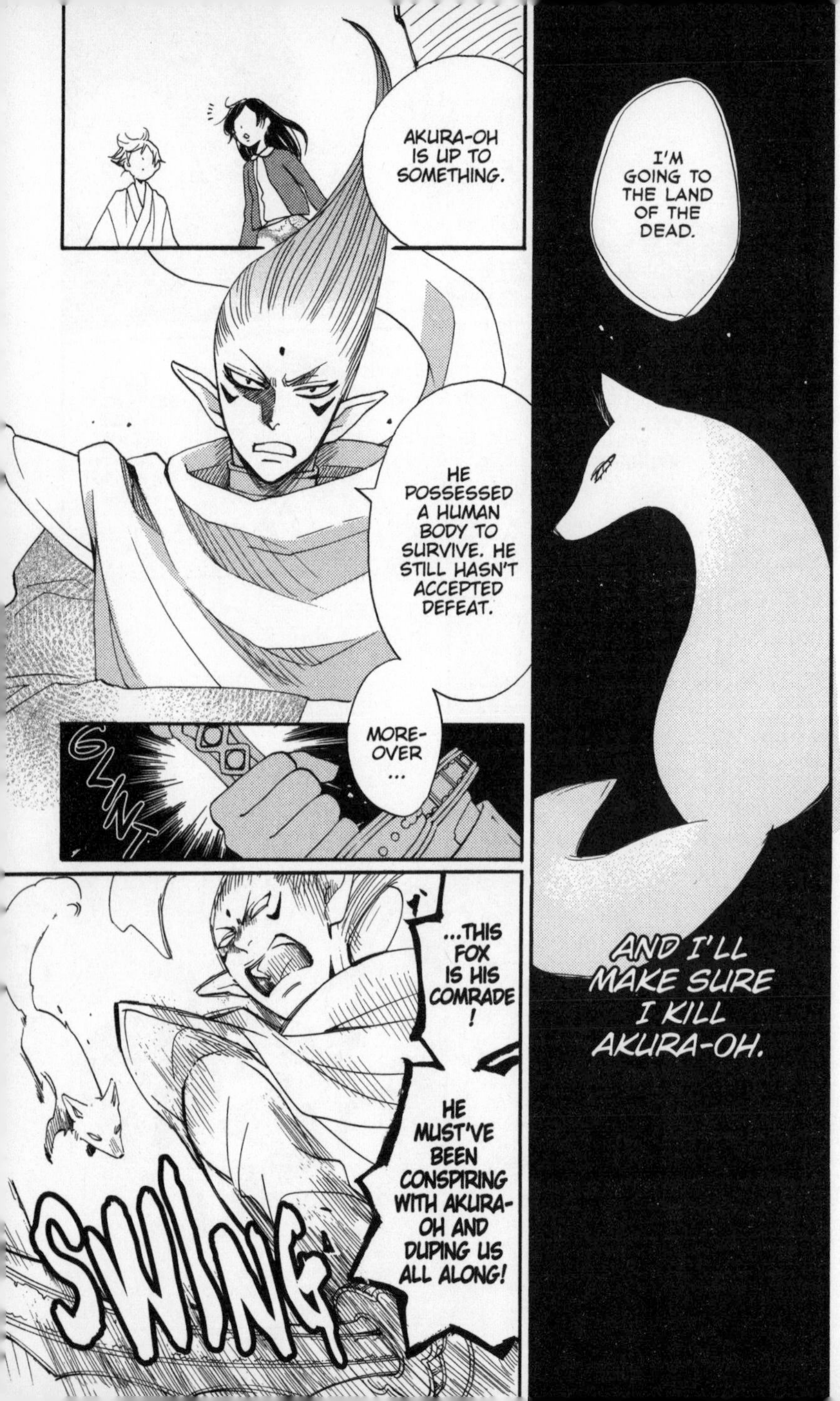
I'M GOING TO THE LAND OF THE DEAD.
AND I'LL MAKE SURE I KILL AKURA-OH.
AKURA-OH IS UP TO SOMETHING.
HE POSSESSED A HUMAN BODY TO SURVIVE. HE STILL HASN'T ACCEPTED DEFEAT.
MORE-OVER ...
GLINT
...THIS FOX IS HIS COMRADE!
HE MUST'VE BEEN CONSPIRING WITH AKURA-OH AND DUPING US ALL ALONG!
SWING

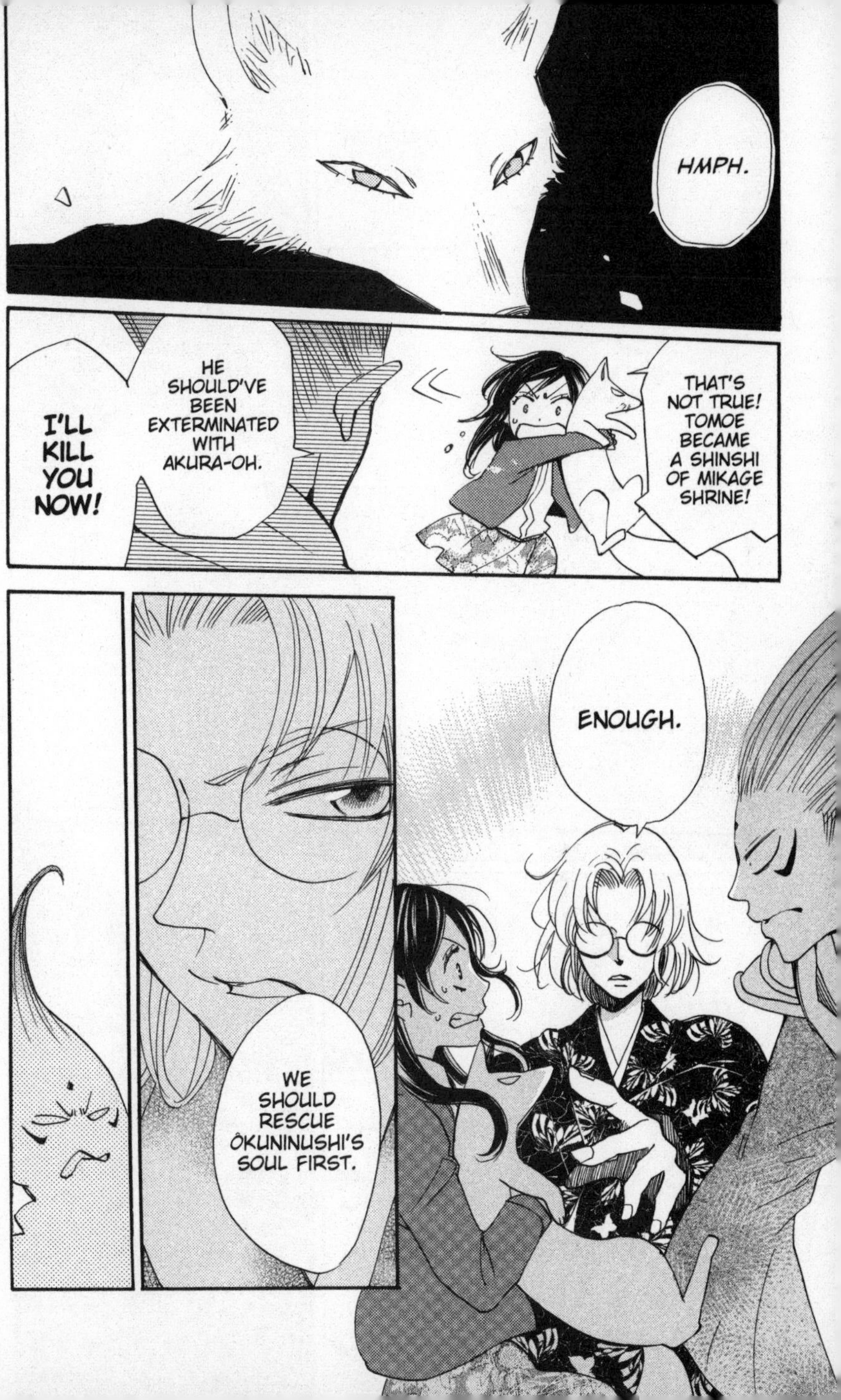
HMPH.
THAT'S NOT TRUE! TOMOE BECAME A SHINSHI OF MIKAGE SHRINE!
HE SHOULD'VE BEEN EXTERMINATED WITH AKURA-OH.
I'LL KILL YOU NOW!
ENOUGH.
WE SHOULD RESCUE ÔKUNINUSHI'S SOUL FIRST.

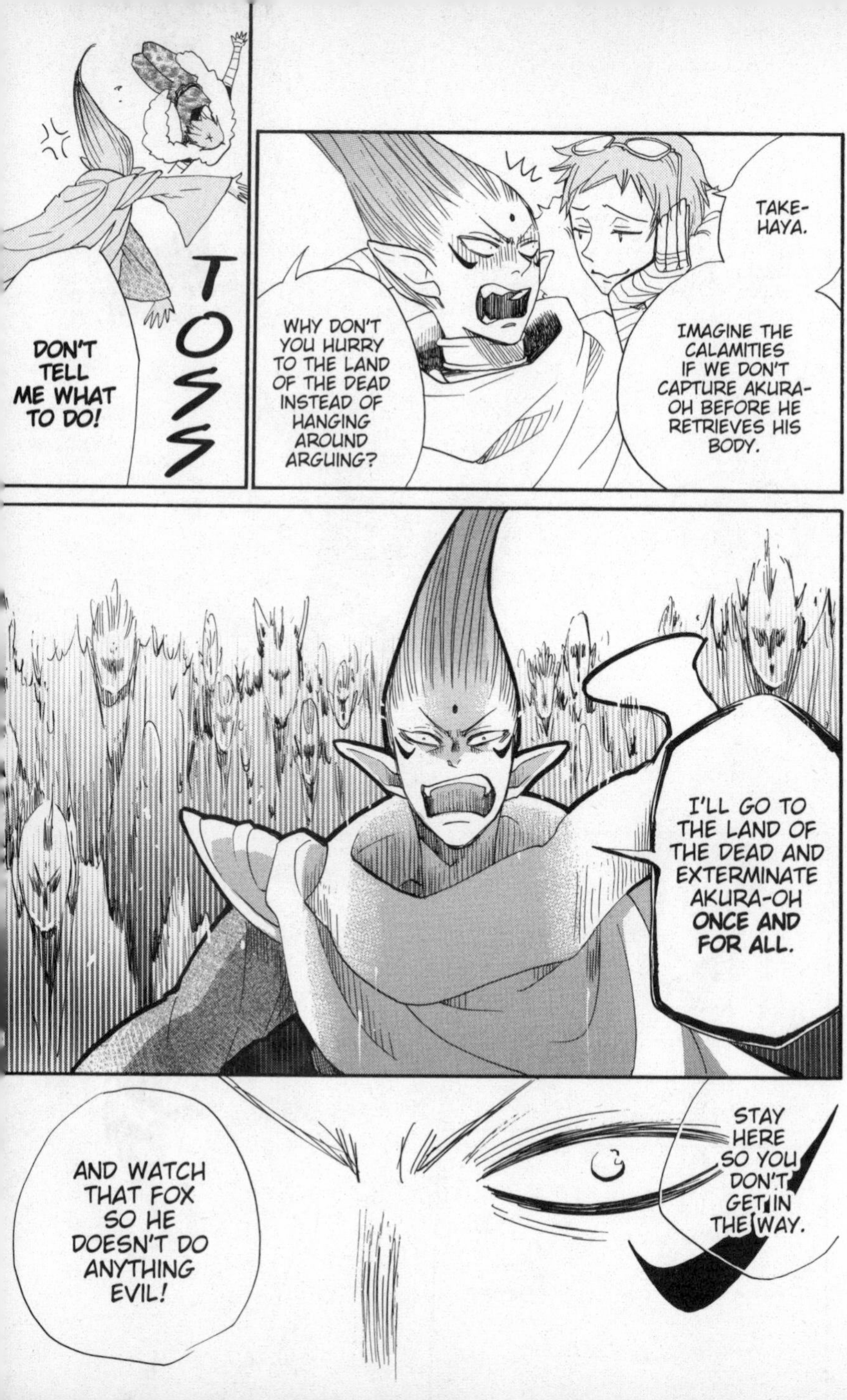
TAKE-HAYA.
IMAGINE THE CALAMITIES IF WE DON'T CAPTURE AKURA-OH BEFORE HE RETRIEVES HIS BODY.
WHY DON'T YOU HURRY TO THE LAND OF THE DEAD INSTEAD OF HANGING AROUND ARGUING?
TOSS
DON'T TELL ME WHAT TO DO!
I'LL GO TO THE LAND OF THE DEAD AND EXTERMINATE AKURA-OH ONCE AND FOR ALL.
STAY HERE SO YOU DON'T GET IN THE WAY.
AND WATCH THAT FOX SO HE DOESN'T DO ANYTHING EVIL!

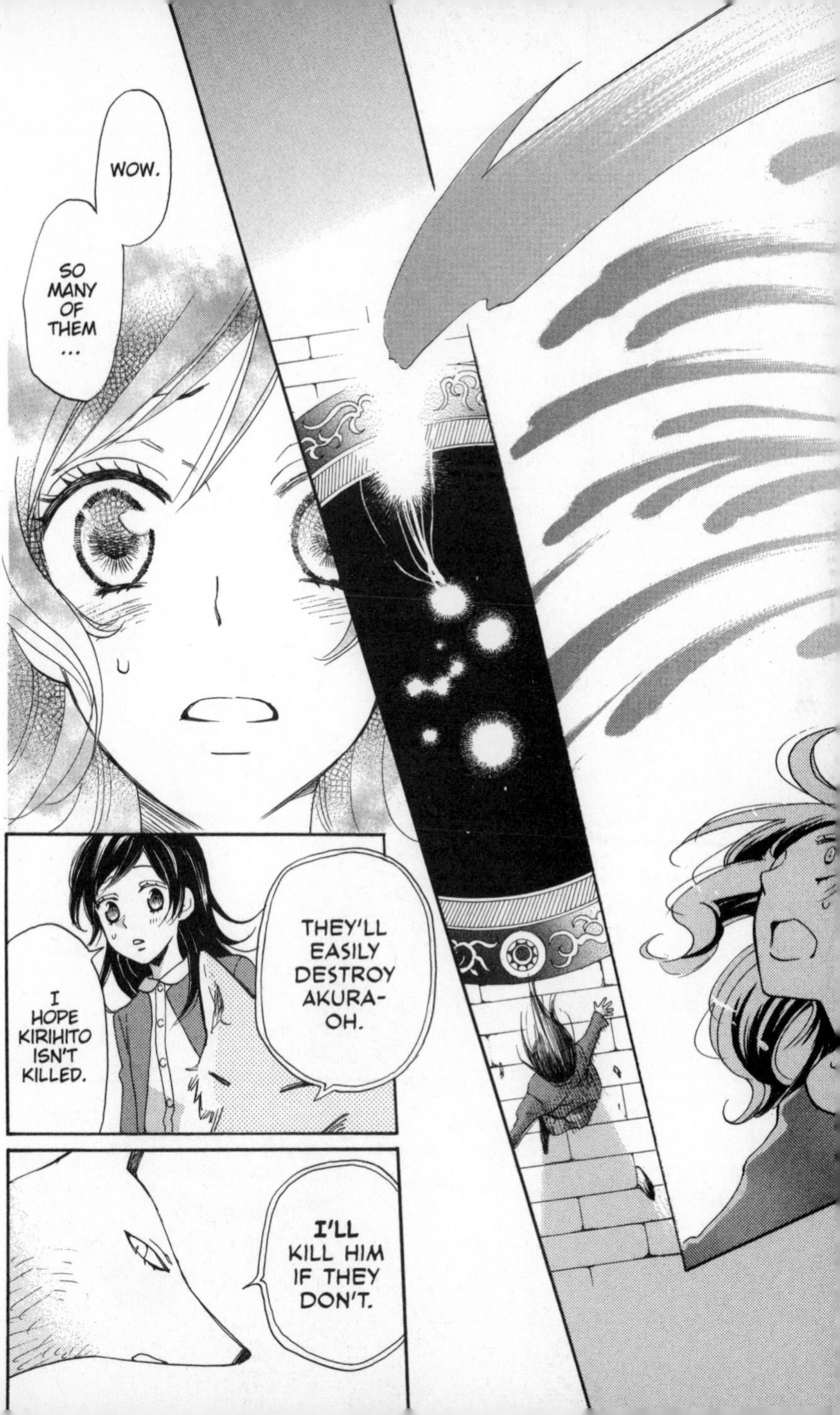
WOW.
SO MANY OF THEM...
THEY'LL EASILY DESTROY AKURA-OH.
I HOPE KIRIHITO ISN'T KILLED.
I'LL KILL HIM IF THEY DON'T.

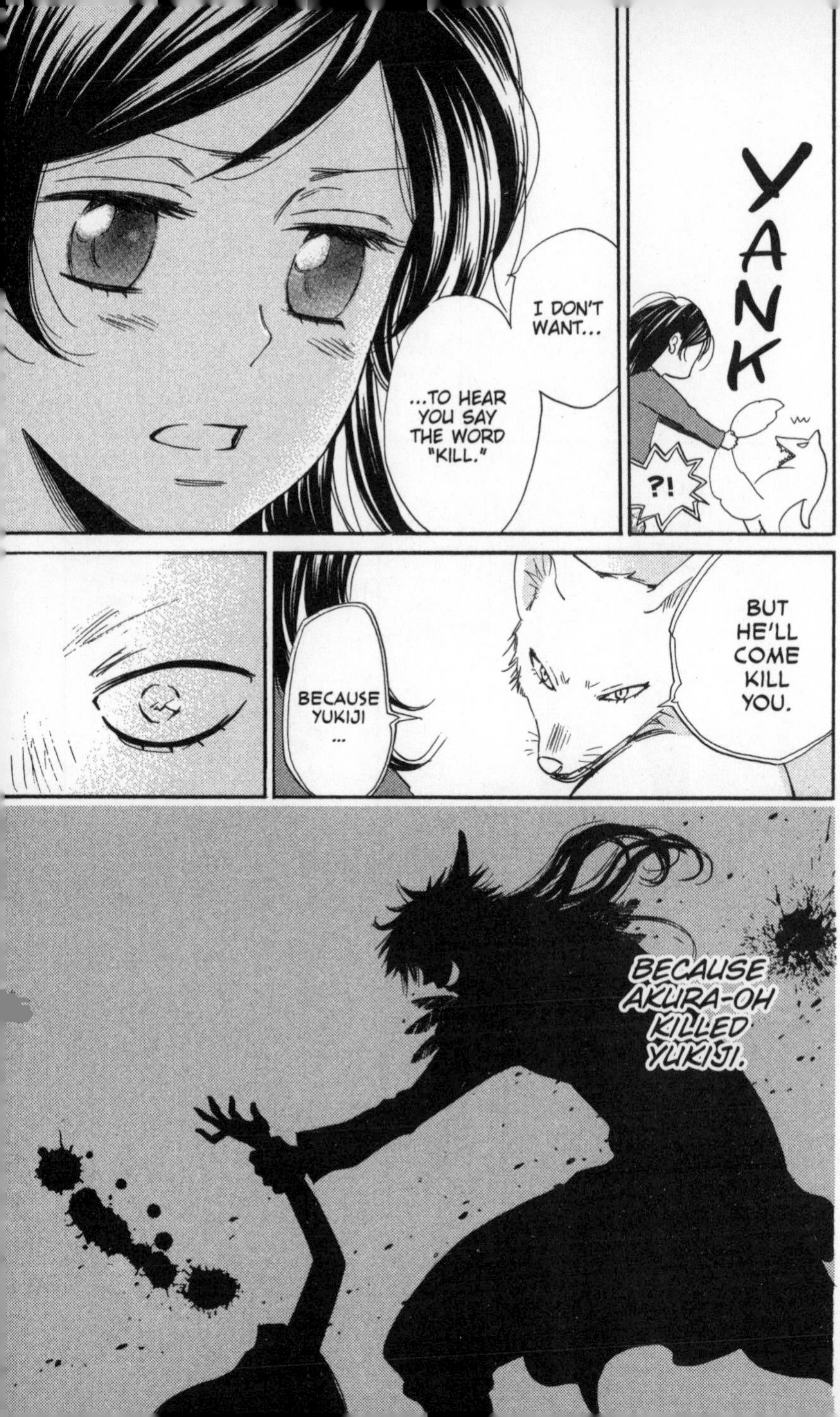
YANK
?!
I DON'T WANT...
...TO HEAR YOU SAY THE WORD "KILL."
BUT HE'LL COME KILL YOU.
BECAUSE YUKIJI ...
BECAUSE AKURA-OH KILLED YUKIJI.

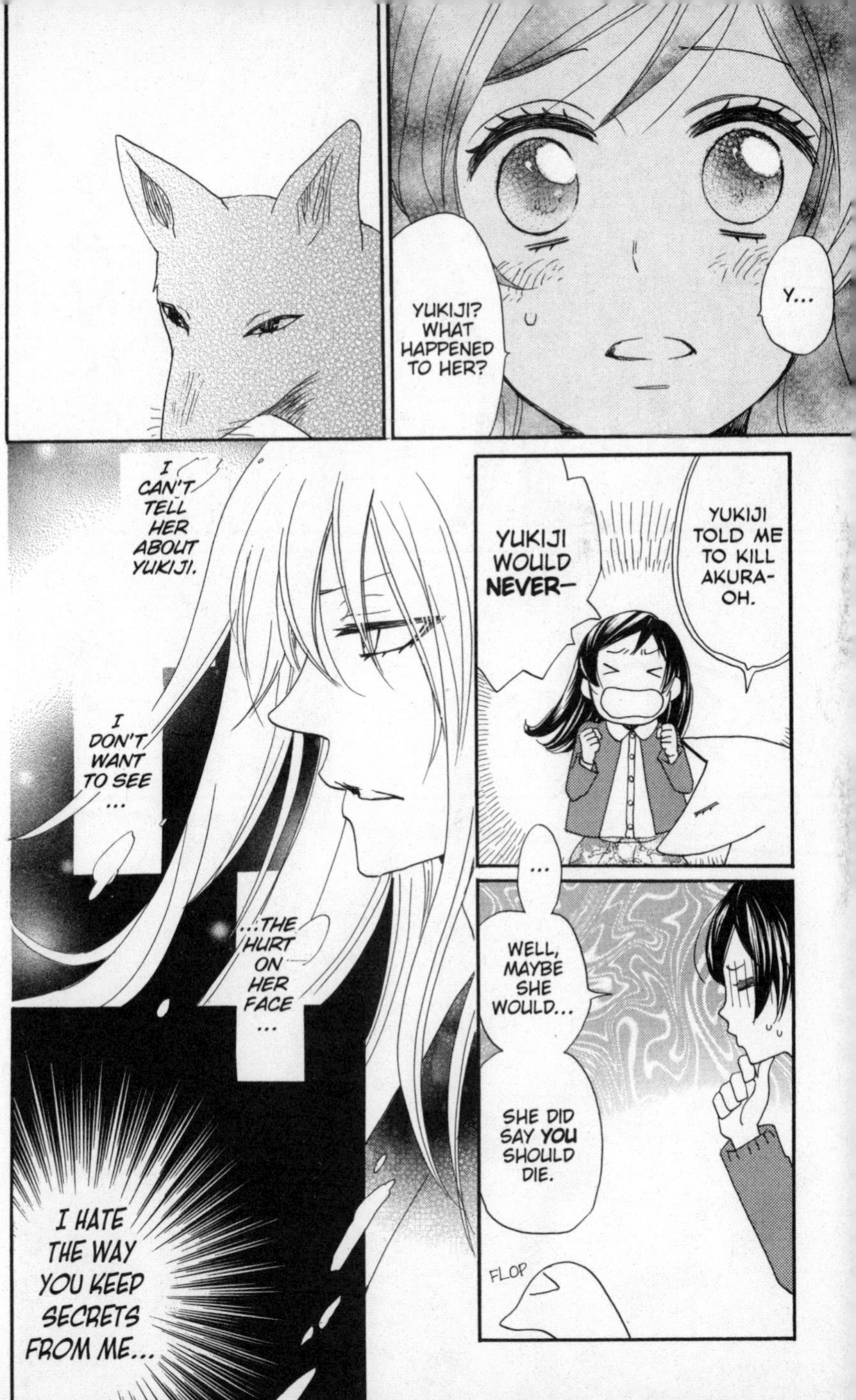
Y...
YUKIJI? WHAT HAPPENED TO HER?
YUKIJI TOLD ME TO KILL AKURA-OH.
YUKIJI WOULD **NEVER**—
...
WELL, MAYBE SHE WOULD...
SHE DID SAY **YOU** SHOULD DIE.
FLOP
I CAN'T TELL HER ABOUT YUKIJI.
I DON'T WANT TO SEE...
...THE HURT ON HER FACE...
I HATE THE WAY YOU KEEP SECRETS FROM ME...

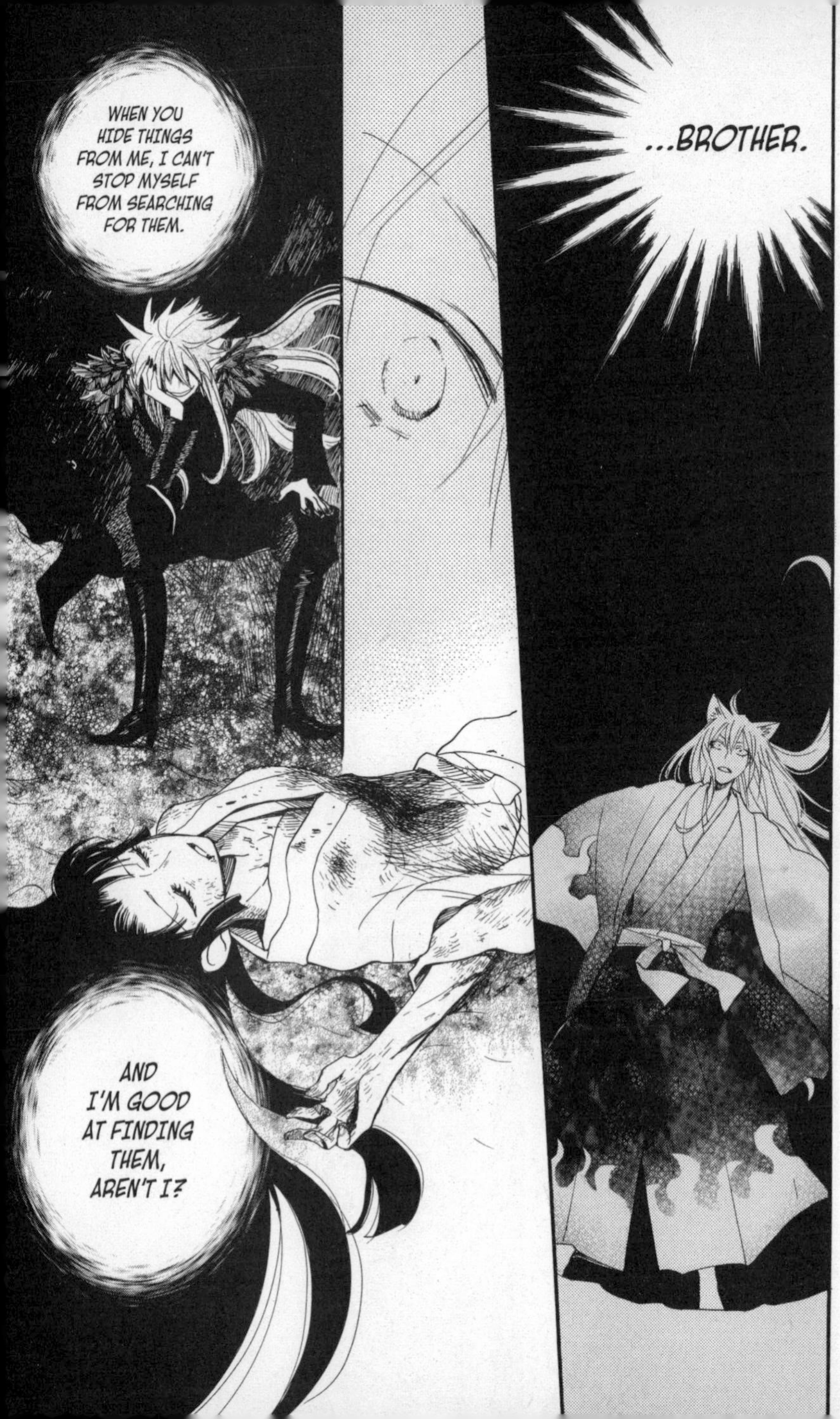
...BROTHER.
WHEN YOU HIDE THINGS FROM ME, I CAN'T STOP MYSELF FROM SEARCHING FOR THEM.
AND I'M GOOD AT FINDING THEM, AREN'T I?

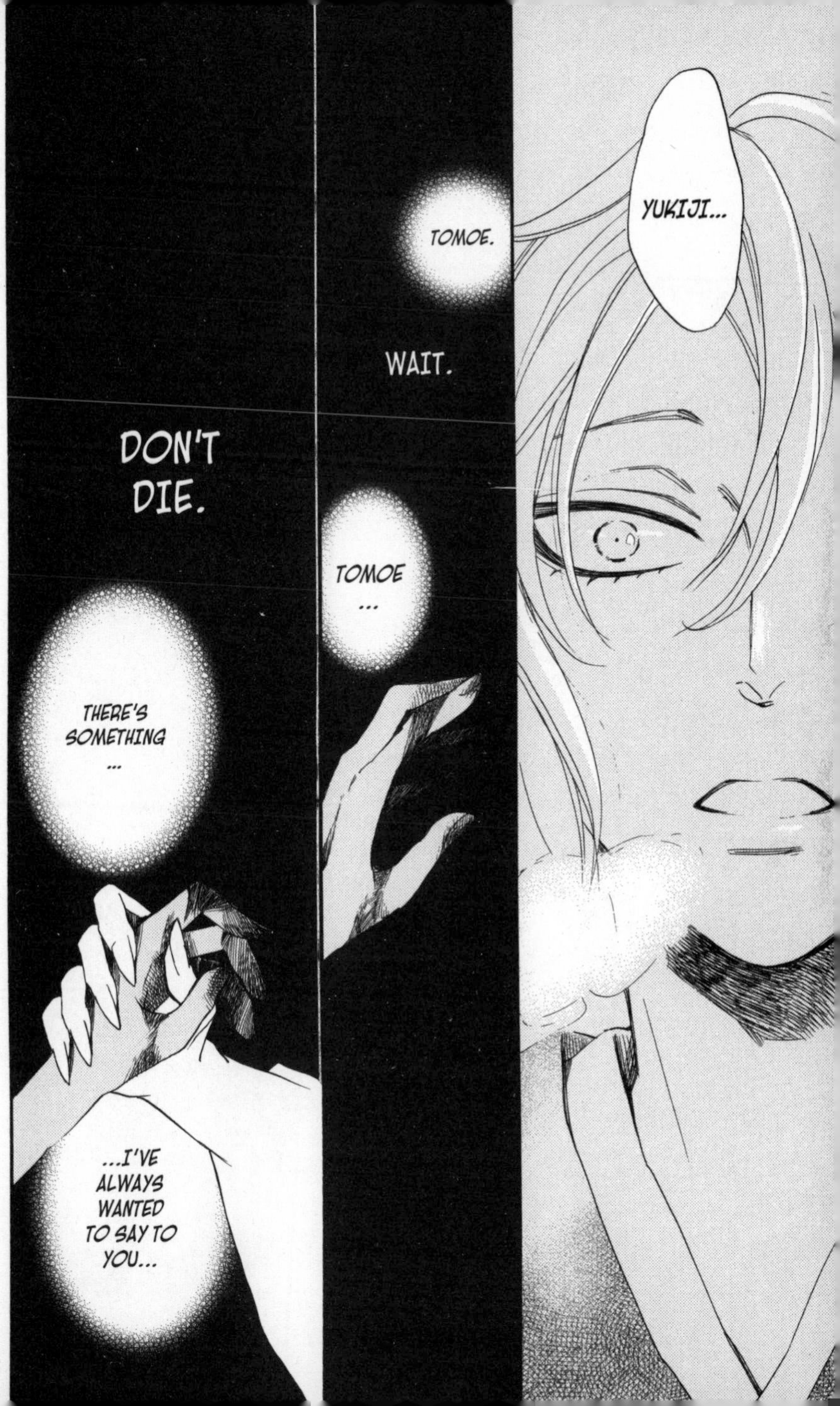
YUKIJI...
TOMOE.
WAIT.
TOMOE ...
DON'T DIE.
THERE'S SOMETHING ...
...I'VE ALWAYS WANTED TO SAY TO YOU...

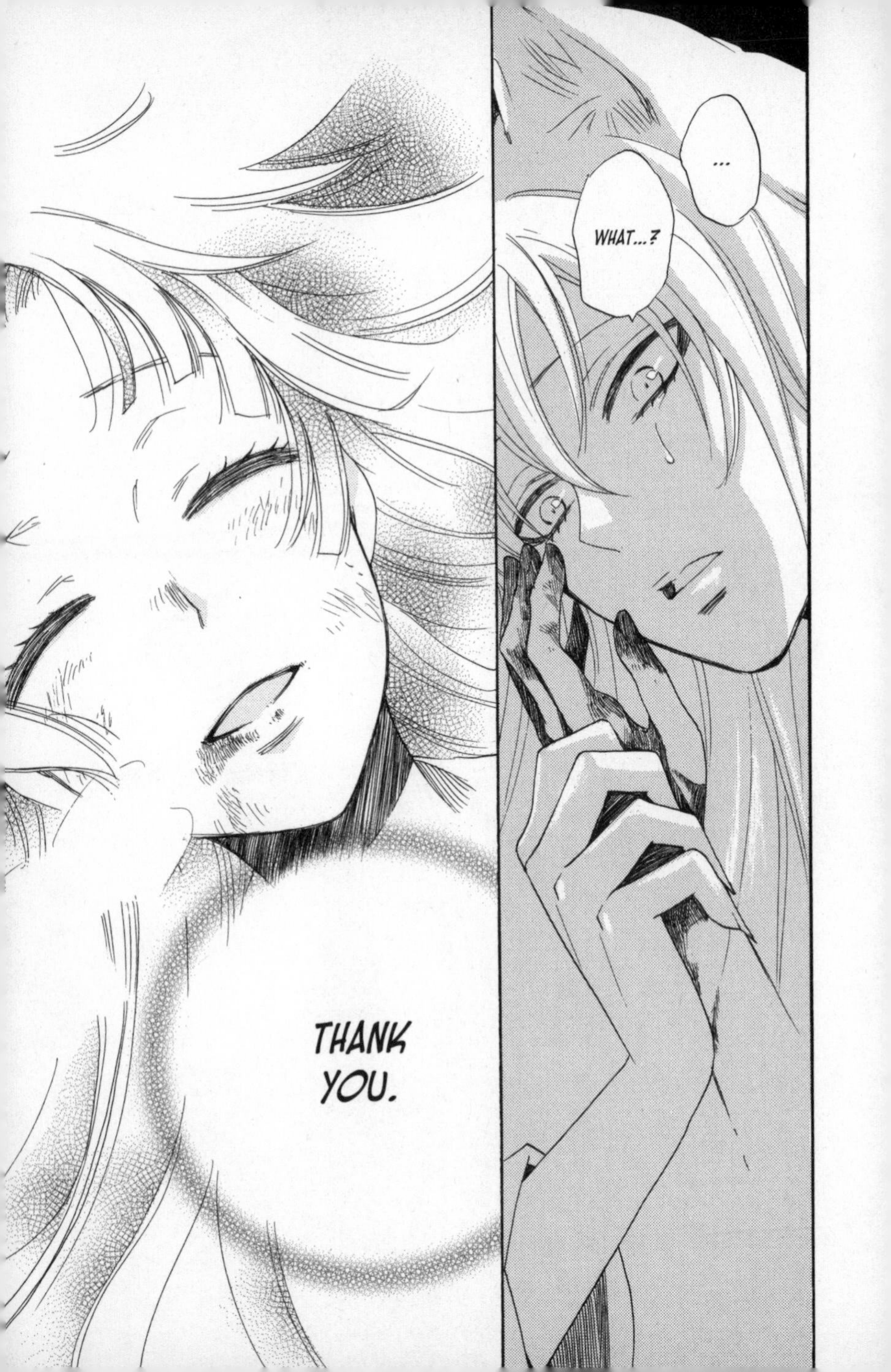
...
WHAT...?
THANK YOU.

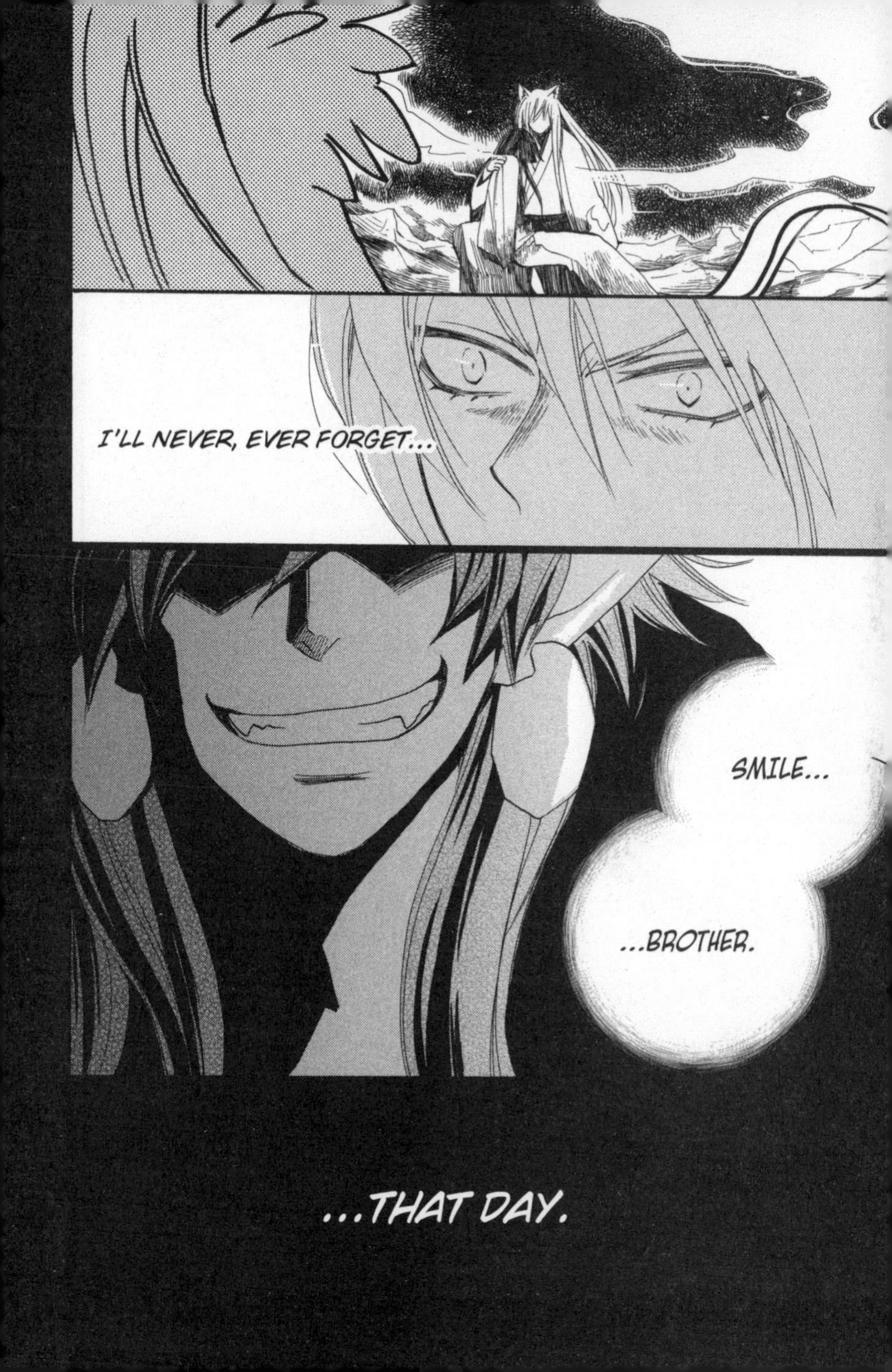
I'LL NEVER, EVER FORGET...
SMILE...
...BROTHER.
...THAT DAY.

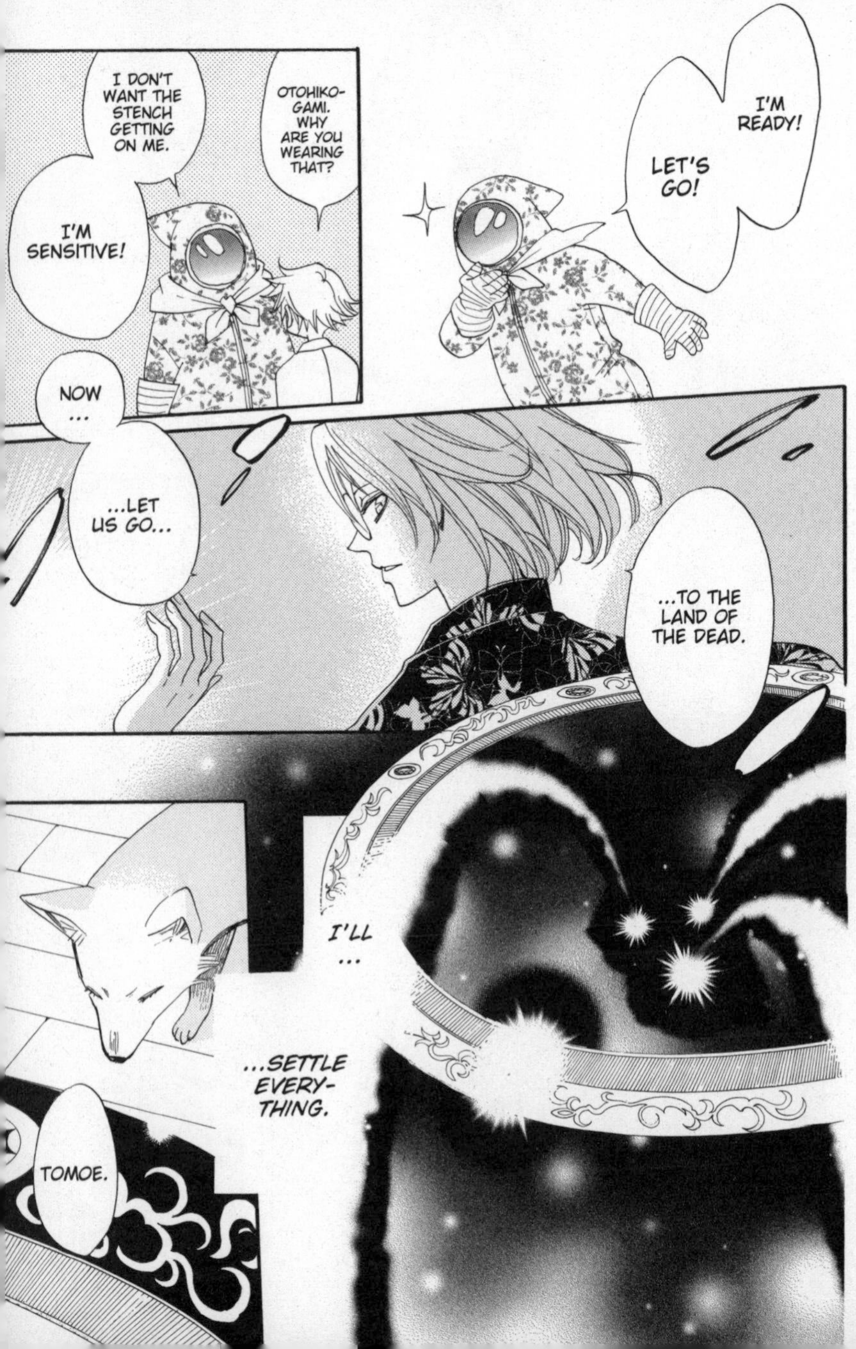
I'M READY!
LET'S GO!
OTOHIKO-GAMI. WHY ARE YOU WEARING THAT?
I DON'T WANT THE STENCH GETTING ON ME.
I'M SENSITIVE!
NOW...
...LET US GO...
...TO THE LAND OF THE DEAD.
I'LL...
...SETTLE EVERY-THING.
TOMOE.

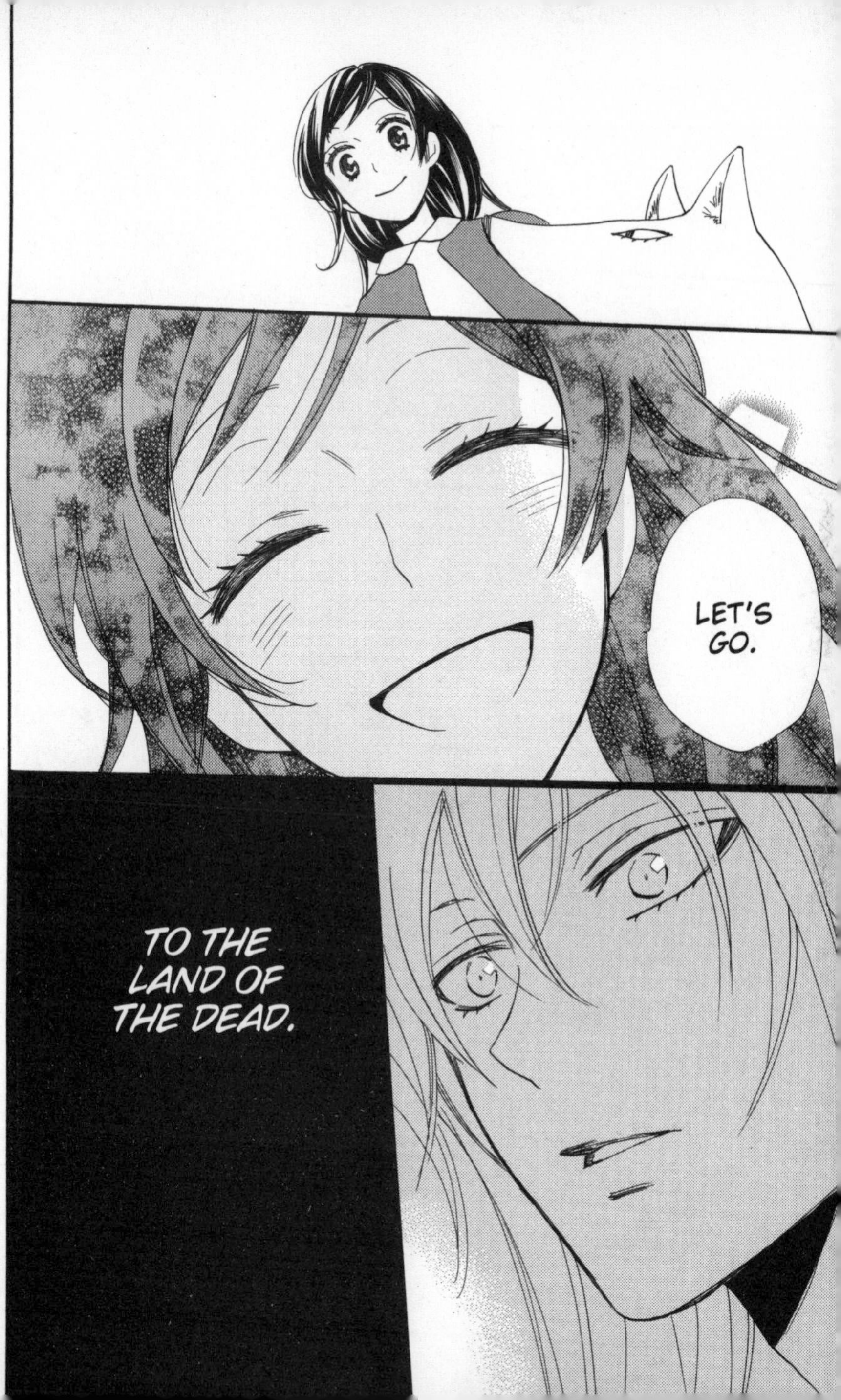
LET'S GO.
TO THE LAND OF THE DEAD.

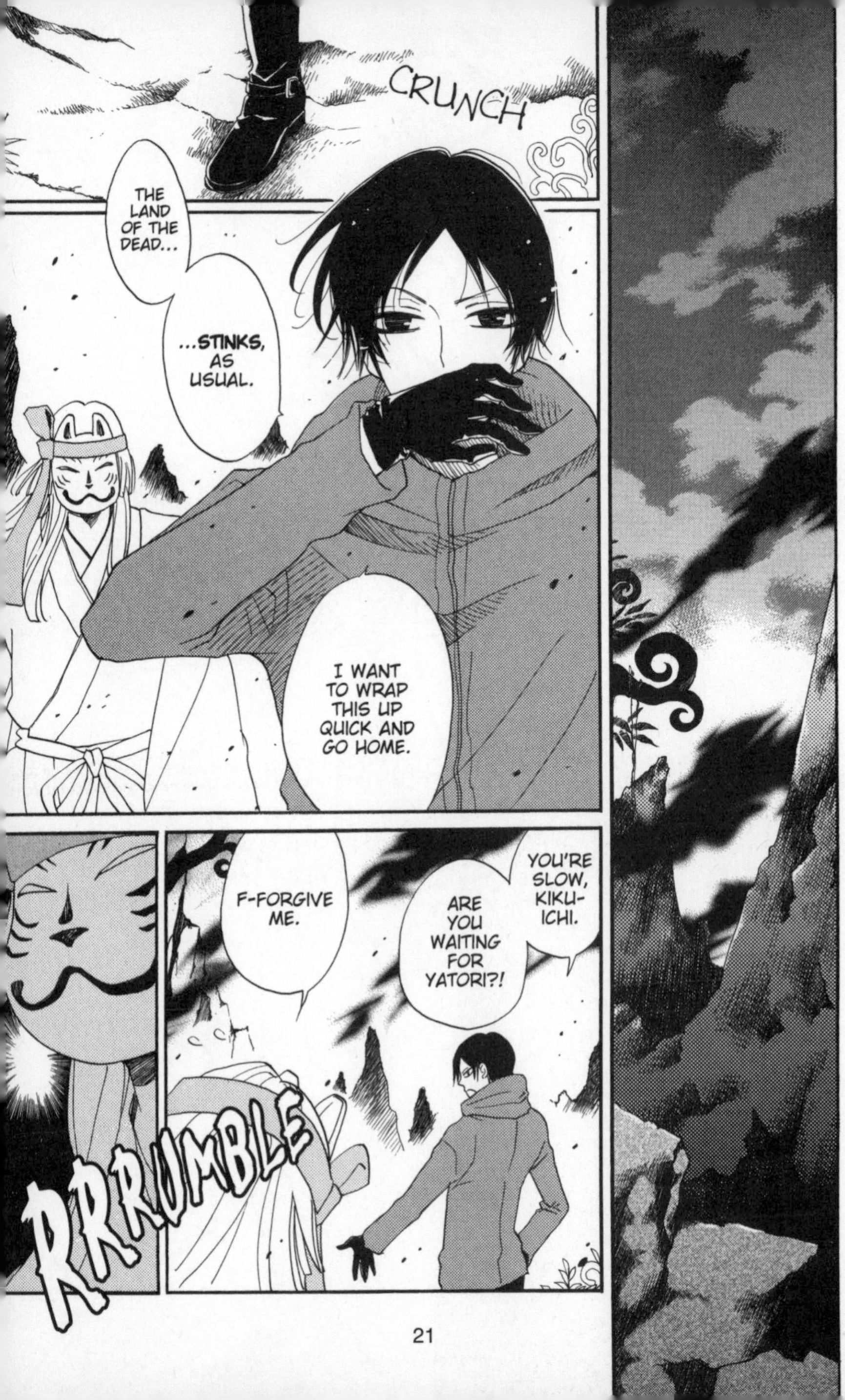
CRUNCH
THE LAND OF THE DEAD...
...STINKS, AS USUAL.
I WANT TO WRAP THIS UP QUICK AND GO HOME.
YOU'RE SLOW, KIKU-ICHI.
ARE YOU WAITING FOR YATORI?!
F-FORGIVE ME.
RRRUMBLE

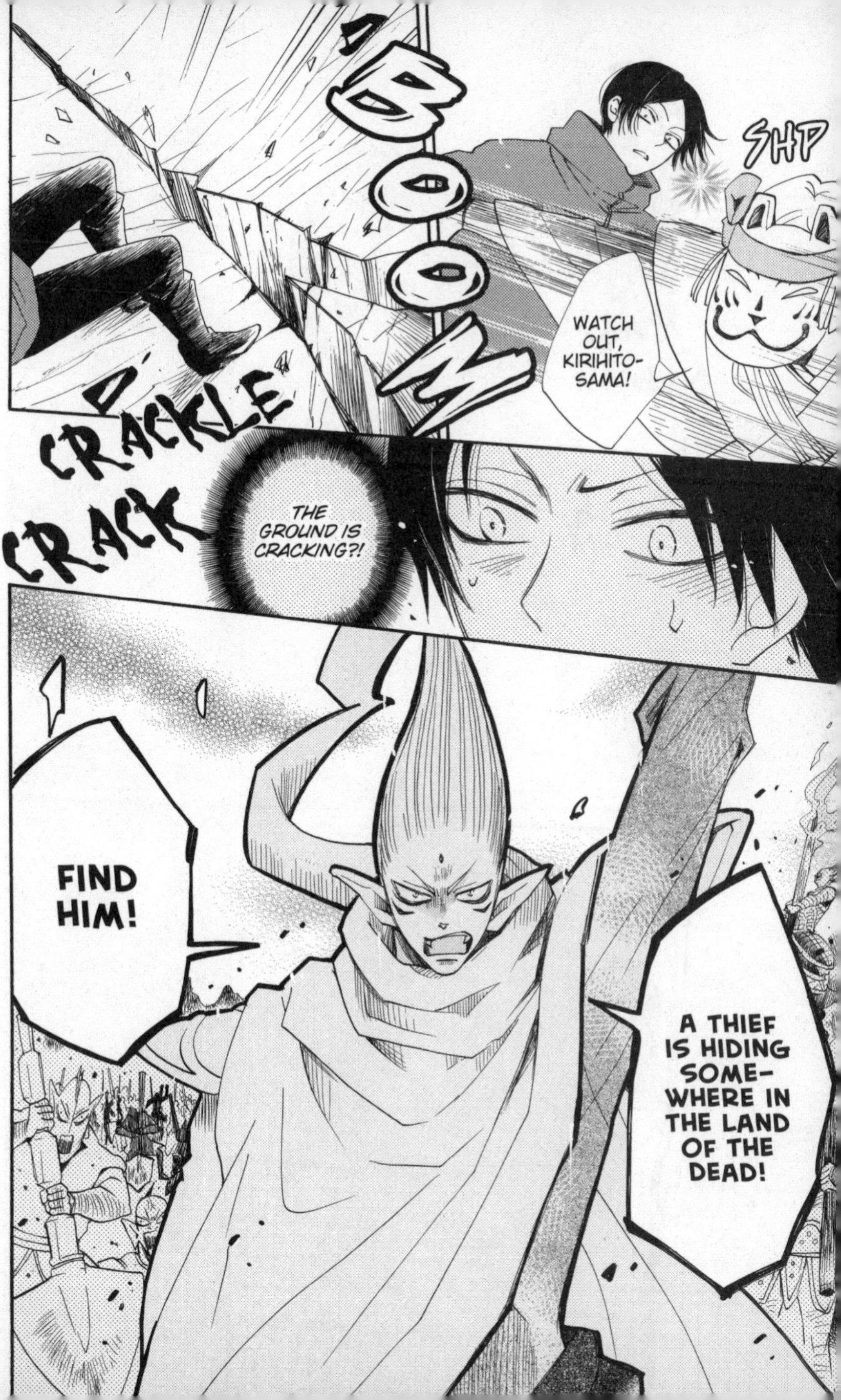
SHP
WATCH OUT, KIRIHITO-SAMA!
BOOM
CRACKLE
THE GROUND IS CRACKING?!
CRACK
A THIEF IS HIDING SOME-WHERE IN THE LAND OF THE DEAD!
FIND HIM!

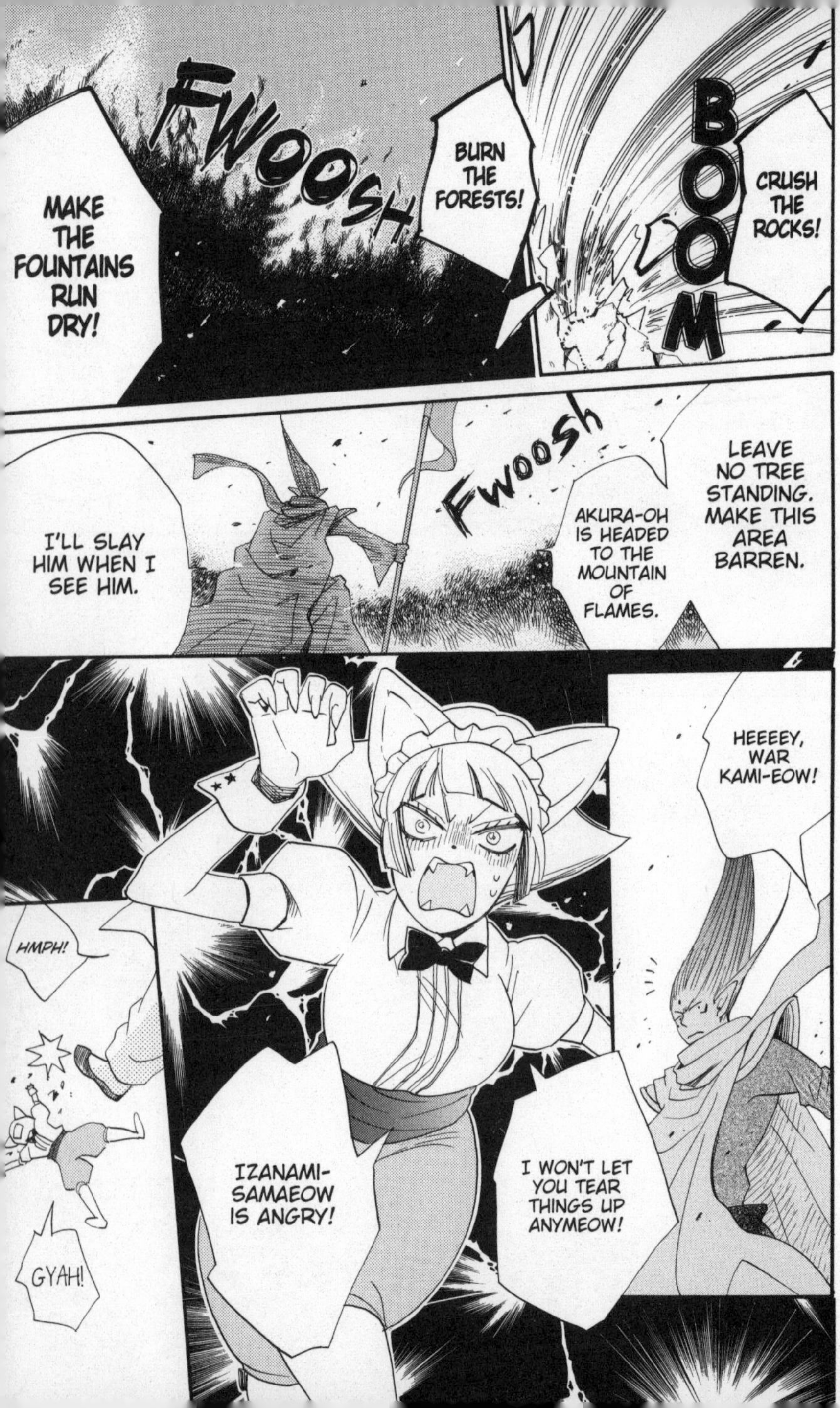
CRUSH THE ROCKS!
BOOM
BURN THE FORESTS!
FWOOSH
MAKE THE FOUNTAINS RUN DRY!
LEAVE NO TREE STANDING. MAKE THIS AREA BARREN.
AKURA-OH IS HEADED TO THE MOUNTAIN OF FLAMES.
FWOOSH
I'LL SLAY HIM WHEN I SEE HIM.
HEEEEY, WAR KAMI-EOW!
I WON'T LET YOU TEAR THINGS UP ANYMEOW!
IZANAMI-SAMAEOW IS ANGRY!
HMPH!
GYAH!

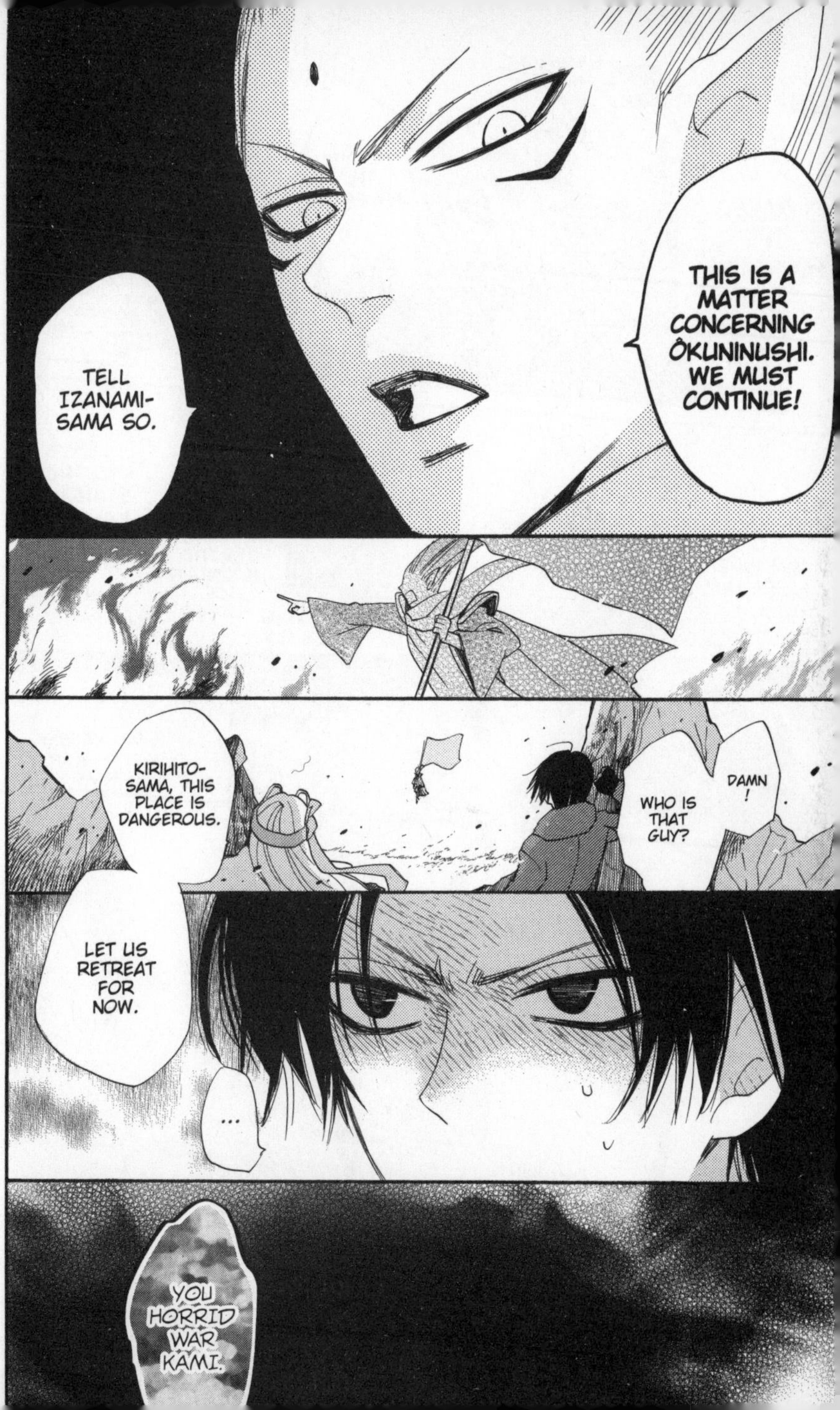
THIS IS A MATTER CONCERNING ÔKUNINUSHI. WE MUST CONTINUE!
TELL IZANAMI-SAMA SO.
DAMN!
WHO IS THAT GUY?
KIRIHITO-SAMA, THIS PLACE IS DANGEROUS.
LET US RETREAT FOR NOW.
...
YOU HORRID WAR KAMI.

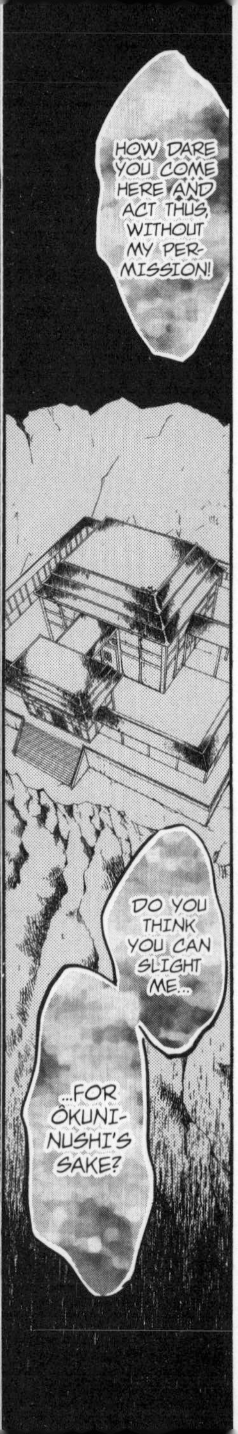
HOW DARE YOU COME HERE AND ACT THUS, WITHOUT MY PER-MISSION!
DO YOU THINK YOU CAN SLIGHT ME...
...FOR ŌKUNI-NUSHI'S SAKE?

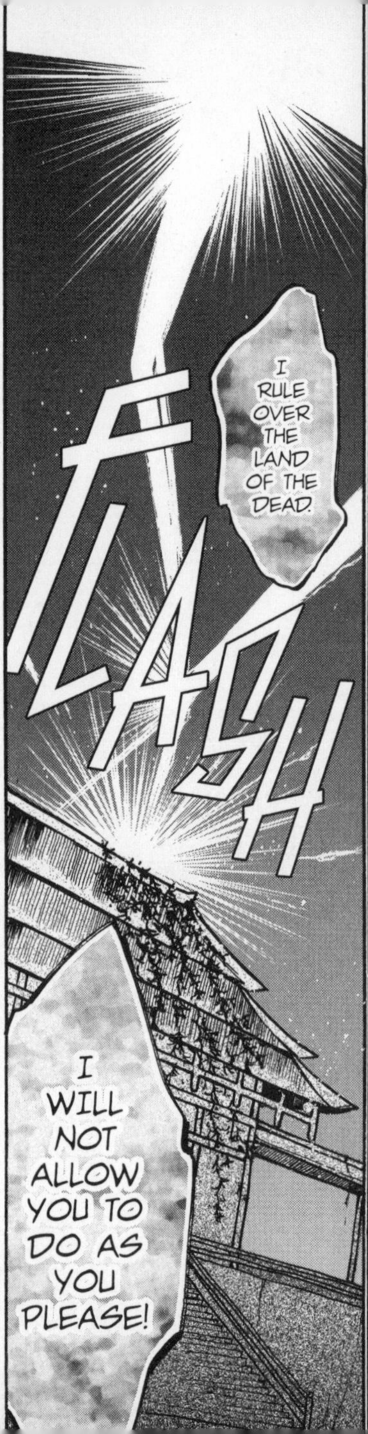
FLASH
I RULE OVER THE LAND OF THE DEAD.
I WILL NOT ALLOW YOU TO DO AS YOU PLEASE!

Hello!

Thank you for picking up this volume of Kamisama Kiss!!

THANK YOU!

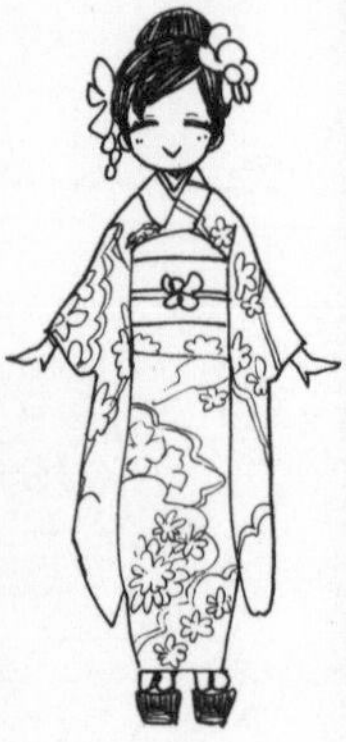

Enjoy your reading!

~Juli

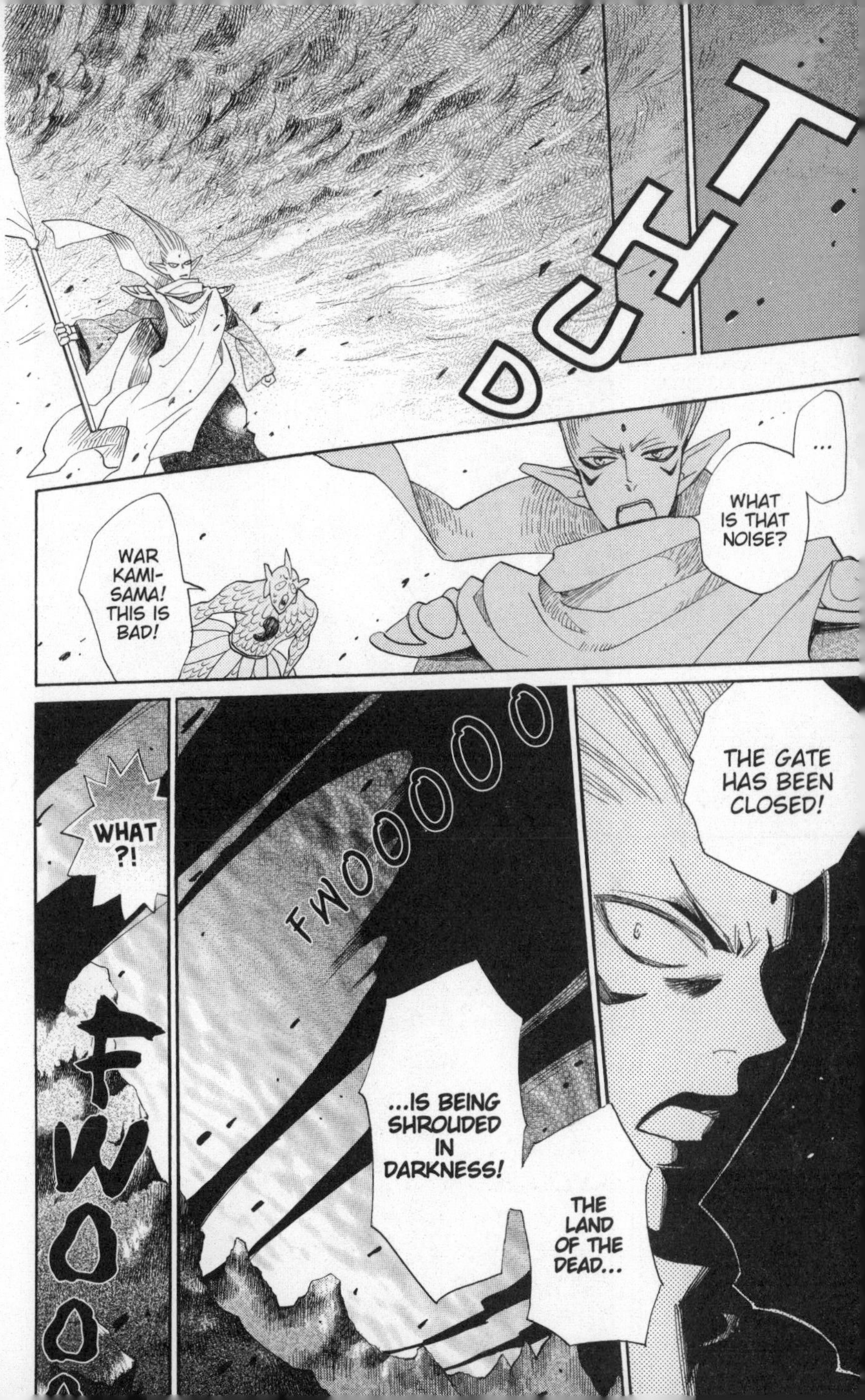
DCHT
...
WHAT IS THAT NOISE?
WAR KAMI-SAMA! THIS IS BAD!
THE GATE HAS BEEN CLOSED!
THE LAND OF THE DEAD...
...IS BEING SHROUDED IN DARKNESS!
FWOOOOOO
WHAT?!
FWOO

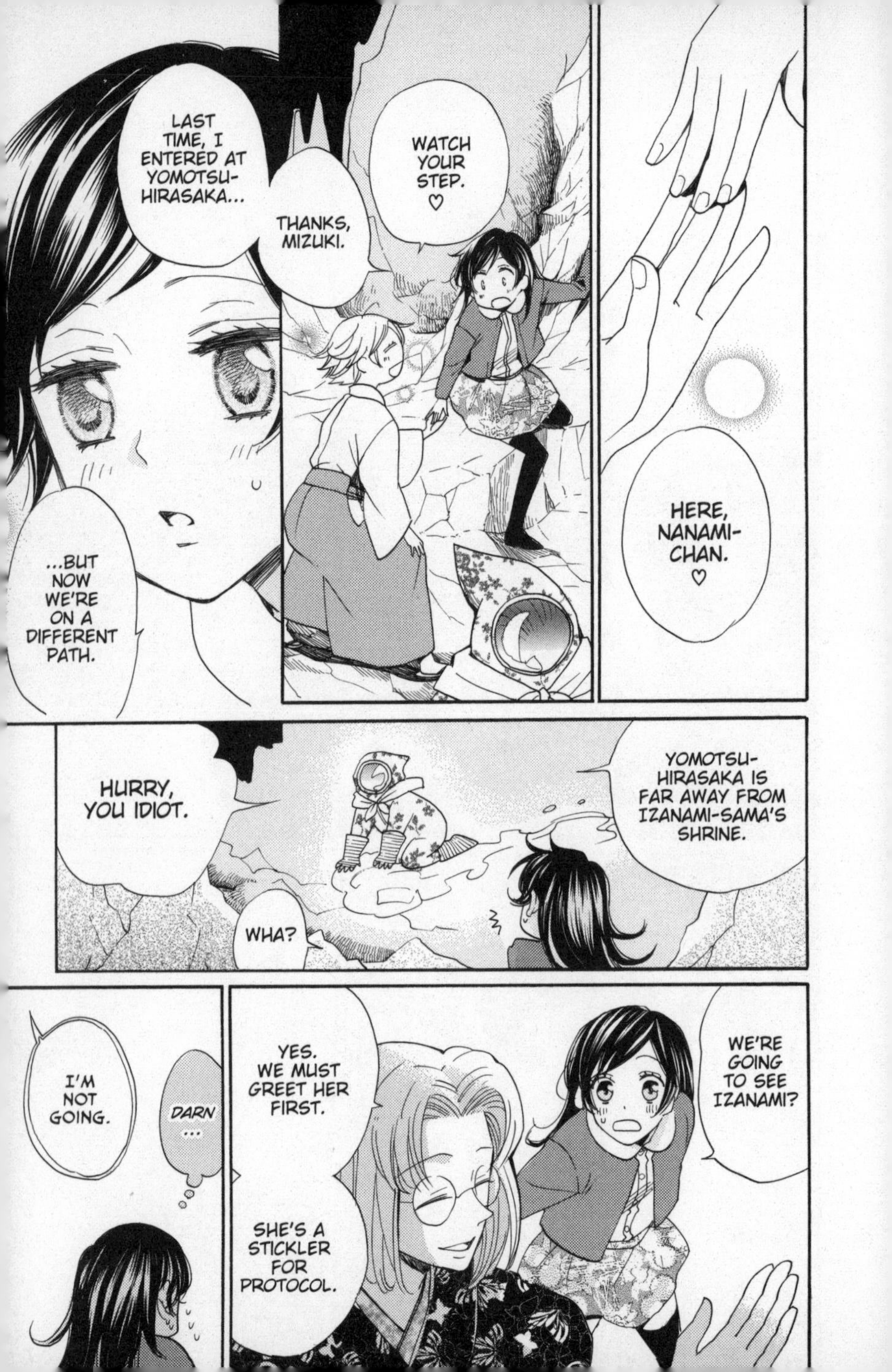
HERE, NANAMI-CHAN. ♡
WATCH YOUR STEP. ♡
THANKS, MIZUKI.
LAST TIME, I ENTERED AT YOMOTSU-HIRASAKA...
...BUT NOW WE'RE ON A DIFFERENT PATH.
YOMOTSU-HIRASAKA IS FAR AWAY FROM IZANAMI-SAMA'S SHRINE.
HURRY, YOU IDIOT.
WHA?
WE'RE GOING TO SEE IZANAMI?
YES. WE MUST GREET HER FIRST.
SHE'S A STICKLER FOR PROTOCOL.
I'M NOT GOING.
DARN...

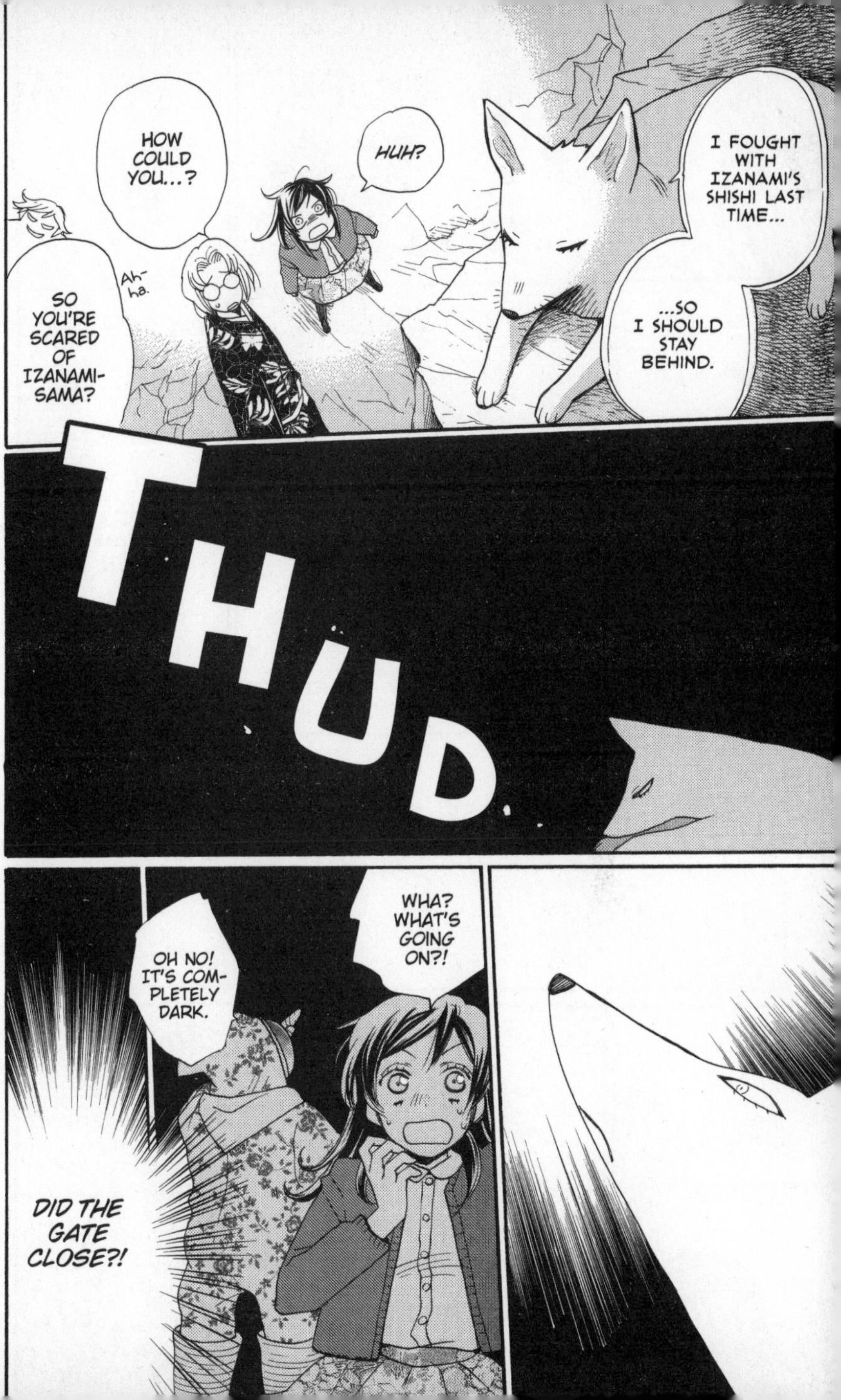
I FOUGHT WITH IZANAMI'S SHISHI LAST TIME...
...SO I SHOULD STAY BEHIND.
HUH?
HOW COULD YOU...?
Ah-ha.
SO YOU'RE SCARED OF IZANAMI-SAMA?
THUD
WHA? WHAT'S GOING ON?!
OH NO! IT'S COM-PLETELY DARK.
DID THE GATE CLOSE?!

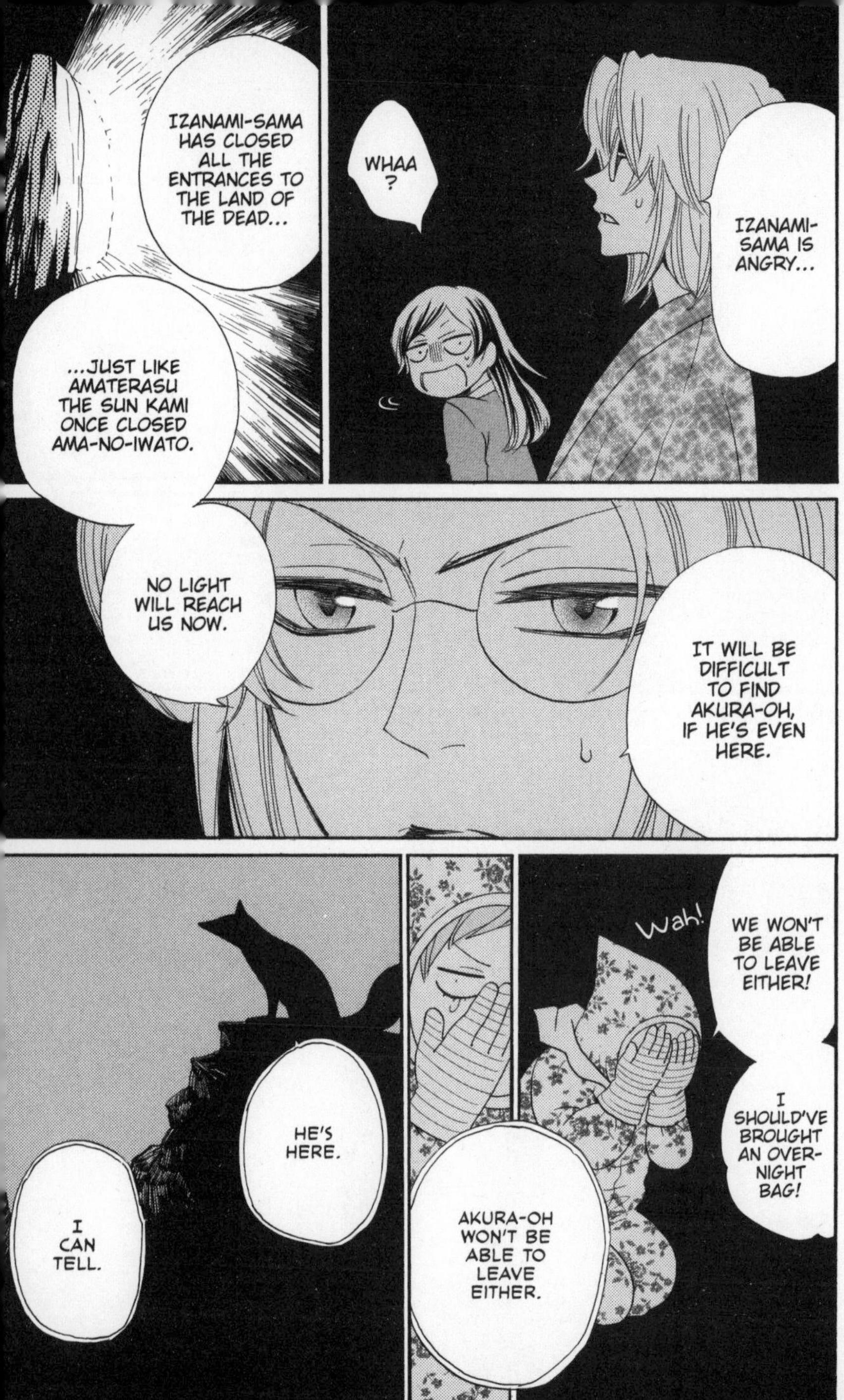
IZANAMI-SAMA IS ANGRY...
WHAA?
IZANAMI-SAMA HAS CLOSED ALL THE ENTRANCES TO THE LAND OF THE DEAD...
...JUST LIKE AMATERASU THE SUN KAMI ONCE CLOSED AMA-NO-IWATO.
NO LIGHT WILL REACH US NOW.
IT WILL BE DIFFICULT TO FIND AKURA-OH, IF HE'S EVEN HERE.
Wah!
WE WON'T BE ABLE TO LEAVE EITHER!
I SHOULD'VE BROUGHT AN OVER-NIGHT BAG!
AKURA-OH WON'T BE ABLE TO LEAVE EITHER.
HE'S HERE.
I CAN TELL.

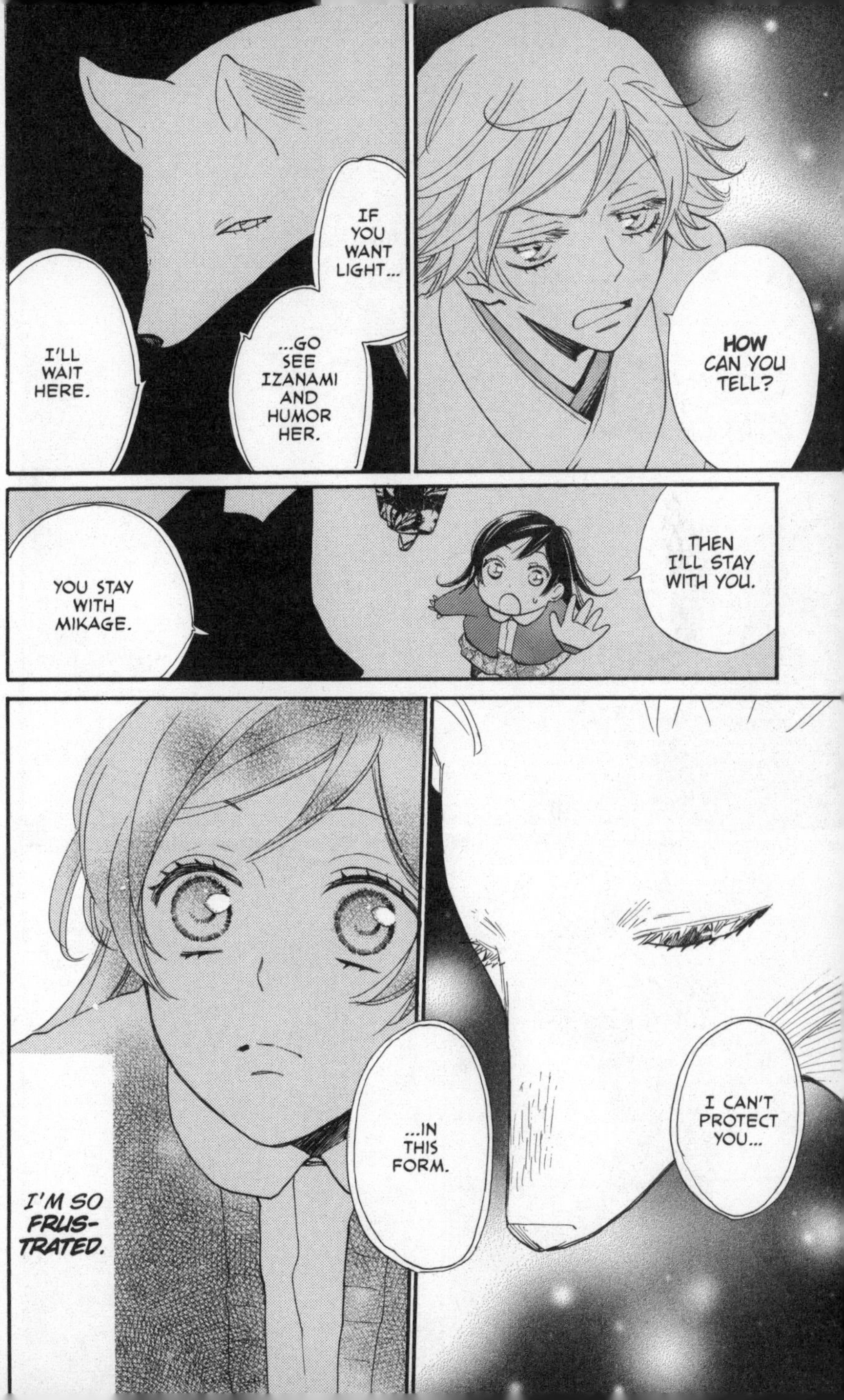
HOW CAN YOU TELL?
IF YOU WANT LIGHT...
...GO SEE IZANAMI AND HUMOR HER.
I'LL WAIT HERE.
THEN I'LL STAY WITH YOU.
YOU STAY WITH MIKAGE.
I CAN'T PROTECT YOU...
...IN THIS FORM.
I'M SO FRUS-TRATED.

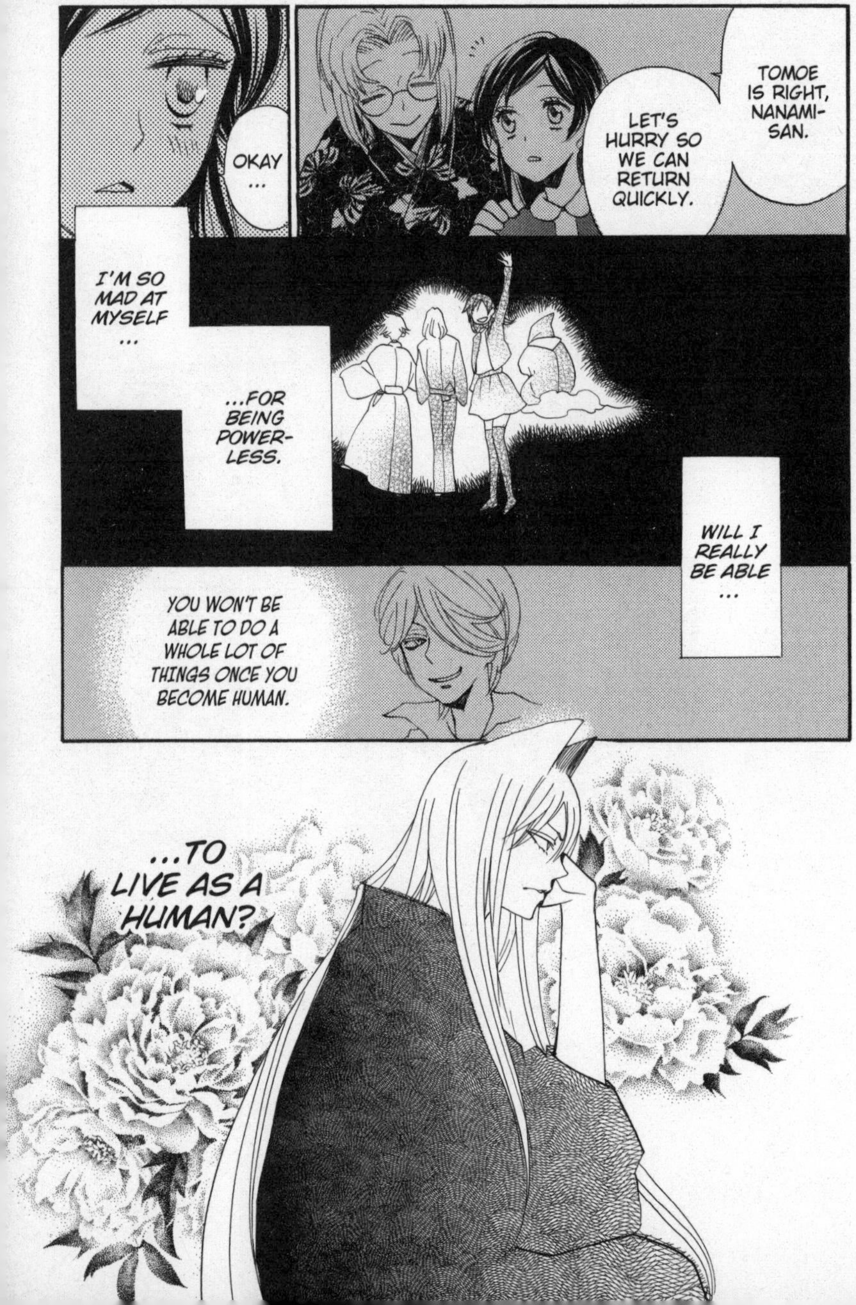
TOMOE IS RIGHT, NANAMI-SAN.
LET'S HURRY SO WE CAN RETURN QUICKLY.
OKAY ...
I'M SO MAD AT MYSELF ...
...FOR BEING POWERLESS.
WILL I REALLY BE ABLE ...
YOU WON'T BE ABLE TO DO A WHOLE LOT OF THINGS ONCE YOU BECOME HUMAN.
...TO LIVE AS A HUMAN?

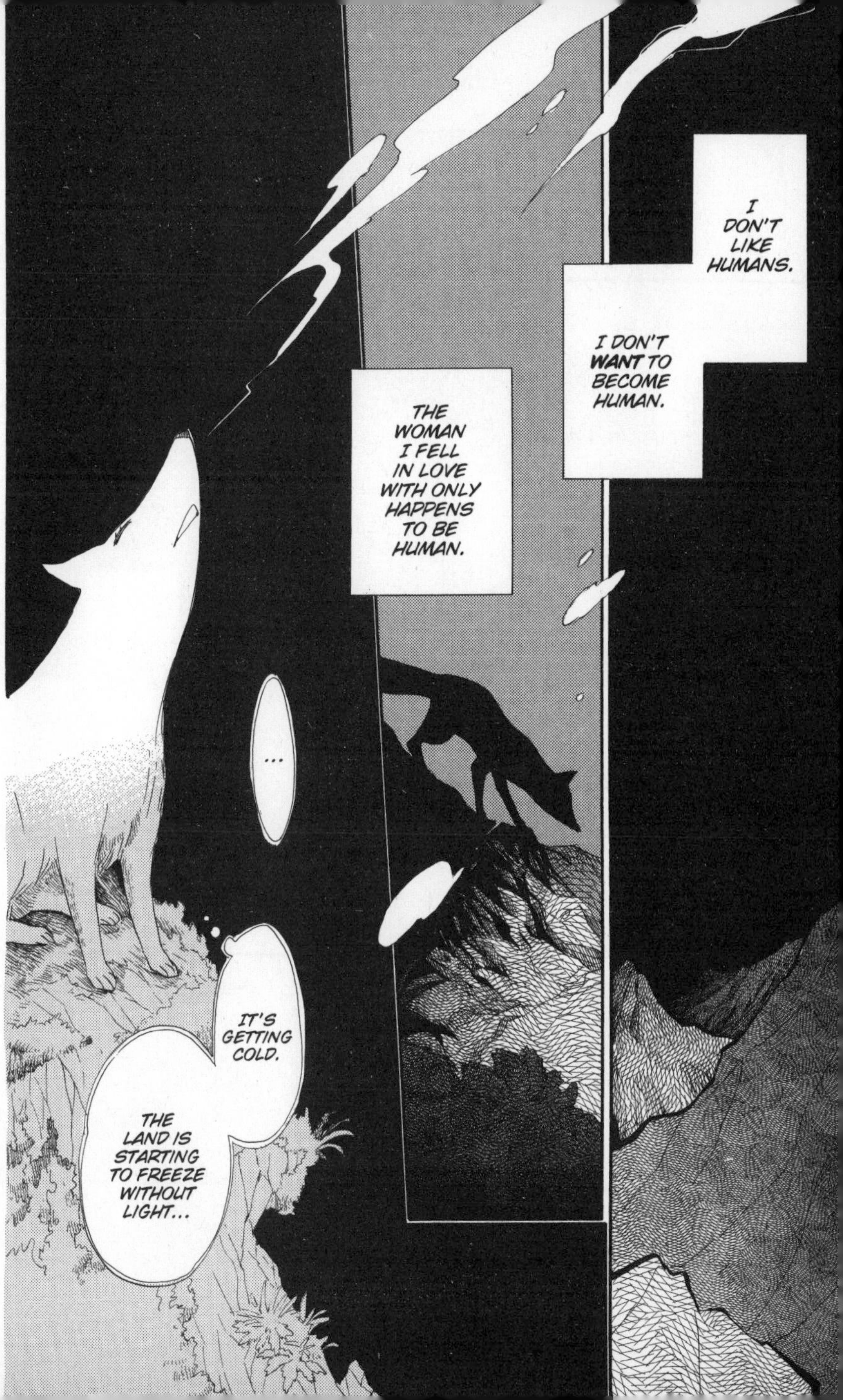
I DON'T LIKE HUMANS.
I DON'T WANT TO BECOME HUMAN.
THE WOMAN I FELL IN LOVE WITH ONLY HAPPENS TO BE HUMAN.
...
IT'S GETTING COLD.
THE LAND IS STARTING TO FREEZE WITHOUT LIGHT...

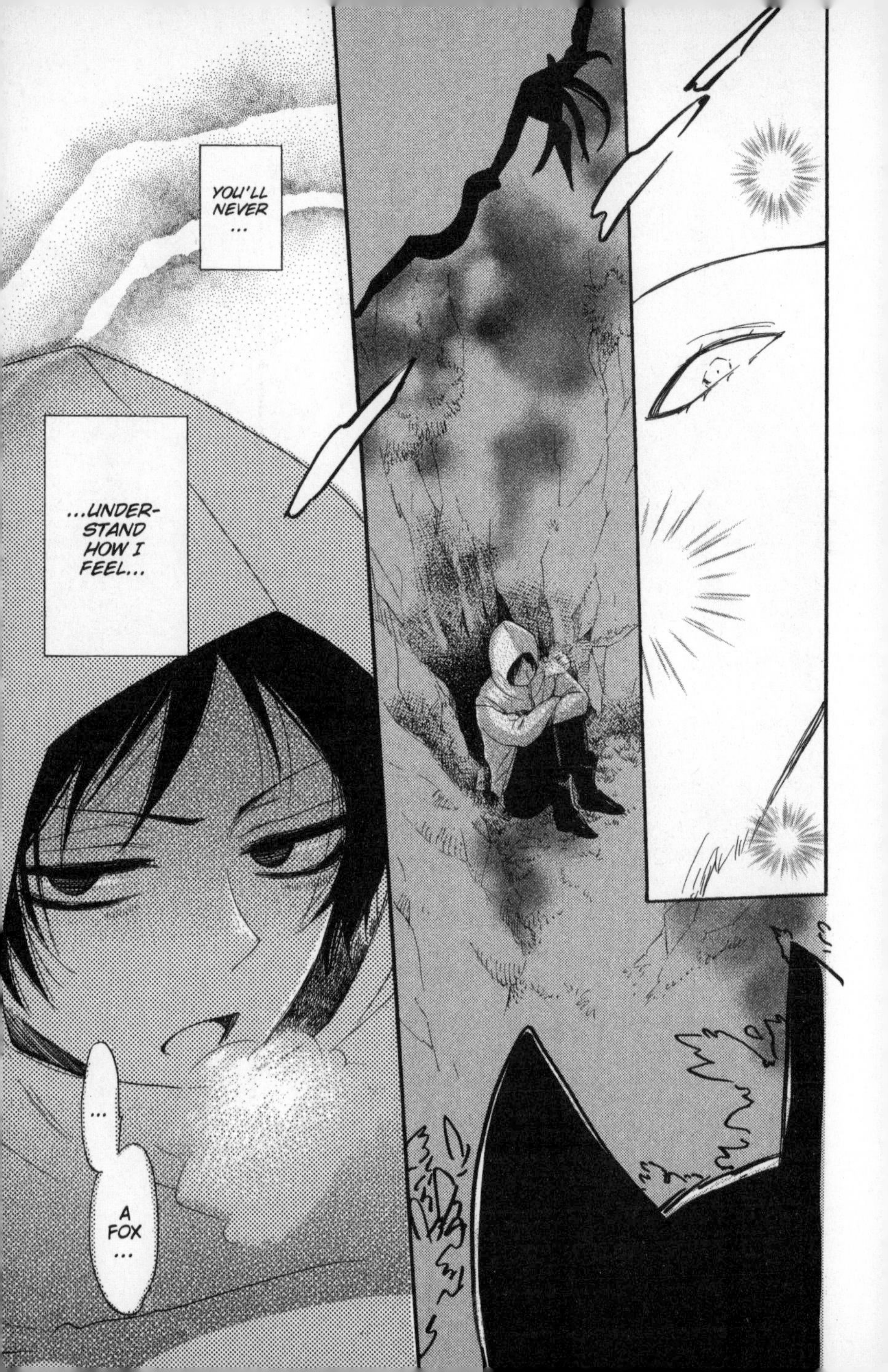
YOU'LL NEVER ...
...UNDER-STAND HOW I FEEL...
...
A FOX ...

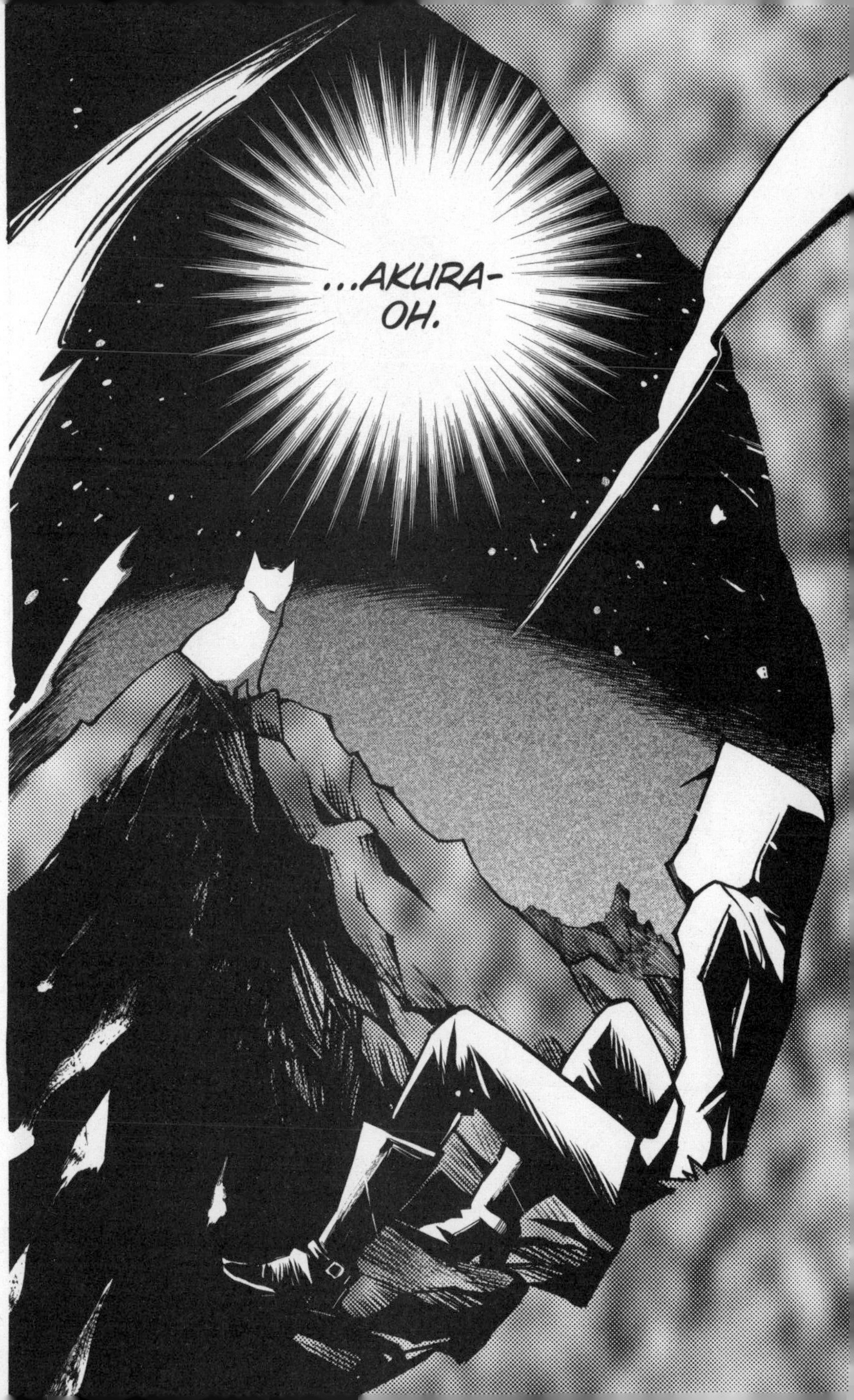
...AKURA-
OH.

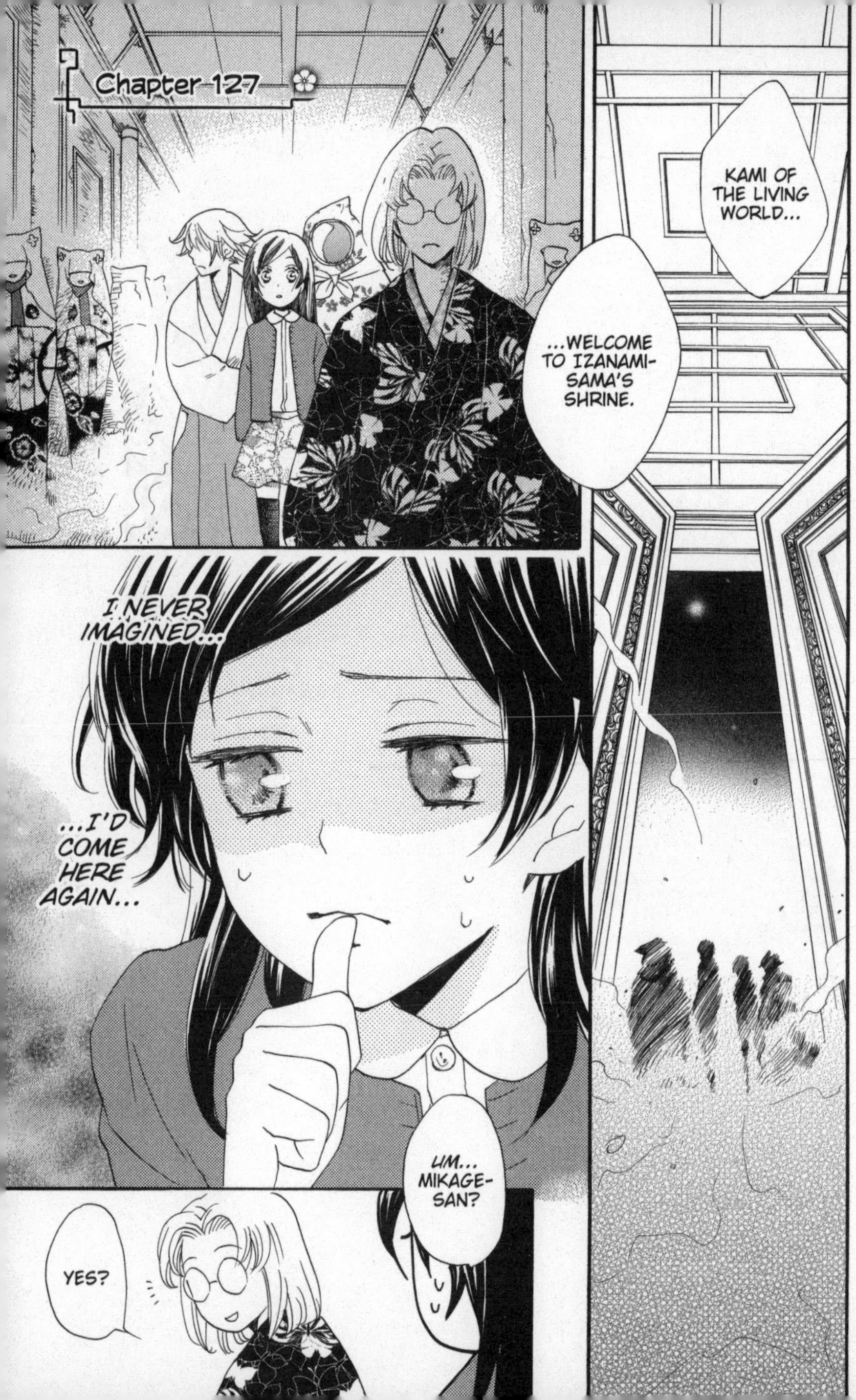
Chapter 127
KAMI OF THE LIVING WORLD...
...WELCOME TO IZANAMI-SAMA'S SHRINE.
I NEVER IMAGINED...
...I'D COME HERE AGAIN...
UM... MIKAGE-SAN?
YES?

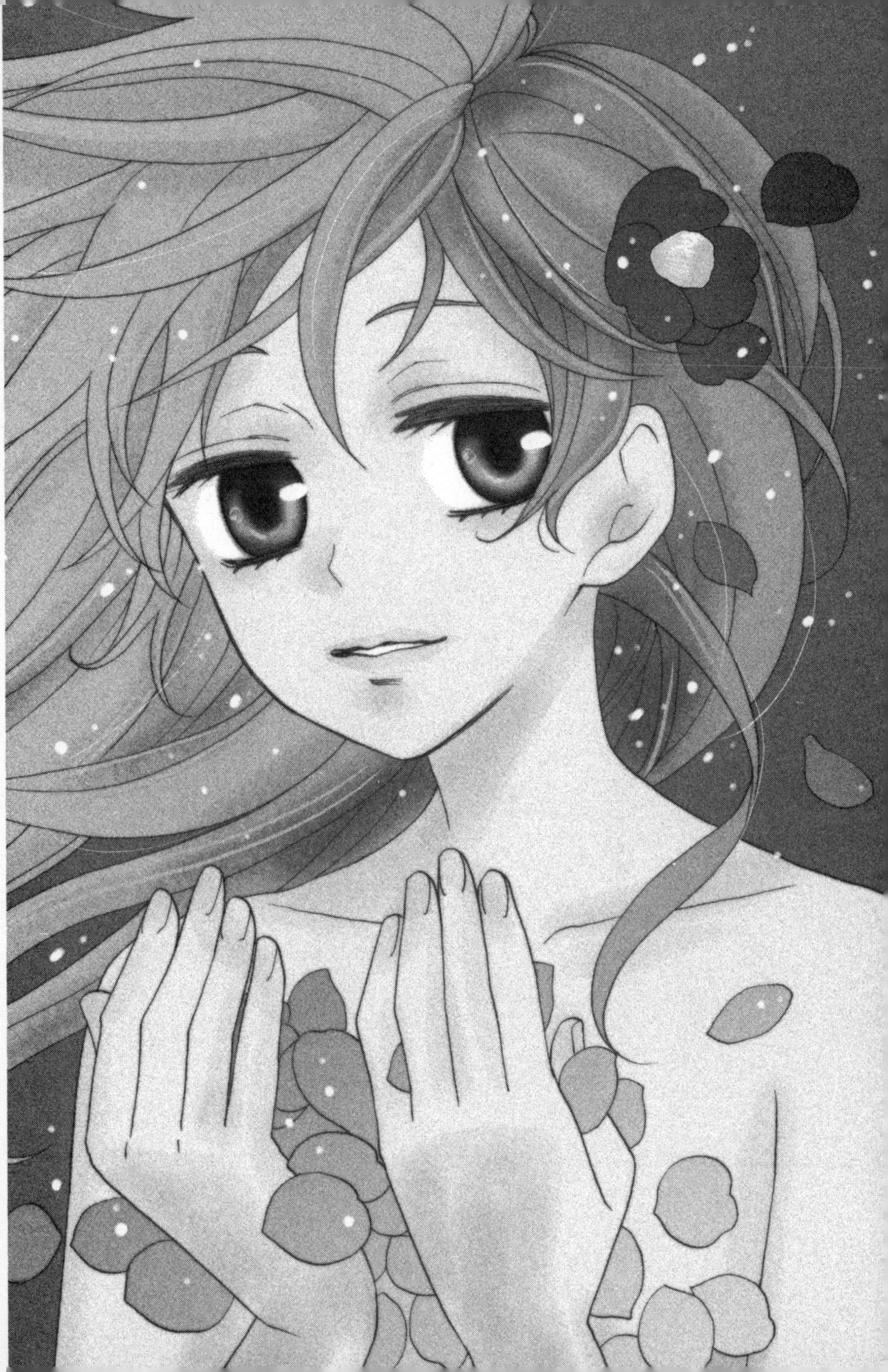

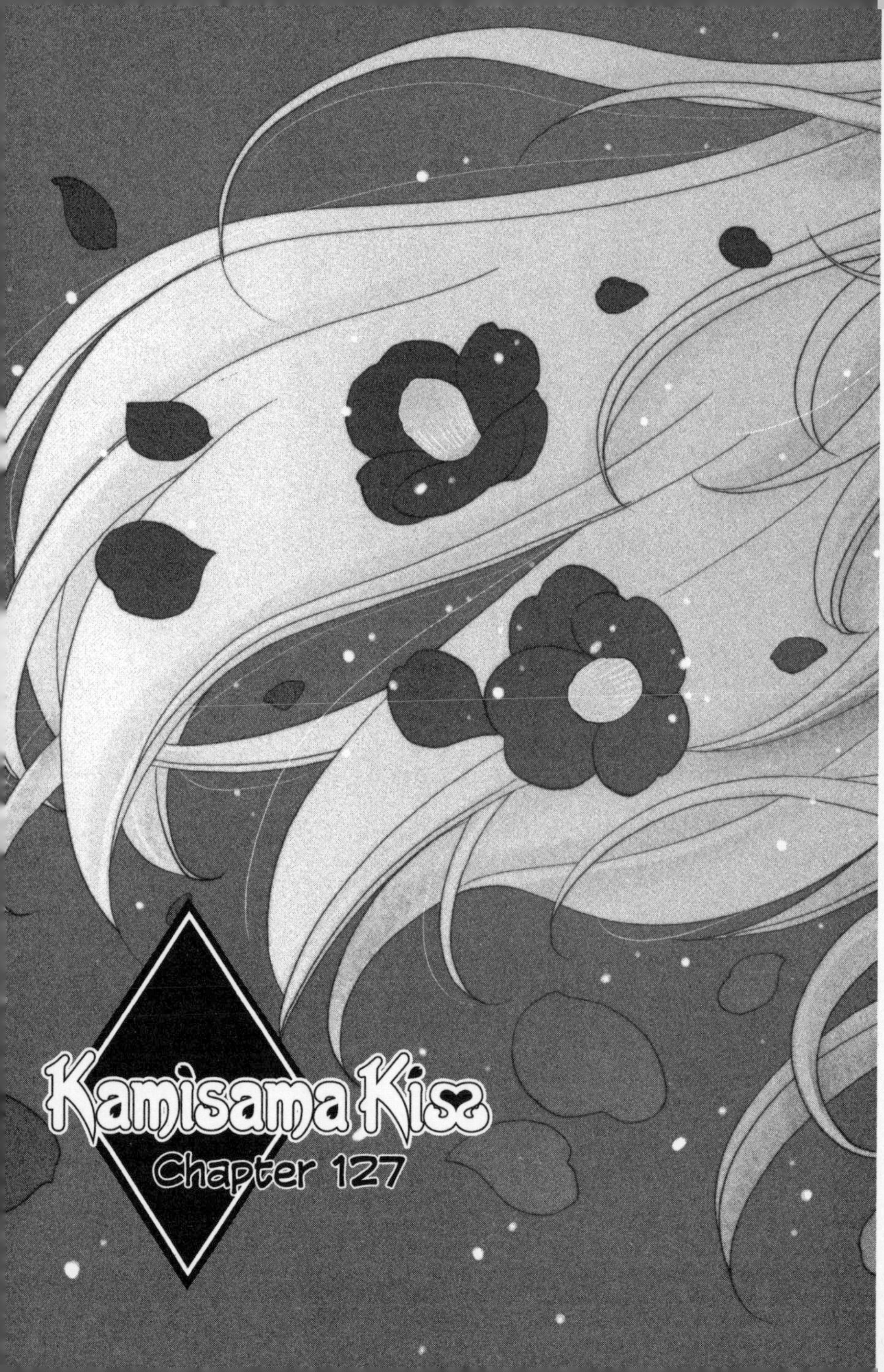
Kamisama Kiss
Chapter 127

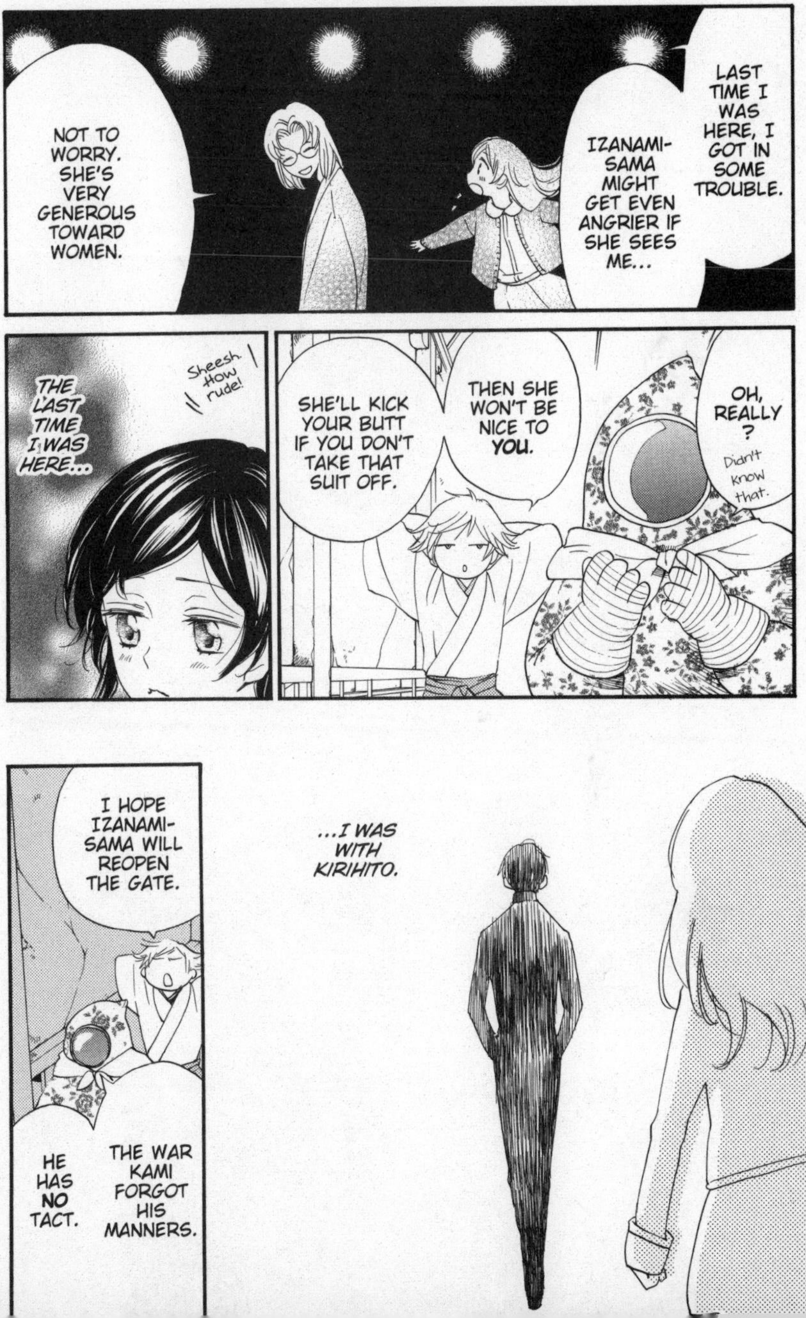
LAST TIME I WAS HERE, I GOT IN SOME TROUBLE.
IZANAMI-SAMA MIGHT GET EVEN ANGRIER IF SHE SEES ME...
NOT TO WORRY. SHE'S VERY GENEROUS TOWARD WOMEN.
OH, REALLY?
Didn't know that.
THEN SHE WON'T BE NICE TO YOU.
SHE'LL KICK YOUR BUTT IF YOU DON'T TAKE THAT SUIT OFF.
Sheesh. How rude!
THE LAST TIME I WAS HERE...
...I WAS WITH KIRIHITO.
I HOPE IZANAMI-SAMA WILL REOPEN THE GATE.
THE WAR KAMI FORGOT HIS MANNERS.
HE HAS NO TACT.

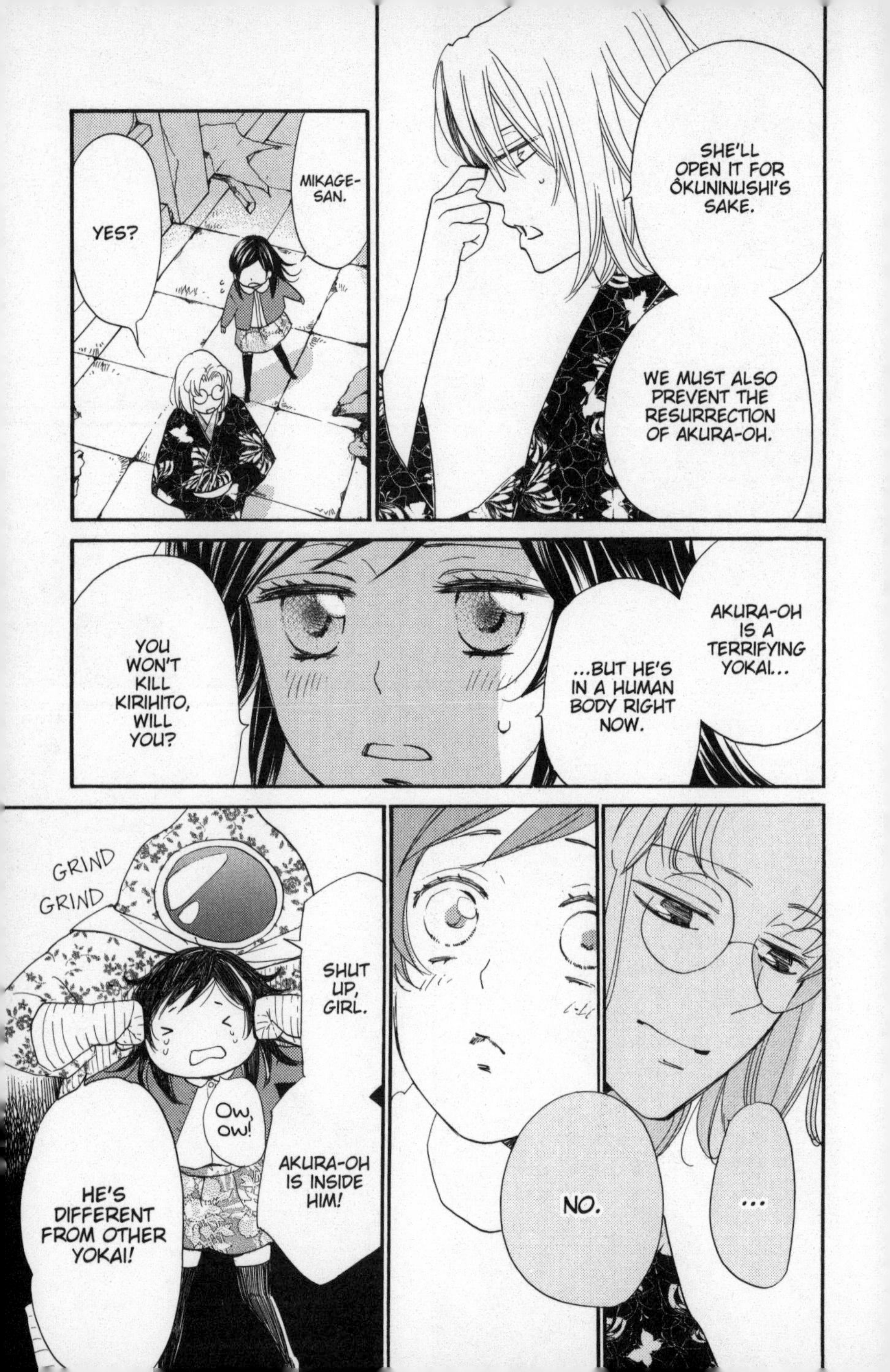
SHE'LL OPEN IT FOR ÔKUNINUSHI'S SAKE.
WE MUST ALSO PREVENT THE RESURRECTION OF AKURA-OH.
MIKAGE-SAN.
YES?
AKURA-OH IS A TERRIFYING YOKAI...
...BUT HE'S IN A HUMAN BODY RIGHT NOW.
YOU WON'T KILL KIRIHITO, WILL YOU?
...
NO.
SHUT UP, GIRL.
GRIND GRIND
Ow, ow!
AKURA-OH IS INSIDE HIM!
HE'S DIFFERENT FROM OTHER YOKAI!

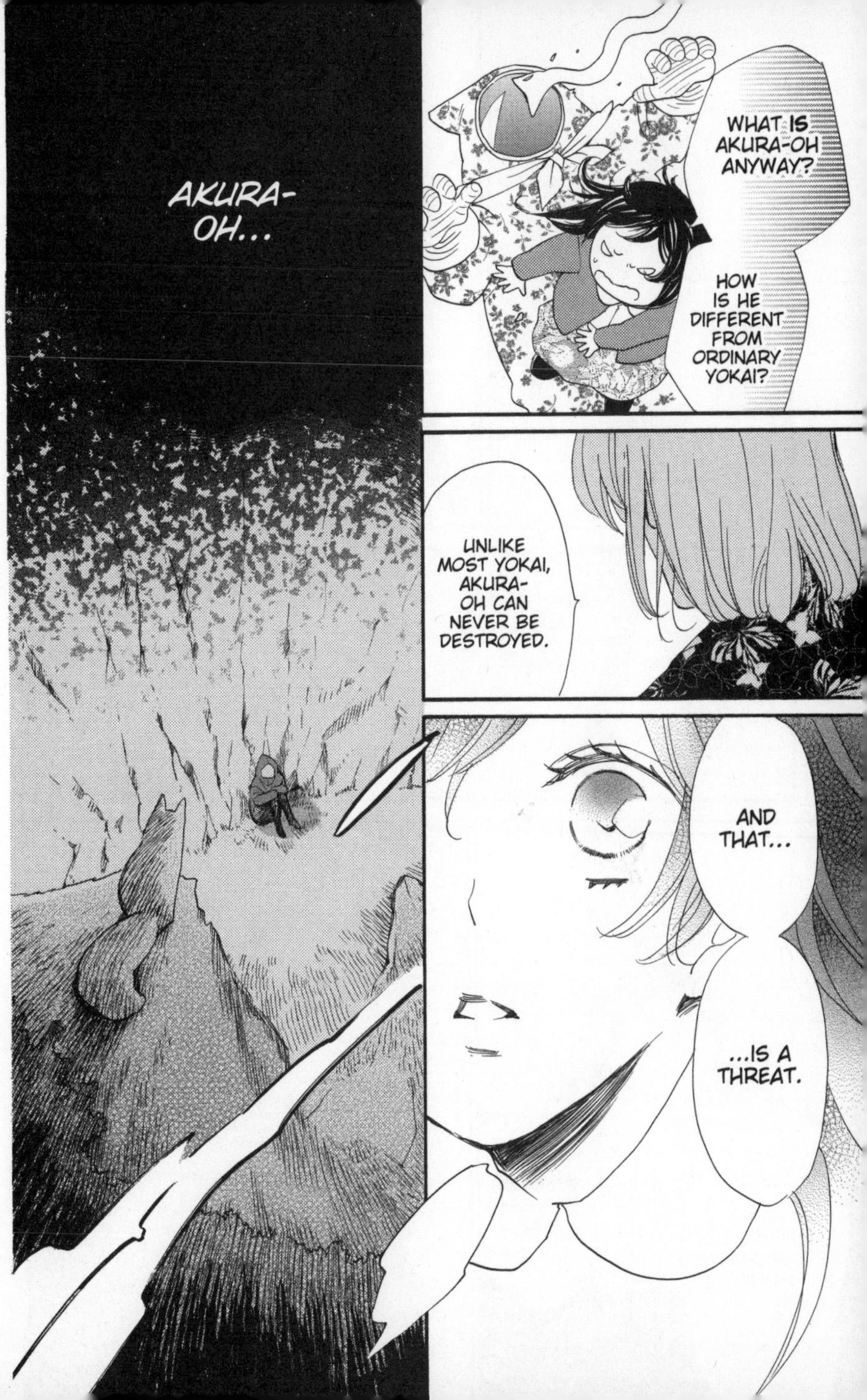
WHAT IS AKURA-OH ANYWAY?
HOW IS HE DIFFERENT FROM ORDINARY YOKAI?
UNLIKE MOST YOKAI, AKURA-OH CAN NEVER BE DESTROYED.
AND THAT...
...IS A THREAT.
AKURA-OH...

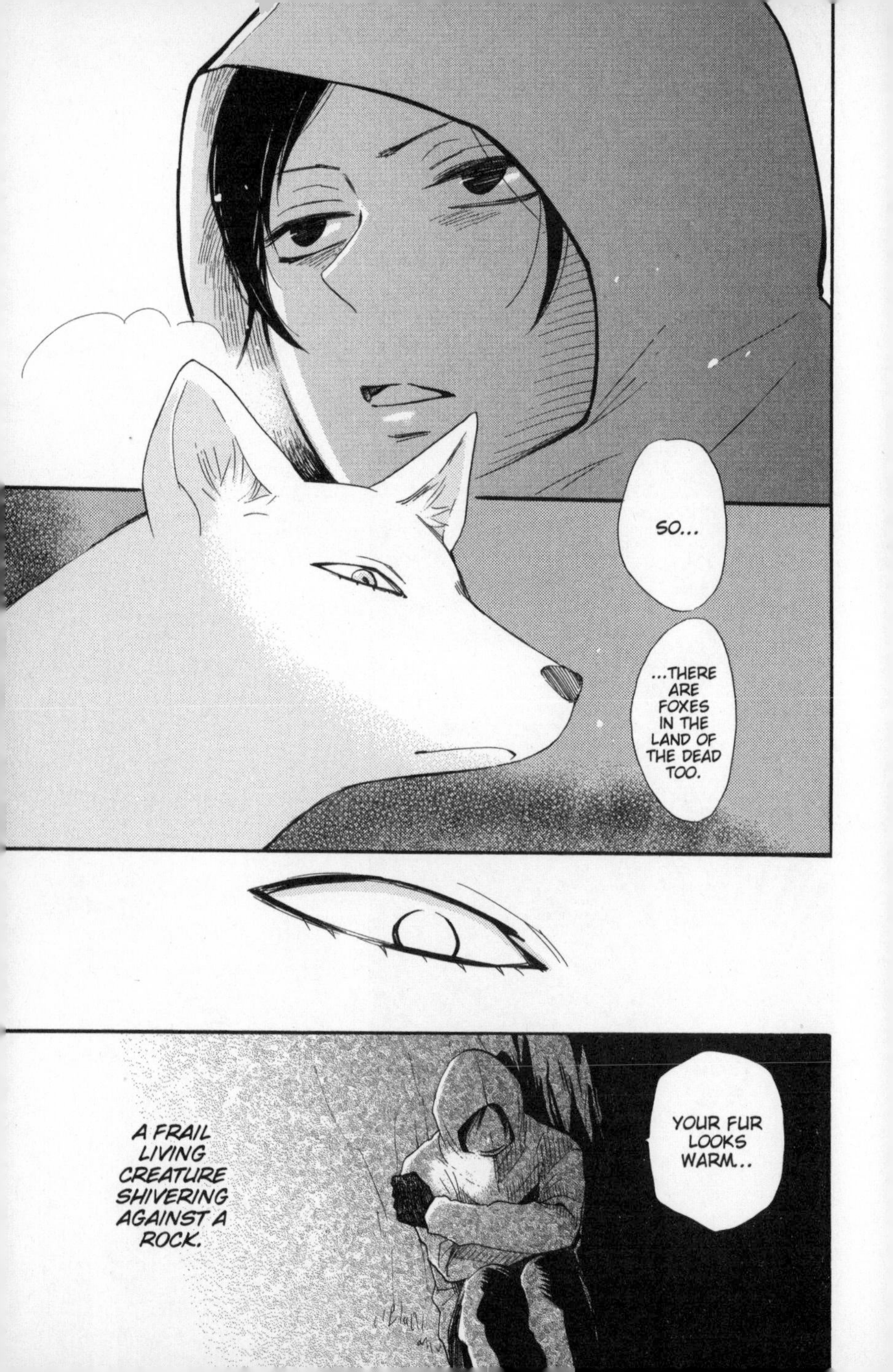
SO...
...THERE ARE FOXES IN THE LAND OF THE DEAD TOO.
YOUR FUR LOOKS WARM..
A FRAIL LIVING CREATURE SHIVERING AGAINST A ROCK.

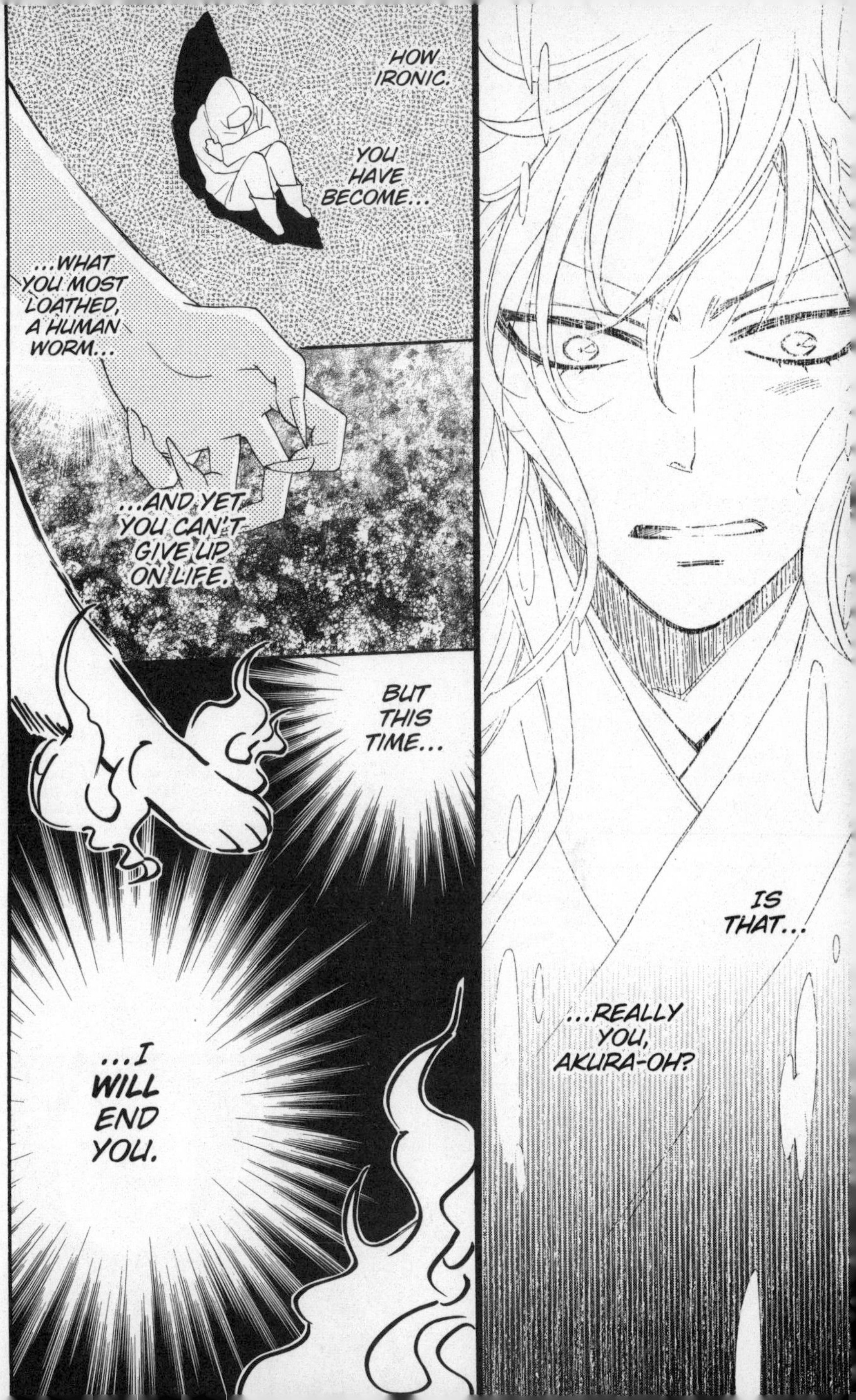
IS THAT...
...REALLY YOU, AKURA-OH?
HOW IRONIC.
YOU HAVE BECOME...
...WHAT YOU MOST LOATHED, A HUMAN WORM...
...AND YET YOU CAN'T GIVE UP ON LIFE.
BUT THIS TIME...
...I **WILL** END YOU.

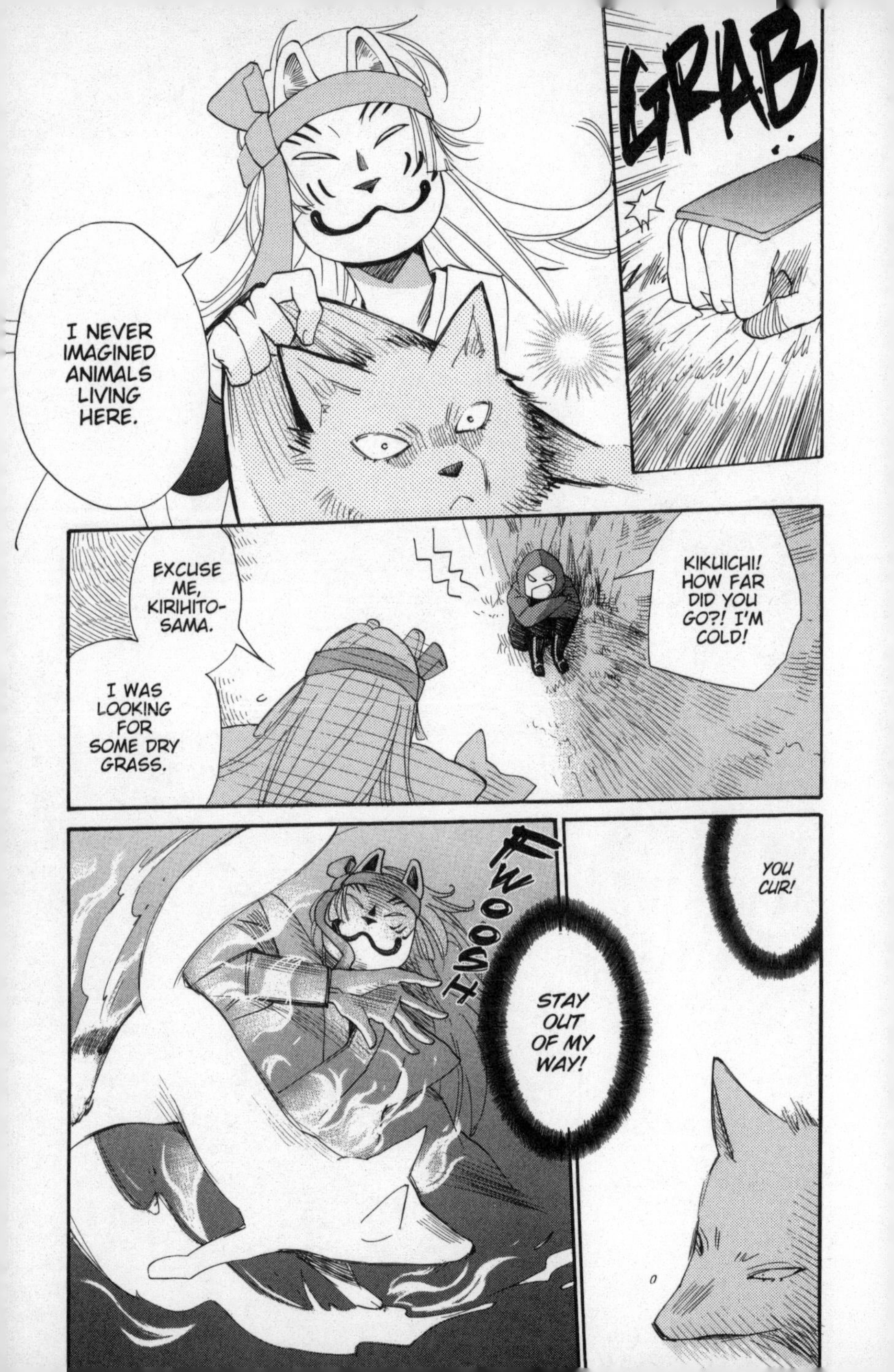
GRAB
I NEVER IMAGINED ANIMALS LIVING HERE.
KIKUICHI! HOW FAR DID YOU GO?! I'M COLD!
EXCUSE ME, KIRIHITO-SAMA.
I WAS LOOKING FOR SOME DRY GRASS.
YOU CUR!
FWOOSH
STAY OUT OF MY WAY!

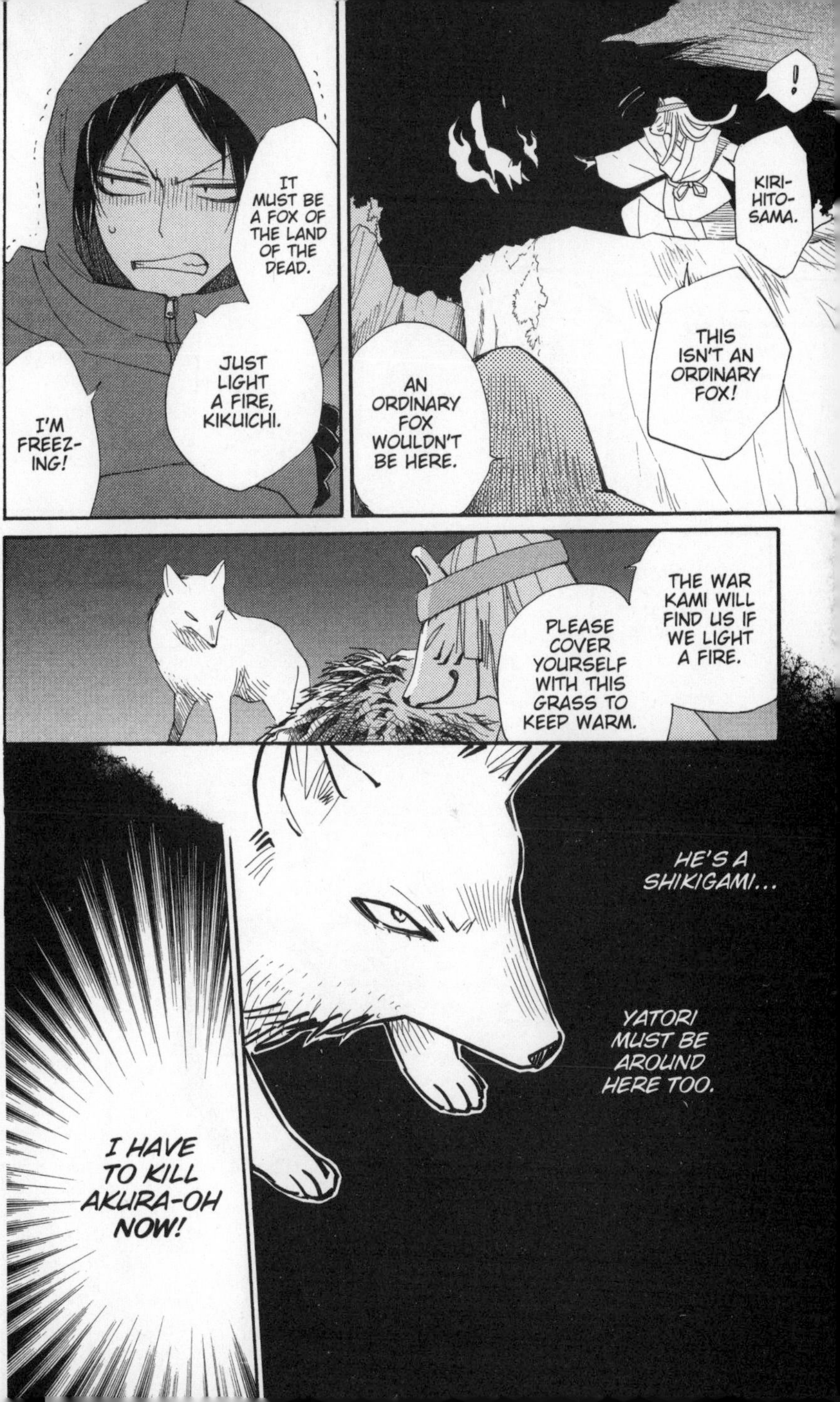
!
KIRI-HITO-SAMA.
THIS ISN'T AN ORDINARY FOX!
AN ORDINARY FOX WOULDN'T BE HERE.
IT MUST BE A FOX OF THE LAND OF THE DEAD.
JUST LIGHT A FIRE, KIKUICHI.
I'M FREEZ-ING!
THE WAR KAMI WILL FIND US IF WE LIGHT A FIRE.
PLEASE COVER YOURSELF WITH THIS GRASS TO KEEP WARM.
HE'S A SHIKIGAMI...
YATORI MUST BE AROUND HERE TOO.
I HAVE TO KILL AKURA-OH NOW!

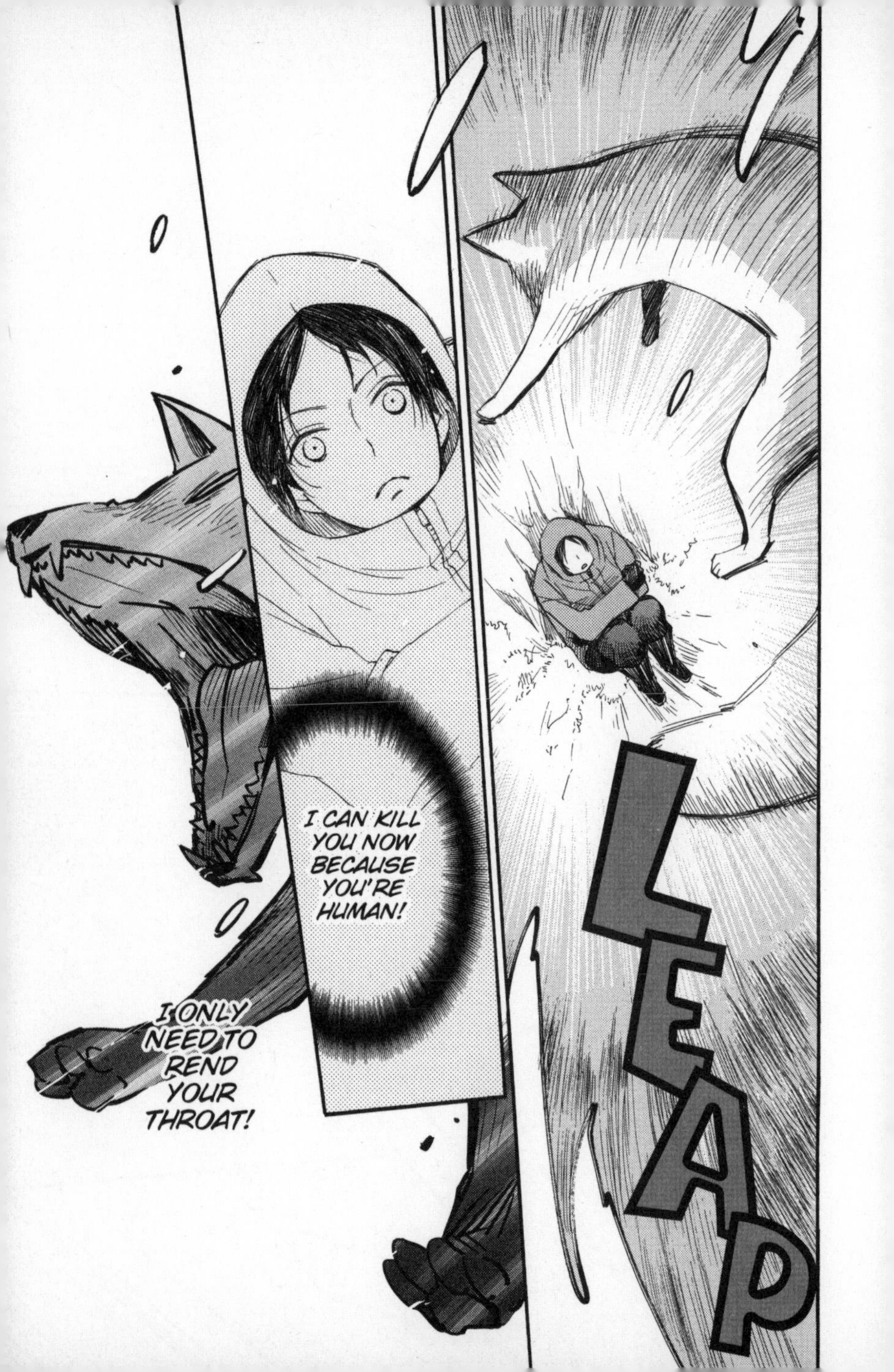
LEAP
I CAN KILL YOU NOW BECAUSE YOU'RE HUMAN!
I ONLY NEED TO REND YOUR THROAT!

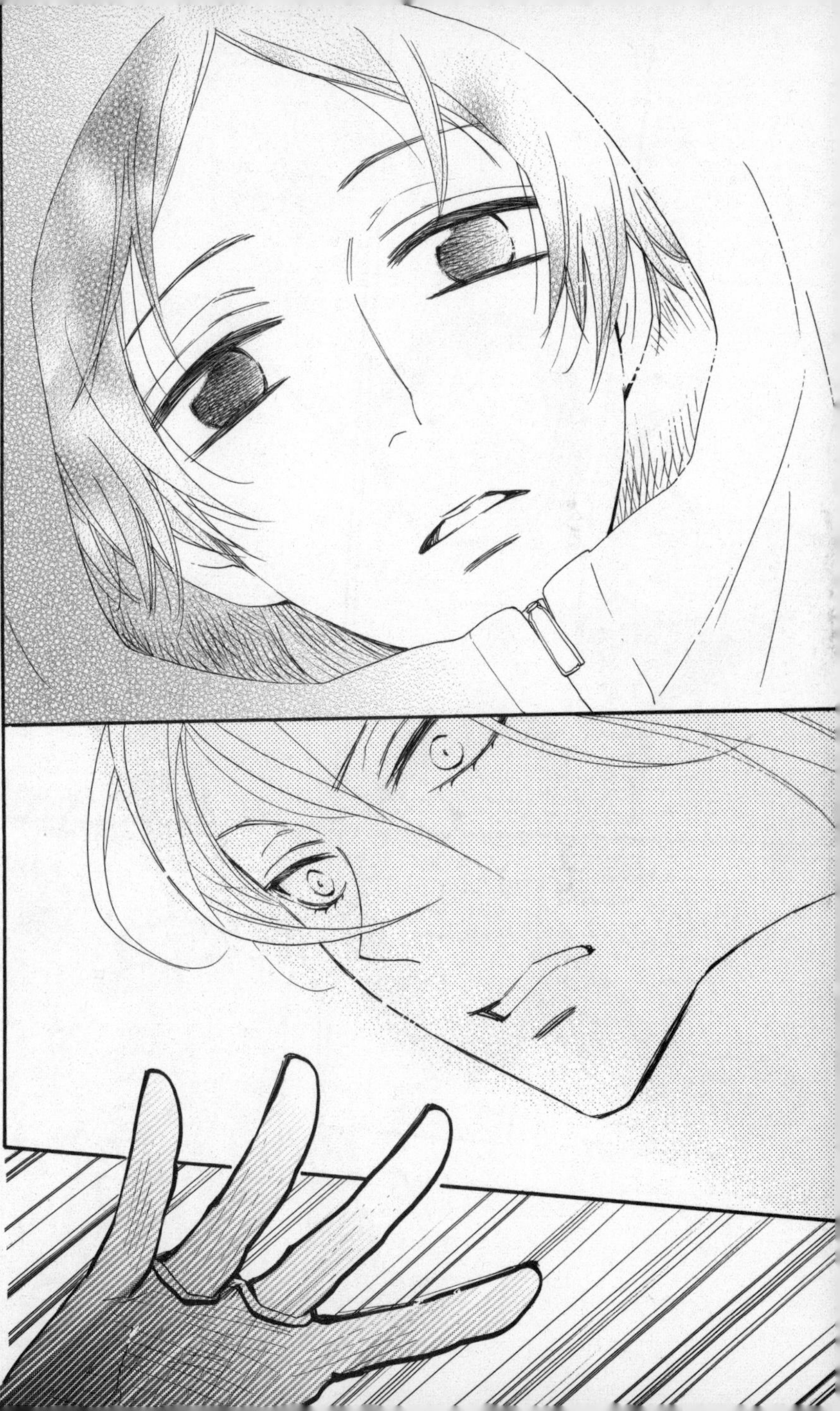

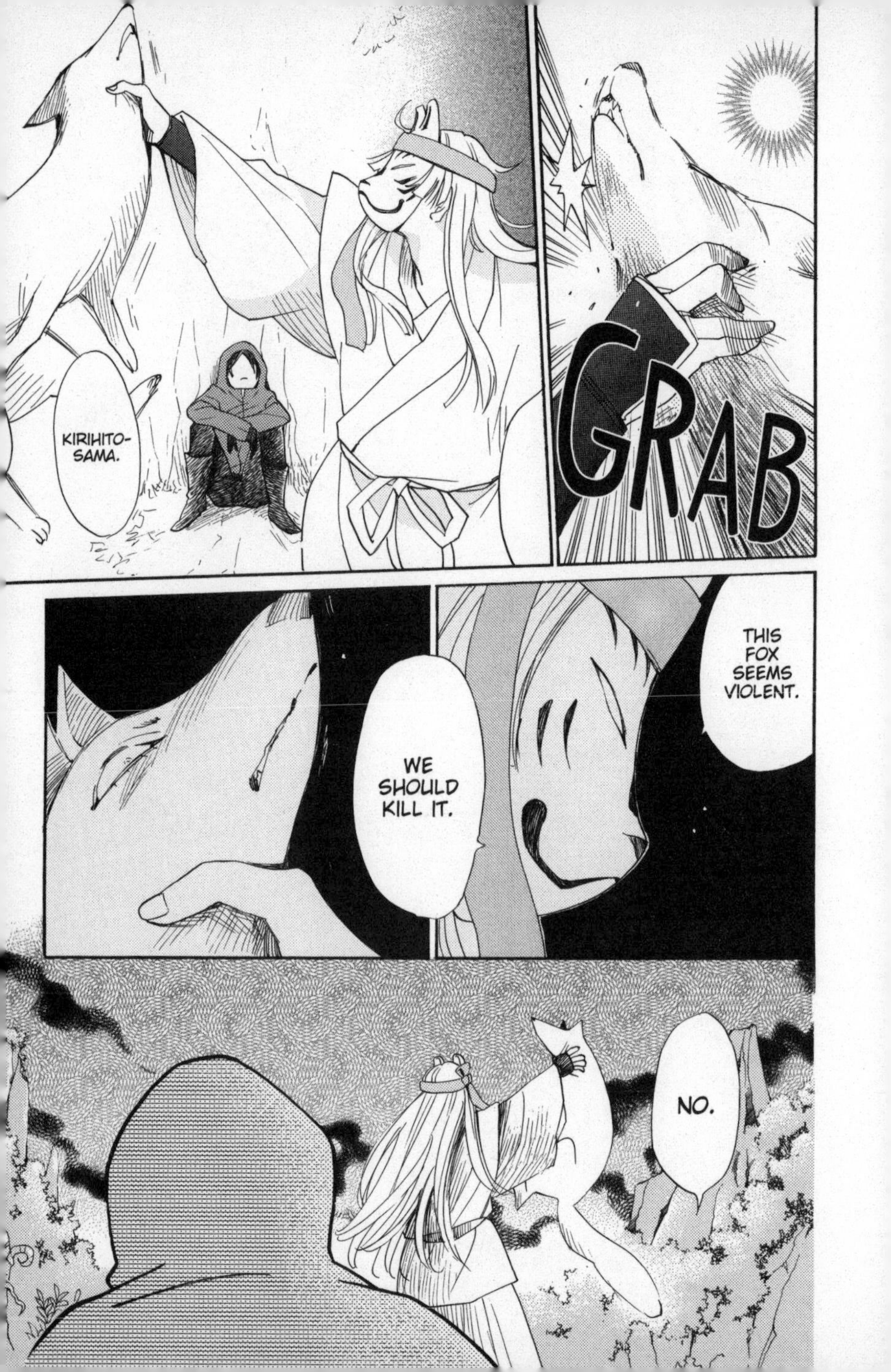
GRAB
KIRIHITO-SAMA.
THIS FOX SEEMS VIOLENT.
WE SHOULD KILL IT.
NO.

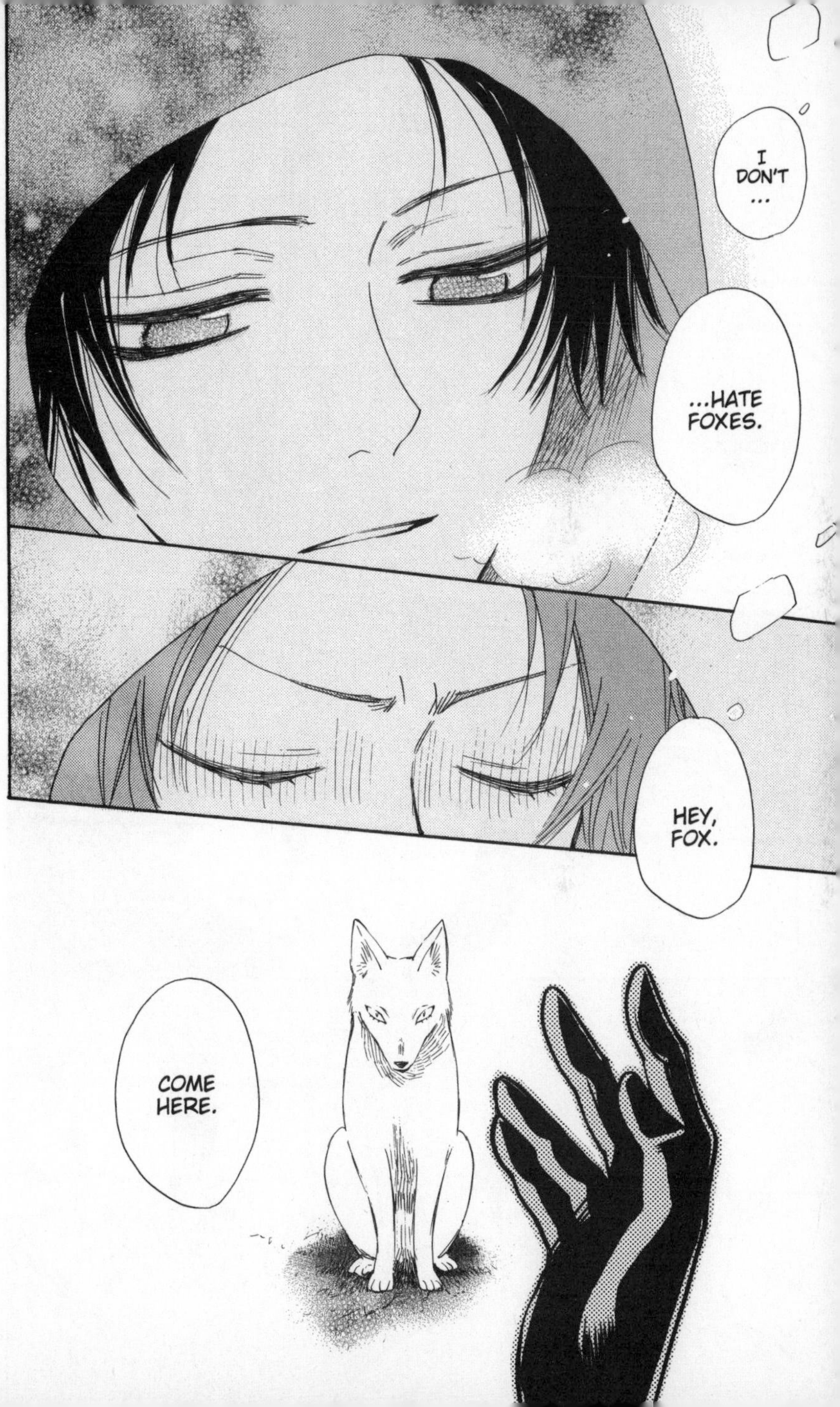
I DON'T ...
...HATE FOXES.
HEY, FOX.
COME HERE.

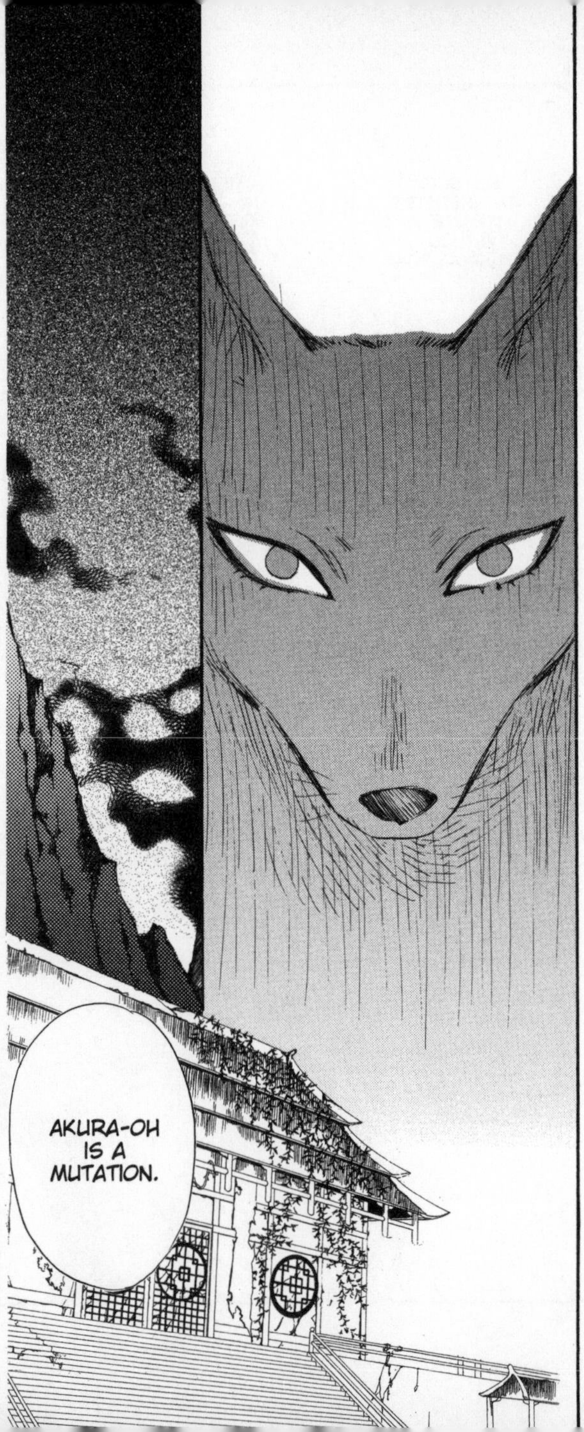
AKURA-OH IS A MUTATION.

I just bought a pair of glasses to protect my eyes.

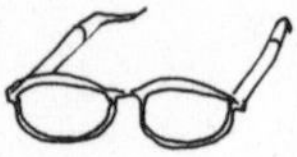

They filter out blue light and I find that reassuring!

I also wear them when I use my smartphone.
I haven't bought glasses in a long time. They've become very light!

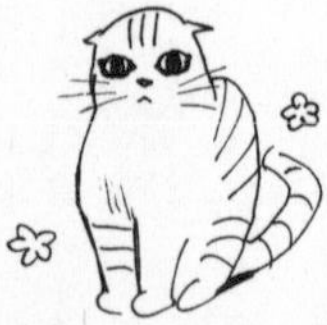

I take care of my cat's eyes too.

I apply eyedrops every day, but the eye goop won't go away.

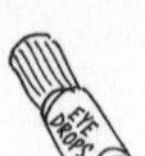
EYE DROPS

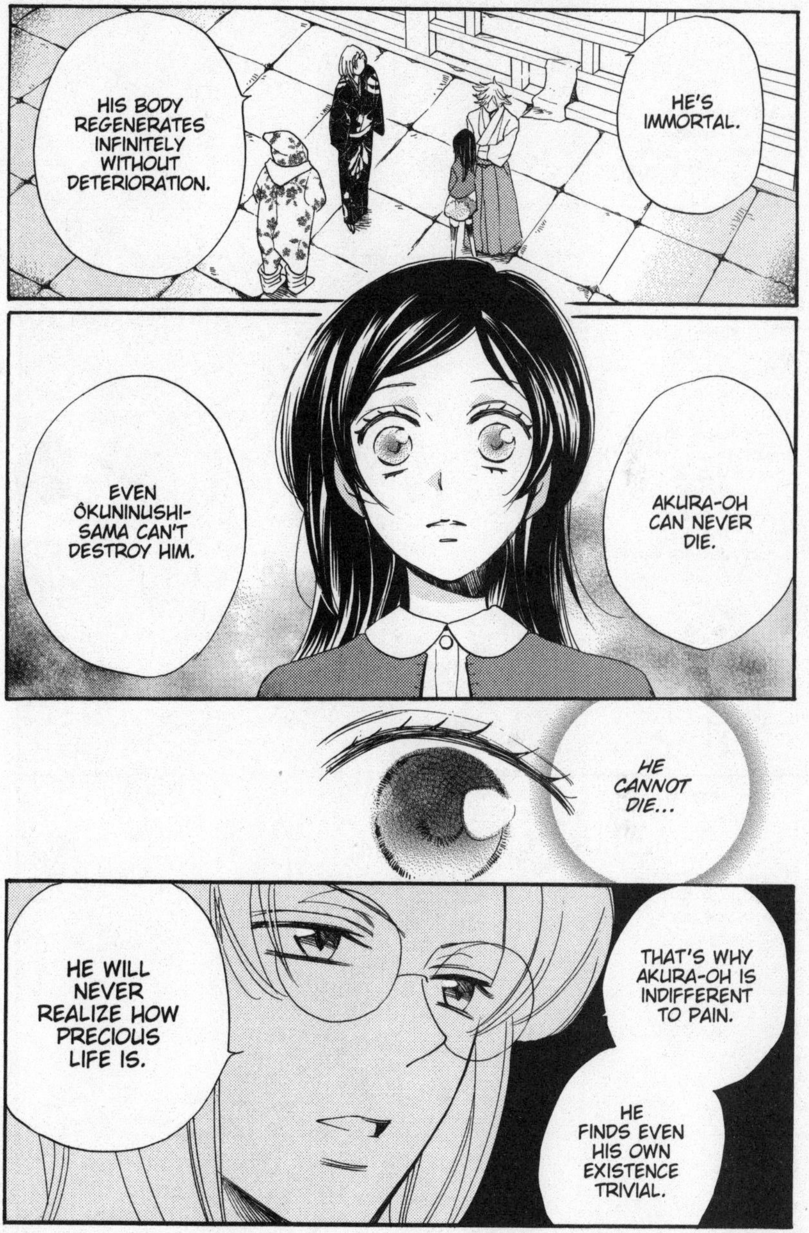
HE'S IMMORTAL.
HIS BODY REGENERATES INFINITELY WITHOUT DETERIORATION.
AKURA-OH CAN NEVER DIE.
EVEN ÔKUNINUSHI-SAMA CAN'T DESTROY HIM.
HE CANNOT DIE...
THAT'S WHY AKURA-OH IS INDIFFERENT TO PAIN.
HE FINDS EVEN HIS OWN EXISTENCE TRIVIAL.
HE WILL NEVER REALIZE HOW PRECIOUS LIFE IS.

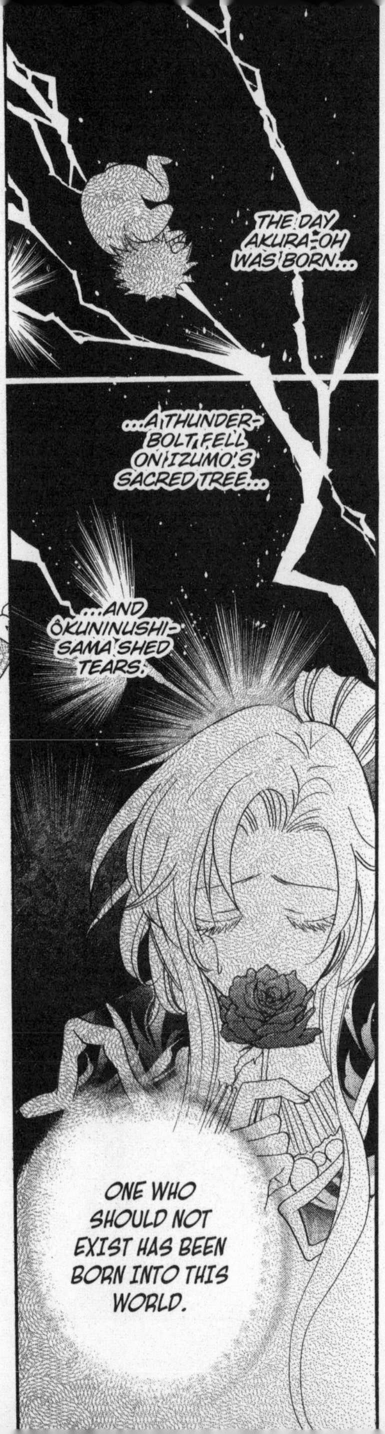
THE DAY AKURA-OH WAS BORN...
...A THUNDER-BOLT FELL ON IZUMO'S SACRED TREE...
...AND ŌKUNINUSHI-SAMA SHED TEARS.
ONE WHO SHOULD NOT EXIST HAS BEEN BORN INTO THIS WORLD.
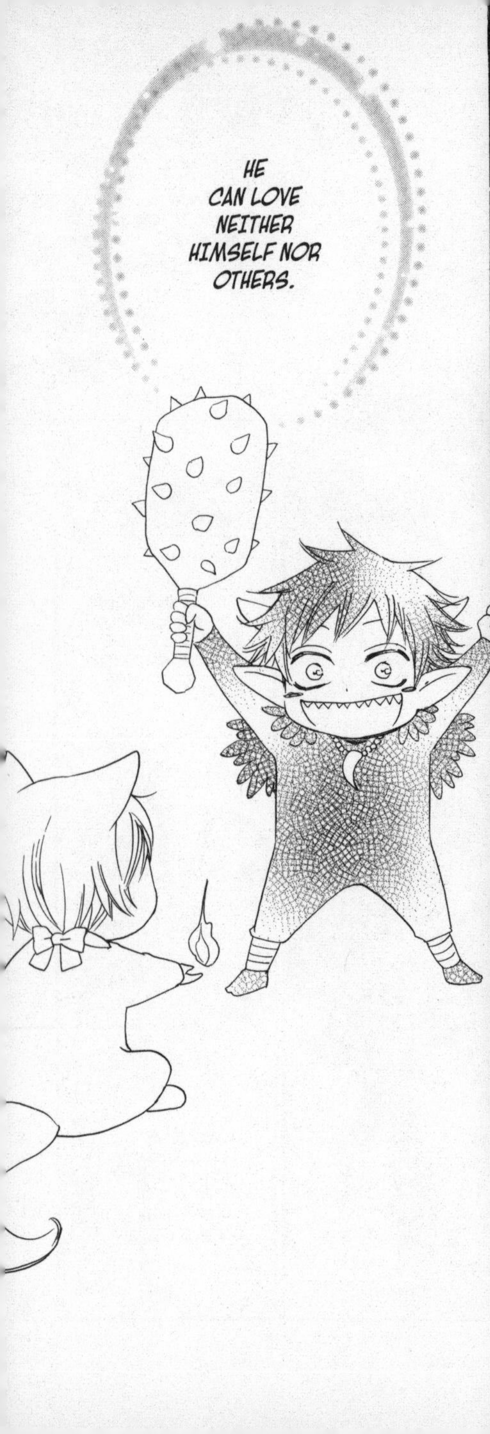
HE CAN LOVE NEITHER HIMSELF NOR OTHERS.

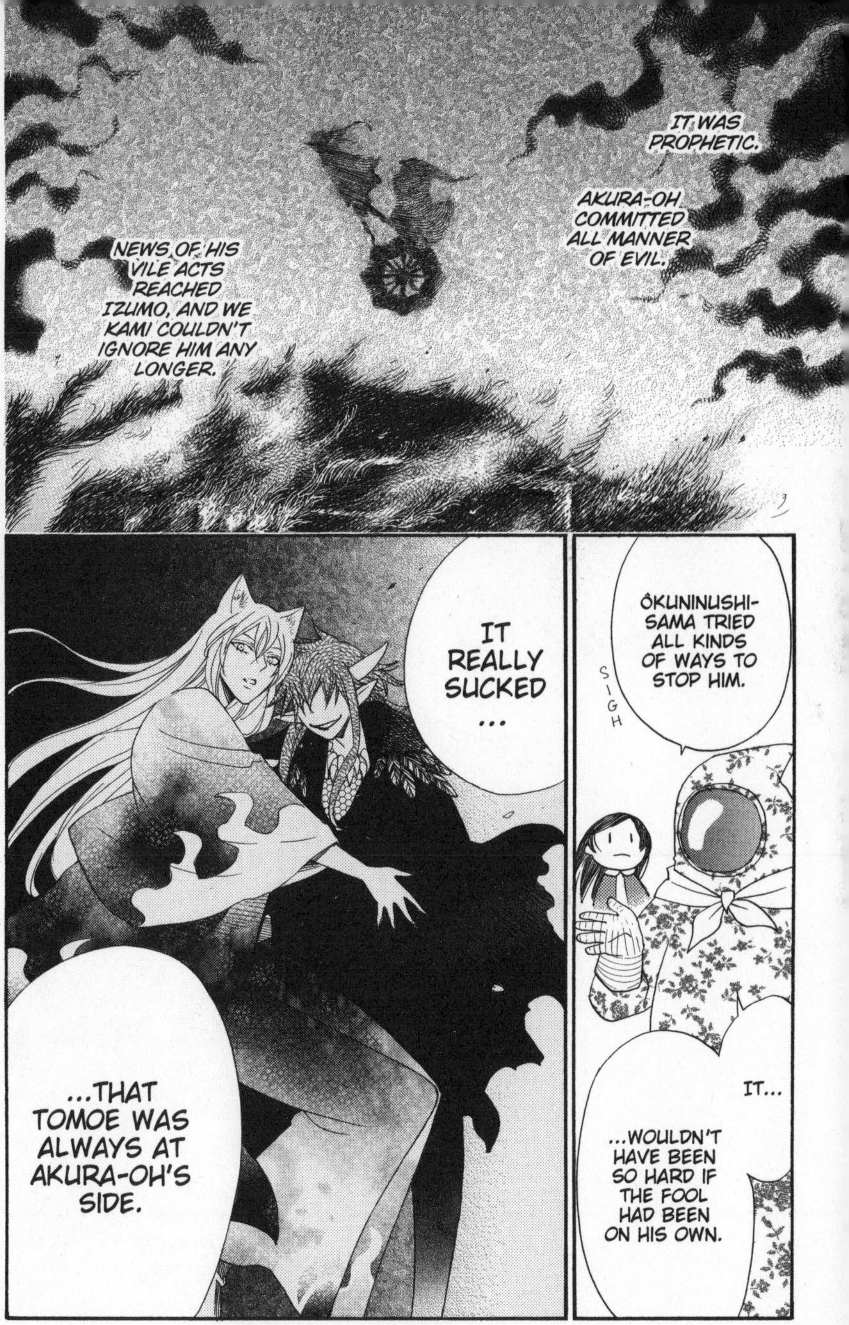
IT WAS PROPHETIC.
AKURA-OH COMMITTED ALL MANNER OF EVIL.
NEWS OF HIS VILE ACTS REACHED IZUMO, AND WE KAMI COULDN'T IGNORE HIM ANY LONGER.
ÔKUNINUSHI-SAMA TRIED ALL KINDS OF WAYS TO STOP HIM.
SIGH
IT...
...WOULDN'T HAVE BEEN SO HARD IF THE FOOL HAD BEEN ON HIS OWN.
IT REALLY SUCKED...
...THAT TOMOE WAS ALWAYS AT AKURA-OH'S SIDE.

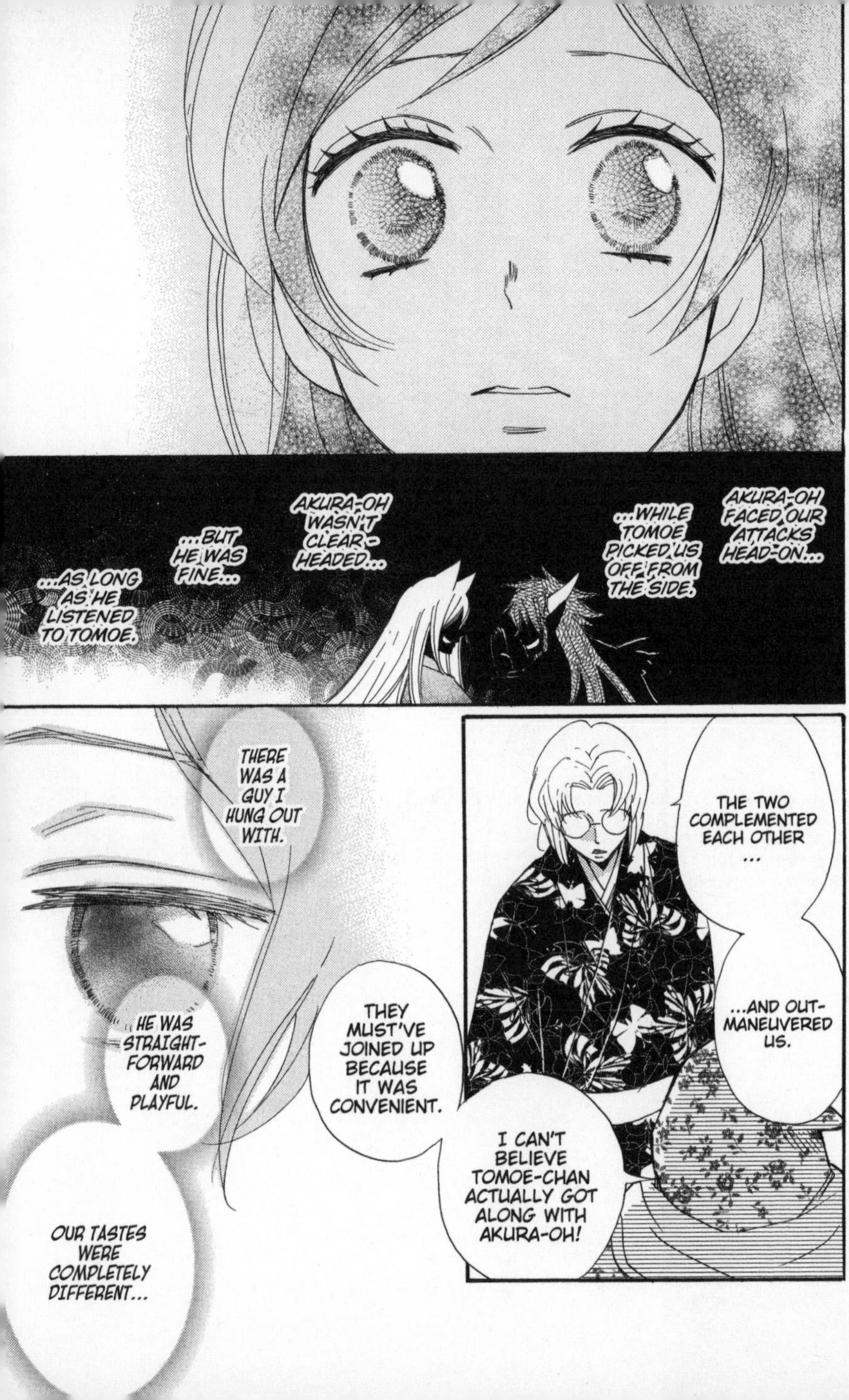
AKURA-OH FACED OUR ATTACKS HEAD-ON...
...WHILE TOMOE PICKED US OFF FROM THE SIDE.
AKURA-OH WASN'T CLEAR-HEADED...
...BUT HE WAS FINE...
...AS LONG AS HE LISTENED TO TOMOE.
THE TWO COMPLEMENTED EACH OTHER ...
...AND OUT-MANEUVERED US.
I CAN'T BELIEVE TOMOE-CHAN ACTUALLY GOT ALONG WITH AKURA-OH!
THEY MUST'VE JOINED UP BECAUSE IT WAS CONVENIENT.
THERE WAS A GUY I HUNG OUT WITH.
HE WAS STRAIGHT-FORWARD AND PLAYFUL.
OUR TASTES WERE COMPLETELY DIFFERENT...

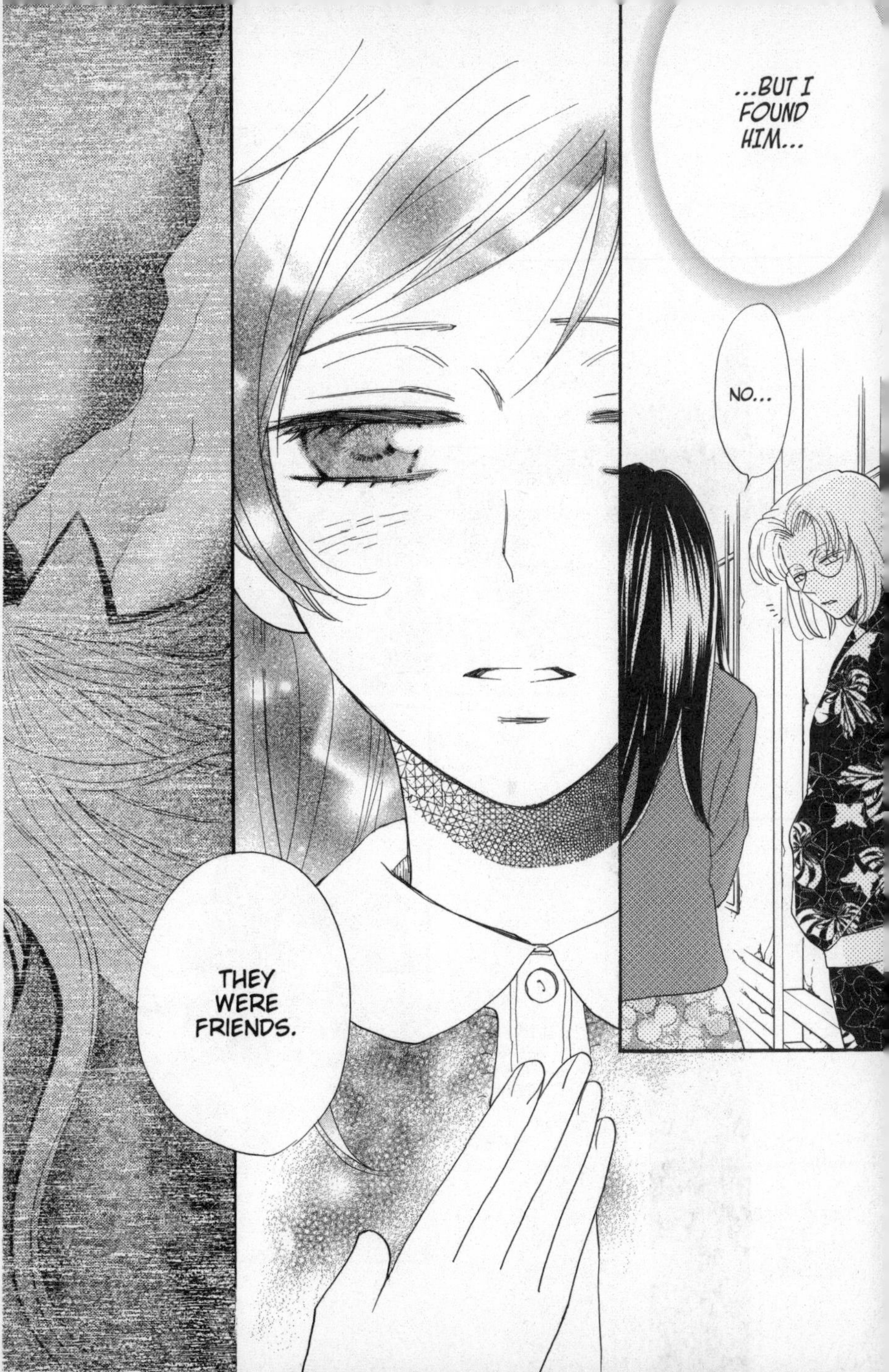
...BUT I FOUND HIM...
NO...
THEY WERE FRIENDS.

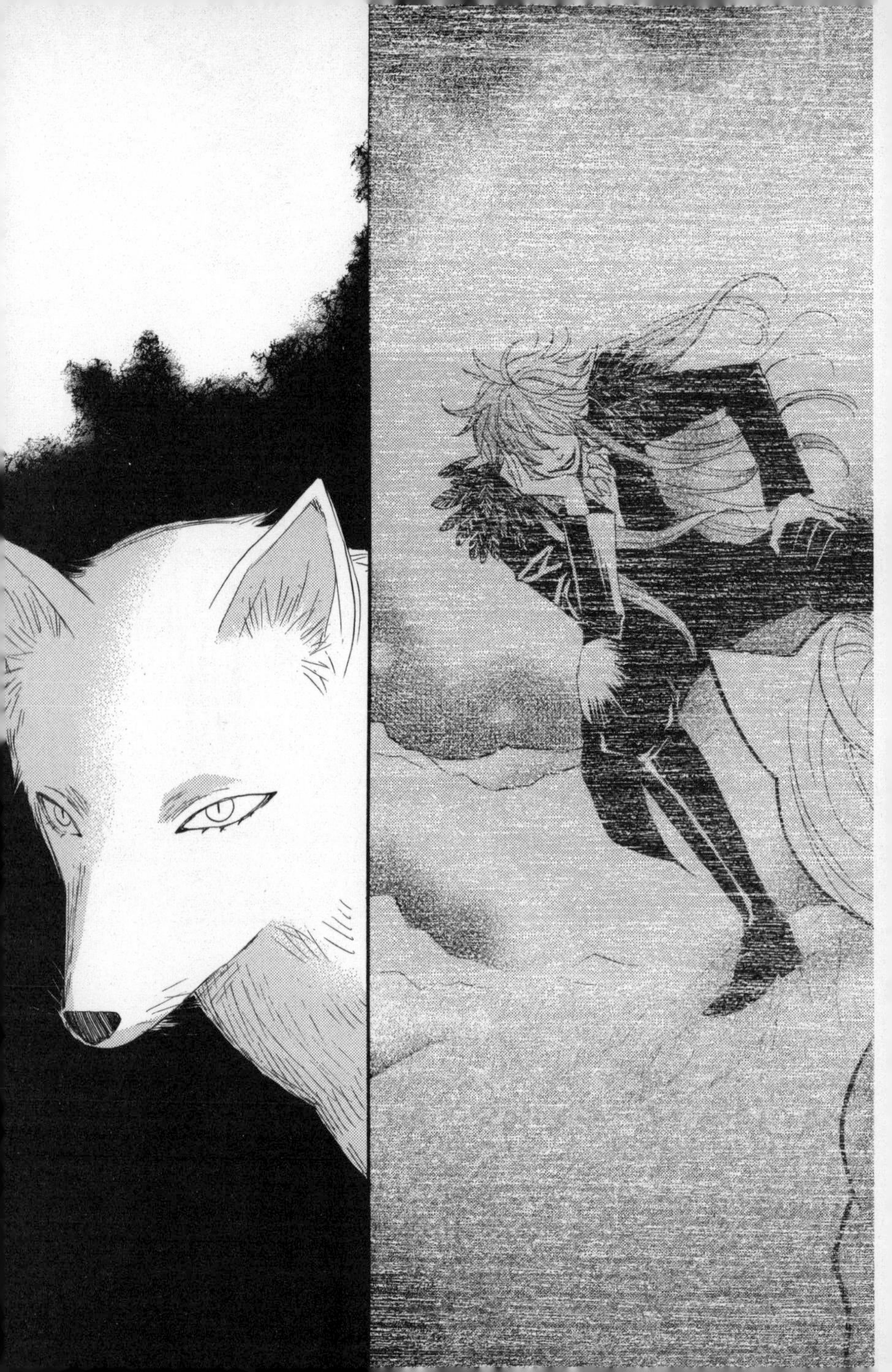

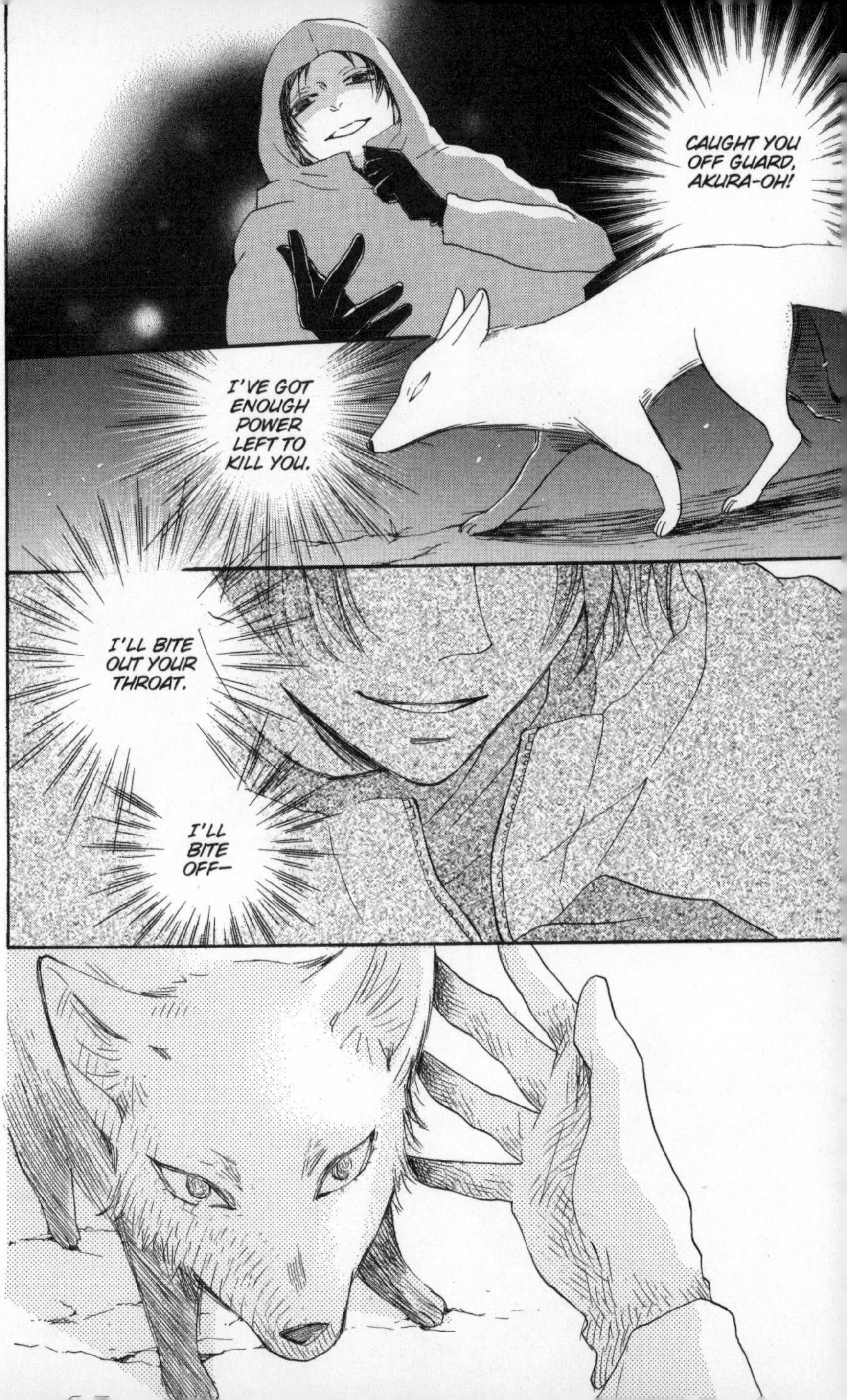
CAUGHT YOU OFF GUARD, AKURA-OH!
I'VE GOT ENOUGH POWER LEFT TO KILL YOU.
I'LL BITE OUT YOUR THROAT.
I'LL BITE OFF—

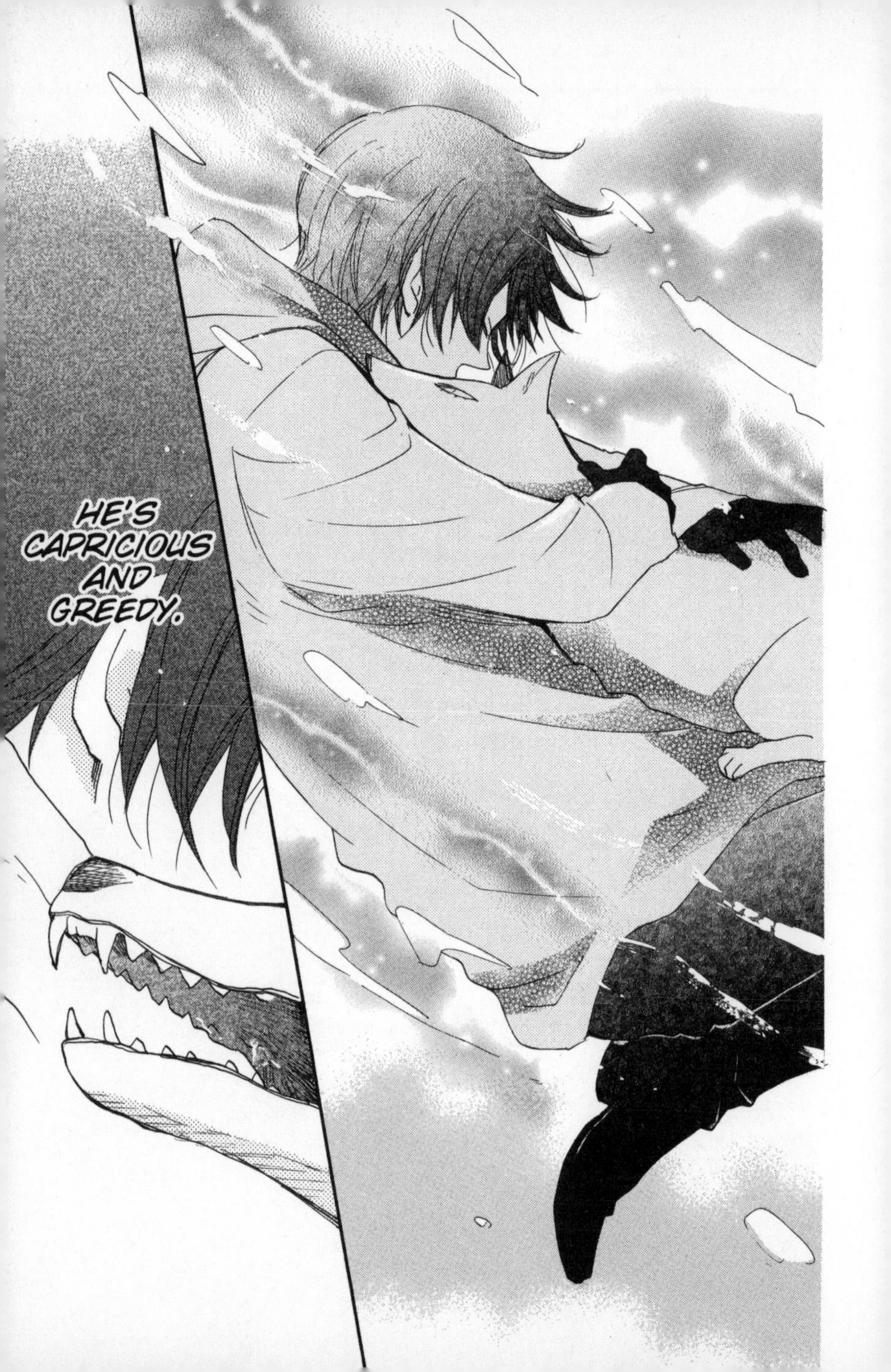
HE'S CAPRICIOUS AND GREEDY.

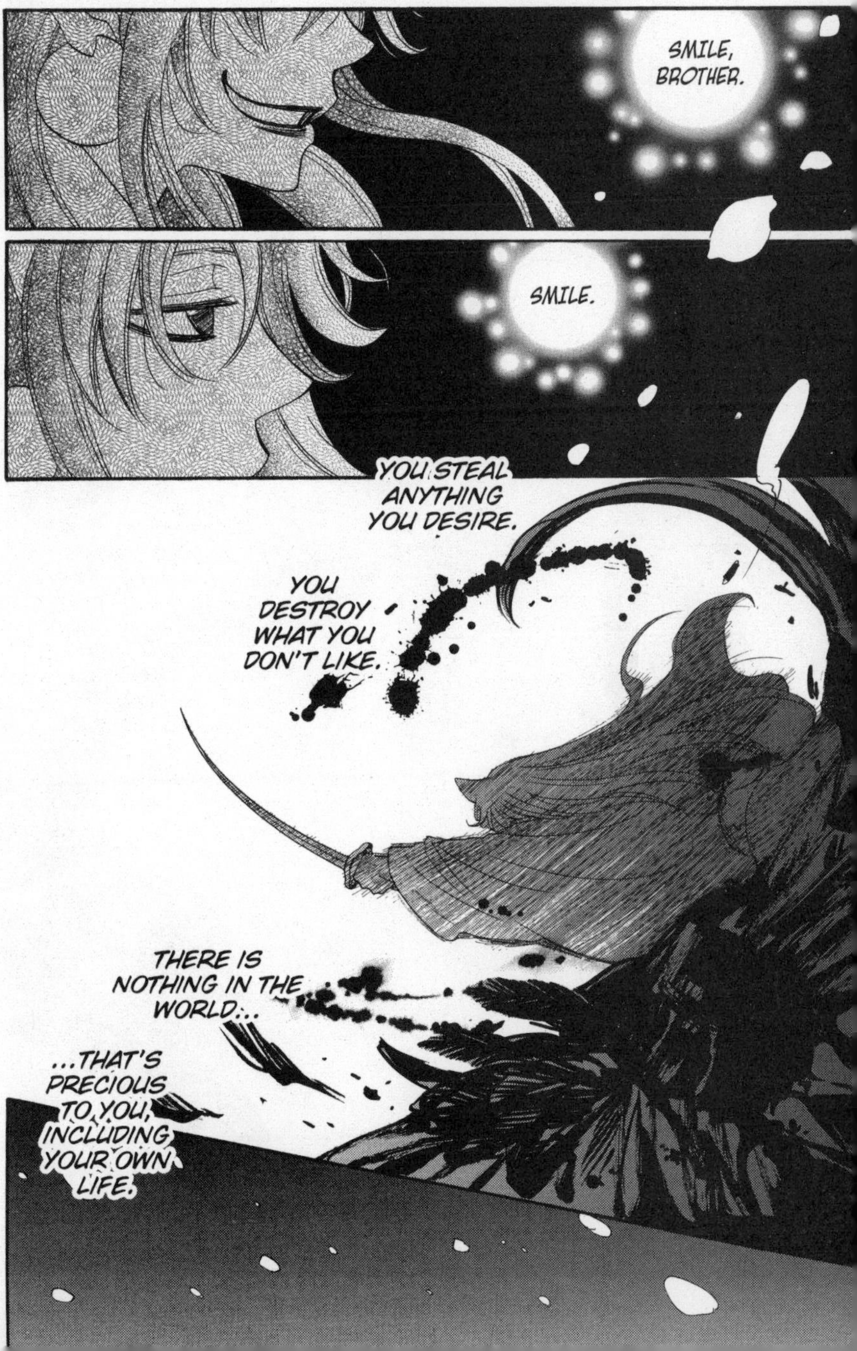
SMILE, BROTHER.
SMILE.
YOU STEAL ANYTHING YOU DESIRE.
YOU DESTROY WHAT YOU DON'T LIKE.
THERE IS NOTHING IN THE WORLD...
...THAT'S PRECIOUS TO YOU, INCLUDING YOUR OWN LIFE.

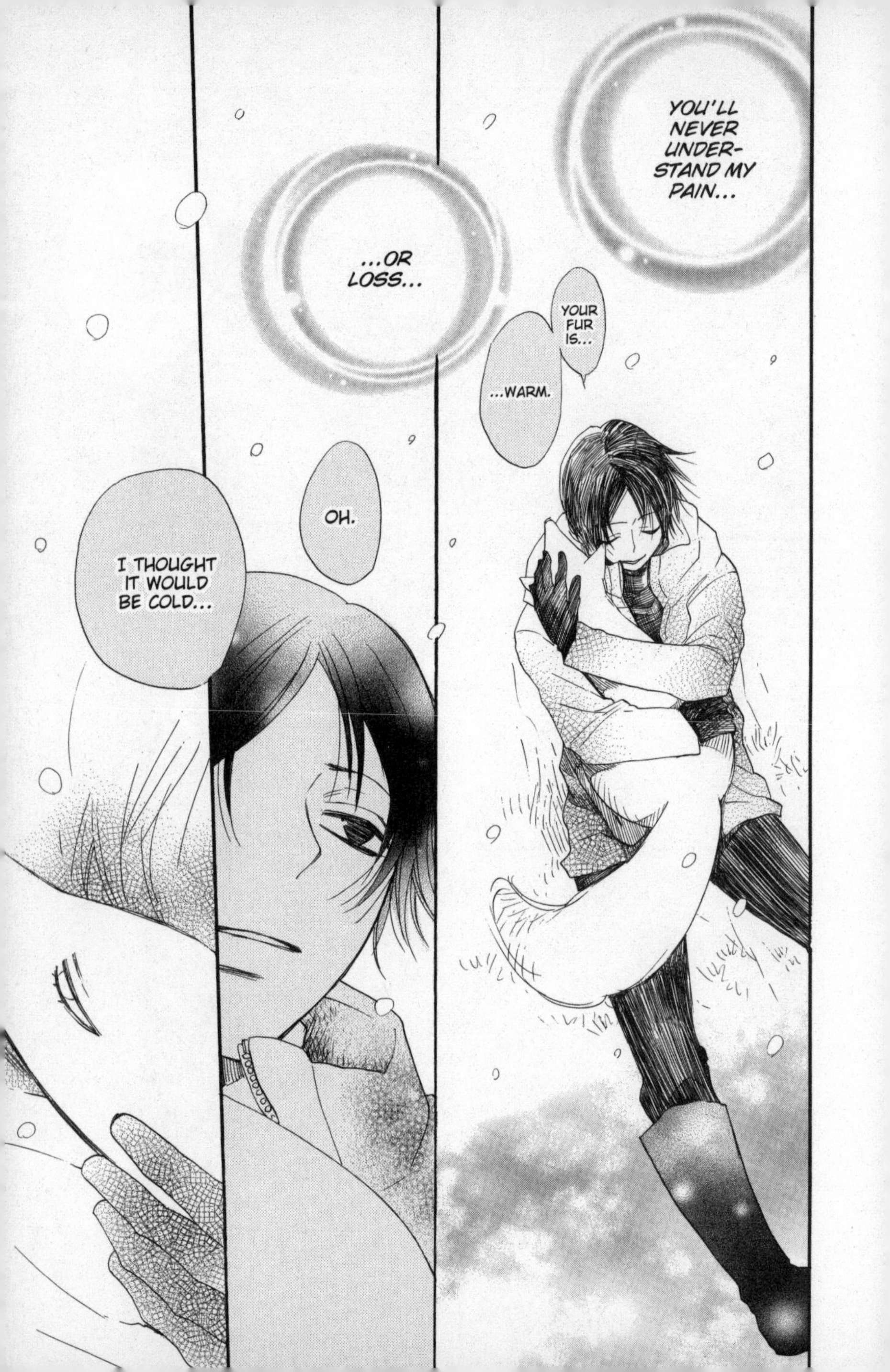
YOU'LL NEVER UNDER-STAND MY PAIN...
YOUR FUR IS...
...WARM.
...OR LOSS...
OH.
I THOUGHT IT WOULD BE COLD...

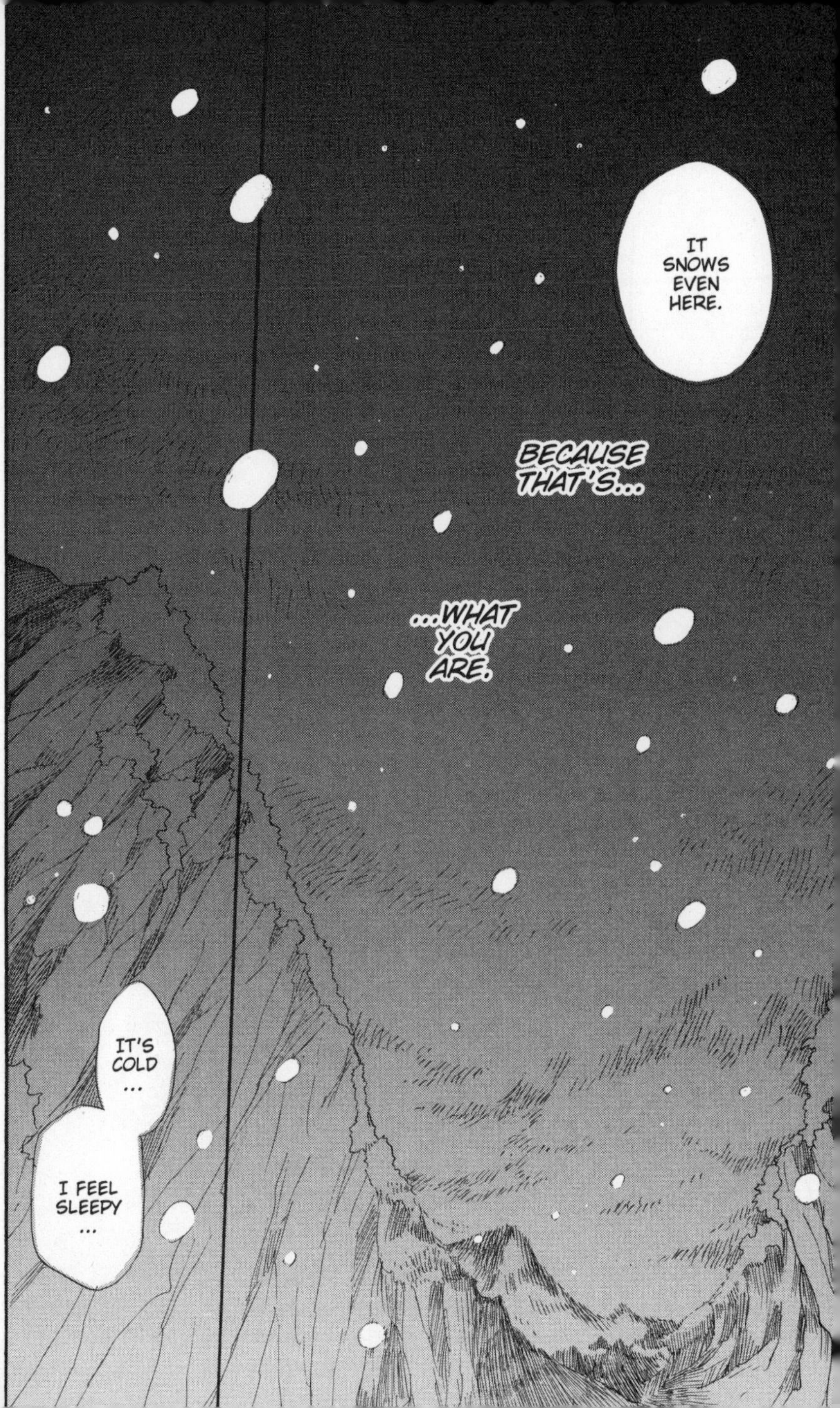
IT SNOWS EVEN HERE.
BECAUSE THAT'S...
...WHAT YOU ARE.
IT'S COLD ...
I FEEL SLEEPY ...

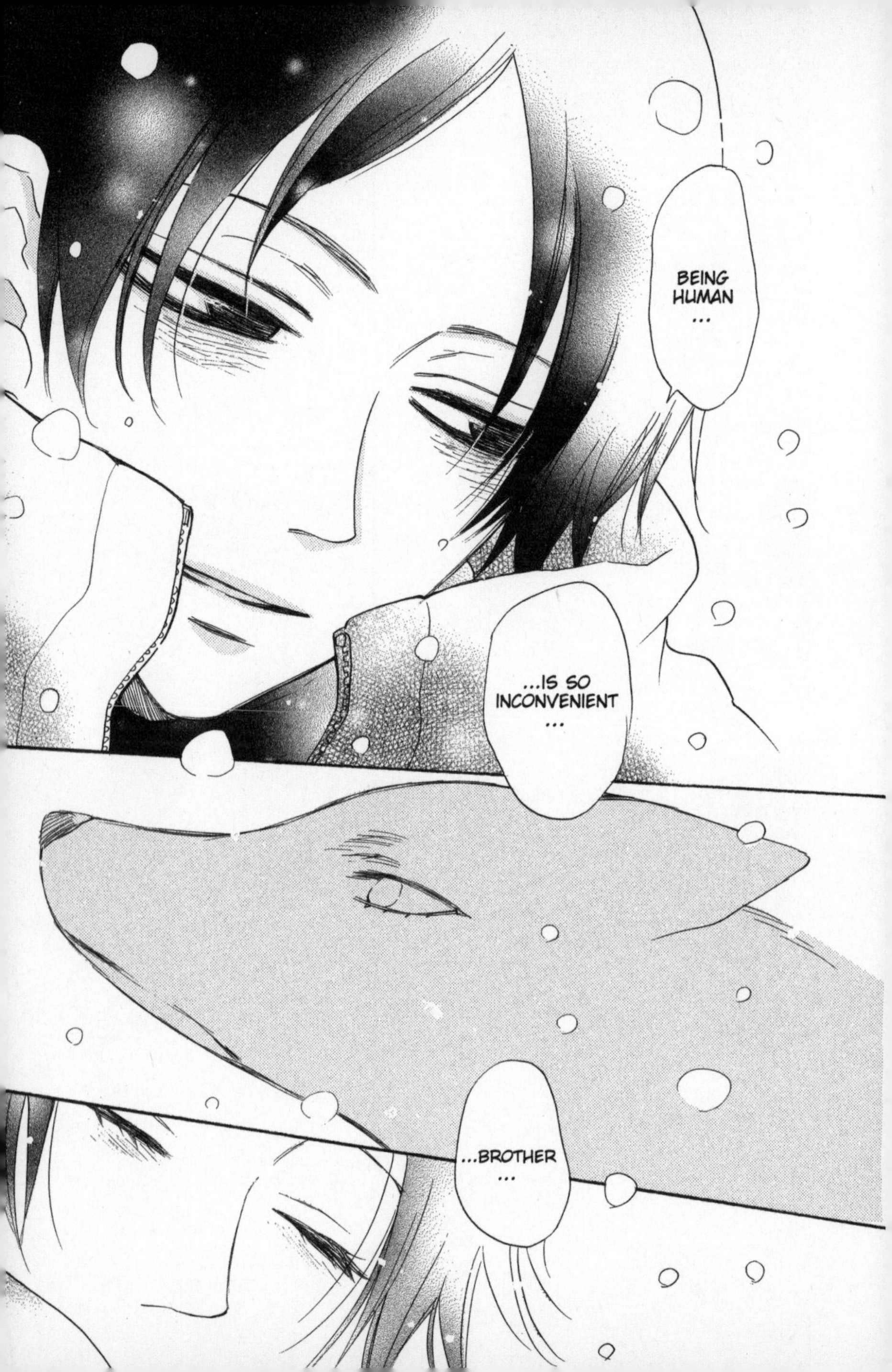
BEING HUMAN...
...IS SO INCONVENIENT...
...BROTHER...

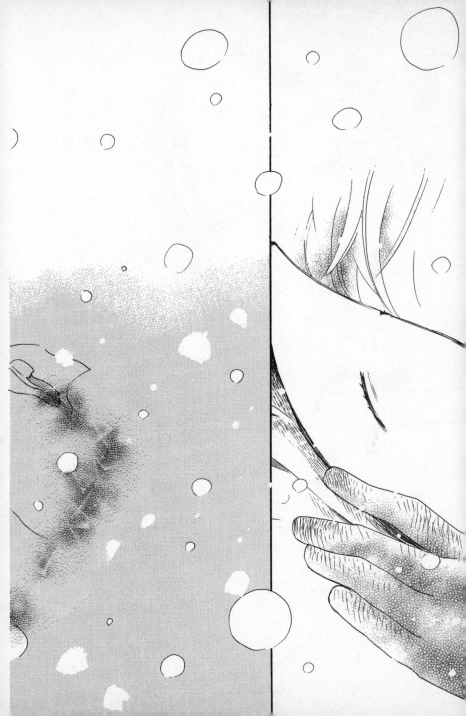

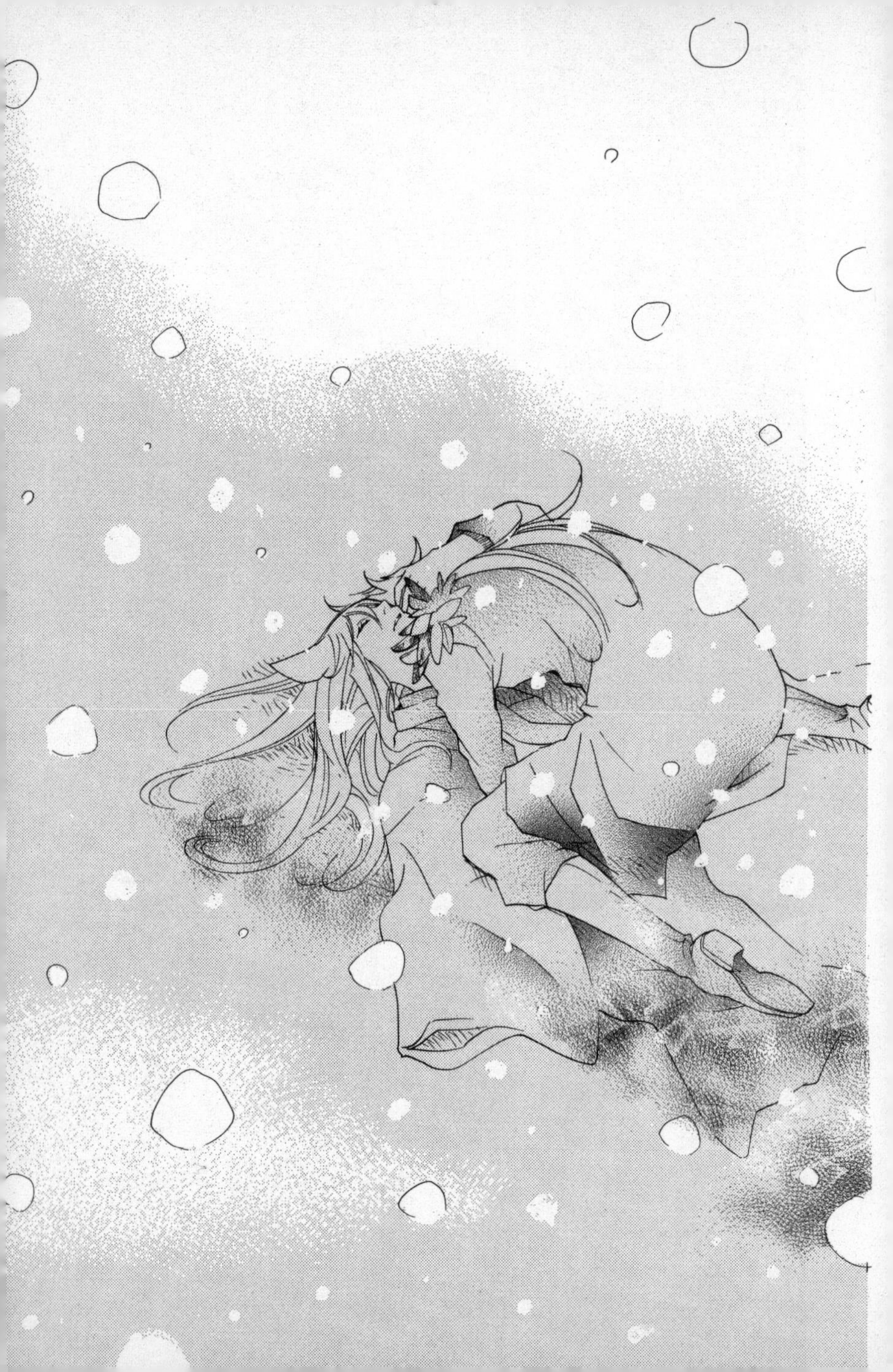

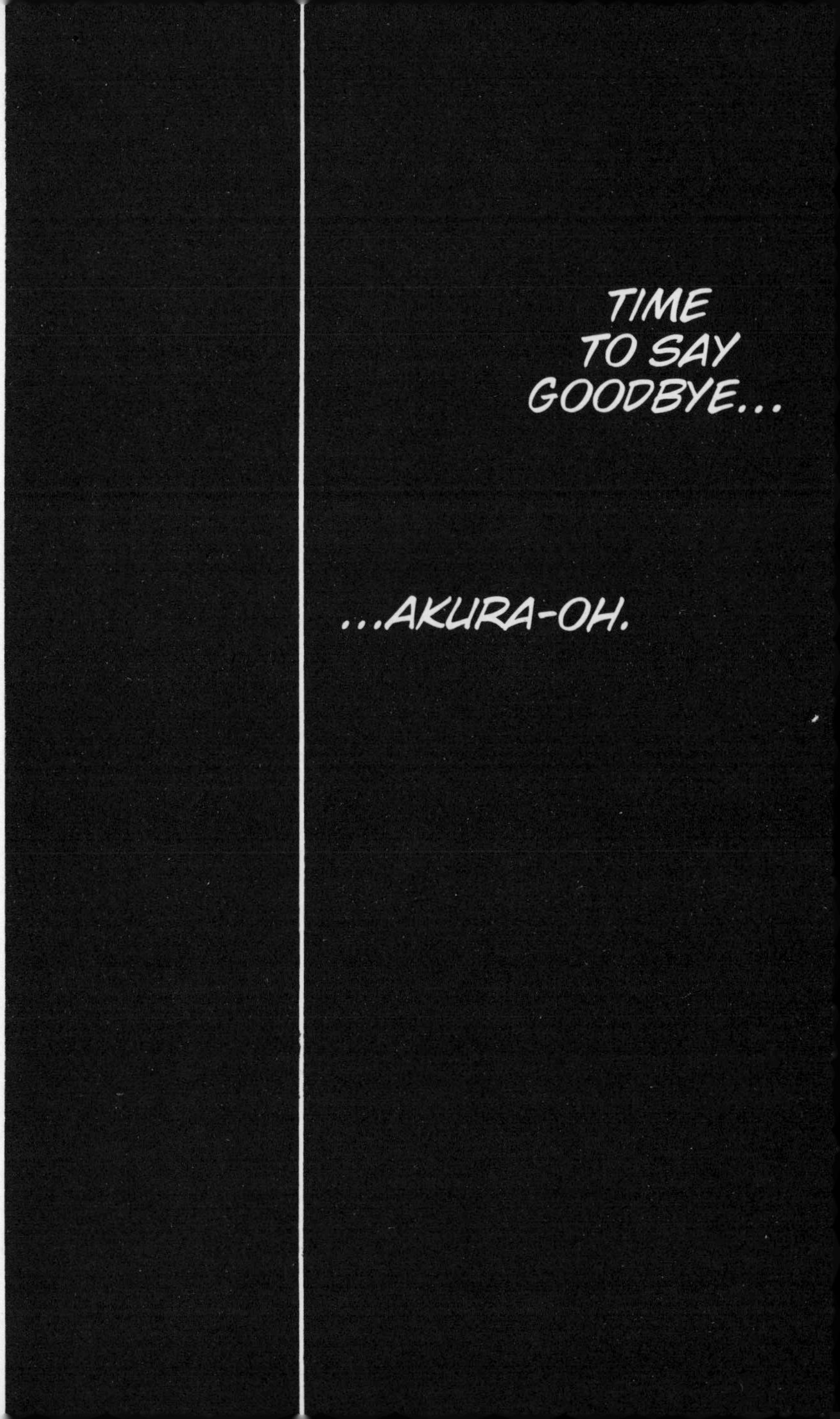
TIME TO SAY GOODBYE...
...AKURA-OH.

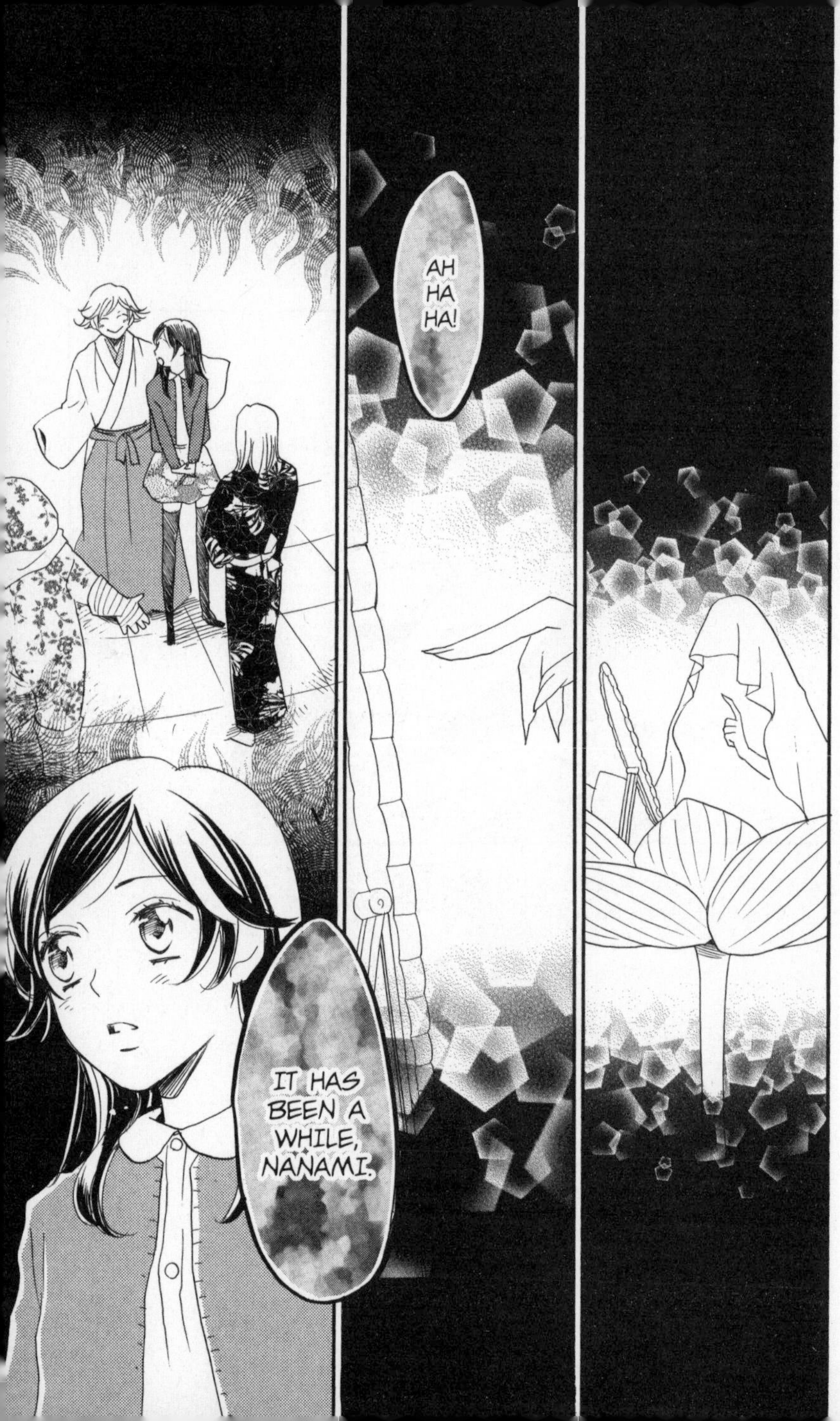
AH HA HA!
IT HAS BEEN A WHILE, NANAMI.

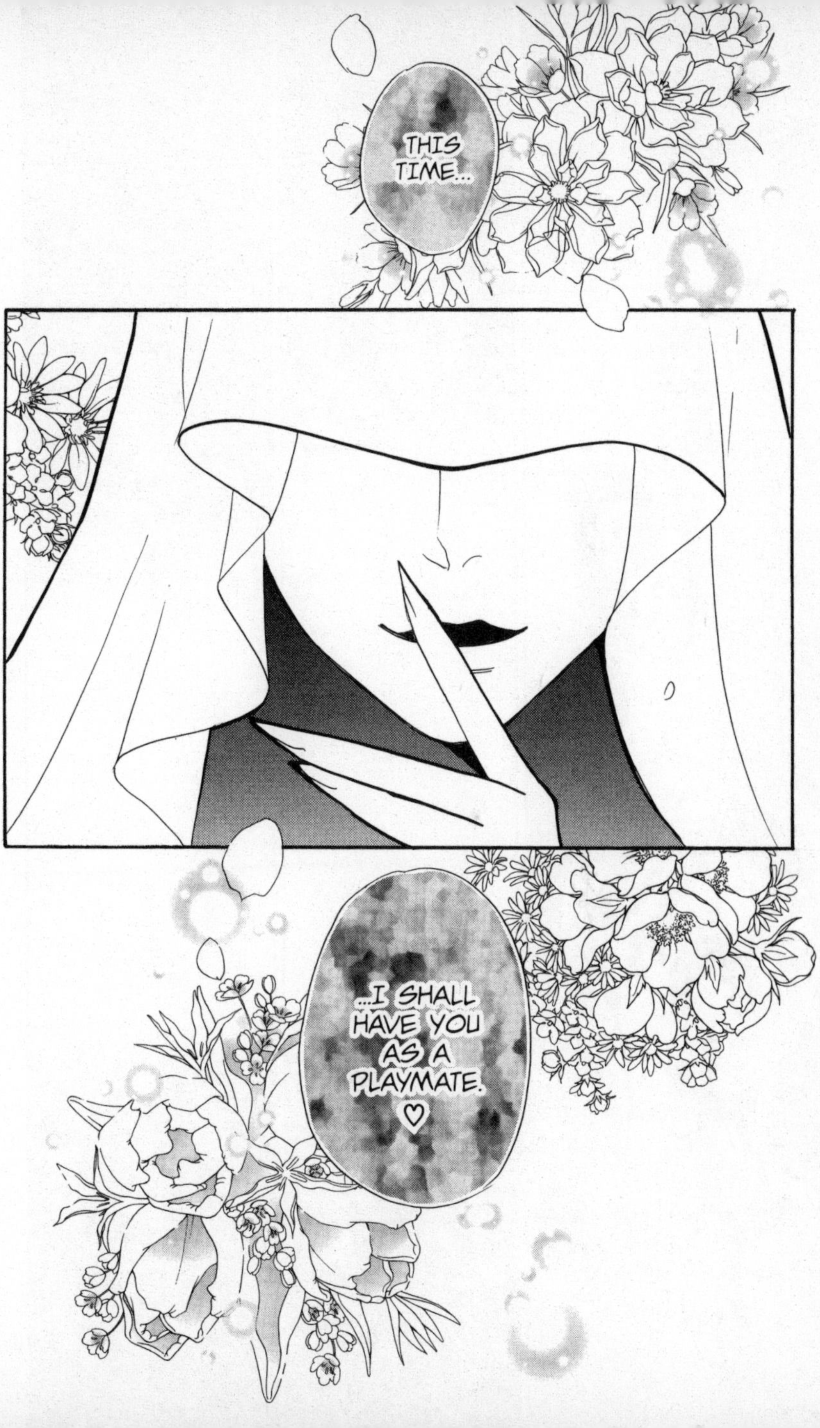
THIS TIME...
...I SHALL HAVE YOU AS A PLAYMATE. ♡

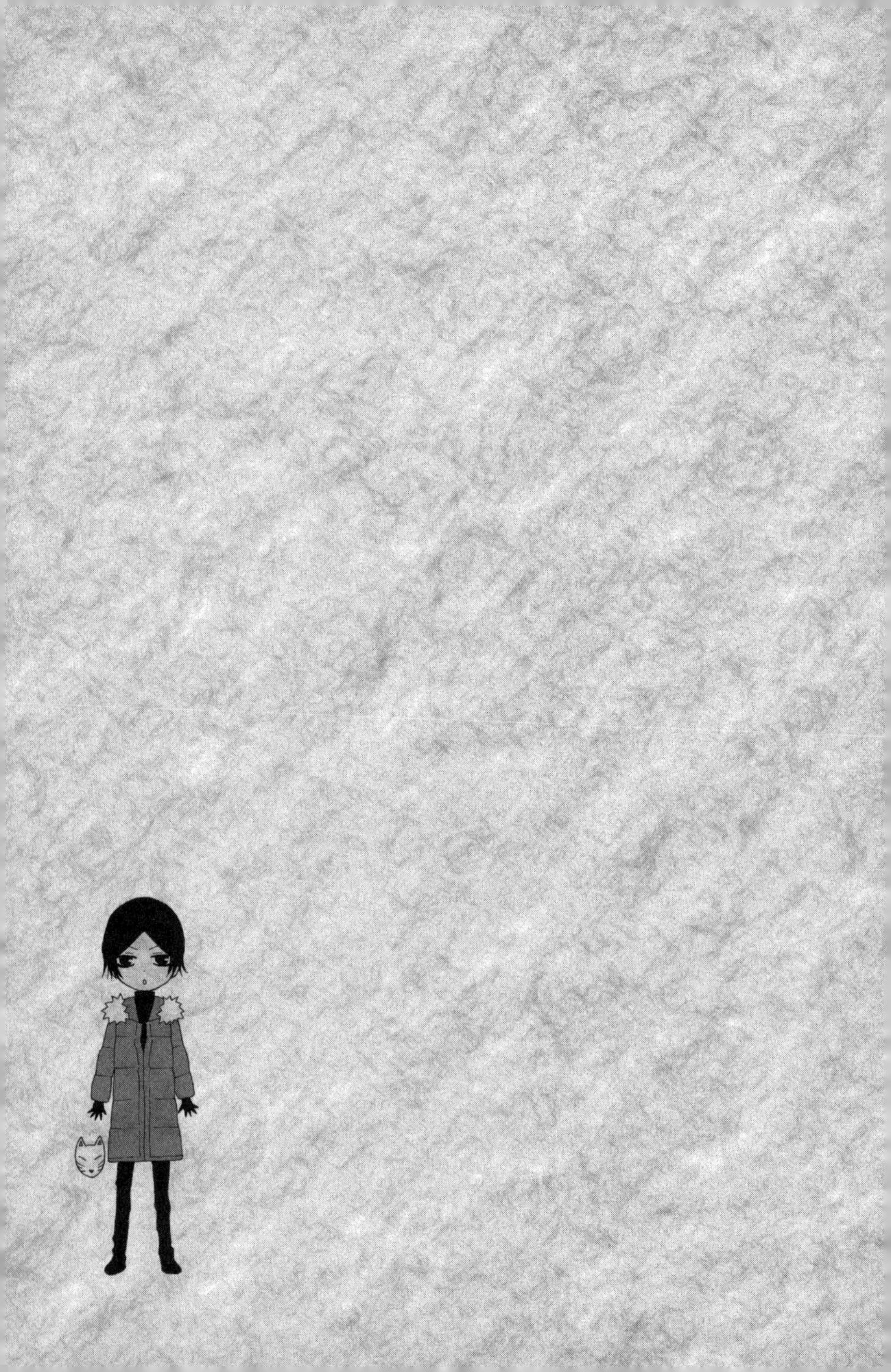

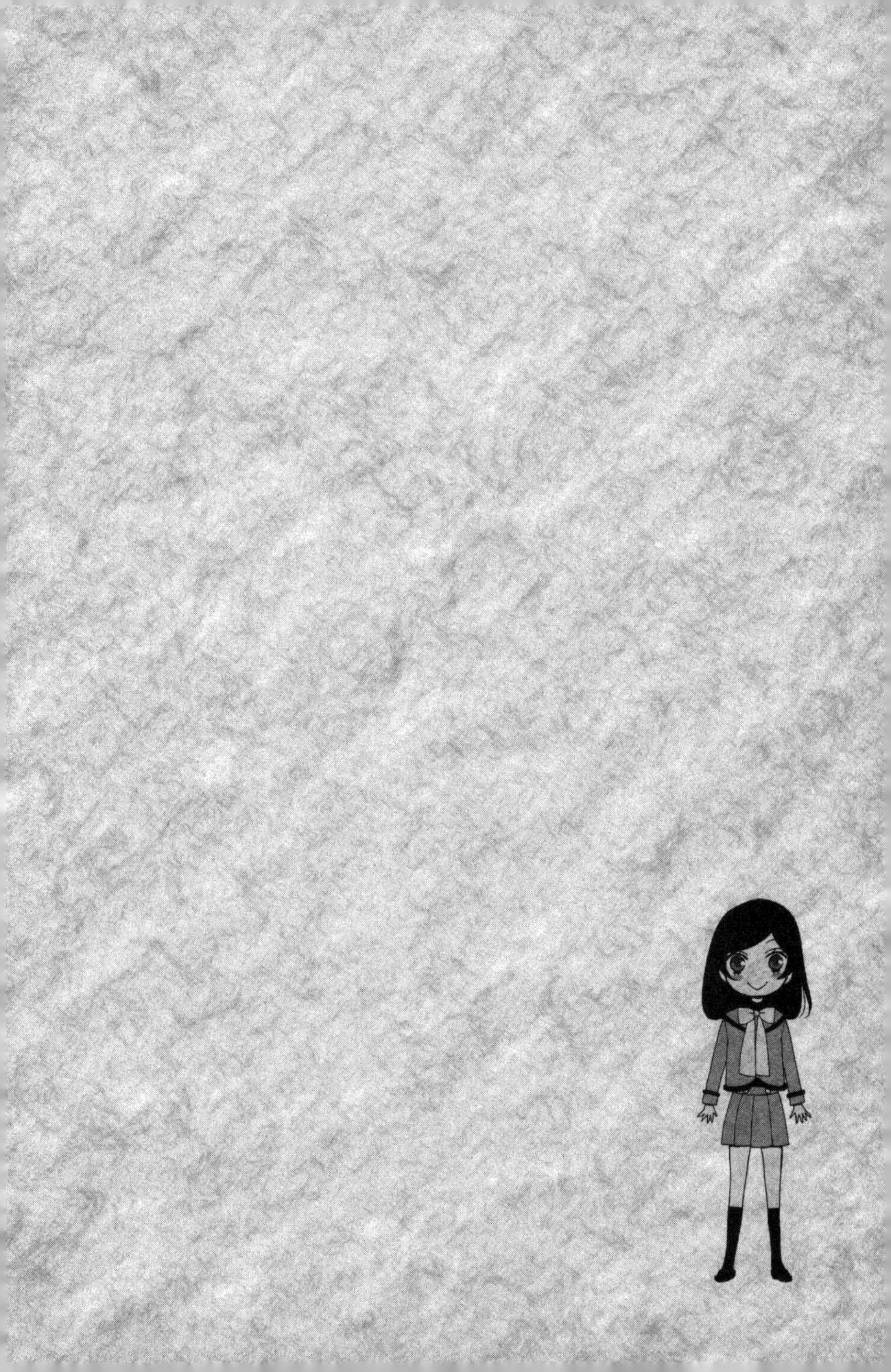

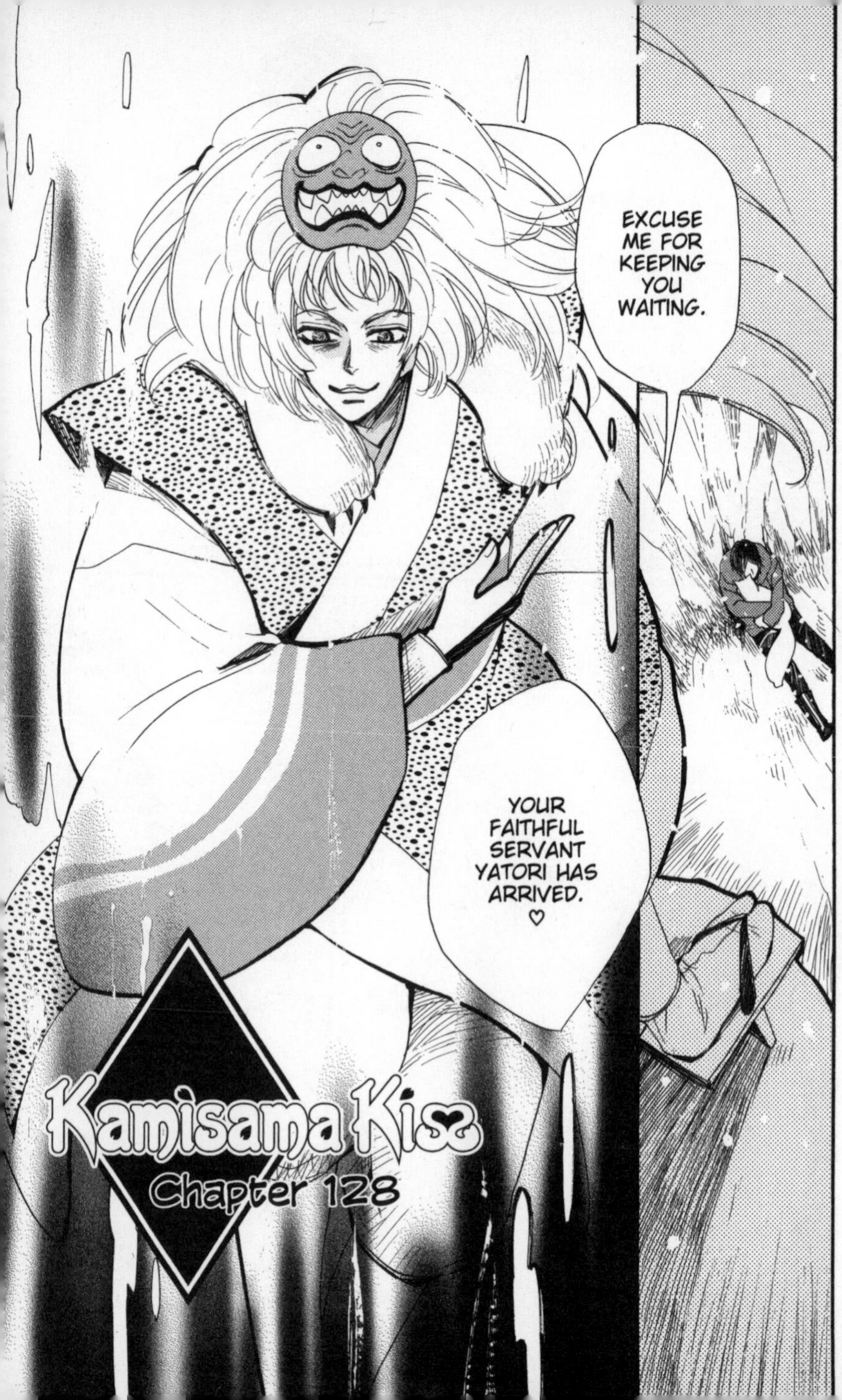
EXCUSE ME FOR KEEPING YOU WAITING.
YOUR FAITHFUL SERVANT YATORI HAS ARRIVED. ♡
Kamisama Kiss
Chapter 128

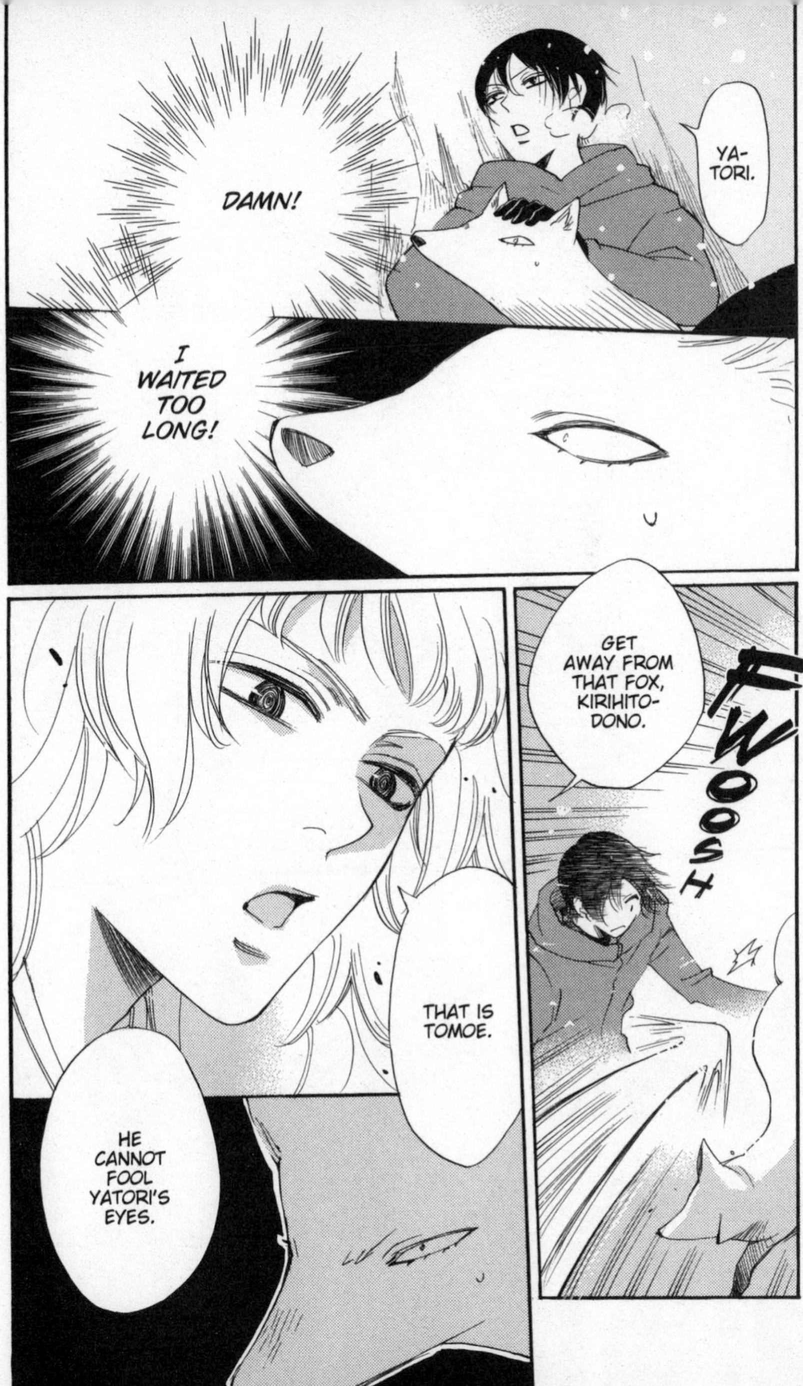
YA-TORI.
DAMN!
I WAITED TOO LONG!
GET AWAY FROM THAT FOX, KIRIHITO-DONO.
FWOOSH
THAT IS TOMOE.
HE CANNOT FOOL YATORI'S EYES.

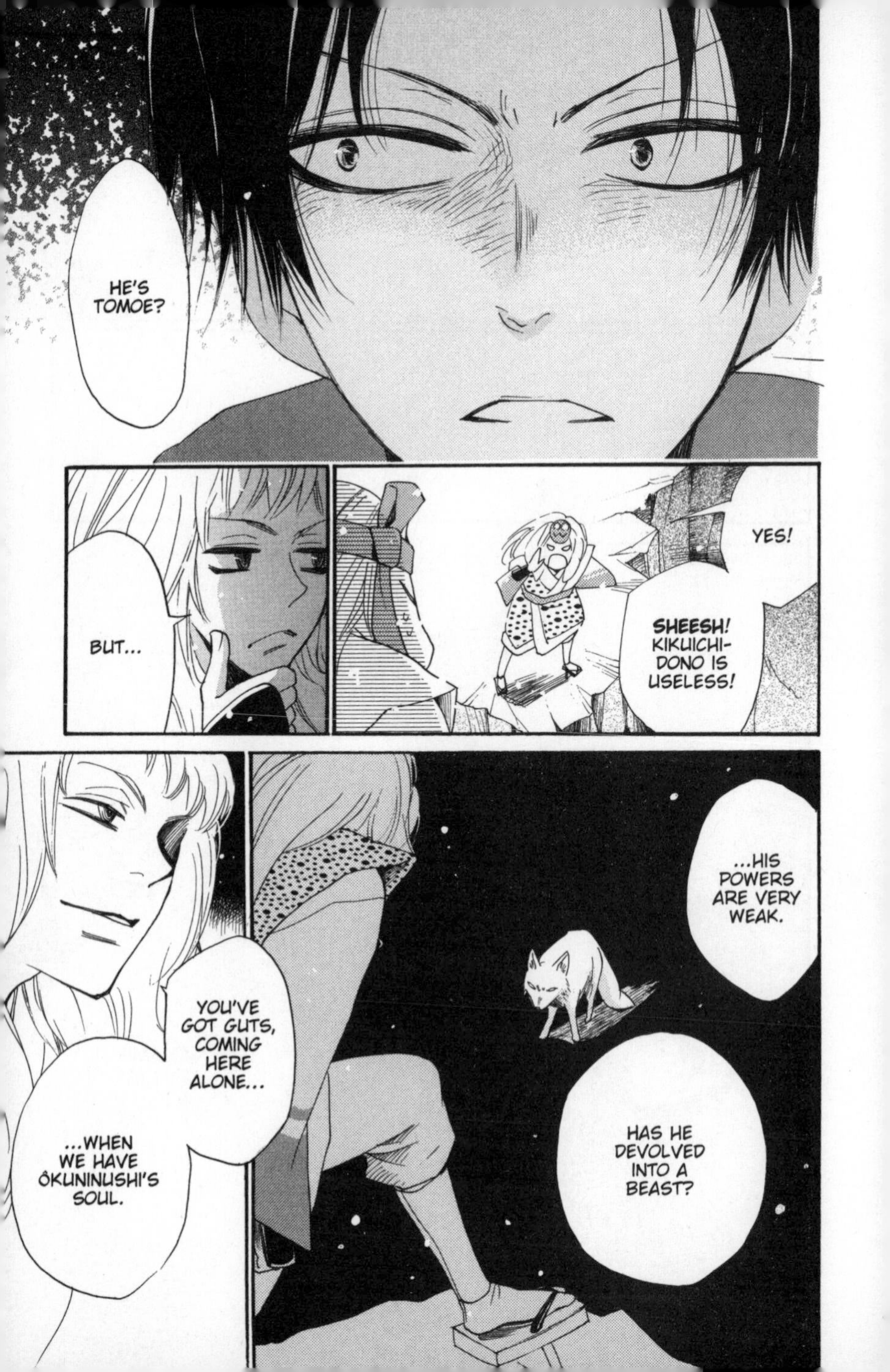

HE'S TOMOE?
YES!
SHEESH! KIKUICHI-DONO IS USELESS!
BUT...
...HIS POWERS ARE VERY WEAK.
HAS HE DEVOLVED INTO A BEAST?
YOU'VE GOT GUTS, COMING HERE ALONE...
...WHEN WE HAVE ÔKUNINUSHI'S SOUL.

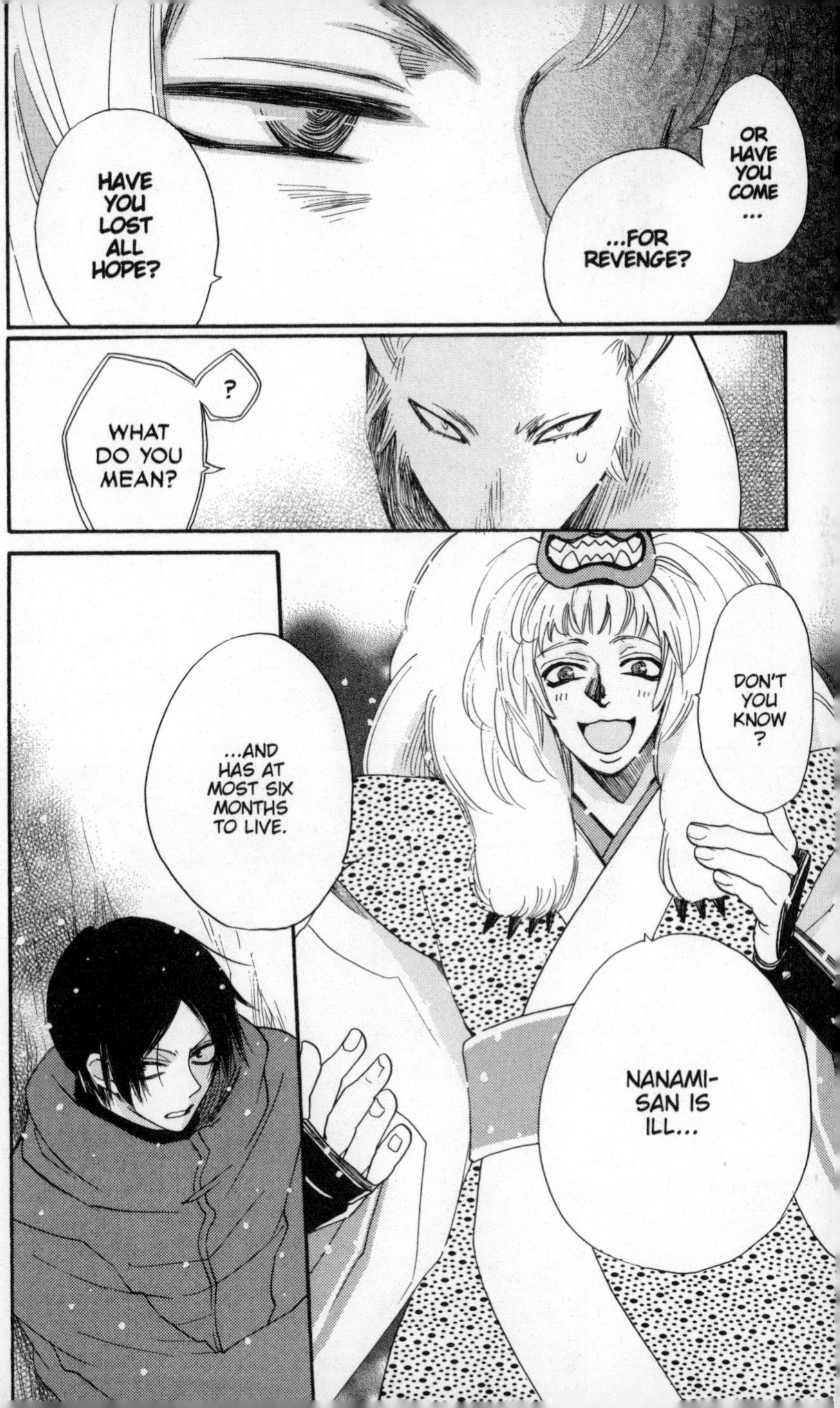
OR HAVE YOU COME...
...FOR REVENGE?
HAVE YOU LOST ALL HOPE?
WHAT DO YOU MEAN?
?
DON'T YOU KNOW?
NANAMI-SAN IS ILL...
...AND HAS AT MOST SIX MONTHS TO LIVE.

DON'T LIE.

I REGRET TO TELL YOU IT'S TRUE.

YOU CANNOT FOOL YATORI'S EYES.

SHE DIDN'T KNOW UNTIL I TOLD HER...

...BUT SHE SEEMED TO UNDERSTAND WHY...

...AND WAS IN TEARS AS SHE ACCEPTED HER FATE.

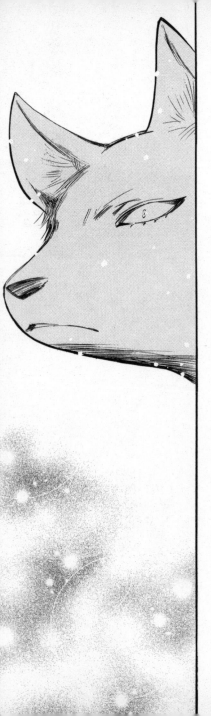

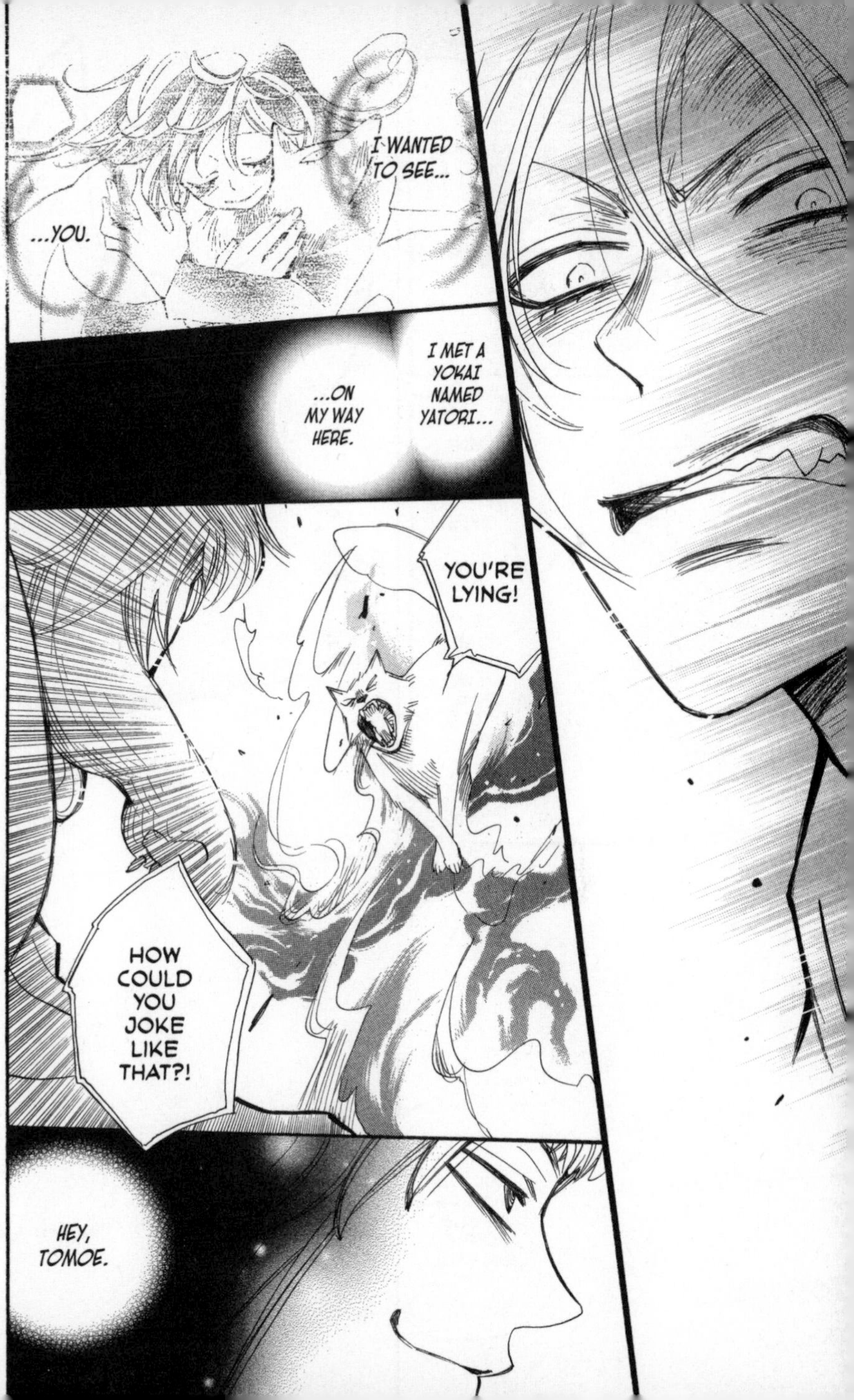
I WANTED TO SEE...
...YOU.
I MET A YOKAI NAMED YATORI...
...ON MY WAY HERE.
YOU'RE LYING!
HOW COULD YOU JOKE LIKE THAT?!
HEY, TOMOE.

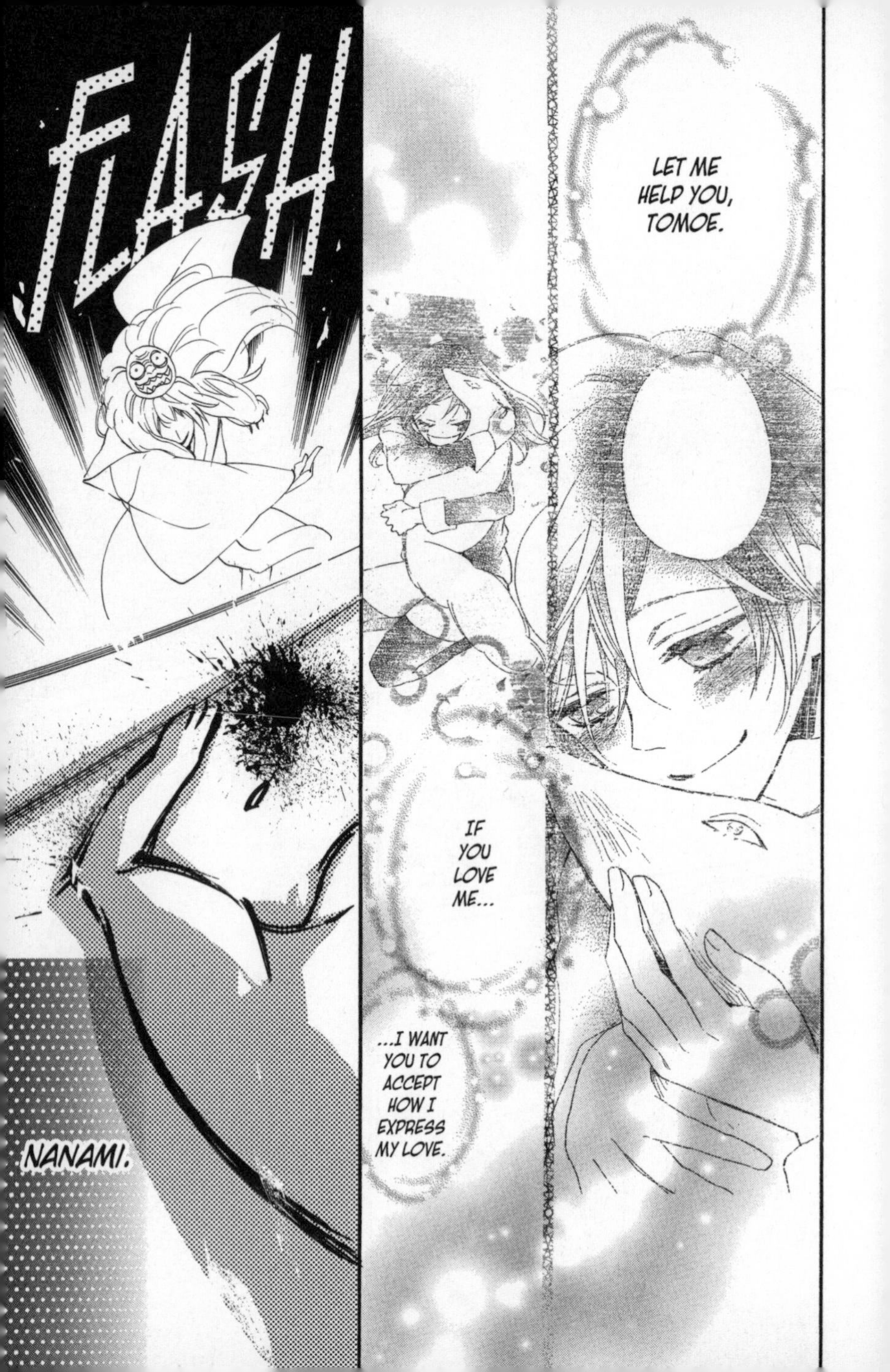
LET ME HELP YOU, TOMOE.
IF YOU LOVE ME...
...I WANT YOU TO ACCEPT HOW I EXPRESS MY LOVE.
FLASH
NANAMI.

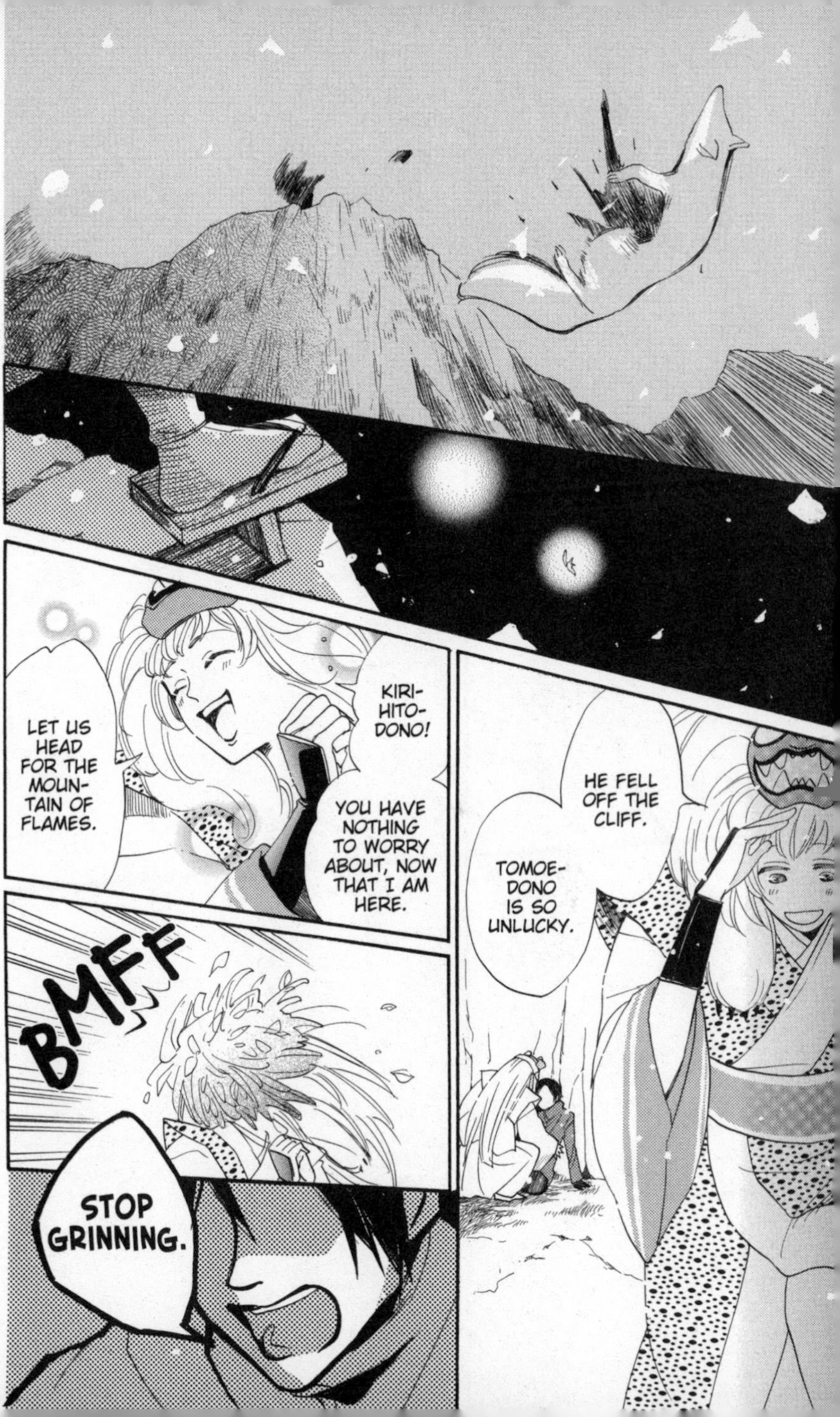
HE FELL OFF THE CLIFF.
TOMOE-DONO IS SO UNLUCKY.
KIRI-HITO-DONO!
YOU HAVE NOTHING TO WORRY ABOUT, NOW THAT I AM HERE.
LET US HEAD FOR THE MOUN-TAIN OF FLAMES.
BMFF
STOP GRINNING.

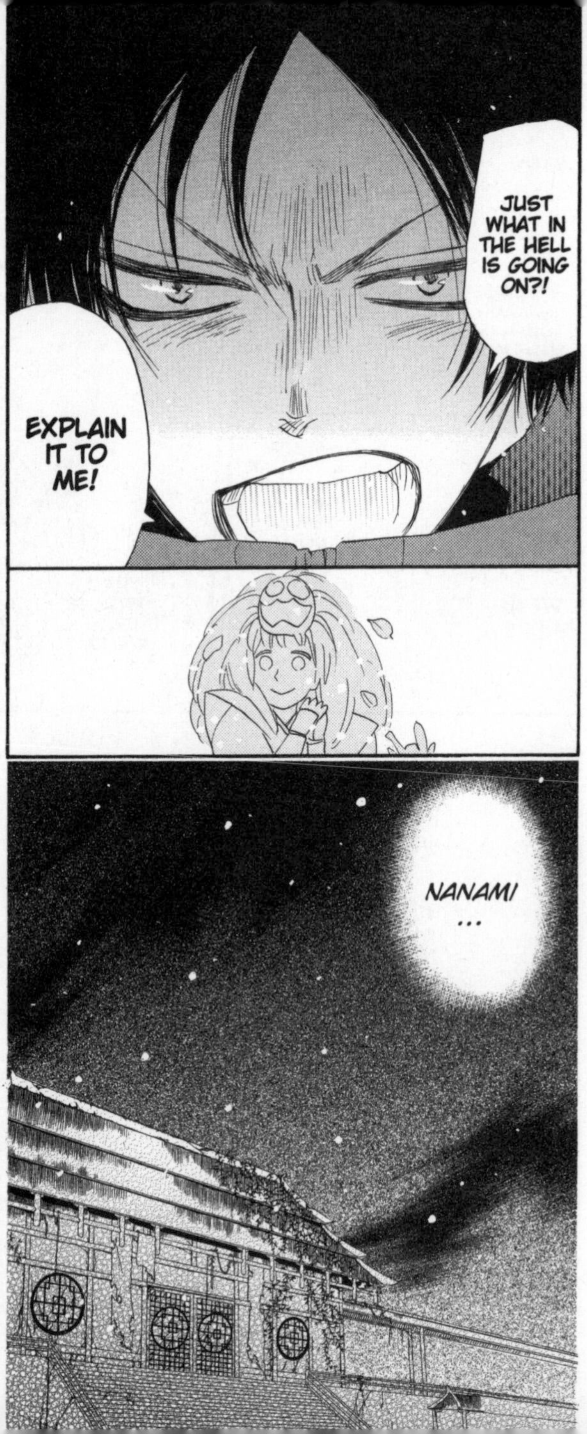
JUST WHAT IN THE HELL IS GOING ON?!
EXPLAIN IT TO ME!
NANAMI ...

My editor went to see a Tasha Tudor exhibition and bought a book for me!

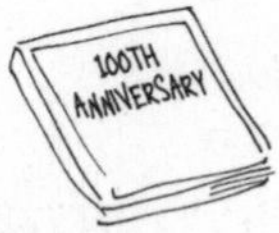
100TH ANNIVERSARY

I feel so happy every time I read it...♡

I didn't know about Tasha (she's an American picture book writer), so I've been buying and reading her other photography books and feeling soooooo happy while reading them.

I live in an apartment, so I don't have a garden, but I really adore lovely gardens like Tasha's.

I plan to open one of her books tonight and fall asleep feeling veeery happy.

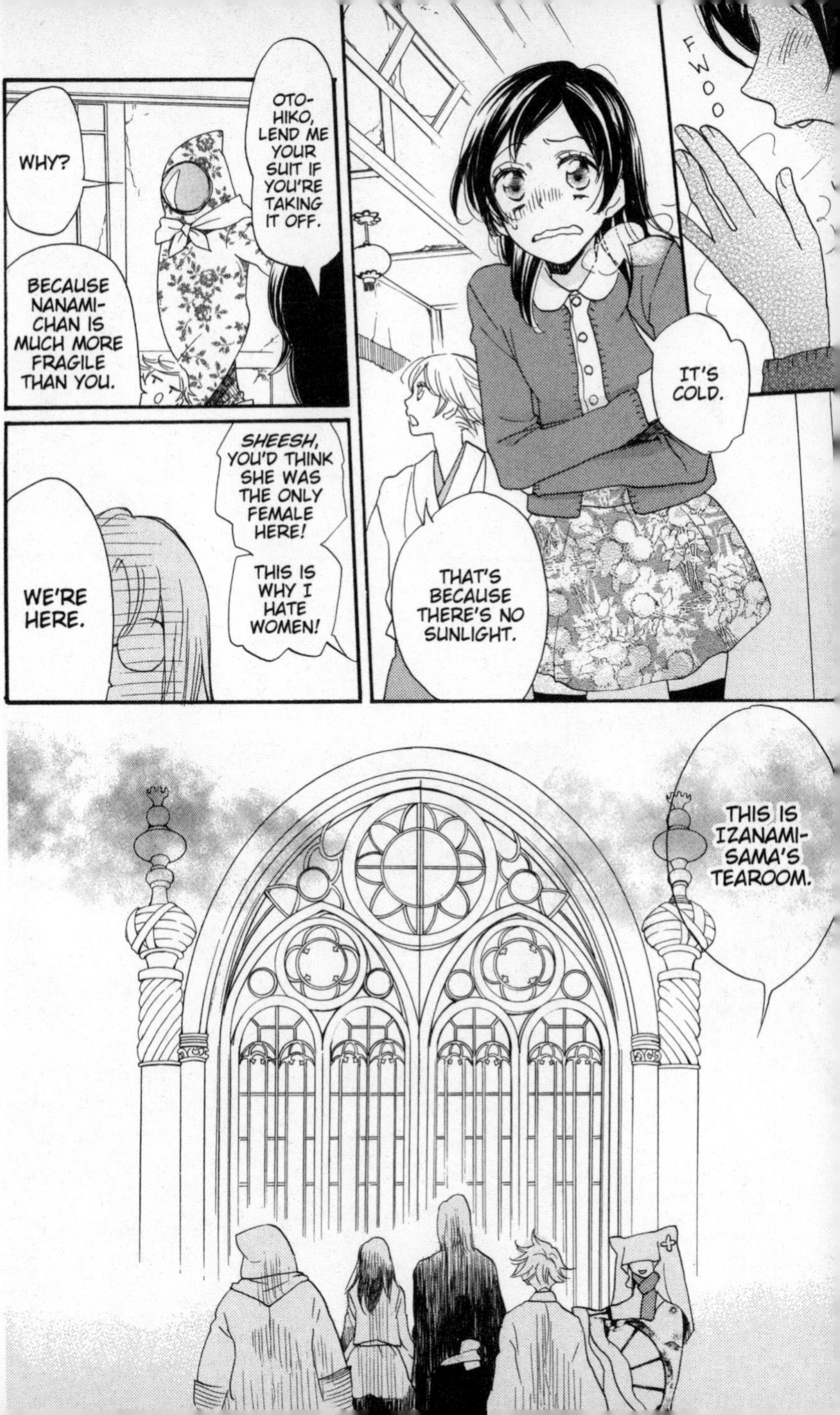
FWOO
IT'S COLD.
THAT'S BECAUSE THERE'S NO SUNLIGHT.
OTO-HIKO, LEND ME YOUR SUIT IF YOU'RE TAKING IT OFF.
WHY?
BECAUSE NANAMI-CHAN IS MUCH MORE FRAGILE THAN YOU.
SHEESH, YOU'D THINK SHE WAS THE ONLY FEMALE HERE!
THIS IS WHY I HATE WOMEN!
WE'RE HERE.
THIS IS IZANAMI-SAMA'S TEAROOM.

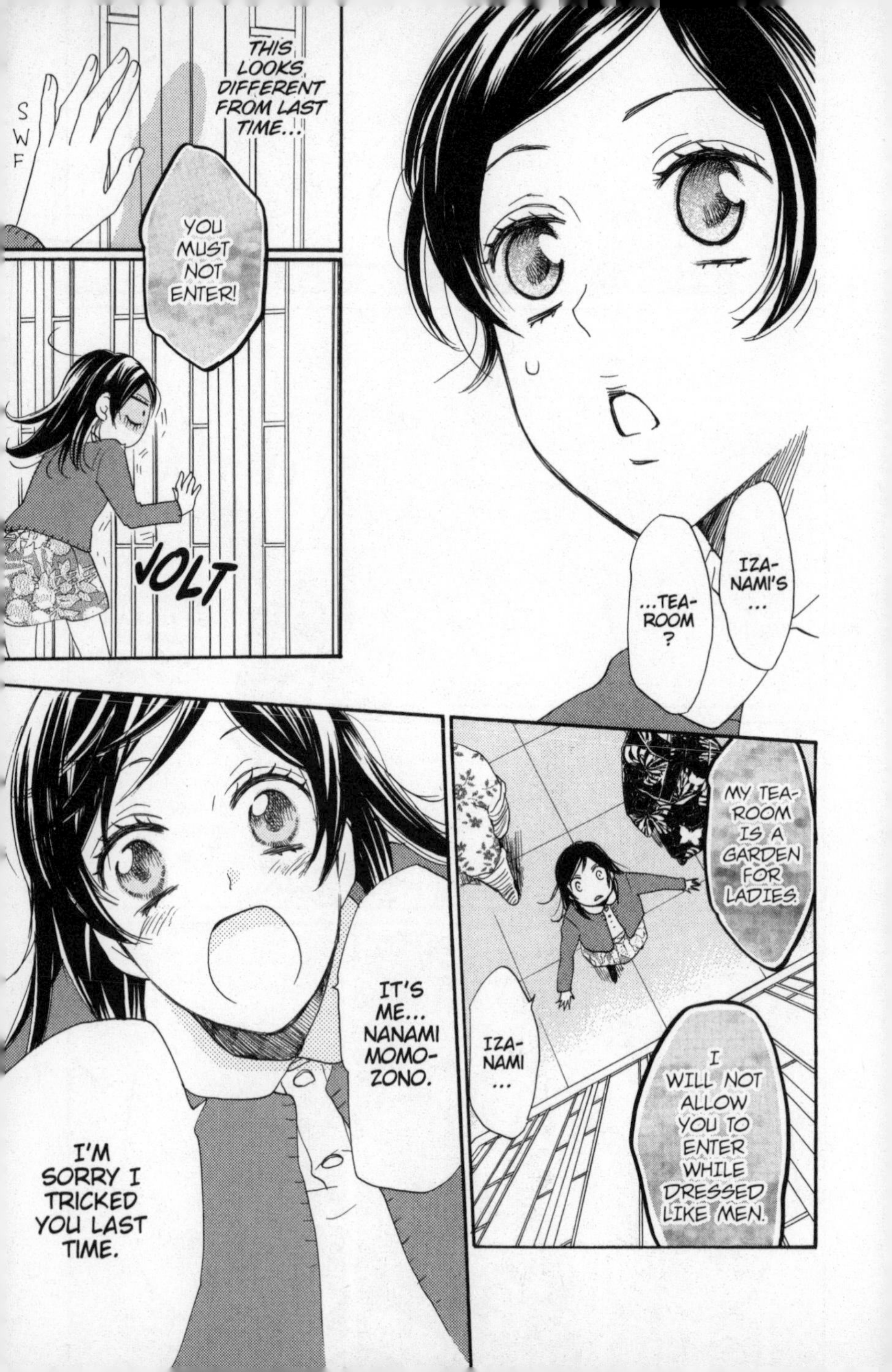
IZA-NAMI'S...
...TEA-ROOM?
THIS LOOKS DIFFERENT FROM LAST TIME...
SWF
YOU MUST NOT ENTER!
JOLT
MY TEA-ROOM IS A GARDEN FOR LADIES.
I WILL NOT ALLOW YOU TO ENTER WHILE DRESSED LIKE MEN.
IZA-NAMI...
IT'S ME... NANAMI MOMO-ZONO.
I'M SORRY I TRICKED YOU LAST TIME.

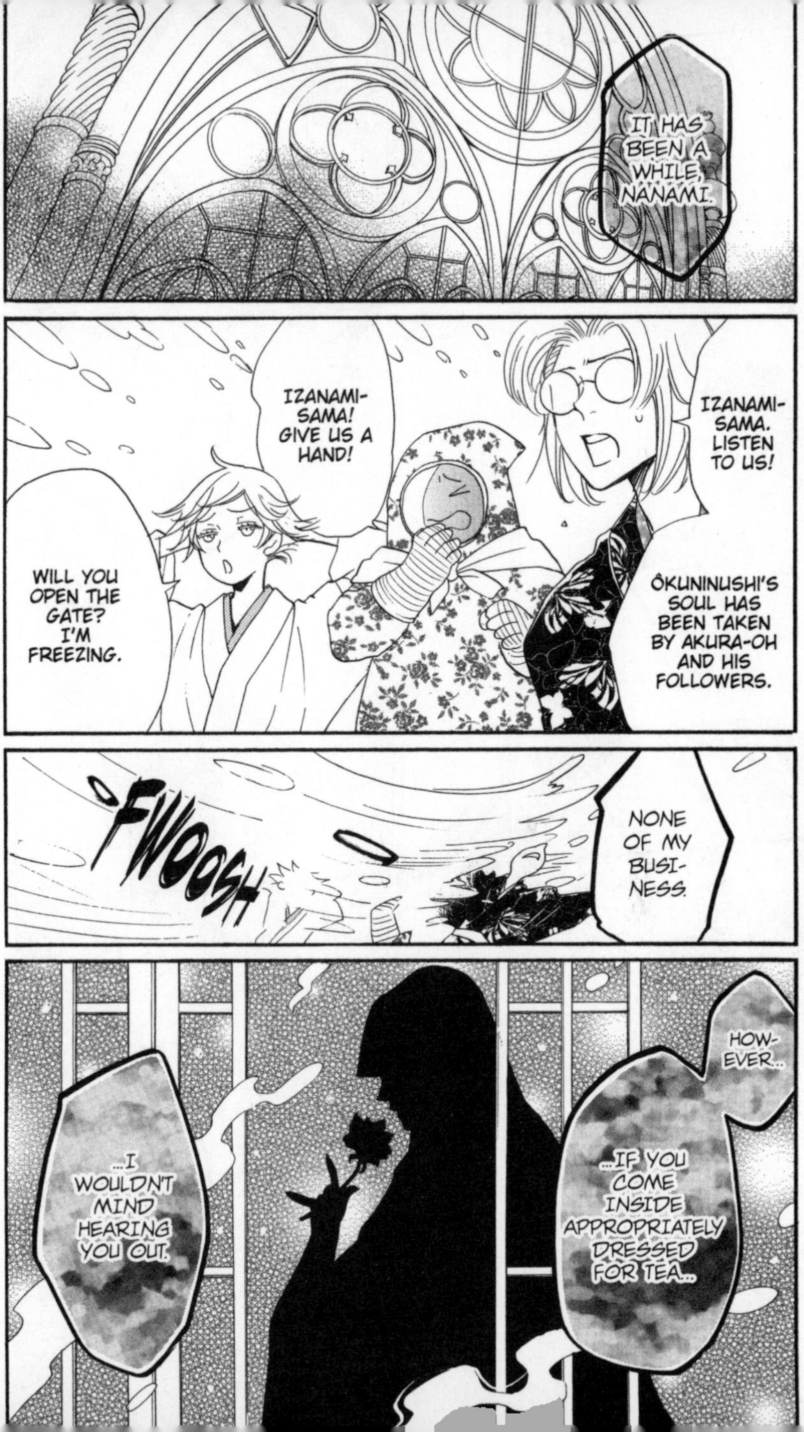
IT HAS BEEN A WHILE, NANAMI.
IZANAMI-SAMA. LISTEN TO US!
ÔKUNINUSHI'S SOUL HAS BEEN TAKEN BY AKURA-OH AND HIS FOLLOWERS.
IZANAMI-SAMA! GIVE US A HAND!
WILL YOU OPEN THE GATE? I'M FREEZING.
NONE OF MY BUSINESS.
FWOOSH
HOW-EVER...
...IF YOU COME INSIDE APPROPRIATELY DRESSED FOR TEA...
...I WOULDN'T MIND HEARING YOU OUT.

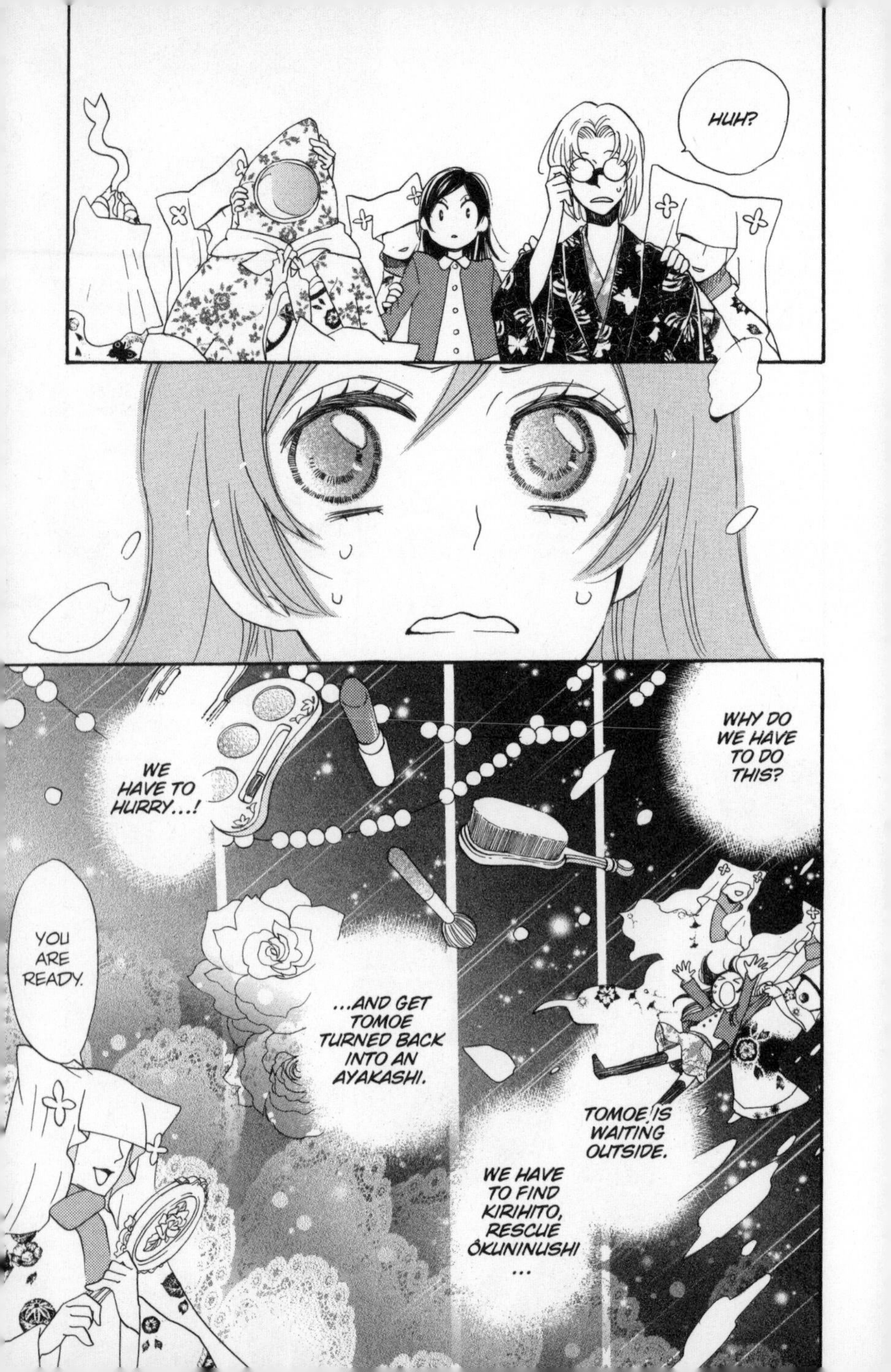
HUH?
WHY DO WE HAVE TO DO THIS?
WE HAVE TO HURRY...!
TOMOE IS WAITING OUTSIDE.
WE HAVE TO FIND KIRIHITO, RESCUE ŌKUNINUSHI...
...AND GET TOMOE TURNED BACK INTO AN AYAKASHI.
YOU ARE READY.

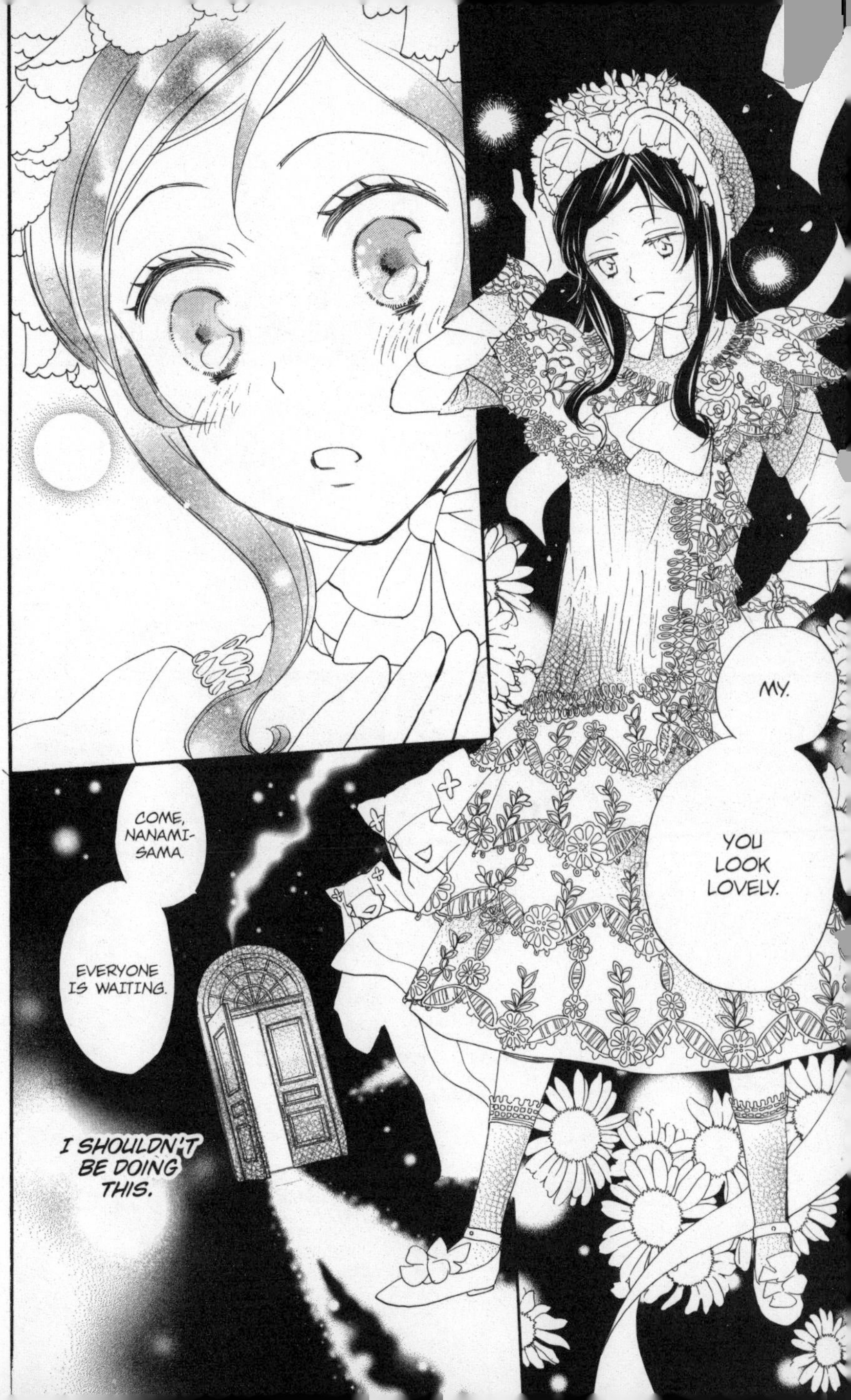
MY.
YOU LOOK LOVELY.
COME, NANAMI-SAMA.
EVERYONE IS WAITING.
I SHOULDN'T BE DOING THIS.

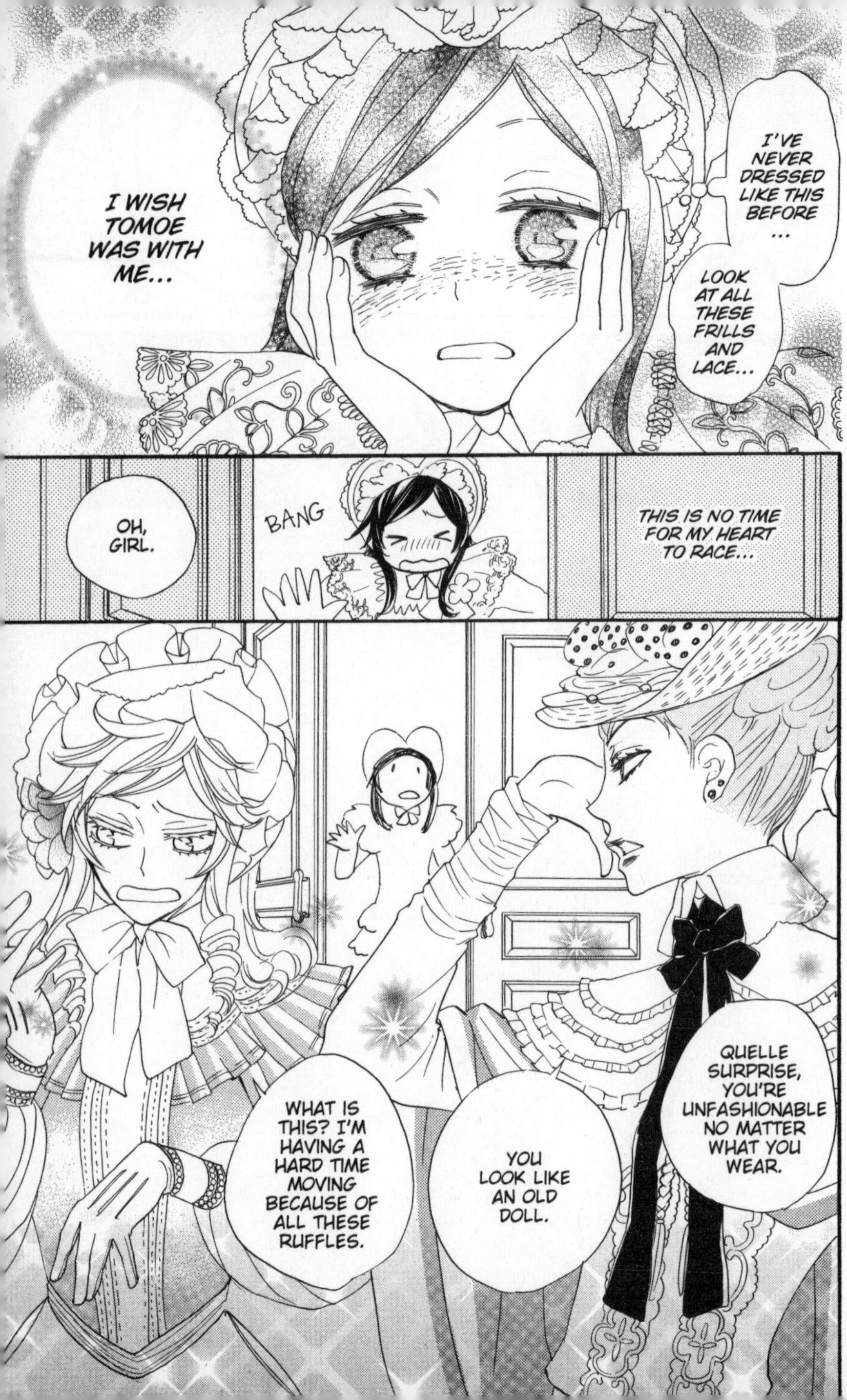
I'VE NEVER DRESSED LIKE THIS BEFORE ...
LOOK AT ALL THESE FRILLS AND LACE...
I WISH TOMOE WAS WITH ME...
THIS IS NO TIME FOR MY HEART TO RACE...
BANG
OH, GIRL.
QUELLE SURPRISE, YOU'RE UNFASHIONABLE NO MATTER WHAT YOU WEAR.
YOU LOOK LIKE AN OLD DOLL.
WHAT IS THIS? I'M HAVING A HARD TIME MOVING BECAUSE OF ALL THESE RUFFLES.

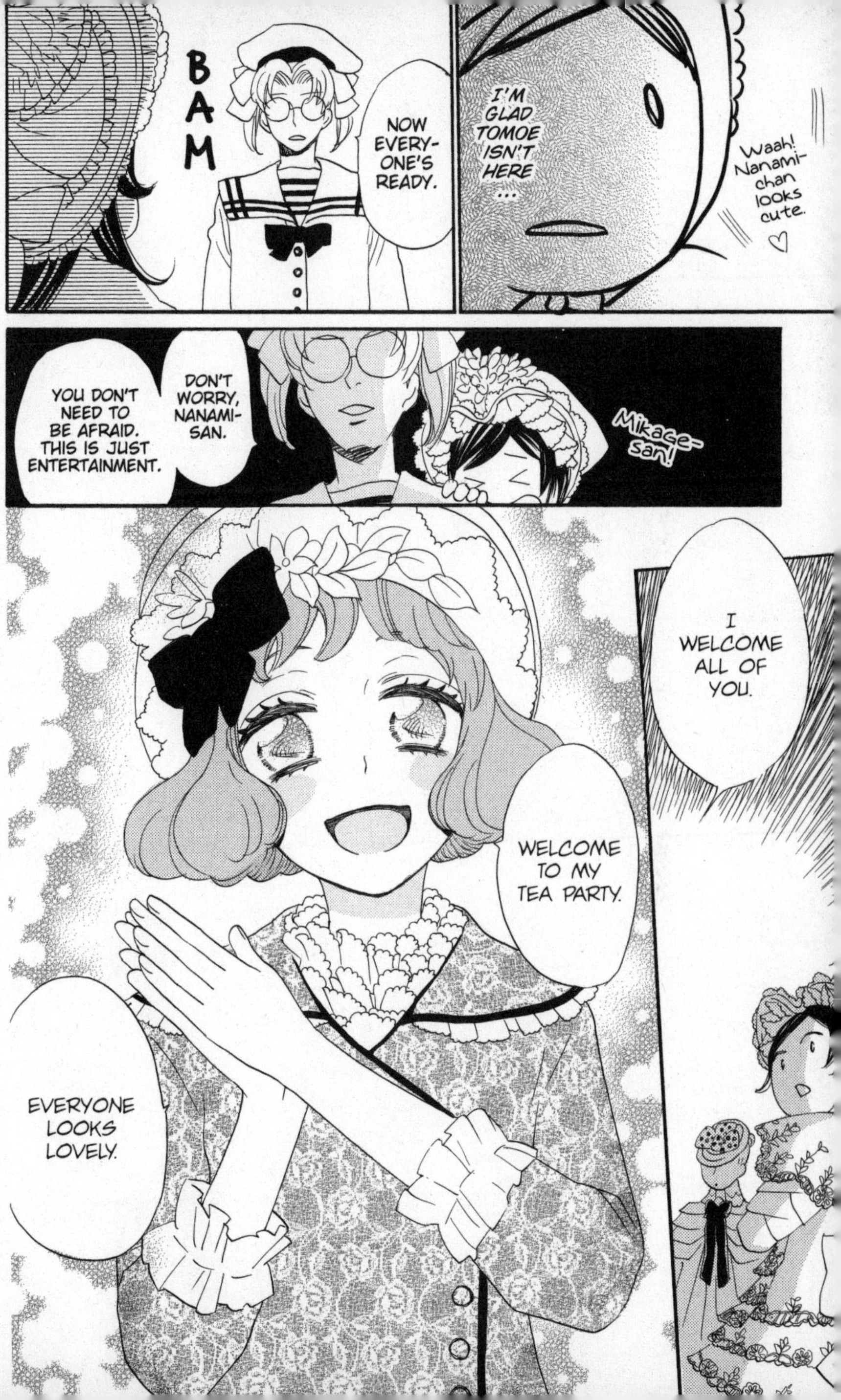
Waah! Nanami-chan looks cute. ♡
I'M GLAD TOMOE ISN'T HERE ...
NOW EVERY-ONE'S READY.
BAM
Mikage-san!
DON'T WORRY, NANAMI-SAN.
YOU DON'T NEED TO BE AFRAID. THIS IS JUST ENTERTAINMENT.
I WELCOME ALL OF YOU.
WELCOME TO MY TEA PARTY.
EVERYONE LOOKS LOVELY.

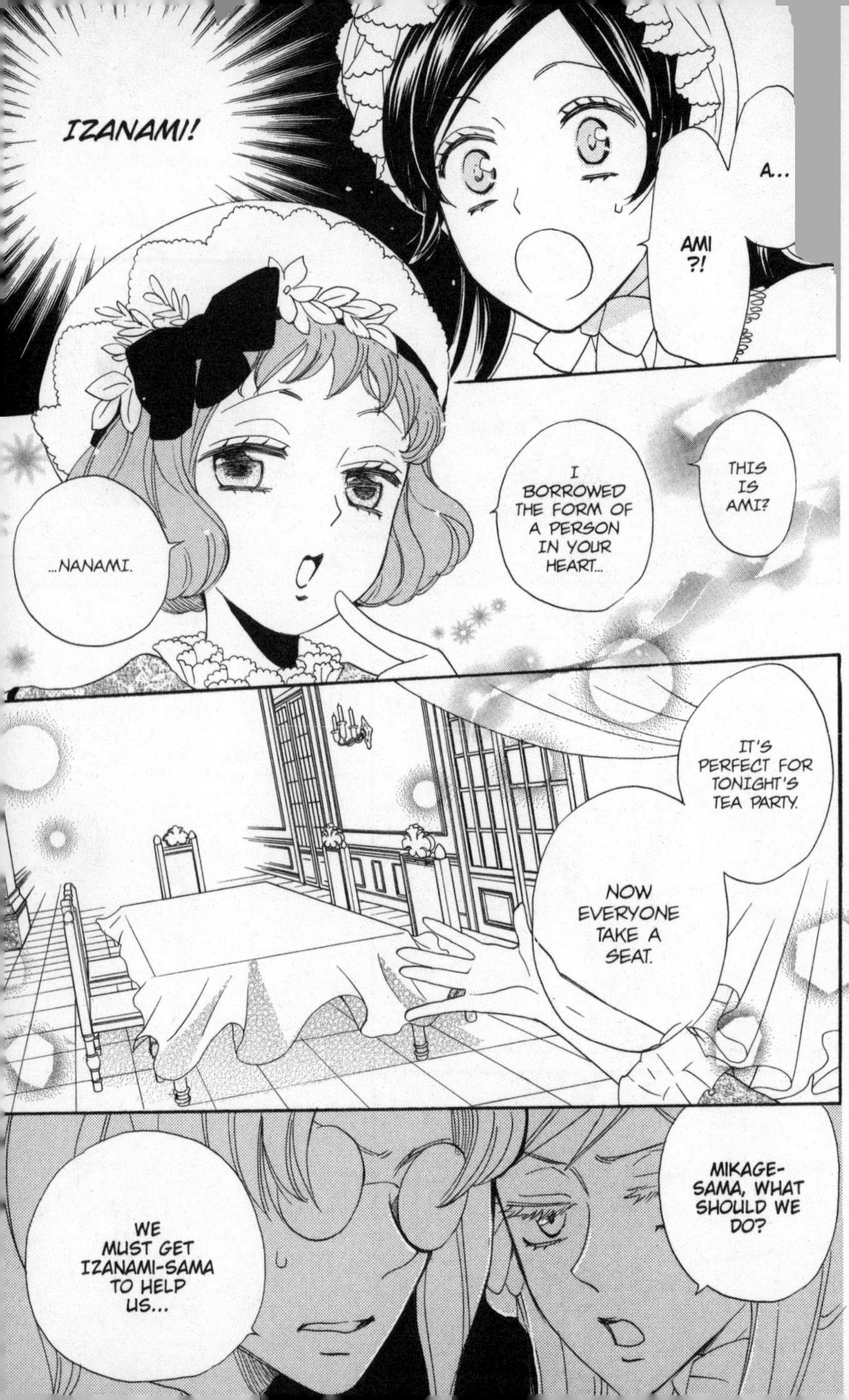
A...
AMI ?!
IZANAMI!
THIS IS AMI?
I BORROWED THE FORM OF A PERSON IN YOUR HEART...
...NANAMI.
IT'S PERFECT FOR TONIGHT'S TEA PARTY.
NOW EVERYONE TAKE A SEAT.
MIKAGE-SAMA, WHAT SHOULD WE DO?
WE MUST GET IZANAMI-SAMA TO HELP US...

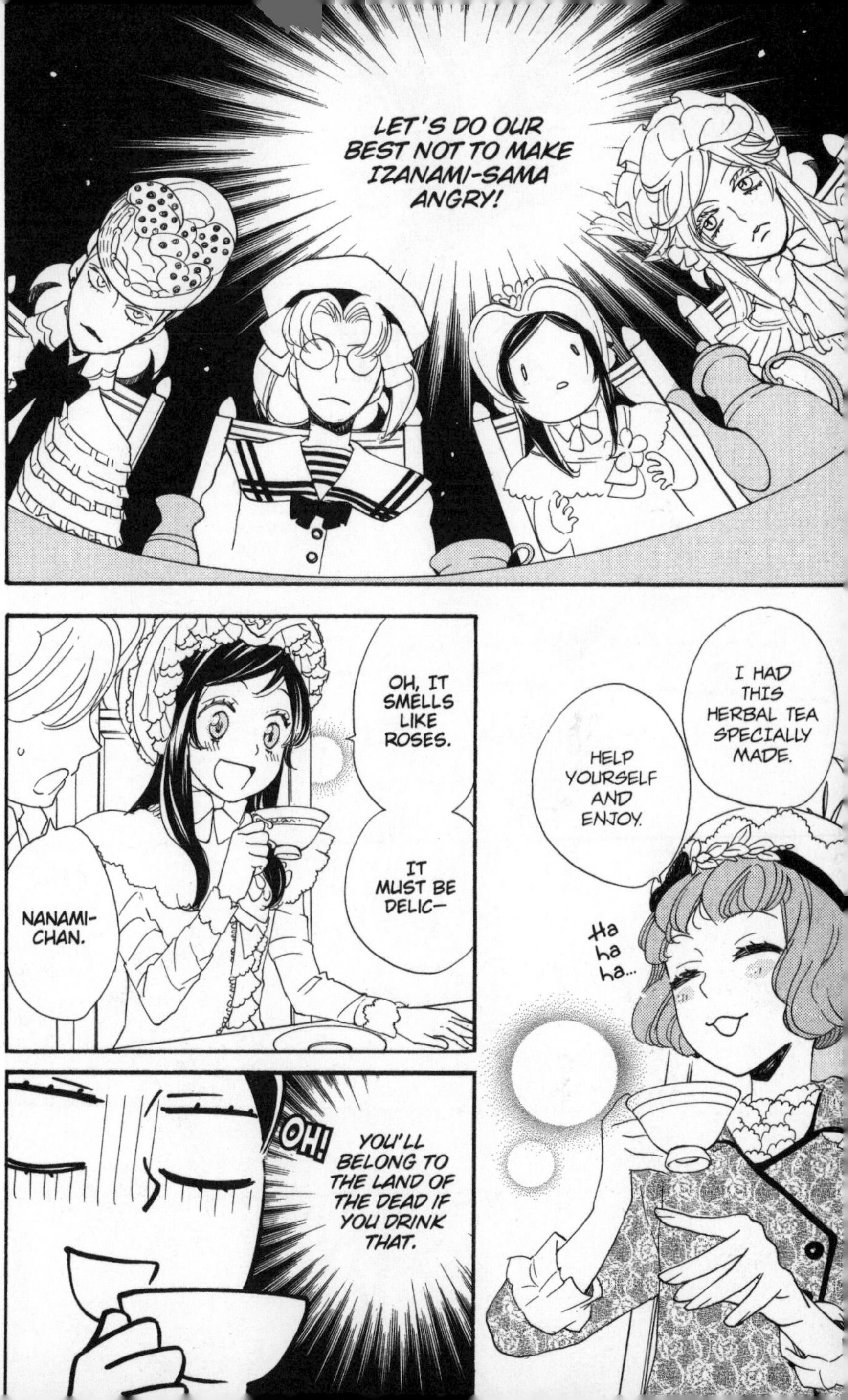
LET'S DO OUR BEST NOT TO MAKE IZANAMI-SAMA ANGRY!
I HAD THIS HERBAL TEA SPECIALLY MADE.
HELP YOURSELF AND ENJOY.
Ha ha ha...
OH, IT SMELLS LIKE ROSES.
IT MUST BE DELIC—
NANAMI-CHAN.
OH!
YOU'LL BELONG TO THE LAND OF THE DEAD IF YOU DRINK THAT.

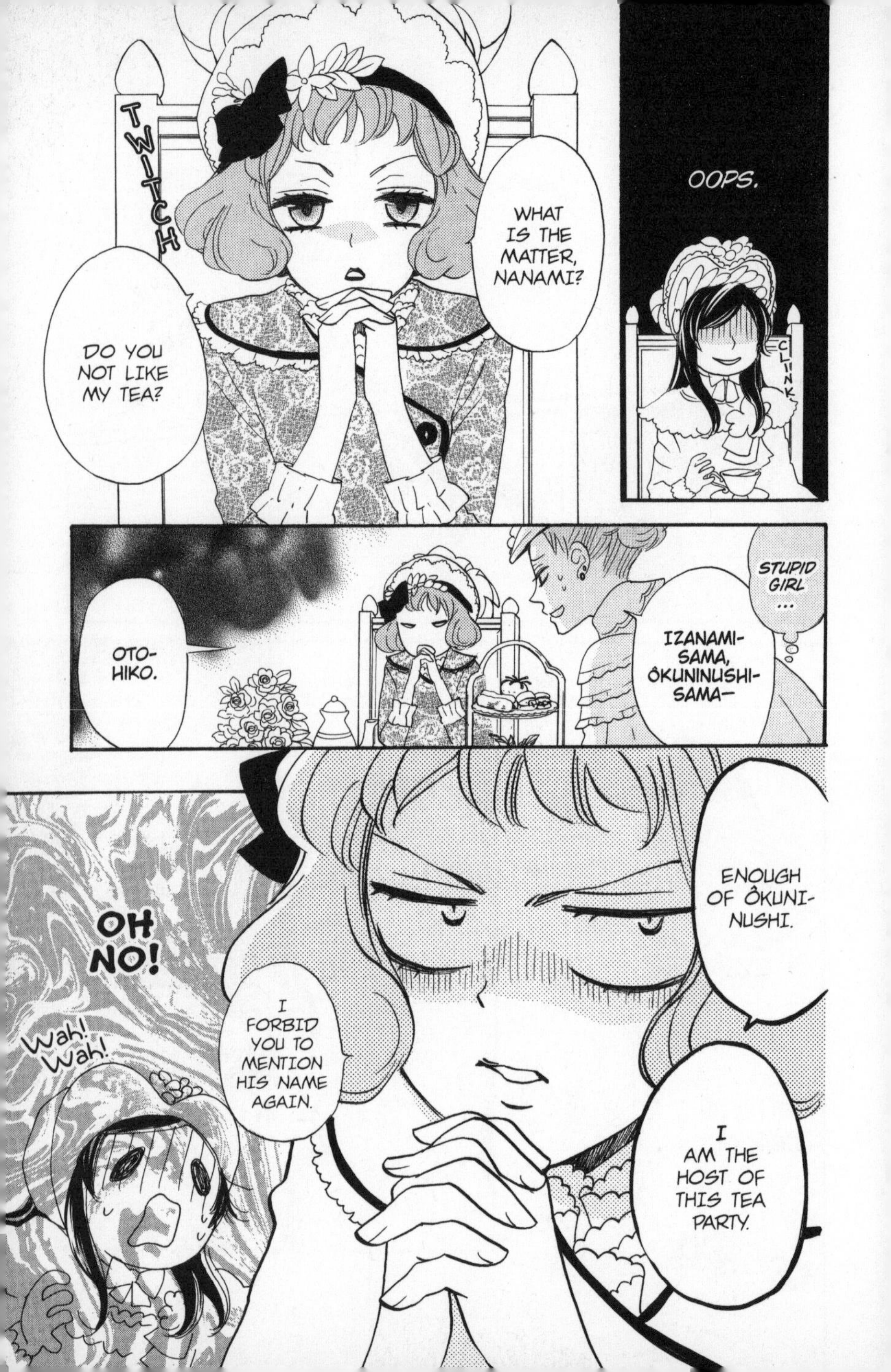
OOPS.
CLINK
TWITCH
WHAT IS THE MATTER, NANAMI?
DO YOU NOT LIKE MY TEA?
STUPID GIRL...
IZANAMI-SAMA, ÔKUNINUSHI-SAMA—
OTO-HIKO.
ENOUGH OF ÔKUNI-NUSHI.
I AM THE HOST OF THIS TEA PARTY.
I FORBID YOU TO MENTION HIS NAME AGAIN.
OH NO!
Wah! Wah!

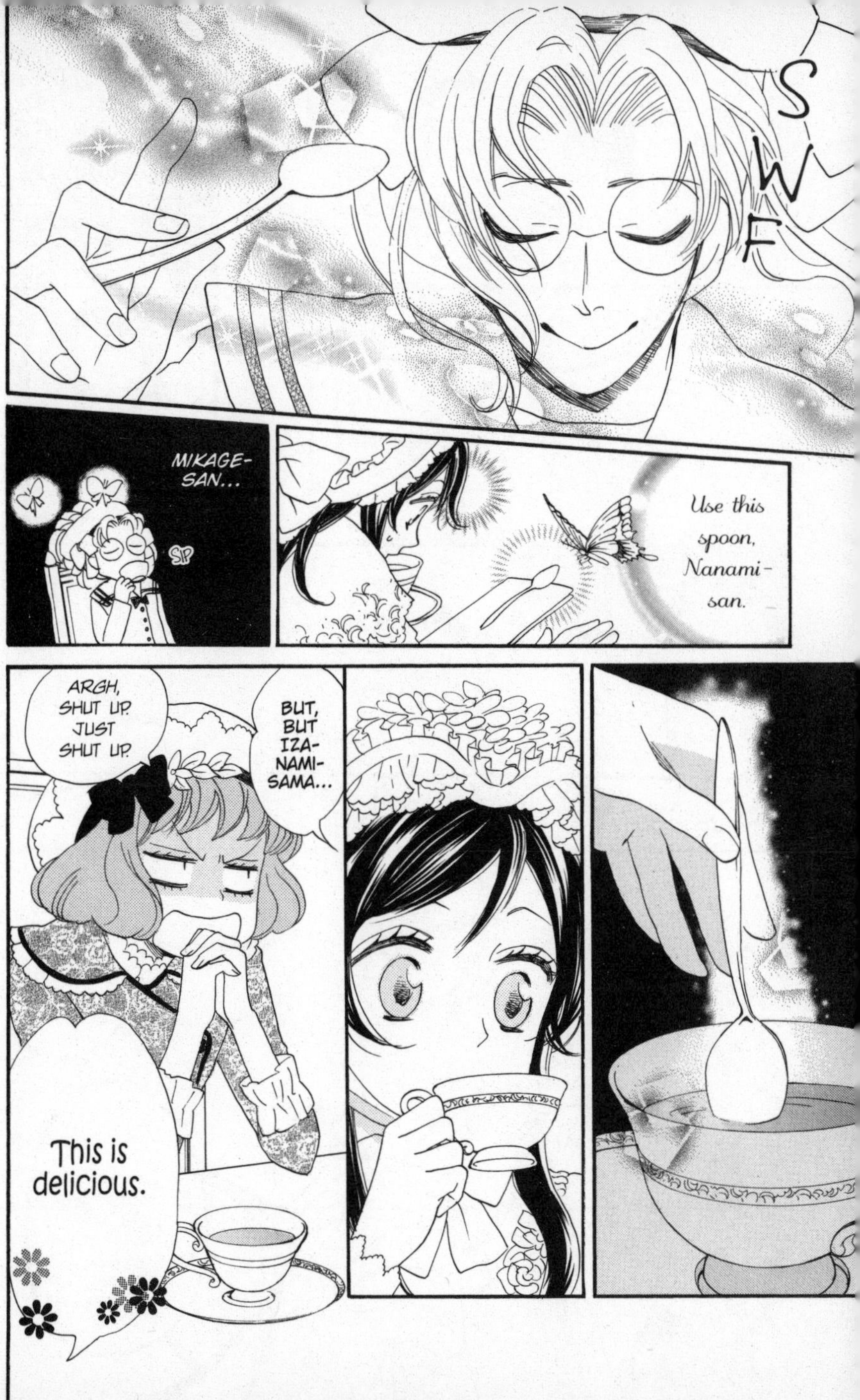
SWF
Use this spoon, Nanami-san.
MIKAGE-SAN...
SIP
BUT, BUT IZA-NAMI-SAMA...
ARGH, SHUT UP. JUST SHUT UP.
This is delicious.

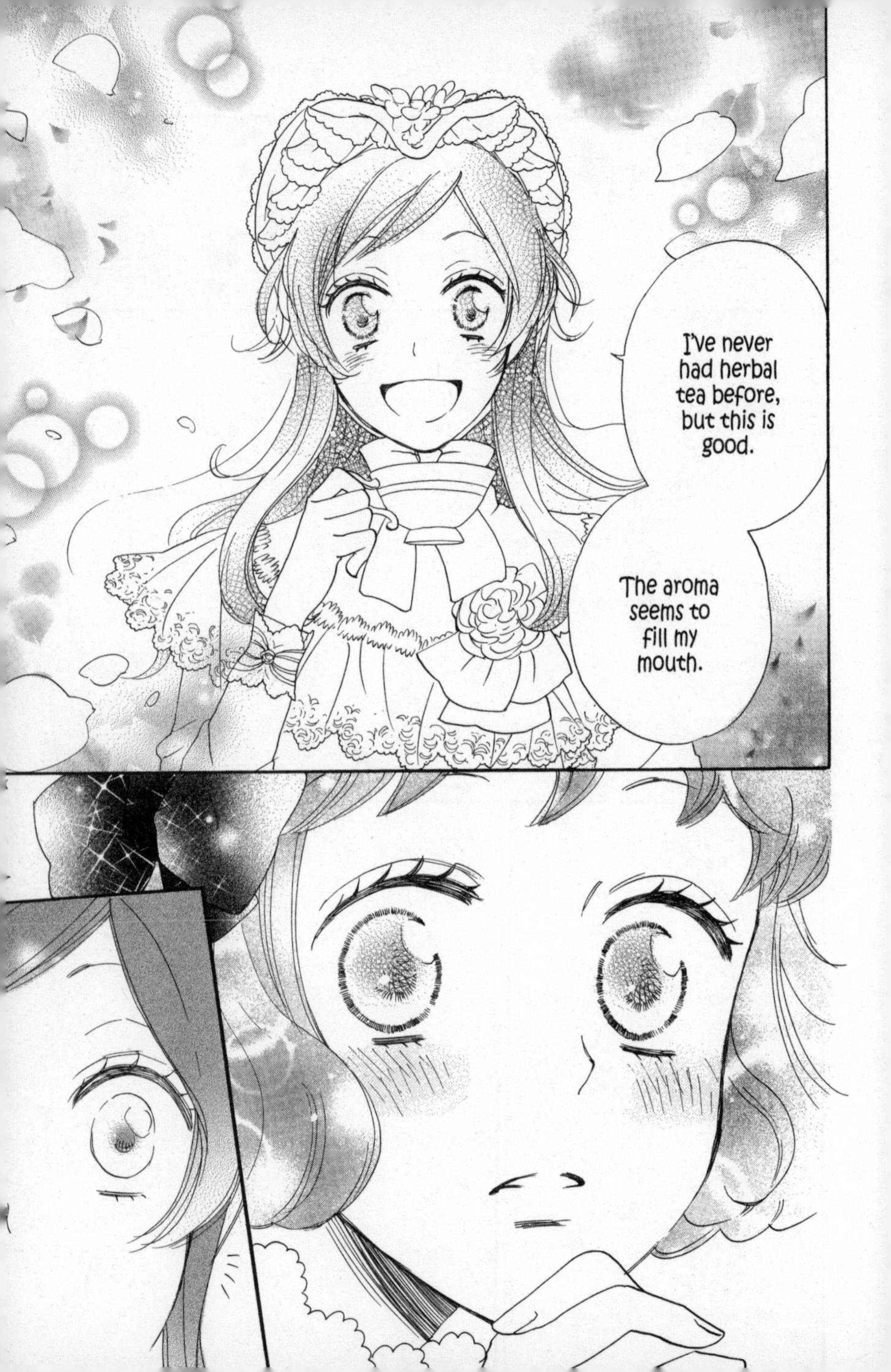
I've never had herbal tea before, but this is good.
The aroma seems to fill my mouth.

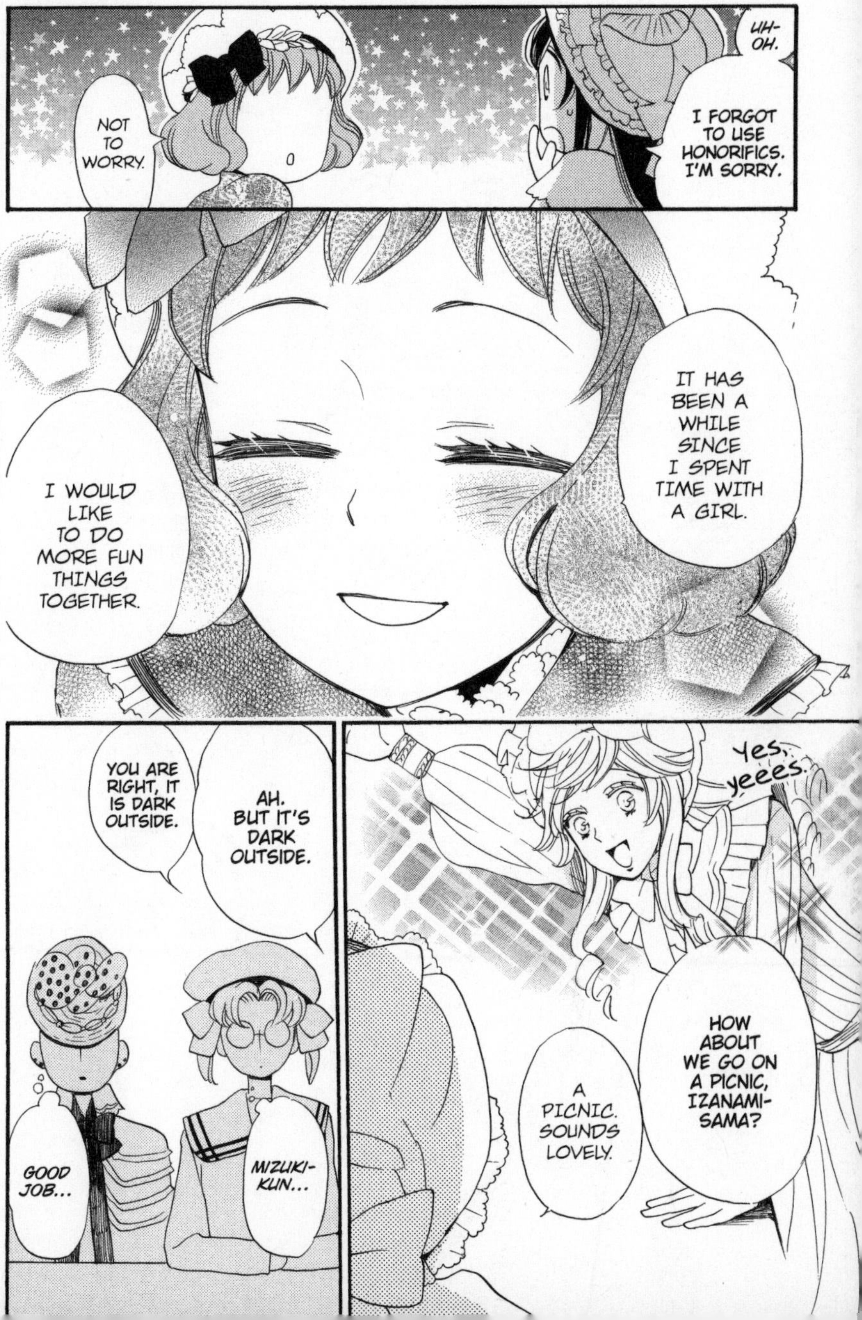
UH-OH.
I FORGOT TO USE HONORIFICS. I'M SORRY.
NOT TO WORRY.
IT HAS BEEN A WHILE SINCE I SPENT TIME WITH A GIRL.
I WOULD LIKE TO DO MORE FUN THINGS TOGETHER.
Yes, yeees.
HOW ABOUT WE GO ON A PICNIC, IZANAMI-SAMA?
A PICNIC. SOUNDS LOVELY.
AH. BUT IT'S DARK OUTSIDE.
YOU ARE RIGHT, IT IS DARK OUTSIDE.
MIZUKI-KUN...
GOOD JOB...

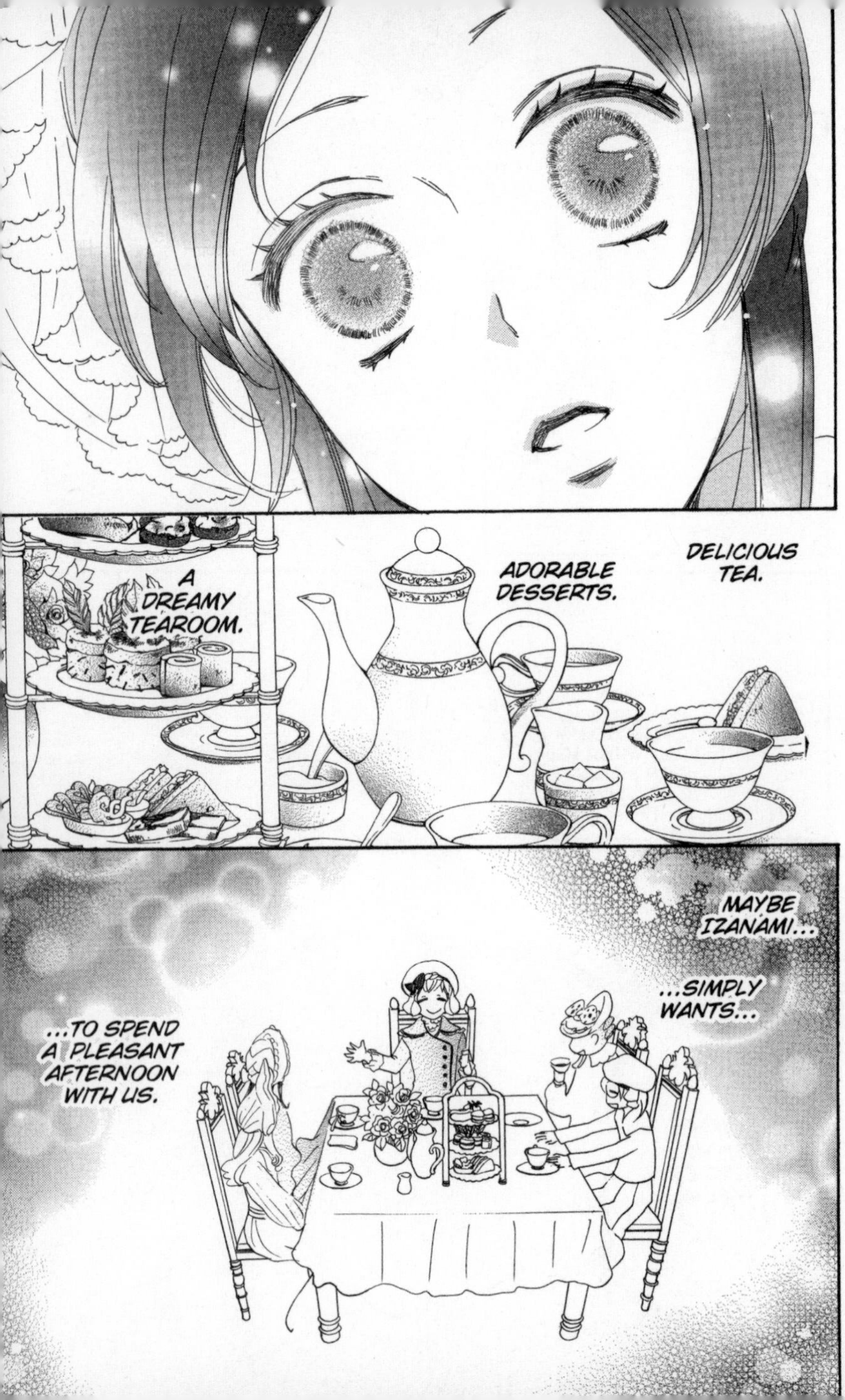
DELICIOUS TEA.
ADORABLE DESSERTS.
A DREAMY TEAROOM.
MAYBE IZANAMI...
...SIMPLY WANTS...
...TO SPEND A PLEASANT AFTERNOON WITH US.

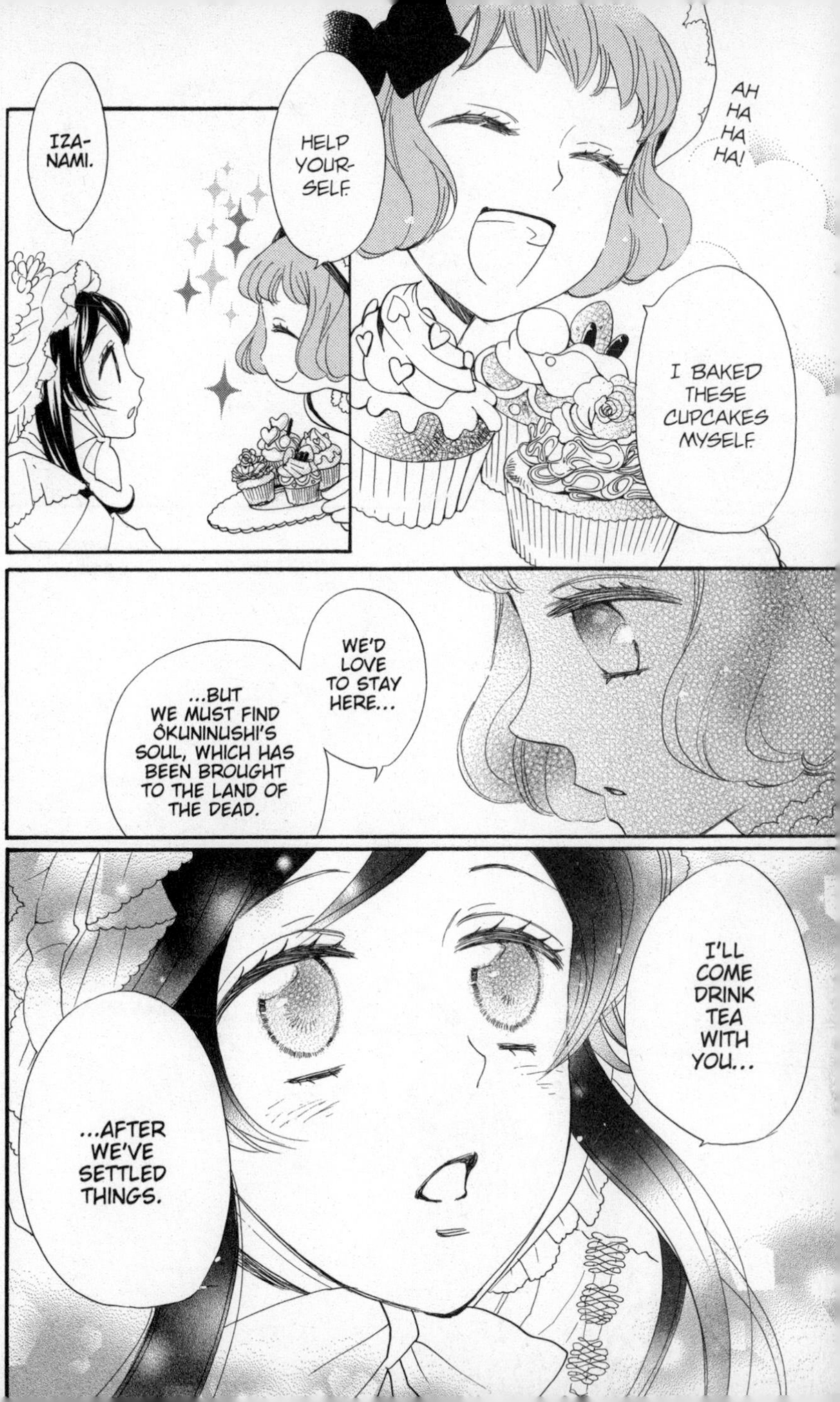

AH HA HA HA!
HELP YOURSELF.
I BAKED THESE CUPCAKES MYSELF.
IZA-NAMI.
WE'D LOVE TO STAY HERE...
...BUT WE MUST FIND ÔKUNINUSHI'S SOUL, WHICH HAS BEEN BROUGHT TO THE LAND OF THE DEAD.
I'LL COME DRINK TEA WITH YOU...
...AFTER WE'VE SETTLED THINGS.

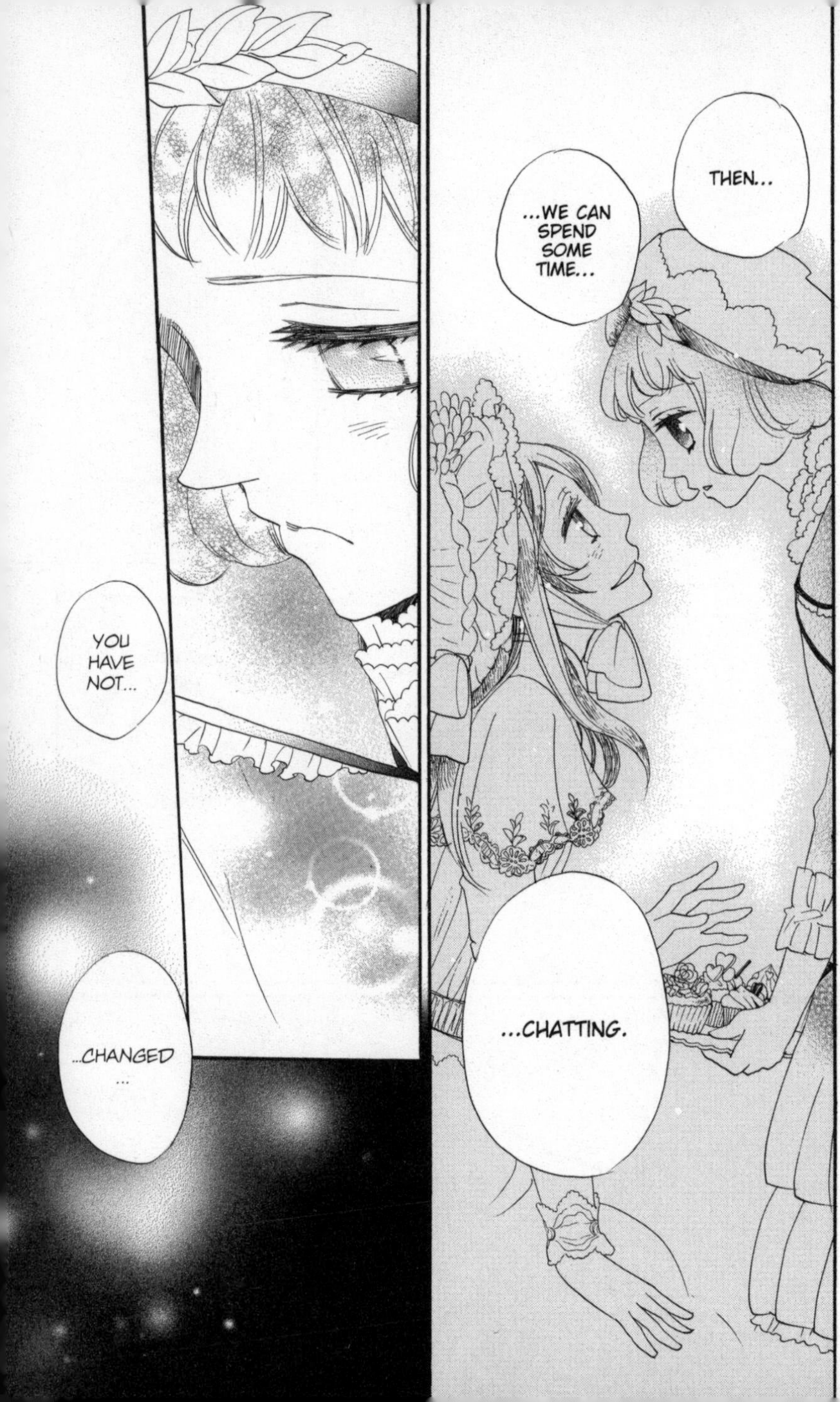
THEN...
...WE CAN SPEND SOME TIME...
...CHATTING.
YOU HAVE NOT...
...CHANGED ...

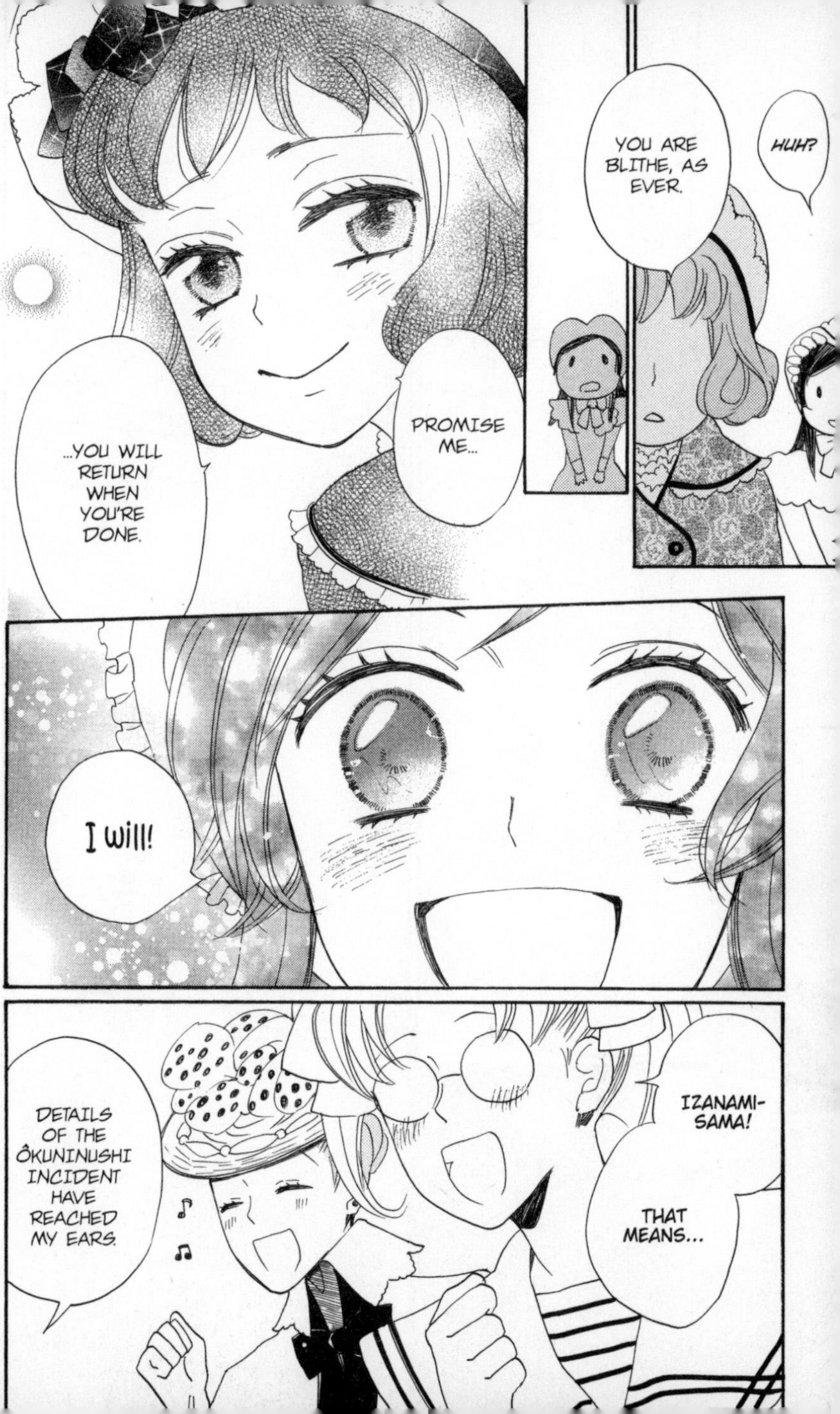
YOU ARE BLITHE, AS EVER.
HUH?
PROMISE ME...
...YOU WILL RETURN WHEN YOU'RE DONE.
I WILL!
IZANAMI-SAMA!
THAT MEANS...
DETAILS OF THE ÔKUNINUSHI INCIDENT HAVE REACHED MY EARS.

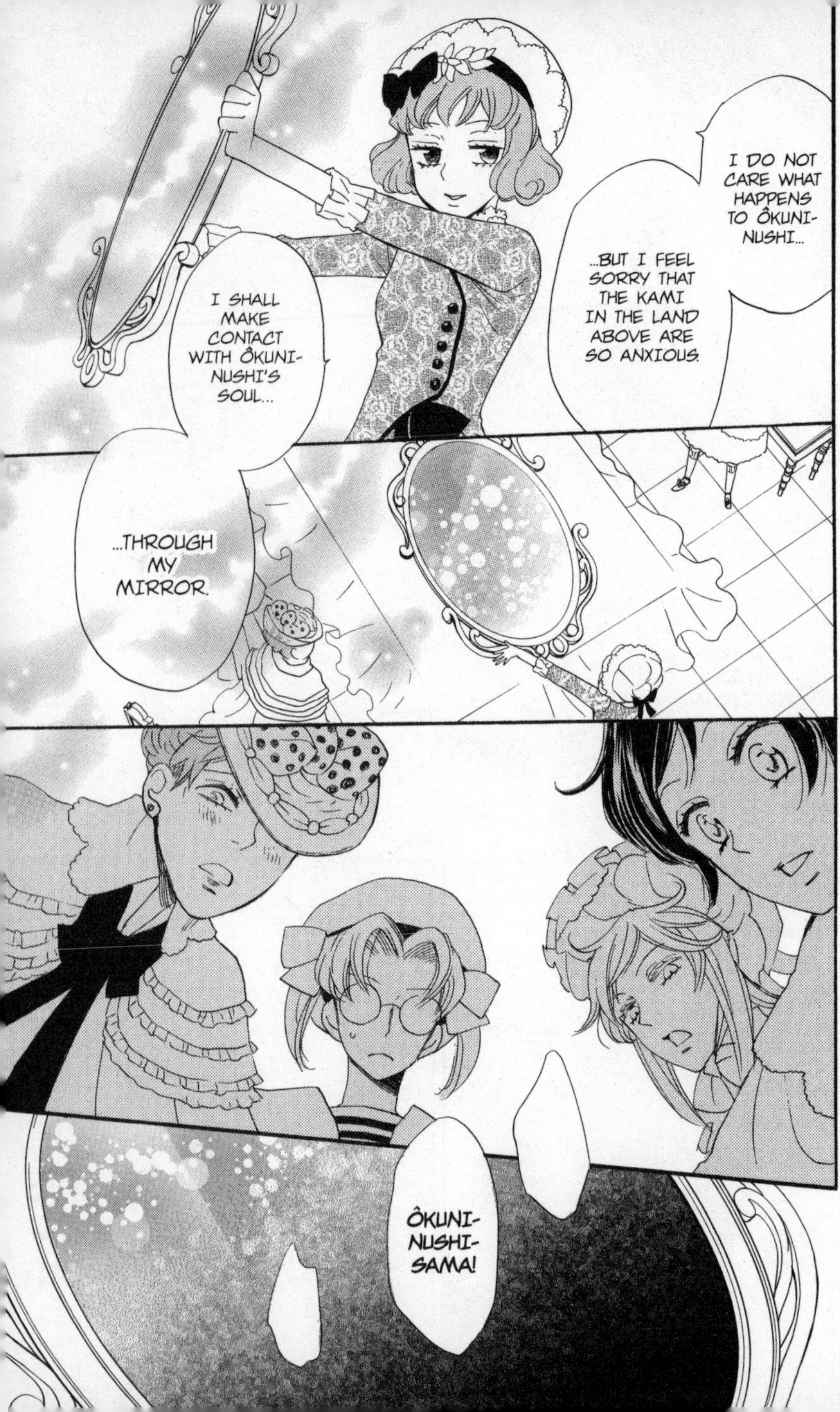
I DO NOT CARE WHAT HAPPENS TO ÔKUNI-NUSHI...
...BUT I FEEL SORRY THAT THE KAMI IN THE LAND ABOVE ARE SO ANXIOUS.
I SHALL MAKE CONTACT WITH ÔKUNI-NUSHI'S SOUL...
...THROUGH MY MIRROR.
ÔKUNI-NUSHI-SAMA!

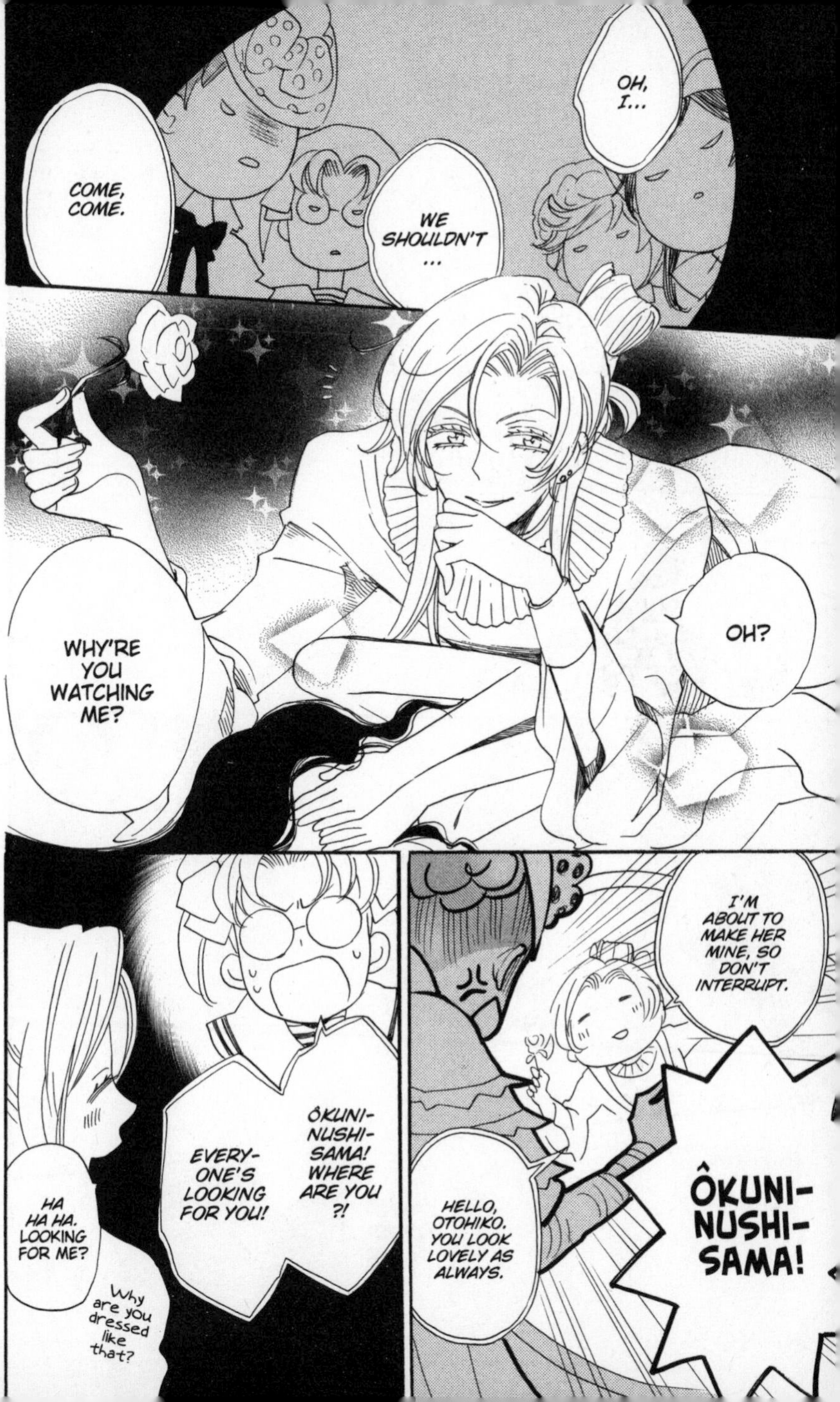
OH, I...
WE SHOULDN'T ...
COME, COME.
OH?
WHY'RE YOU WATCHING ME?
I'M ABOUT TO MAKE HER MINE, SO DON'T INTERRUPT.
ÔKUNI-NUSHI-SAMA!
HELLO, OTOHIKO. YOU LOOK LOVELY AS ALWAYS.
ÔKUNI-NUSHI-SAMA! WHERE ARE YOU ?!
EVERY-ONE'S LOOKING FOR YOU!
HA HA HA. LOOKING FOR ME?
Why are you dressed like that?

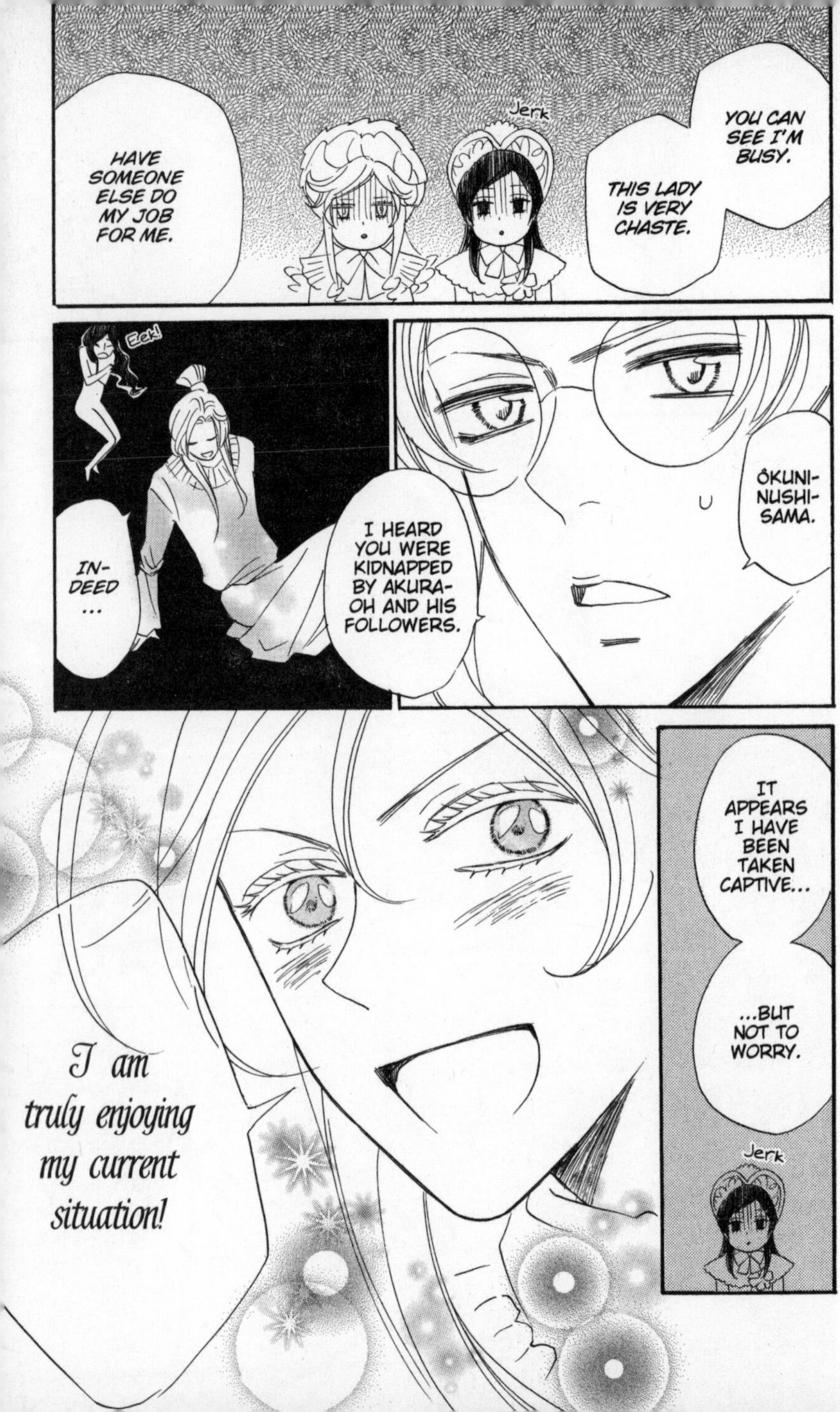
YOU CAN SEE I'M BUSY.
THIS LADY IS VERY CHASTE.
Jerk
HAVE SOMEONE ELSE DO MY JOB FOR ME.
ÔKUNI-NUSHI-SAMA.
I HEARD YOU WERE KIDNAPPED BY AKURA-OH AND HIS FOLLOWERS.
Eek!
IN-DEED...
IT APPEARS I HAVE BEEN TAKEN CAPTIVE...
...BUT NOT TO WORRY.
Jerk
I am truly enjoying my current situation!

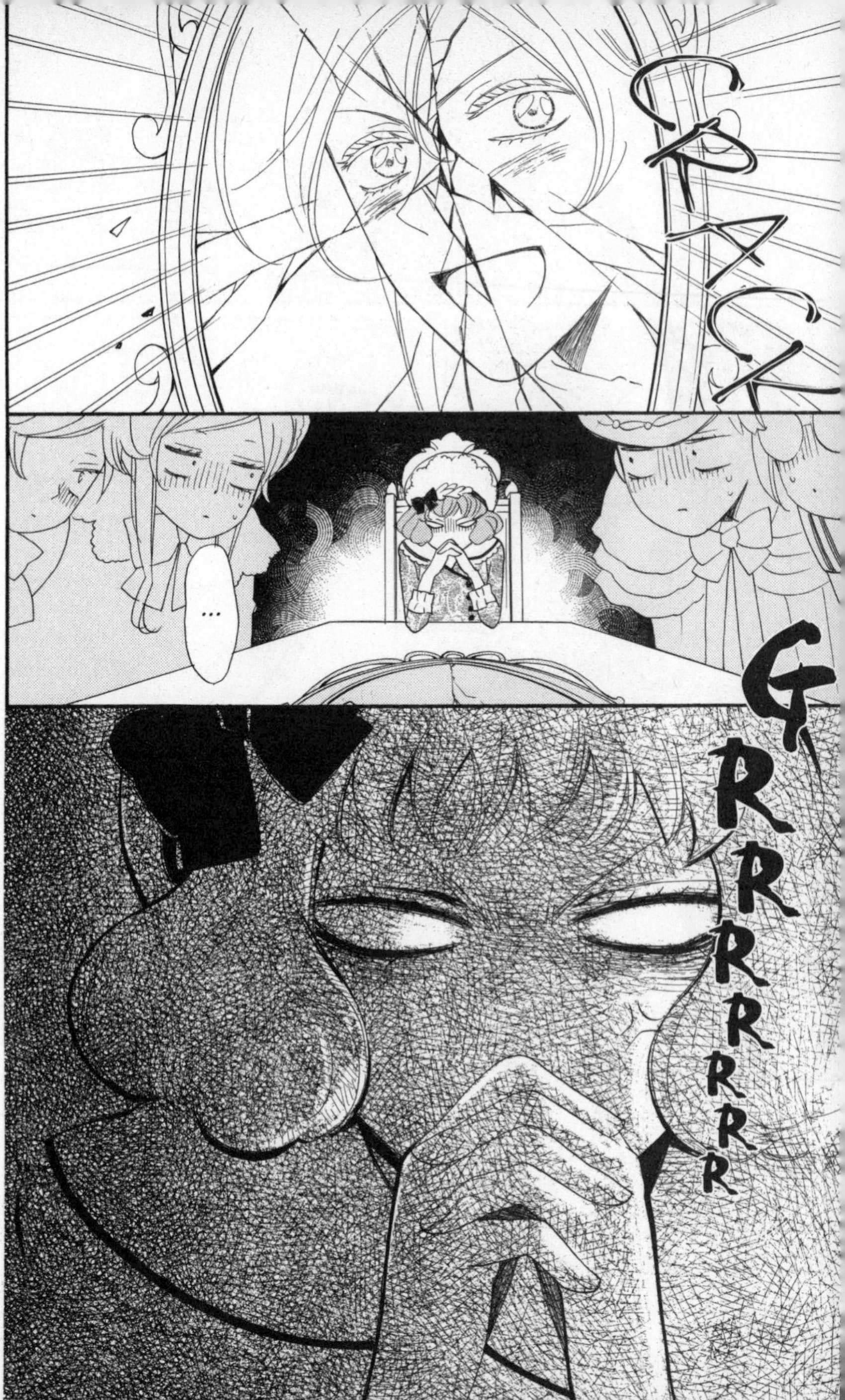
CRACK
...
GRRRRRRR

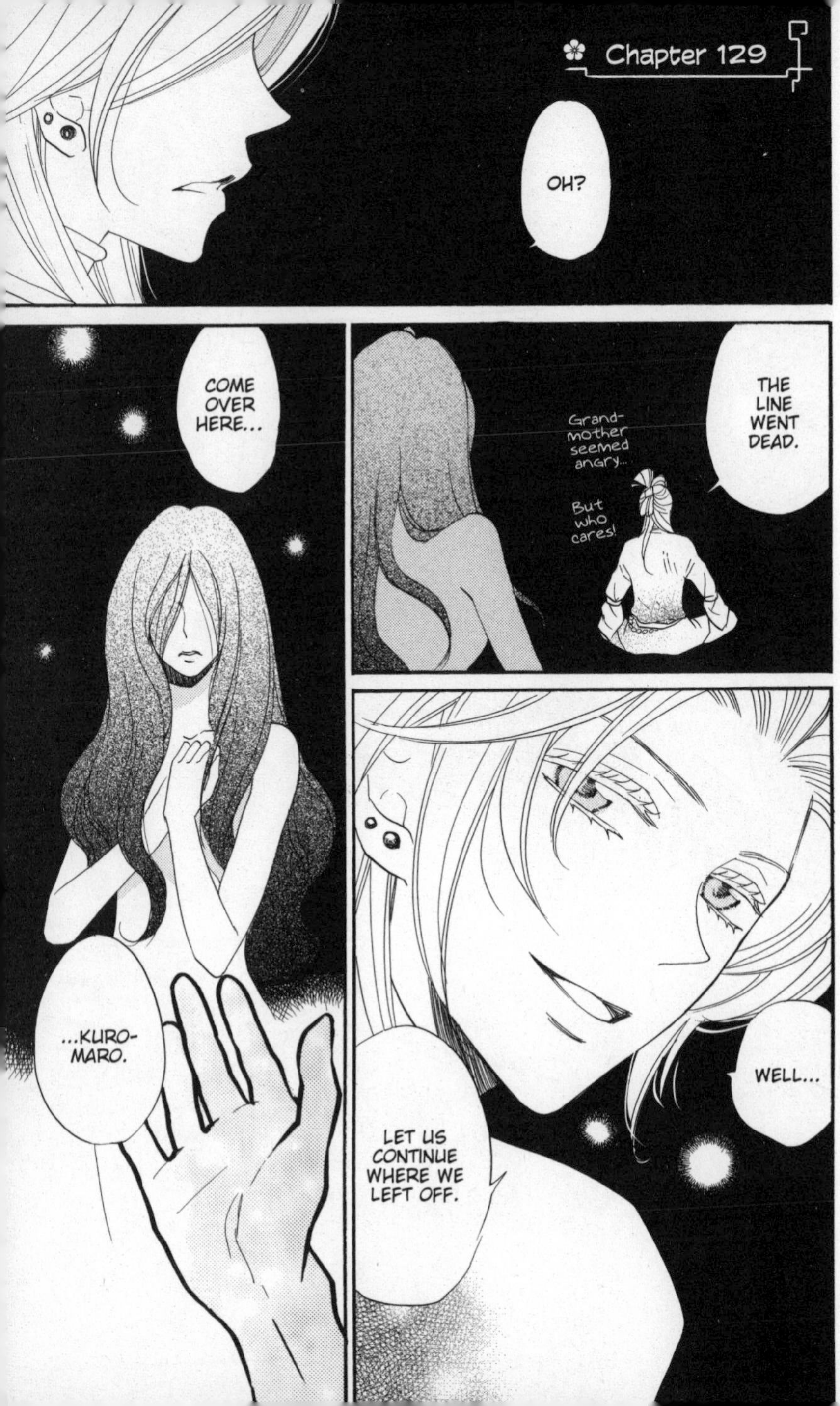
Chapter 129
OH?
THE LINE WENT DEAD.
Grand-mother seemed angry...
But who cares!
WELL...
LET US CONTINUE WHERE WE LEFT OFF.
COME OVER HERE...
...KURO-MARO.

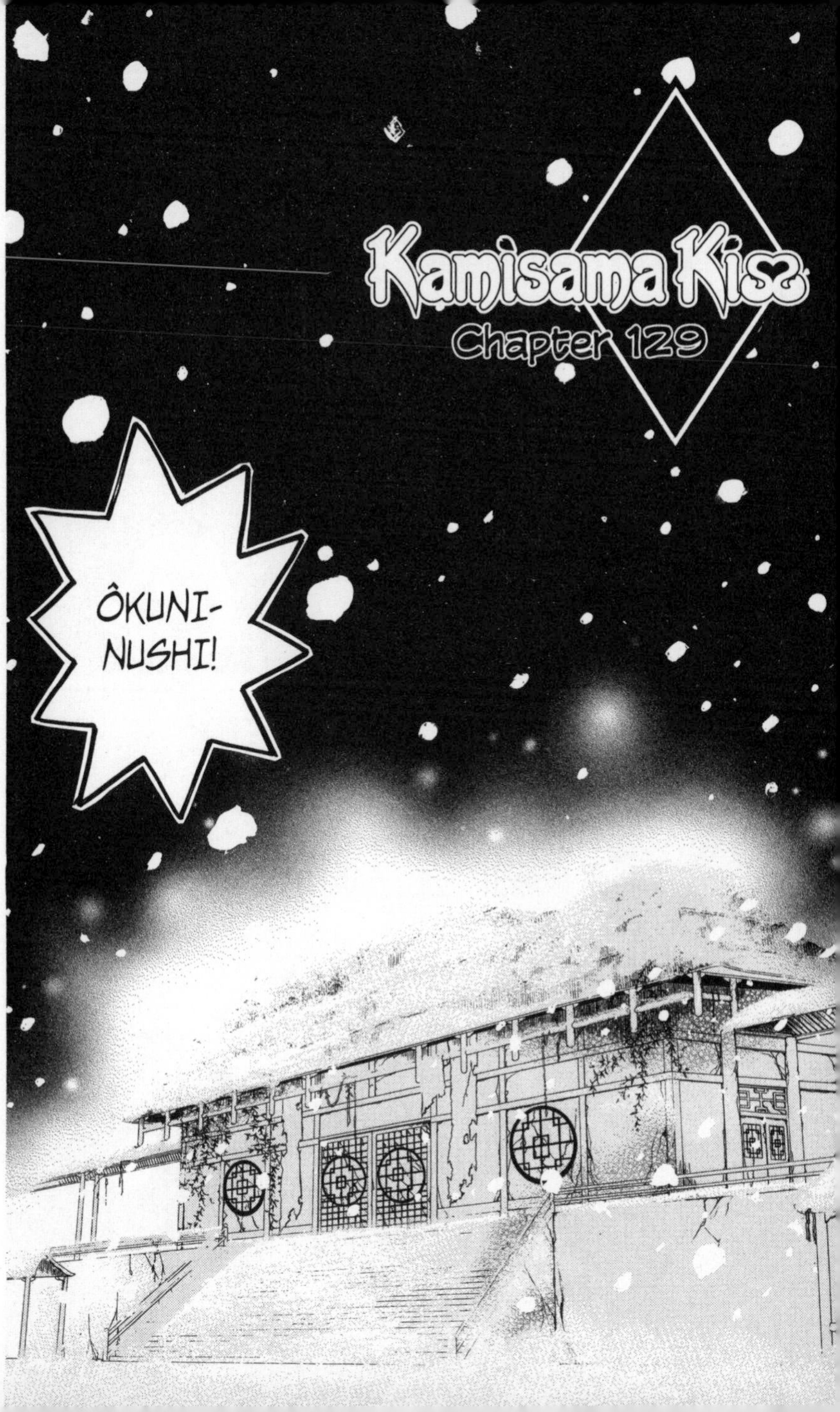
Kamisama Kiss
Chapter 129
ÔKUNI-NUSHI!

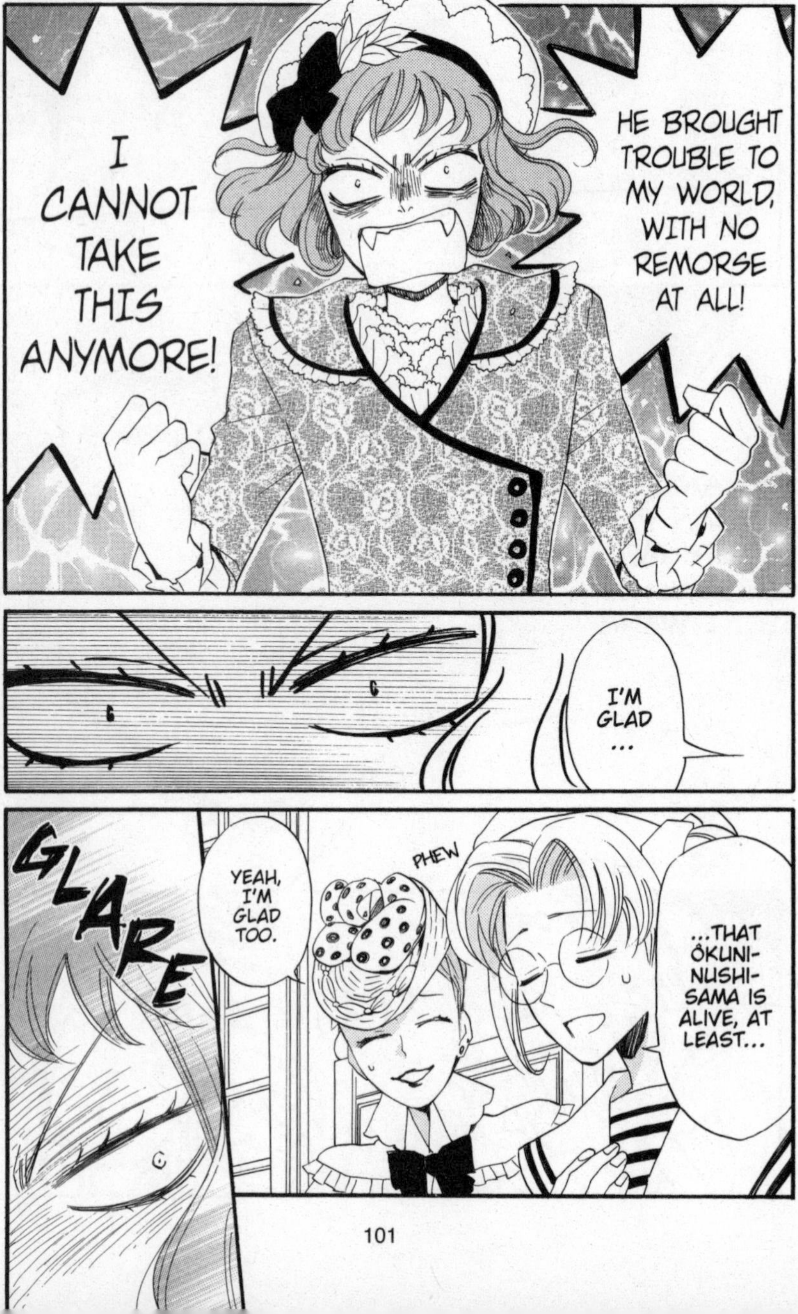
HE BROUGHT TROUBLE TO MY WORLD, WITH NO REMORSE AT ALL!
I CANNOT TAKE THIS ANYMORE!
I'M GLAD ...
...THAT ŌKUNINUSHI-SAMA IS ALIVE, AT LEAST...
PHEW
YEAH, I'M GLAD TOO.
GLARE

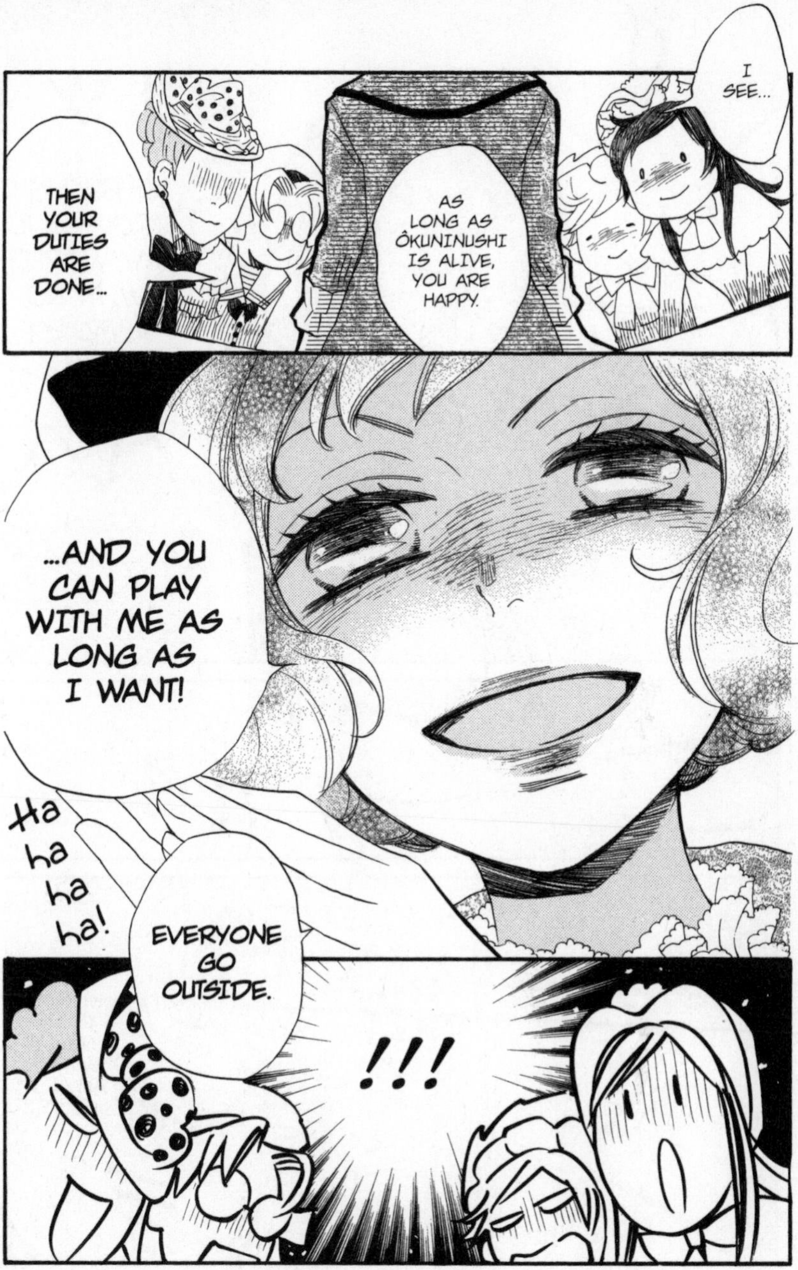
I SEE...
AS LONG AS ÔKUNINUSHI IS ALIVE, YOU ARE HAPPY.
THEN YOUR DUTIES ARE DONE...
...AND YOU CAN PLAY WITH ME AS LONG AS I WANT!
Ha ha ha ha!
EVERYONE GO OUTSIDE.
!!!

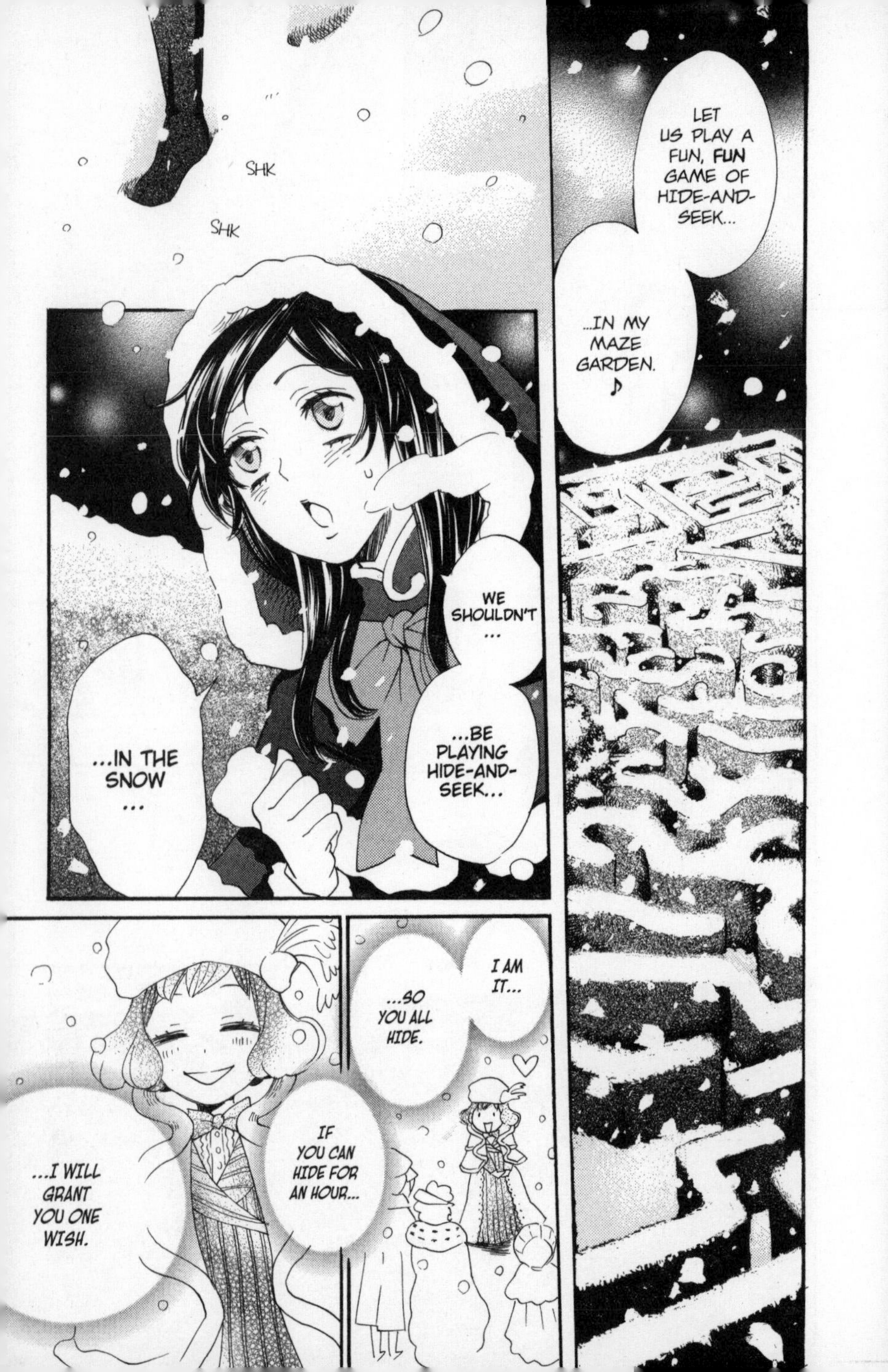
LET US PLAY A FUN, FUN GAME OF HIDE-AND-SEEK...
...IN MY MAZE GARDEN. ♪
SHK
SHK
WE SHOULDN'T...
...BE PLAYING HIDE-AND-SEEK...
...IN THE SNOW...
I AM IT...
...SO YOU ALL HIDE.
IF YOU CAN HIDE FOR AN HOUR...
...I WILL GRANT YOU ONE WISH.

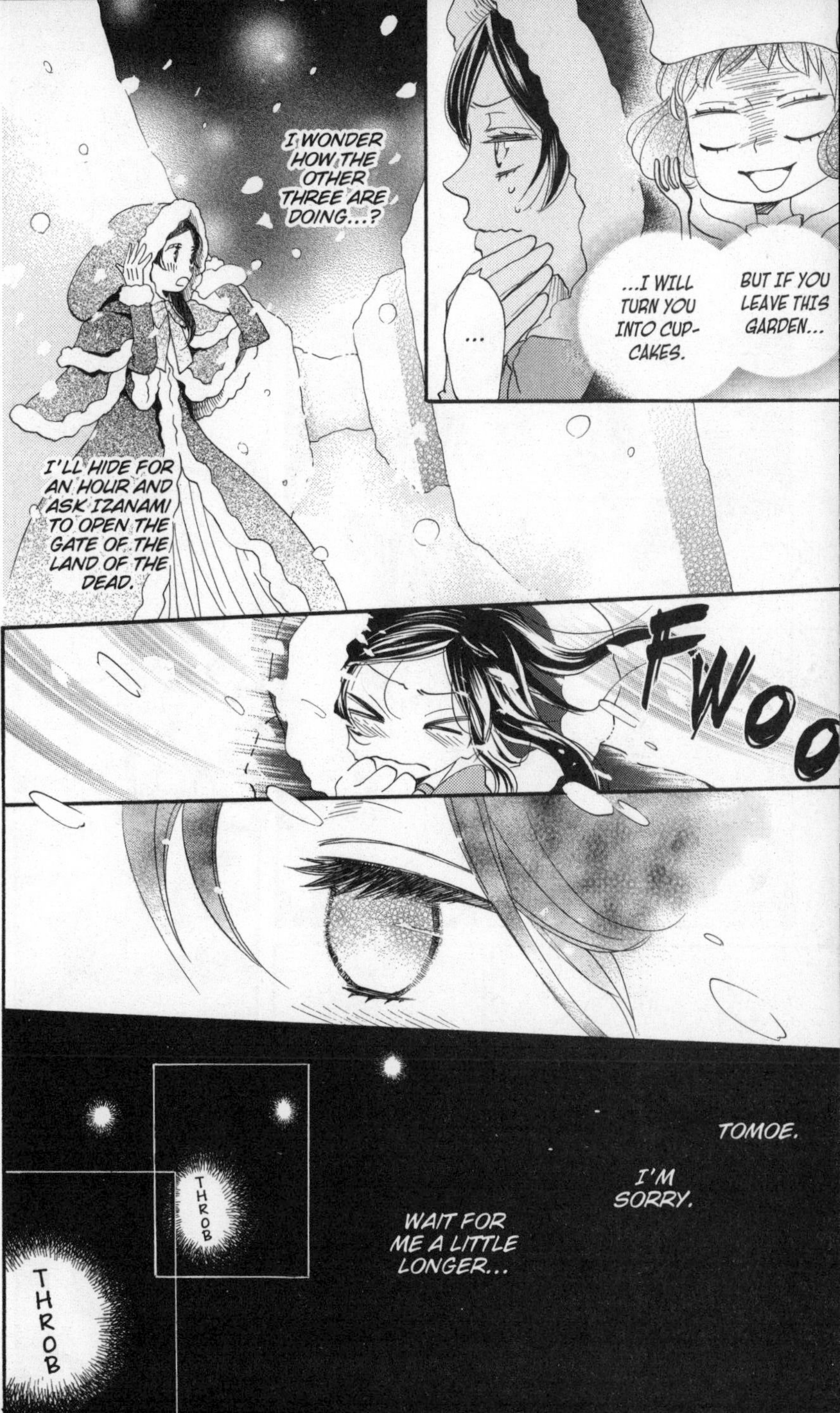
BUT IF YOU LEAVE THIS GARDEN...
...I WILL TURN YOU INTO CUPCAKES.
...
I WONDER HOW THE OTHER THREE ARE DOING...?
I'LL HIDE FOR AN HOUR AND ASK IZANAMI TO OPEN THE GATE OF THE LAND OF THE DEAD.
FWOO
TOMOE.
I'M SORRY.
WAIT FOR ME A LITTLE LONGER...
THROB
THROB

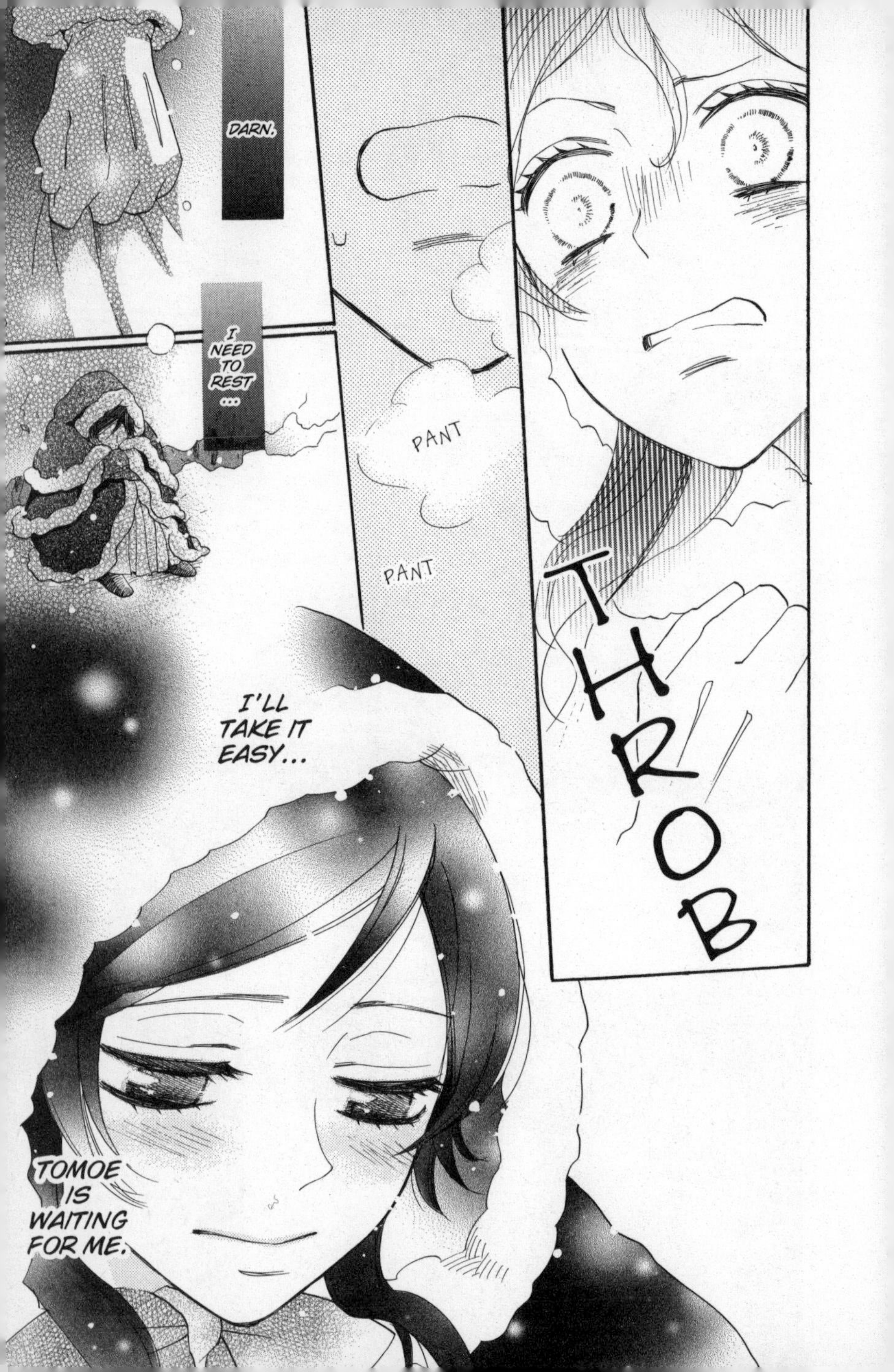
THROB
PANT
PANT
DARN.
I NEED TO REST...
I'LL TAKE IT EASY...
TOMOE IS WAITING FOR ME.

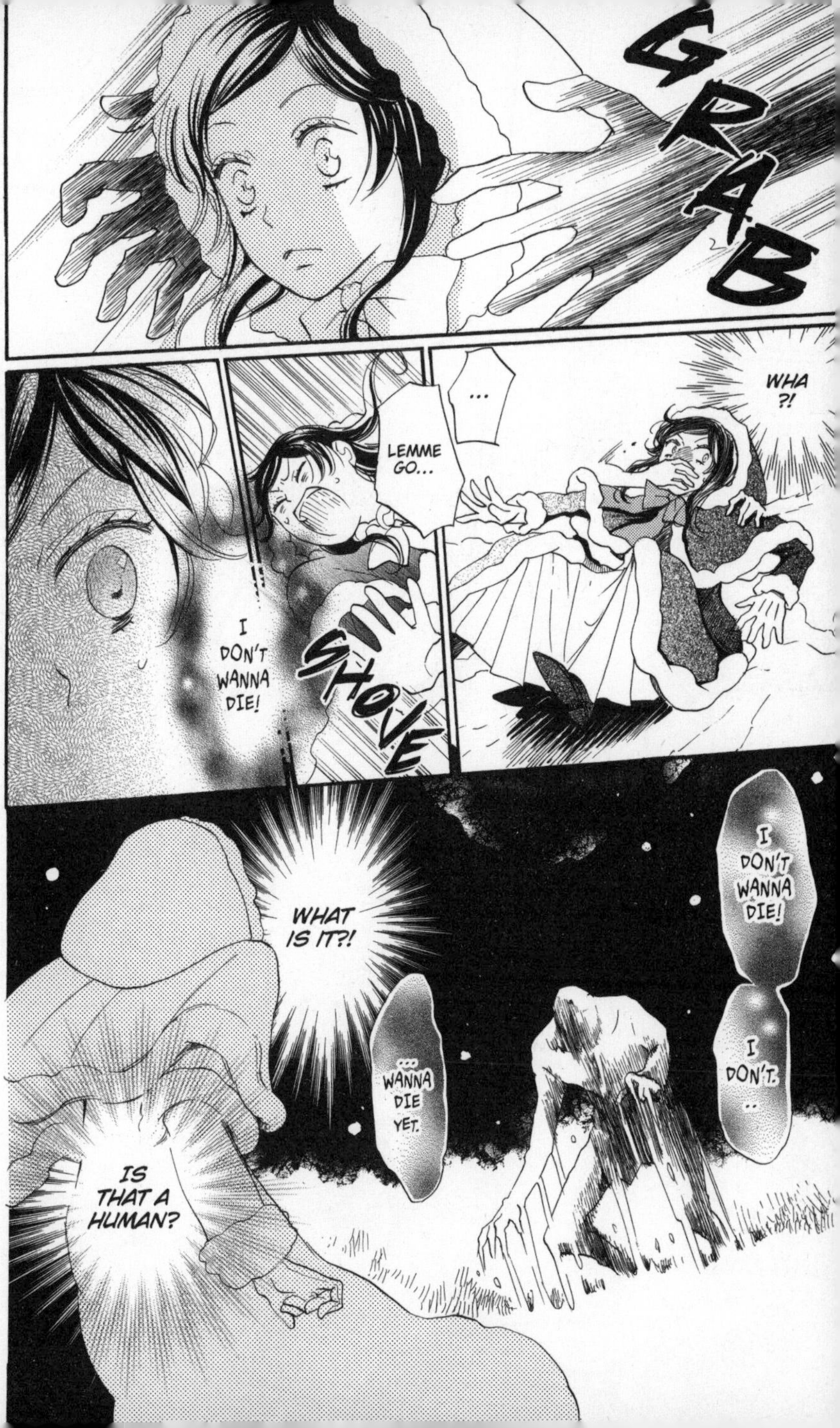
GRAB
WHA?!
...
LEMME GO...
SHOVE
I DON'T WANNA DIE!
I DON'T WANNA DIE!
I DON'T...
...WANNA DIE YET.
WHAT IS IT?!
IS THAT A HUMAN?

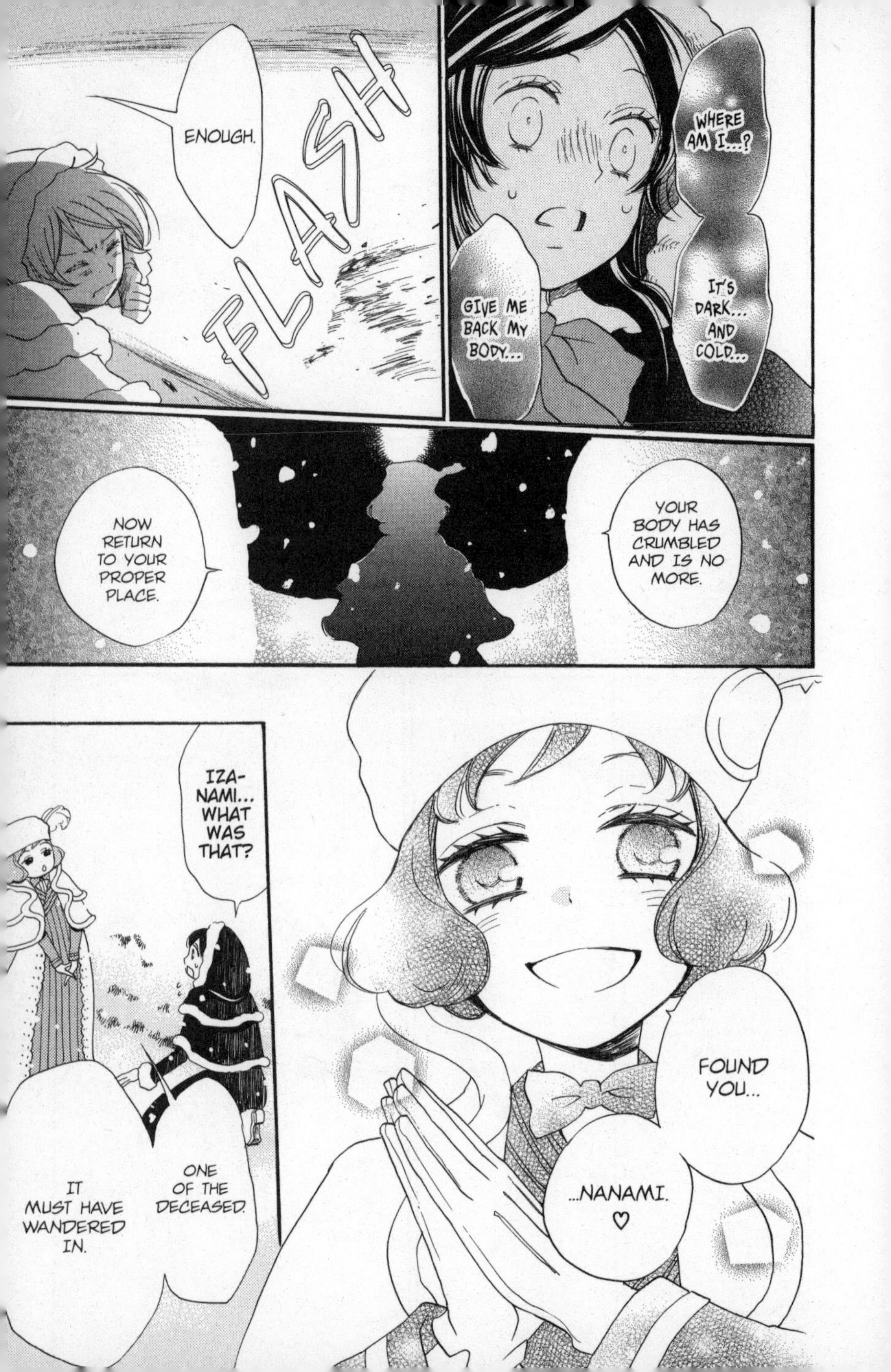
WHERE AM I...?
IT'S DARK... AND COLD...
GIVE ME BACK MY BODY...
ENOUGH.
FLASH
YOUR BODY HAS CRUMBLED AND IS NO MORE.
NOW RETURN TO YOUR PROPER PLACE.
FOUND YOU...
...NANAMI. ♡
IZA-NAMI... WHAT WAS THAT?
ONE OF THE DECEASED.
IT MUST HAVE WANDERED IN.

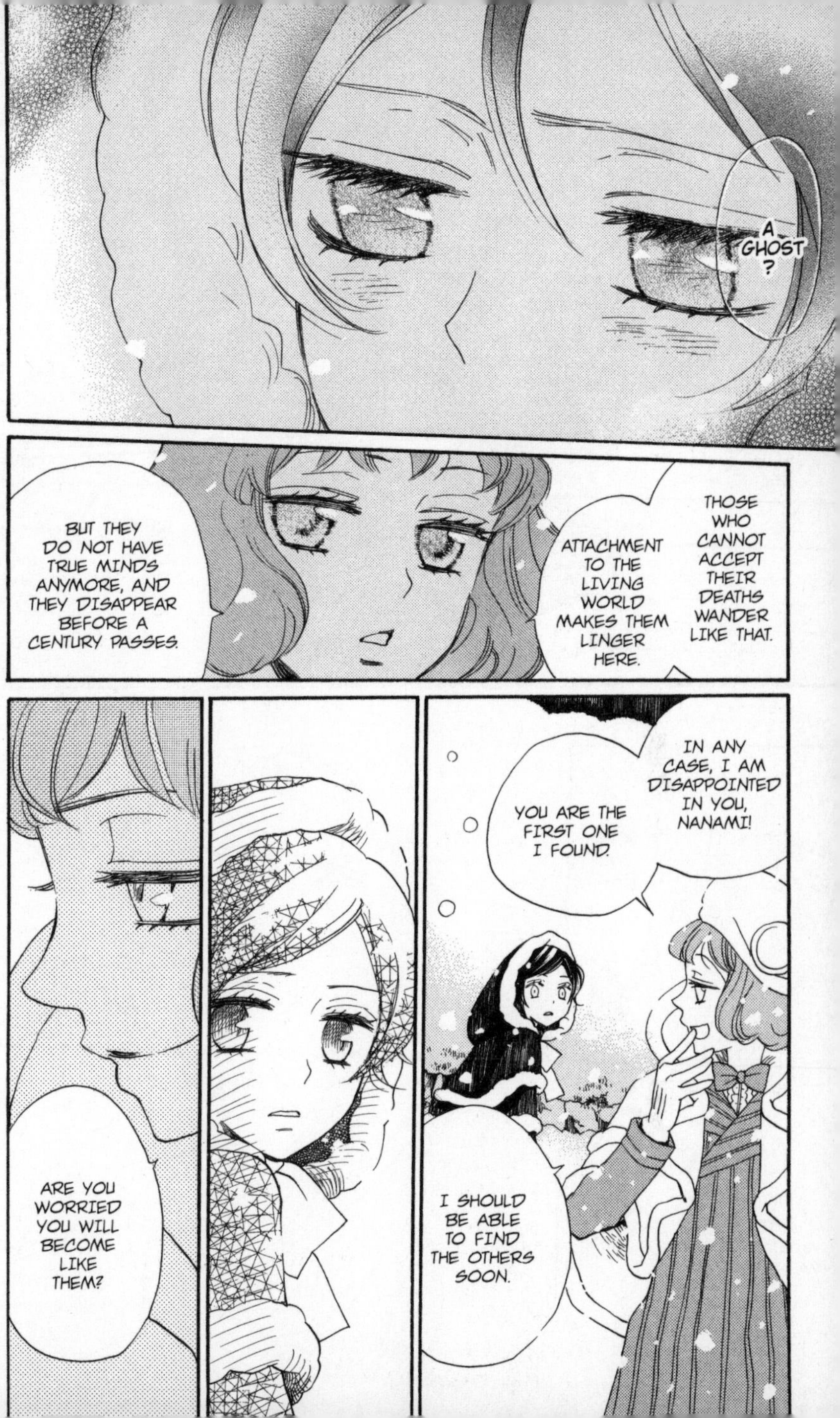
A GHOST?
THOSE WHO CANNOT ACCEPT THEIR DEATHS WANDER LIKE THAT.
ATTACHMENT TO THE LIVING WORLD MAKES THEM LINGER HERE.
BUT THEY DO NOT HAVE TRUE MINDS ANYMORE, AND THEY DISAPPEAR BEFORE A CENTURY PASSES.
IN ANY CASE, I AM DISAPPOINTED IN YOU, NANAMI!
YOU ARE THE FIRST ONE I FOUND.
I SHOULD BE ABLE TO FIND THE OTHERS SOON.
ARE YOU WORRIED YOU WILL BECOME LIKE THEM?

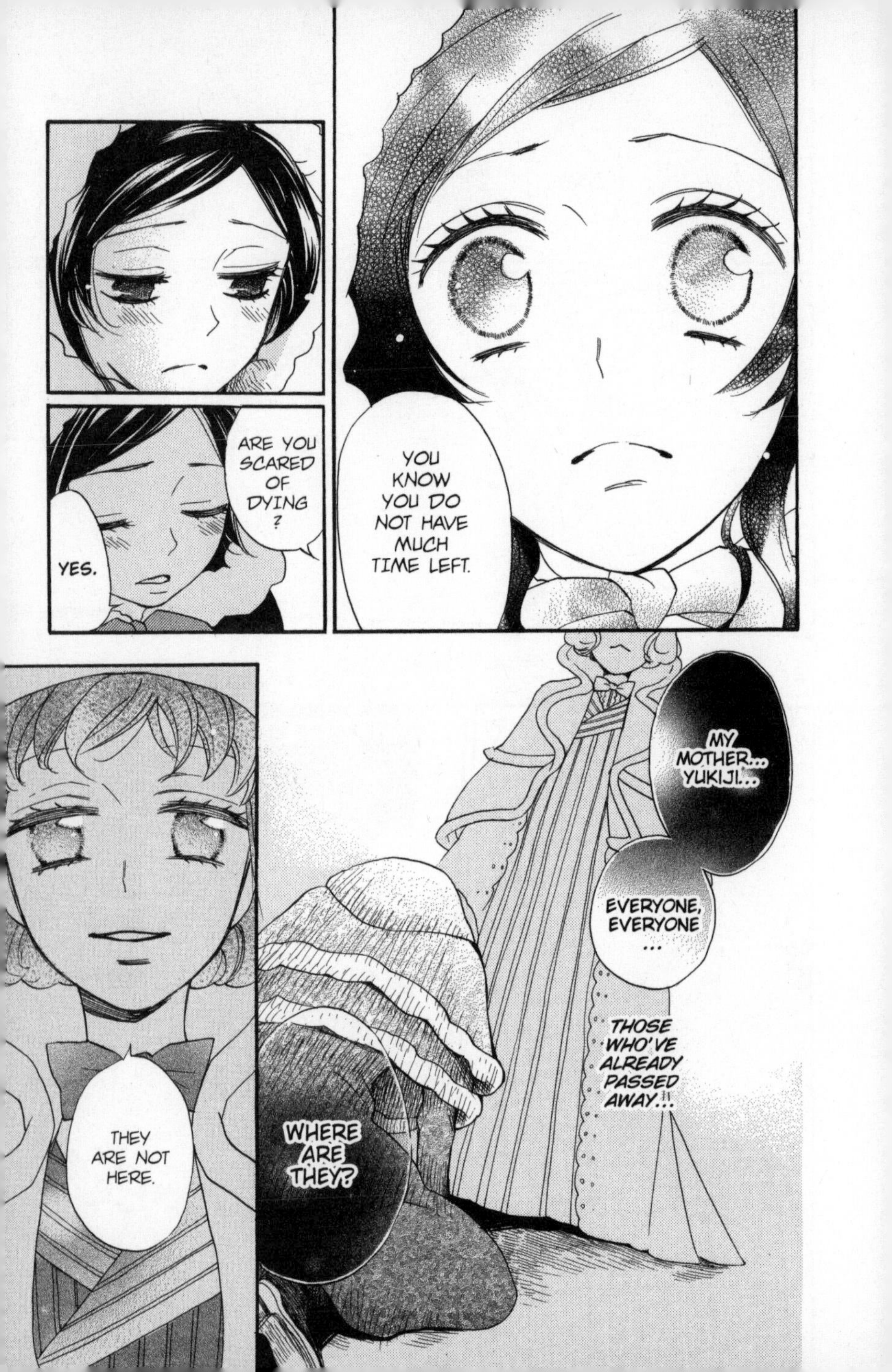
YOU KNOW YOU DO NOT HAVE MUCH TIME LEFT.
ARE YOU SCARED OF DYING?
YES.
MY MOTHER... YUKIJI...
EVERYONE, EVERYONE...
THOSE WHO'VE ALREADY PASSED AWAY...
WHERE ARE THEY?
THEY ARE NOT HERE.

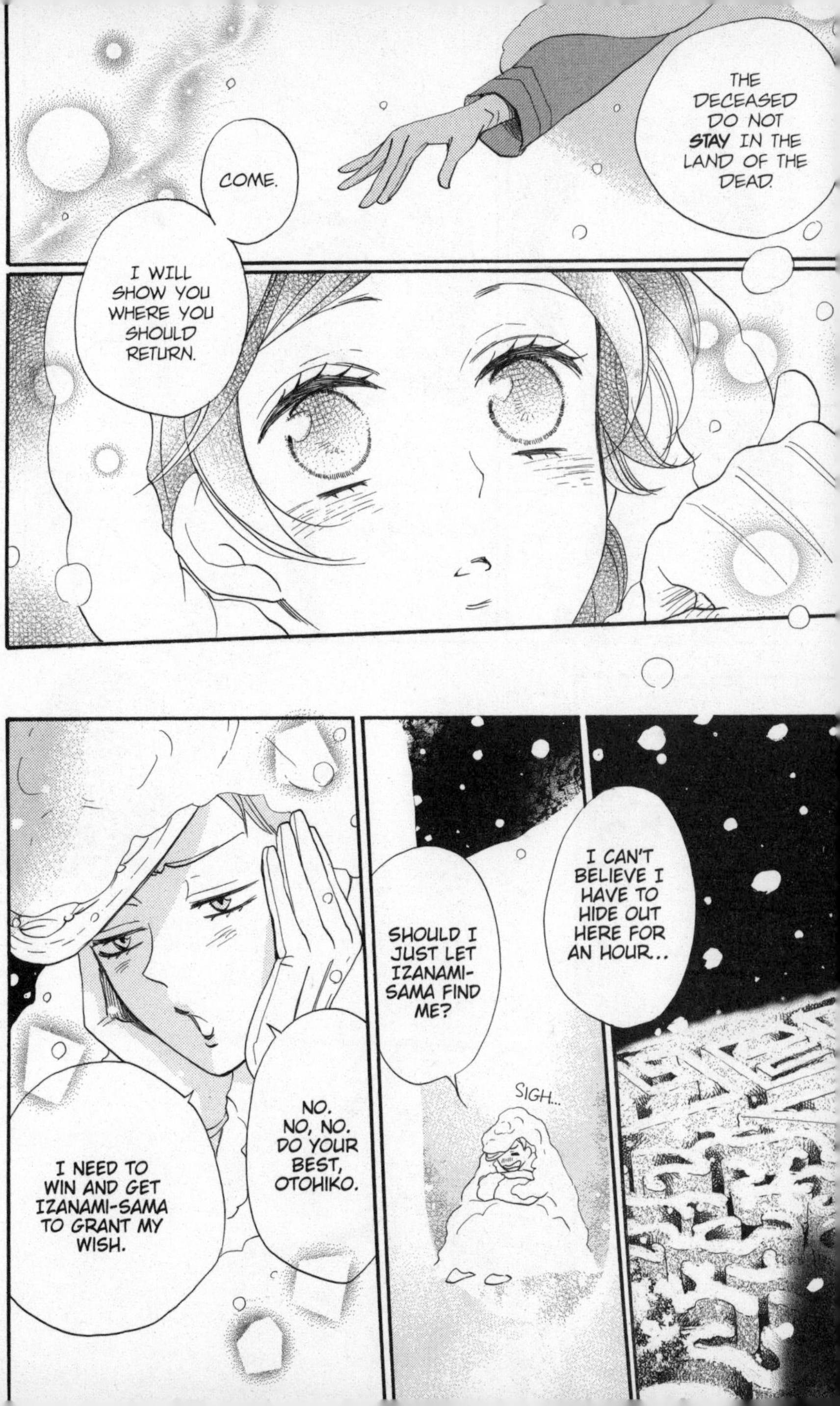
THE DECEASED DO NOT STAY IN THE LAND OF THE DEAD.
COME.
I WILL SHOW YOU WHERE YOU SHOULD RETURN.
I CAN'T BELIEVE I HAVE TO HIDE OUT HERE FOR AN HOUR...
SHOULD I JUST LET IZANAMI-SAMA FIND ME?
SIGH...
NO. NO, NO. DO YOUR BEST, OTOHIKO.
I NEED TO WIN AND GET IZANAMI-SAMA TO GRANT MY WISH.

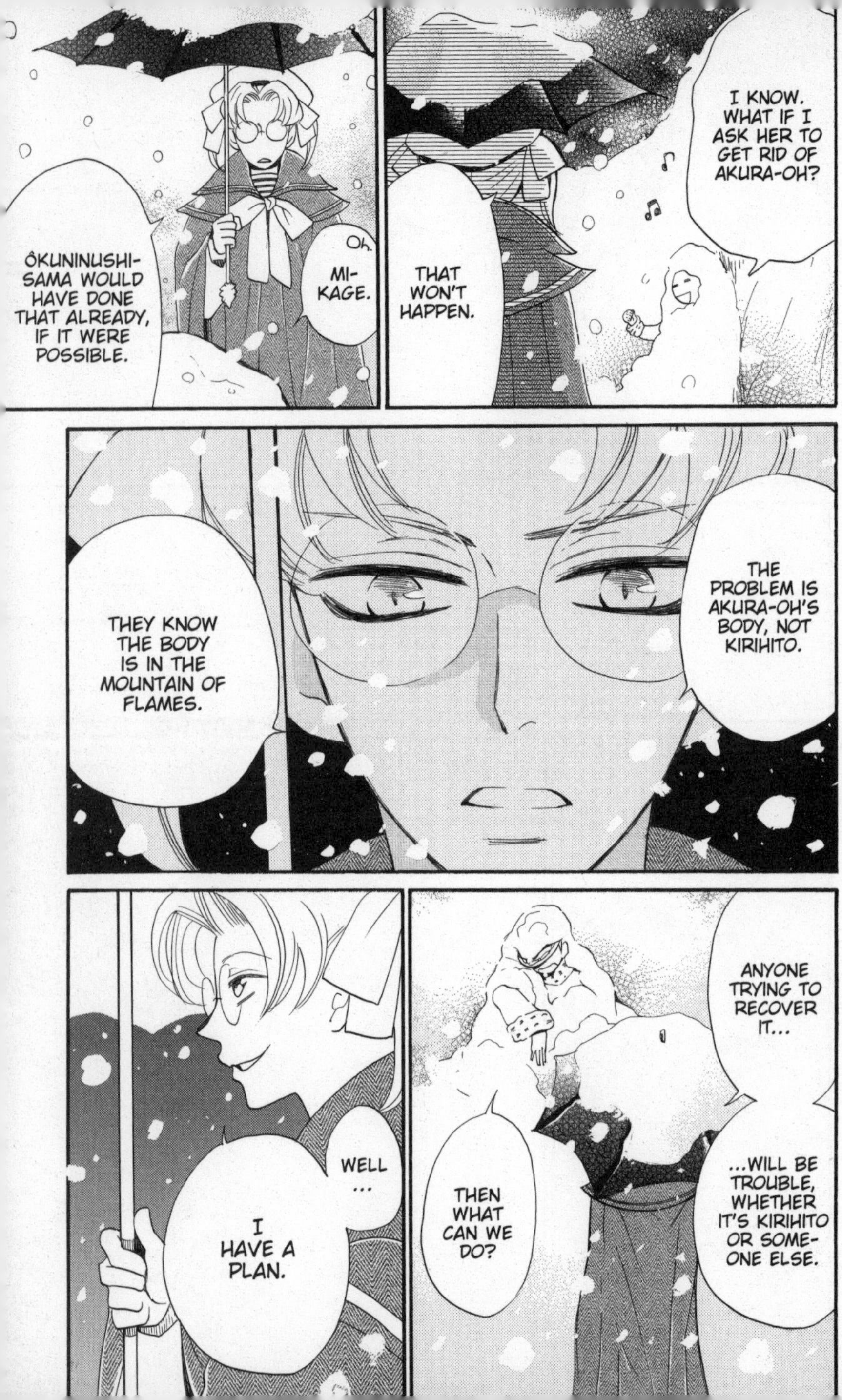
I KNOW. WHAT IF I ASK HER TO GET RID OF AKURA-OH?
THAT WON'T HAPPEN.
Oh.
MI-KAGE.
ÔKUNINUSHI-SAMA WOULD HAVE DONE THAT ALREADY, IF IT WERE POSSIBLE.
THE PROBLEM IS AKURA-OH'S BODY, NOT KIRIHITO.
THEY KNOW THE BODY IS IN THE MOUNTAIN OF FLAMES.
ANYONE TRYING TO RECOVER IT...
...WILL BE TROUBLE, WHETHER IT'S KIRIHITO OR SOME-ONE ELSE.
THEN WHAT CAN WE DO?
WELL...
I HAVE A PLAN.

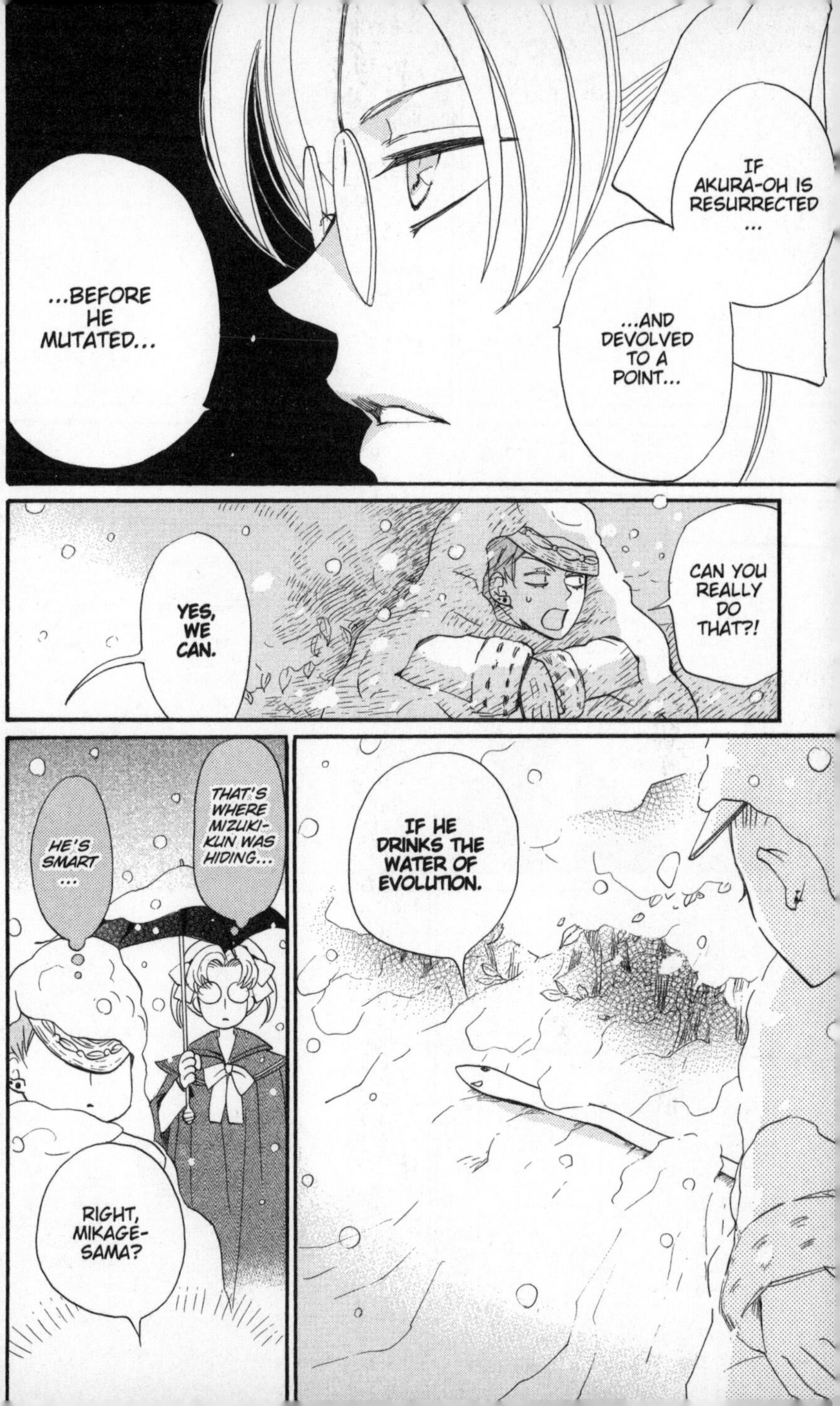
IF AKURA-OH IS RESURRECTED ...
...AND DEVOLVED TO A POINT...
...BEFORE HE MUTATED...
CAN YOU REALLY DO THAT?!
YES, WE CAN.
IF HE DRINKS THE WATER OF EVOLUTION.
THAT'S WHERE MIZUKI-KUN WAS HIDING...
HE'S SMART ...
RIGHT, MIKAGE-SAMA?

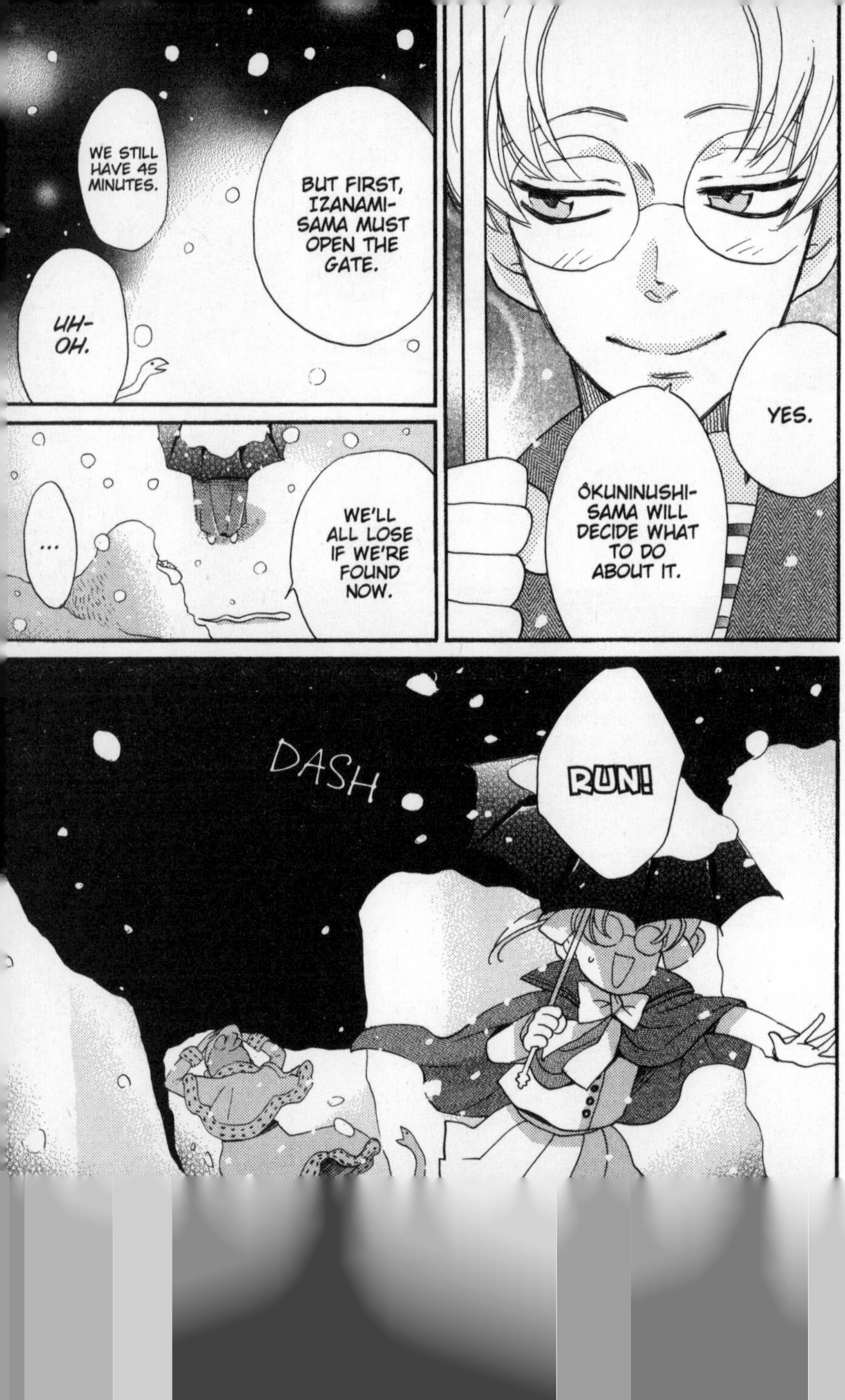
YES.
ŌKUNINUSHI-SAMA WILL DECIDE WHAT TO DO ABOUT IT.
BUT FIRST, IZANAMI-SAMA MUST OPEN THE GATE.
WE STILL HAVE 45 MINUTES.
UH-OH.
WE'LL ALL LOSE IF WE'RE FOUND NOW.
...
RUN!
DASH

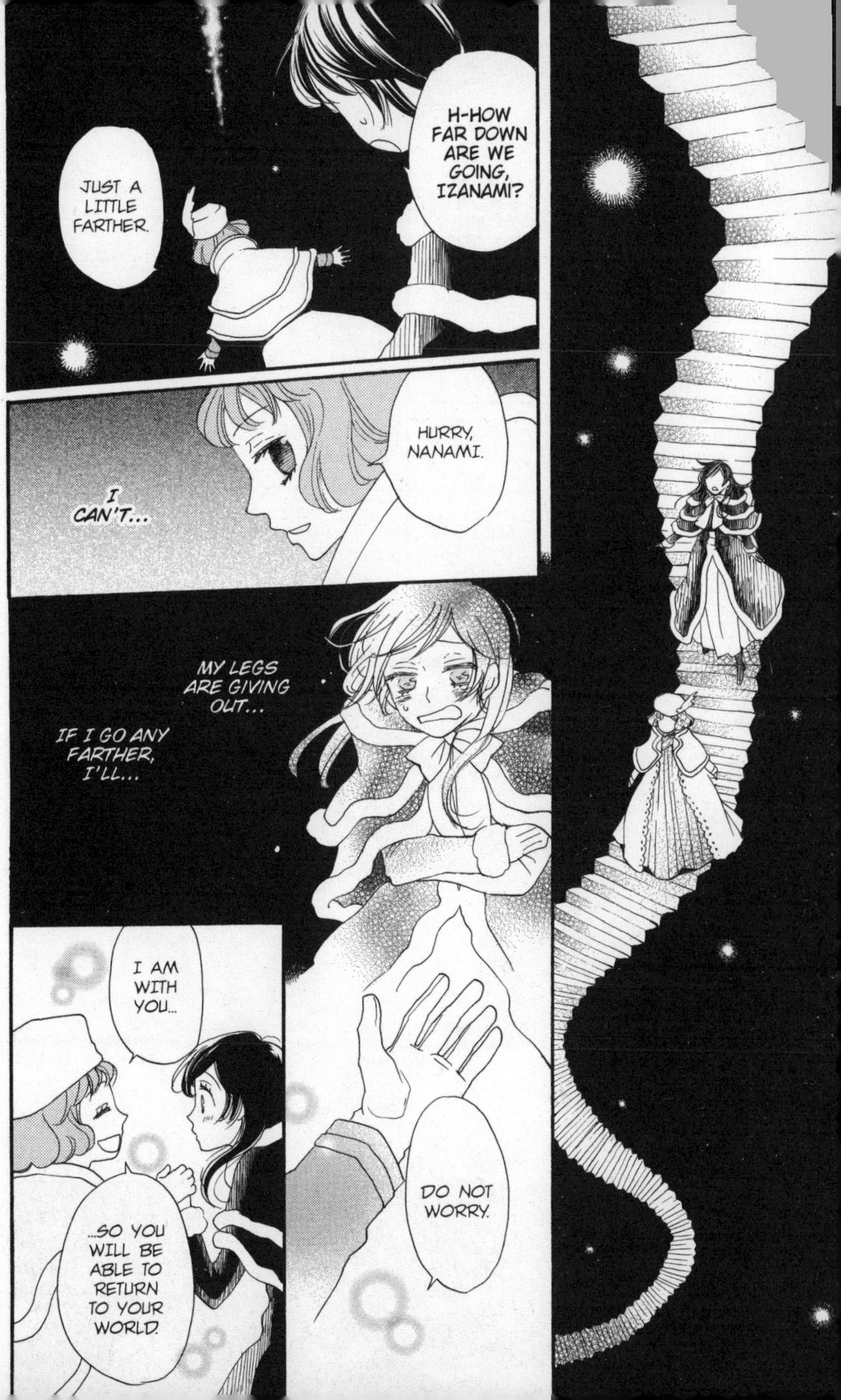
H-HOW FAR DOWN ARE WE GOING, IZANAMI?
JUST A LITTLE FARTHER.
HURRY, NANAMI.
I CAN'T...
MY LEGS ARE GIVING OUT...
IF I GO ANY FARTHER, I'LL...
DO NOT WORRY.
I AM WITH YOU...
...SO YOU WILL BE ABLE TO RETURN TO YOUR WORLD.

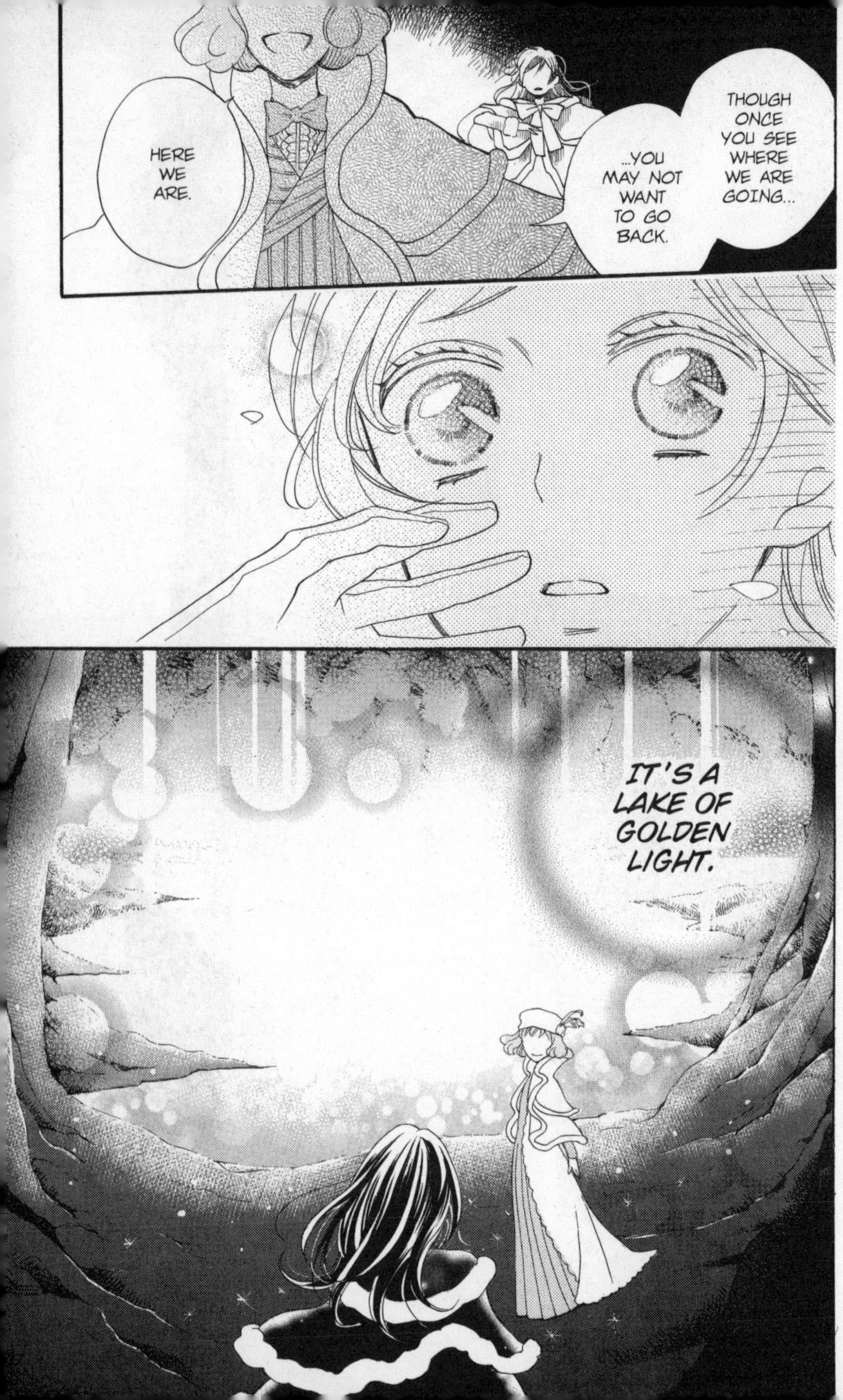
THOUGH ONCE YOU SEE WHERE WE ARE GOING...
...YOU MAY NOT WANT TO GO BACK.
HERE WE ARE.
IT'S A LAKE OF GOLDEN LIGHT.

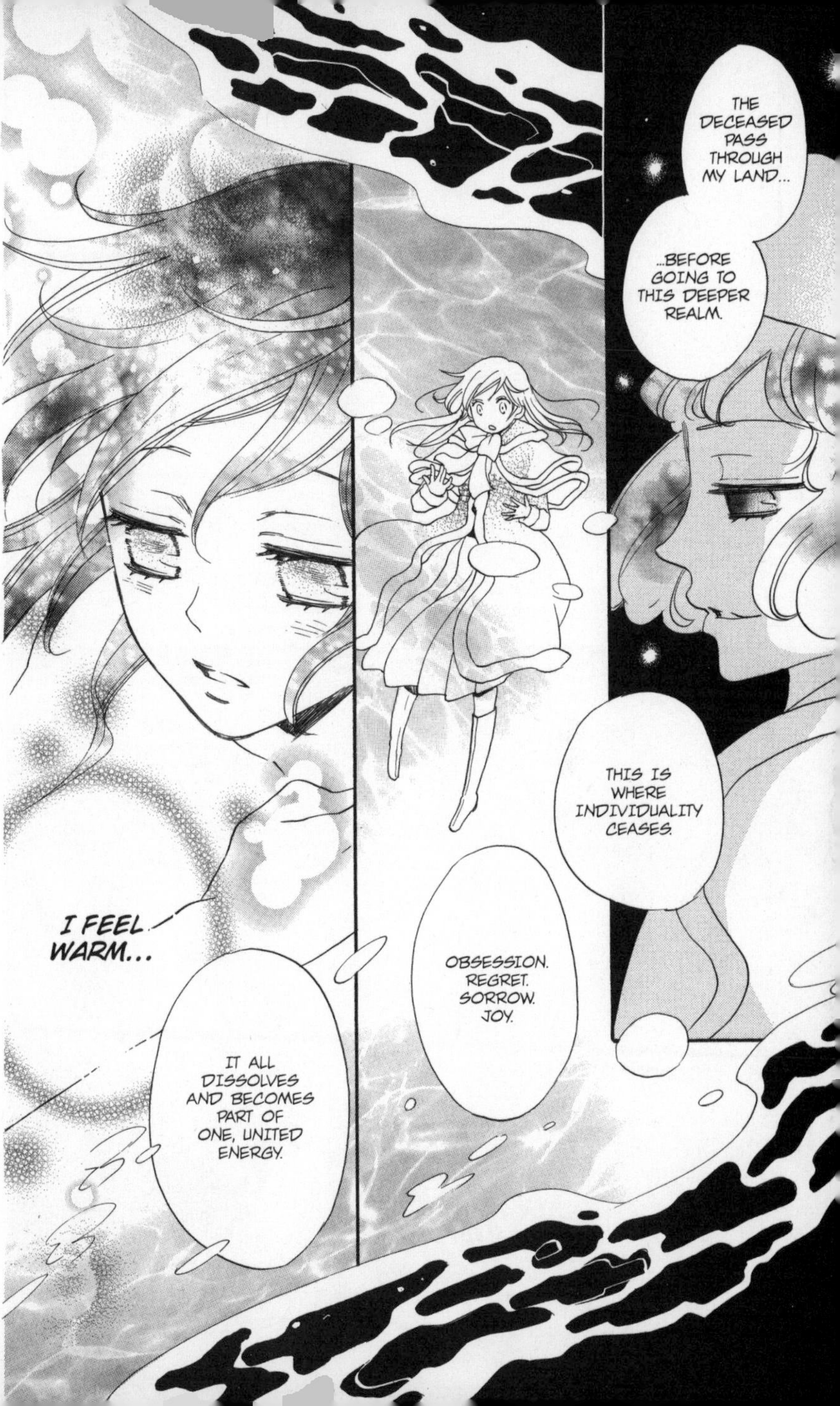
THE DECEASED PASS THROUGH MY LAND...
...BEFORE GOING TO THIS DEEPER REALM.
THIS IS WHERE INDIVIDUALITY CEASES.
OBSESSION. REGRET. SORROW. JOY.
IT ALL DISSOLVES AND BECOMES PART OF ONE, UNITED ENERGY.
I FEEL WARM...

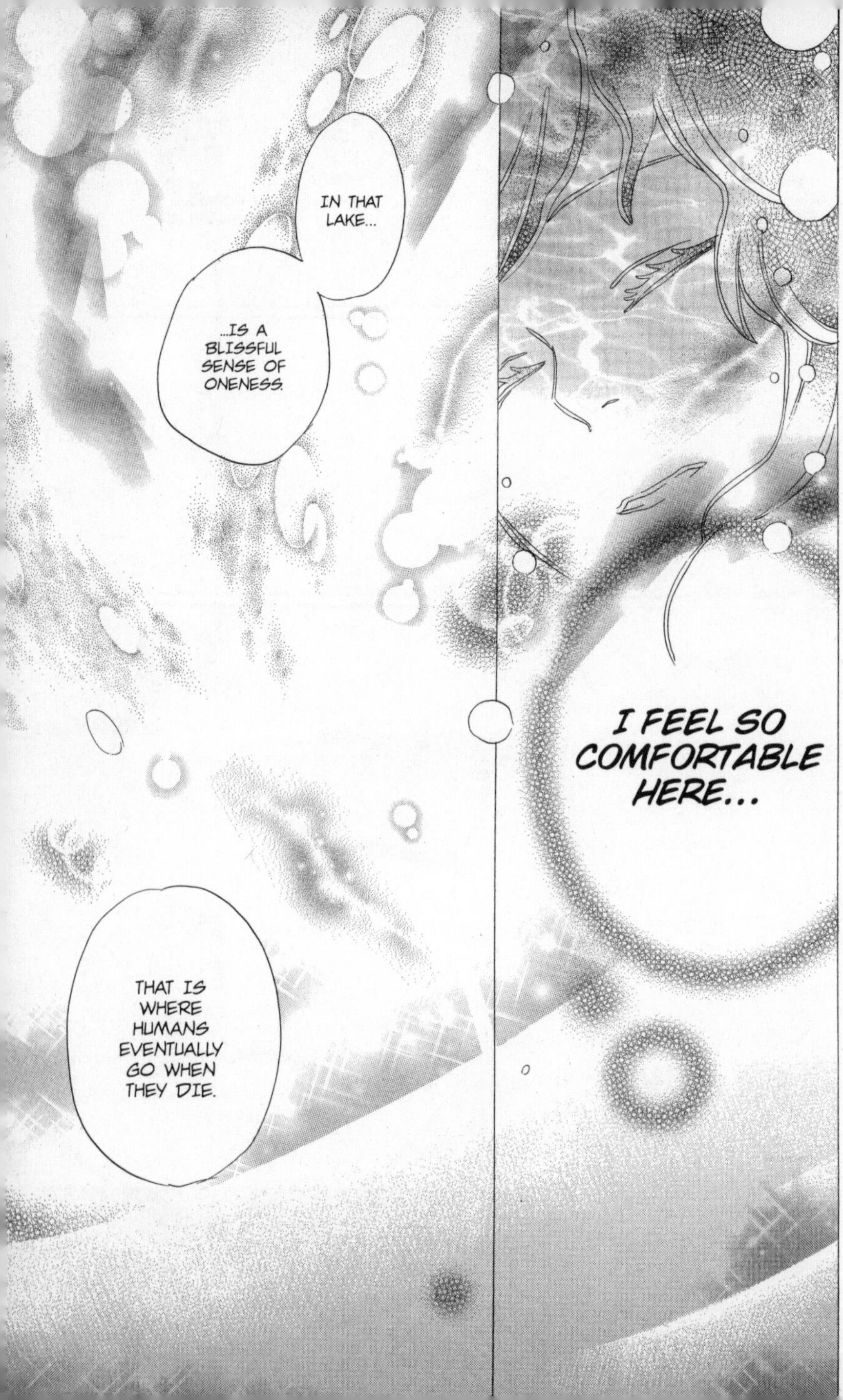
I FEEL SO COMFORTABLE HERE...
IN THAT LAKE...
...IS A BLISSFUL SENSE OF ONENESS.
THAT IS WHERE HUMANS EVENTUALLY GO WHEN THEY DIE.

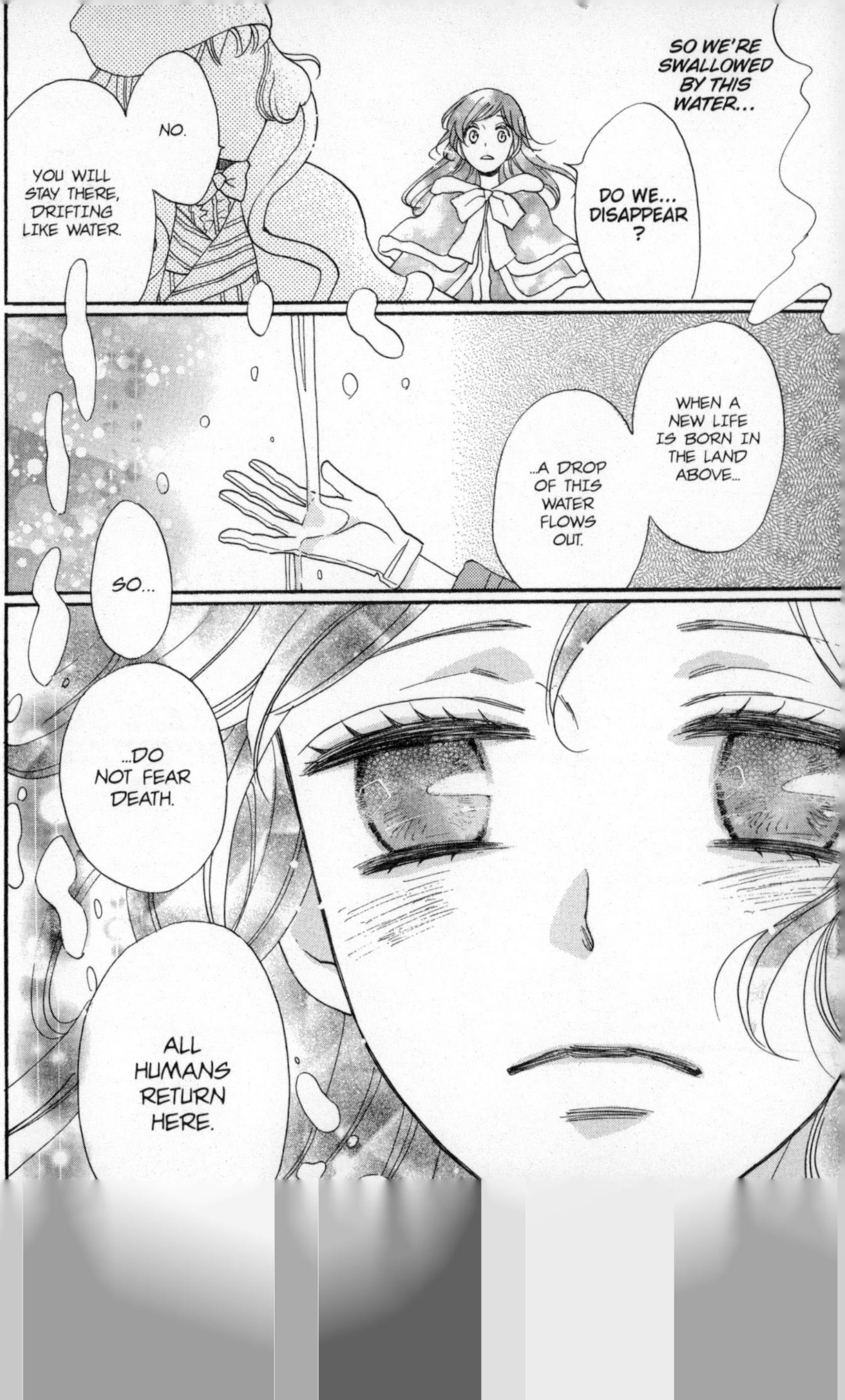
SO WE'RE SWALLOWED BY THIS WATER...
DO WE... DISAPPEAR?
NO.
YOU WILL STAY THERE, DRIFTING LIKE WATER.
WHEN A NEW LIFE IS BORN IN THE LAND ABOVE...
...A DROP OF THIS WATER FLOWS OUT.
SO...
...DO NOT FEAR DEATH.
ALL HUMANS RETURN HERE.

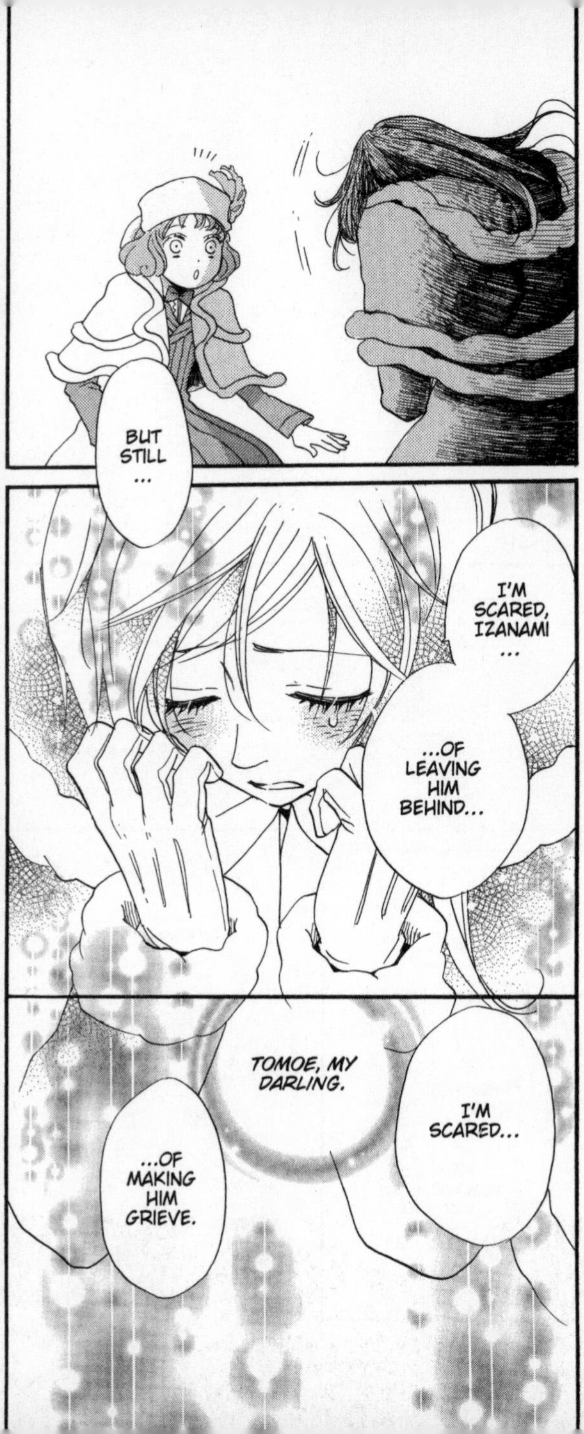
BUT STILL ...
I'M SCARED, IZANAMI ...
...OF LEAVING HIM BEHIND...
I'M SCARED...
TOMOE, MY DARLING.
...OF MAKING HIM GRIEVE.
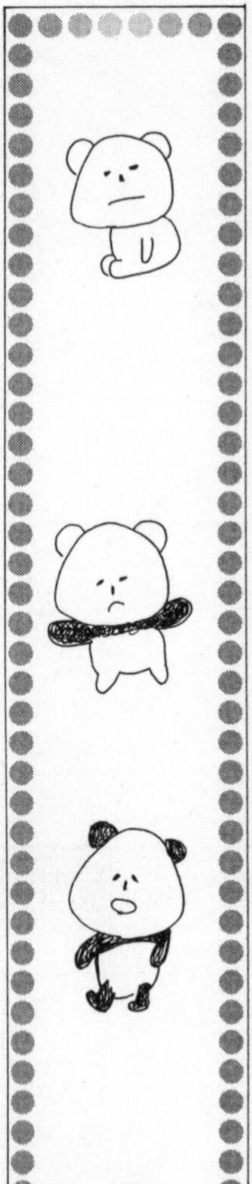

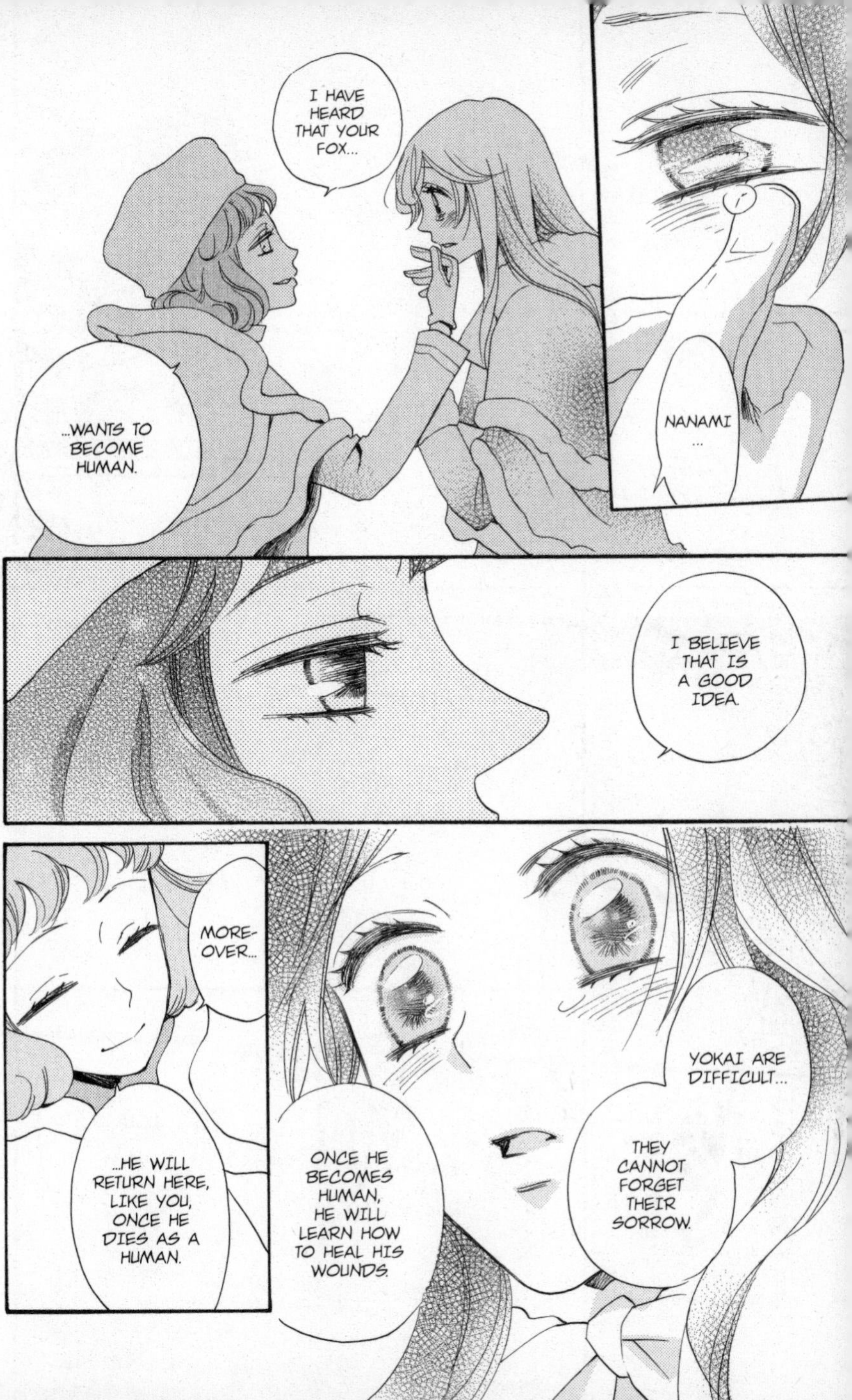

NANAMI...
I HAVE HEARD THAT YOUR FOX...
...WANTS TO BECOME HUMAN.
I BELIEVE THAT IS A GOOD IDEA.
YOKAI ARE DIFFICULT...
THEY CANNOT FORGET THEIR SORROW.
ONCE HE BECOMES HUMAN, HE WILL LEARN HOW TO HEAL HIS WOUNDS.
MORE-OVER...
...HE WILL RETURN HERE, LIKE YOU, ONCE HE DIES AS A HUMAN.

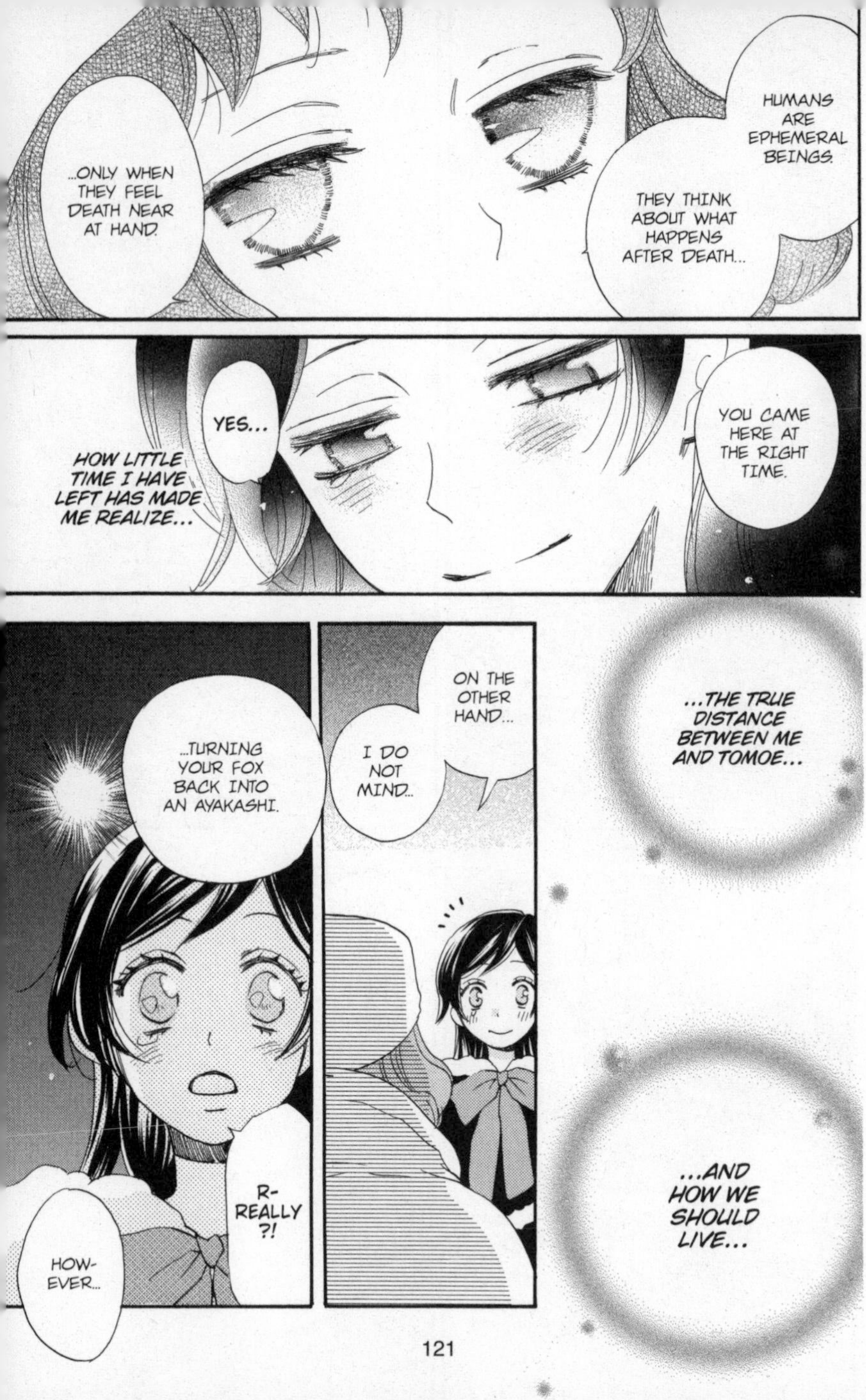
HUMANS ARE EPHEMERAL BEINGS.
THEY THINK ABOUT WHAT HAPPENS AFTER DEATH...
...ONLY WHEN THEY FEEL DEATH NEAR AT HAND.
YOU CAME HERE AT THE RIGHT TIME.
YES...
HOW LITTLE TIME I HAVE LEFT HAS MADE ME REALIZE...
...THE TRUE DISTANCE BETWEEN ME AND TOMOE...
...AND HOW WE SHOULD LIVE...
ON THE OTHER HAND...
I DO NOT MIND...
...TURNING YOUR FOX BACK INTO AN AYAKASHI.
R-REALLY?!
HOW-EVER...

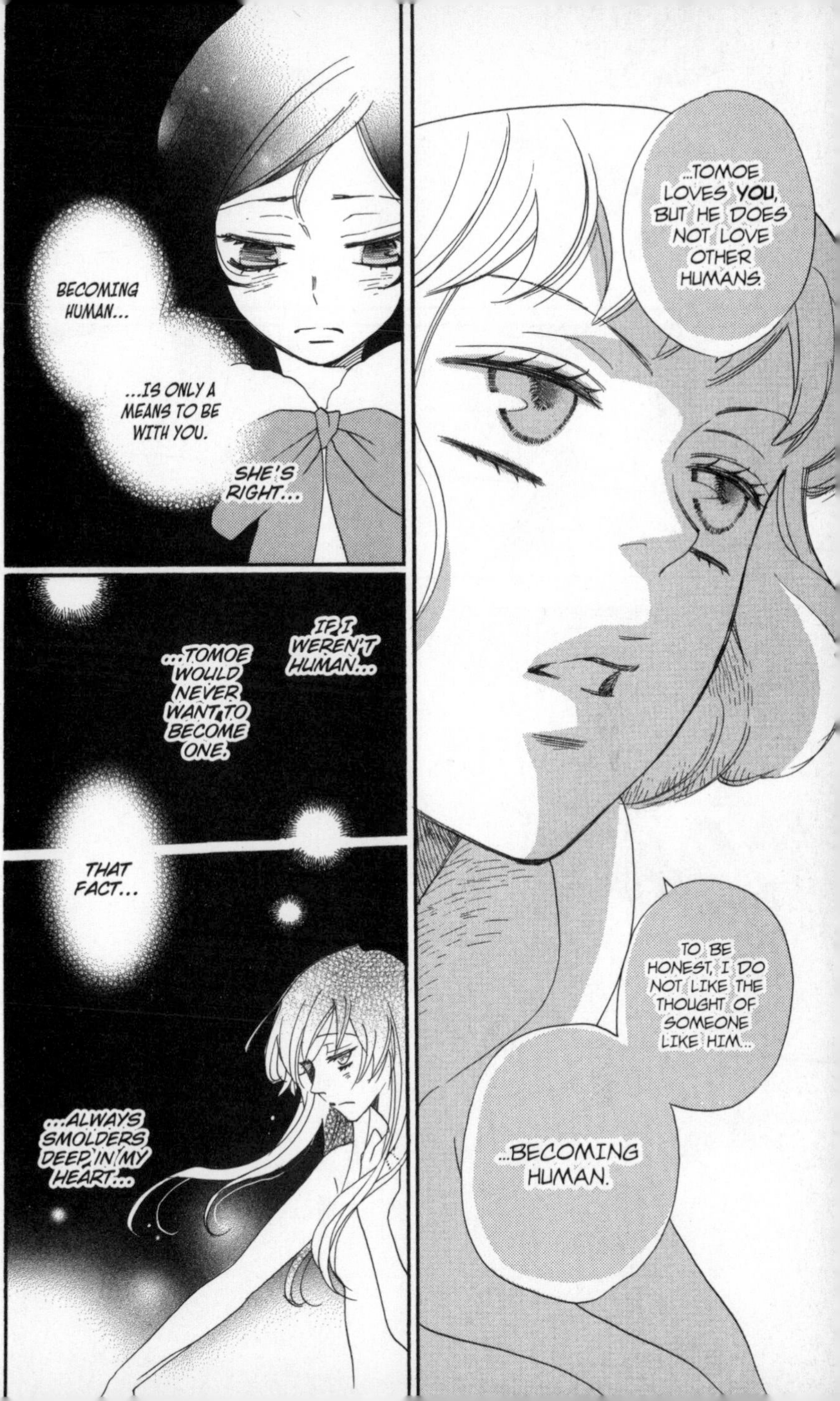
...TOMOE LOVES YOU, BUT HE DOES NOT LOVE OTHER HUMANS.
TO BE HONEST, I DO NOT LIKE THE THOUGHT OF SOMEONE LIKE HIM...
...BECOMING HUMAN.
BECOMING HUMAN...
...IS ONLY A MEANS TO BE WITH YOU.
SHE'S RIGHT...
IF I WEREN'T HUMAN...
...TOMOE WOULD NEVER WANT TO BECOME ONE.
THAT FACT...
...ALWAYS SMOLDERS DEEP IN MY HEART...

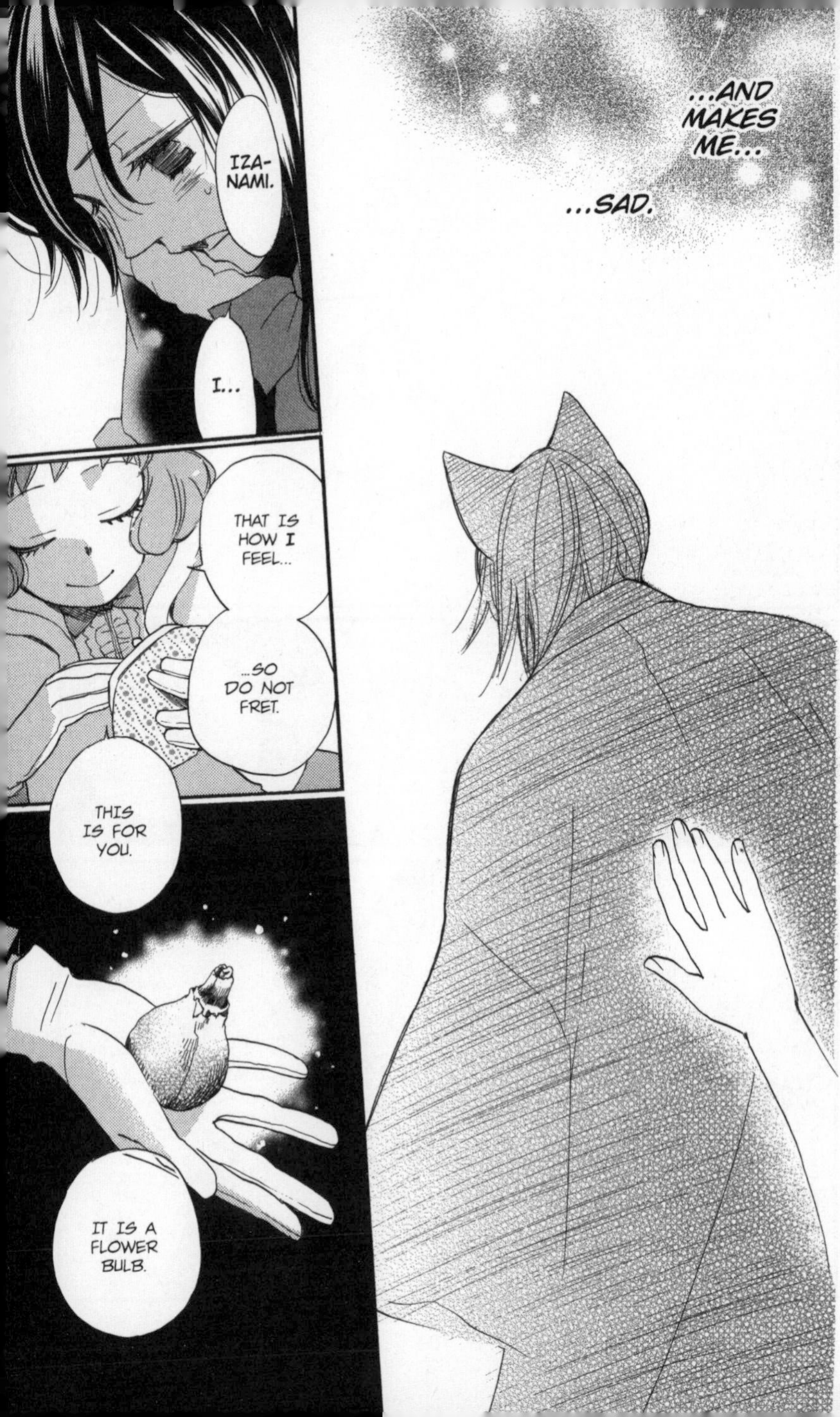
...AND MAKES ME...
...SAD.
IZA-NAMI.
I...
THAT IS HOW I FEEL...
...SO DO NOT FRET.
THIS IS FOR YOU.
IT IS A FLOWER BULB.

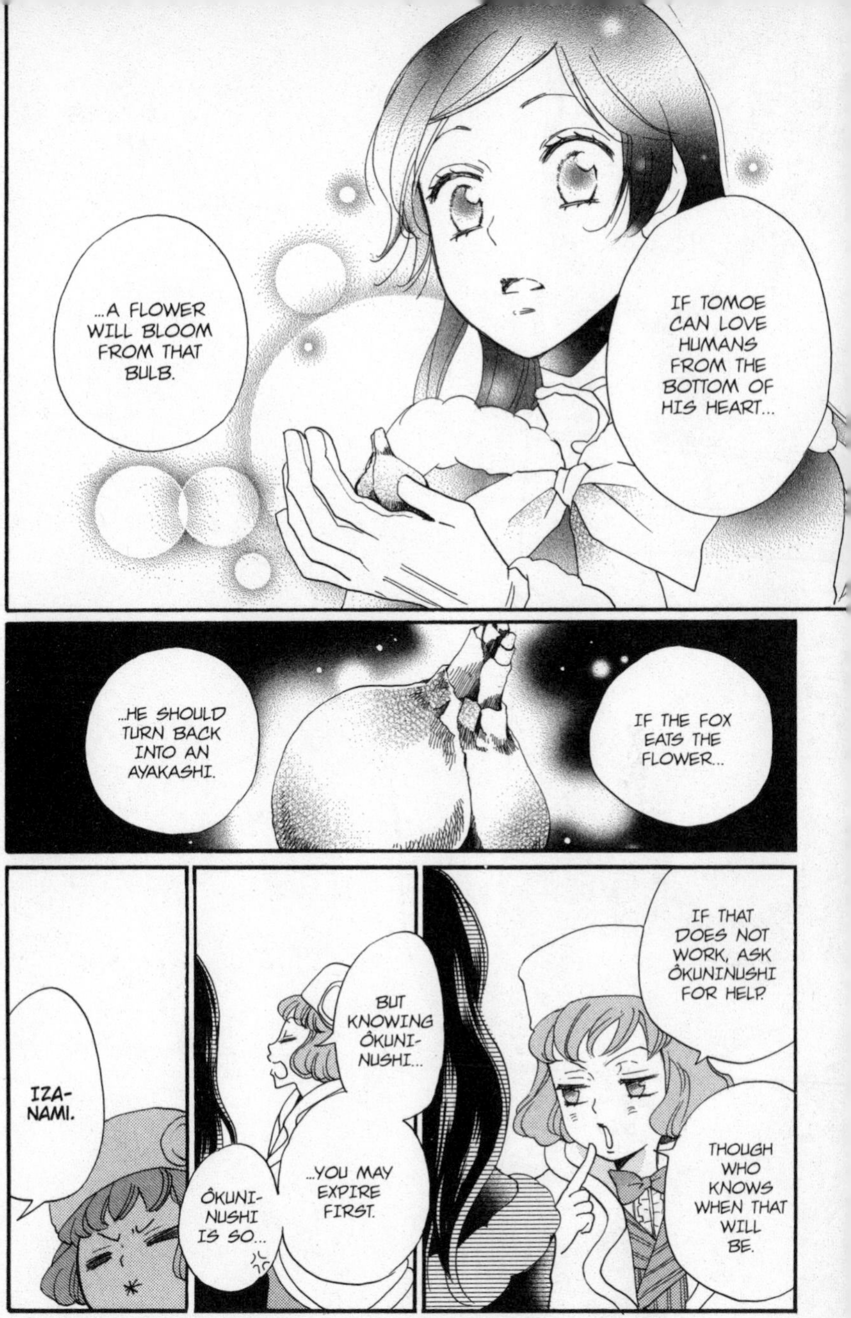
IF TOMOE CAN LOVE HUMANS FROM THE BOTTOM OF HIS HEART...
...A FLOWER WILL BLOOM FROM THAT BULB.
IF THE FOX EATS THE FLOWER...
...HE SHOULD TURN BACK INTO AN AYAKASHI.
IF THAT DOES NOT WORK, ASK ÔKUNINUSHI FOR HELP.
THOUGH WHO KNOWS WHEN THAT WILL BE.
BUT KNOWING ÔKUNI-NUSHI...
...YOU MAY EXPIRE FIRST.
ÔKUNI-NUSHI IS SO...
IZA-NAMI.

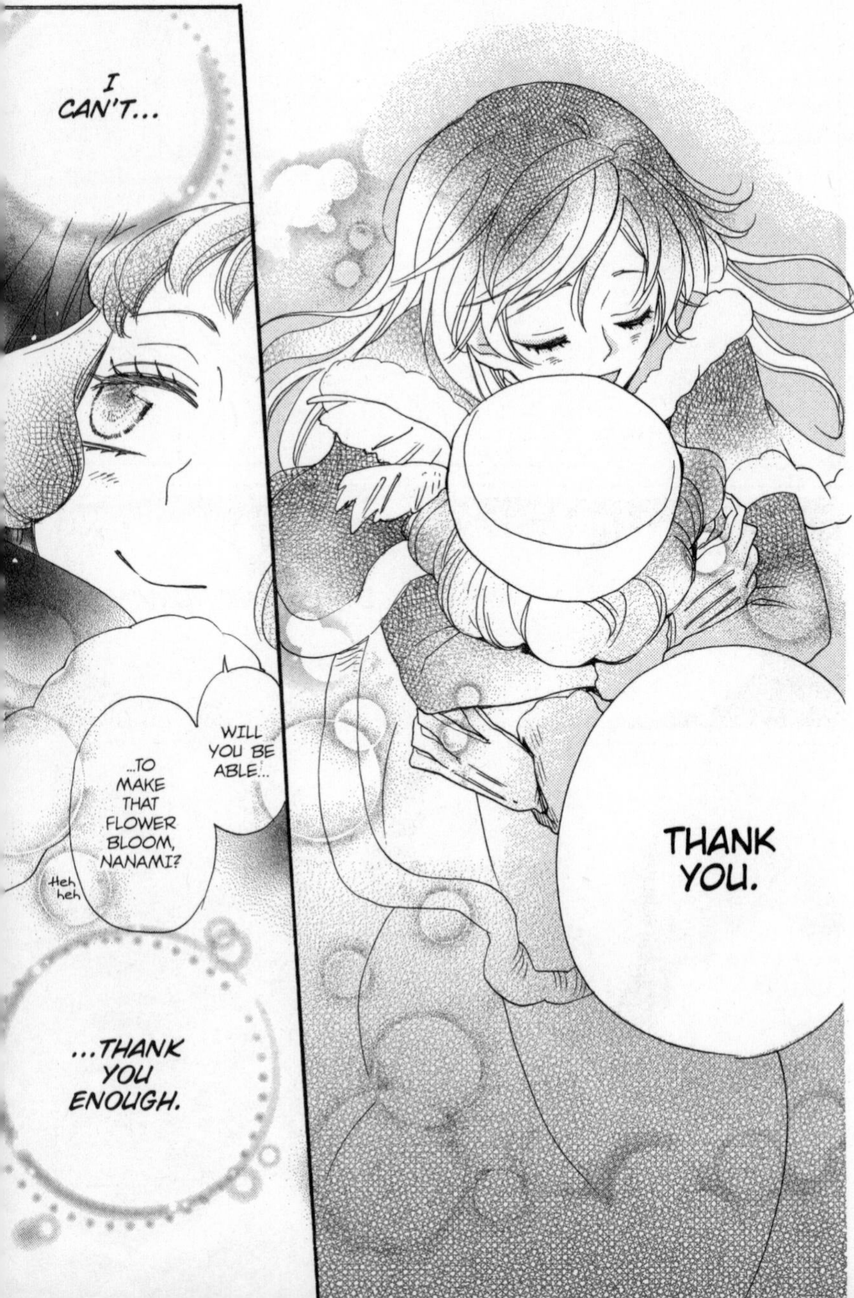

THANK YOU.
I CAN'T...
WILL YOU BE ABLE...
...TO MAKE THAT FLOWER BLOOM, NANAMI?
Heh heh
...THANK YOU ENOUGH.

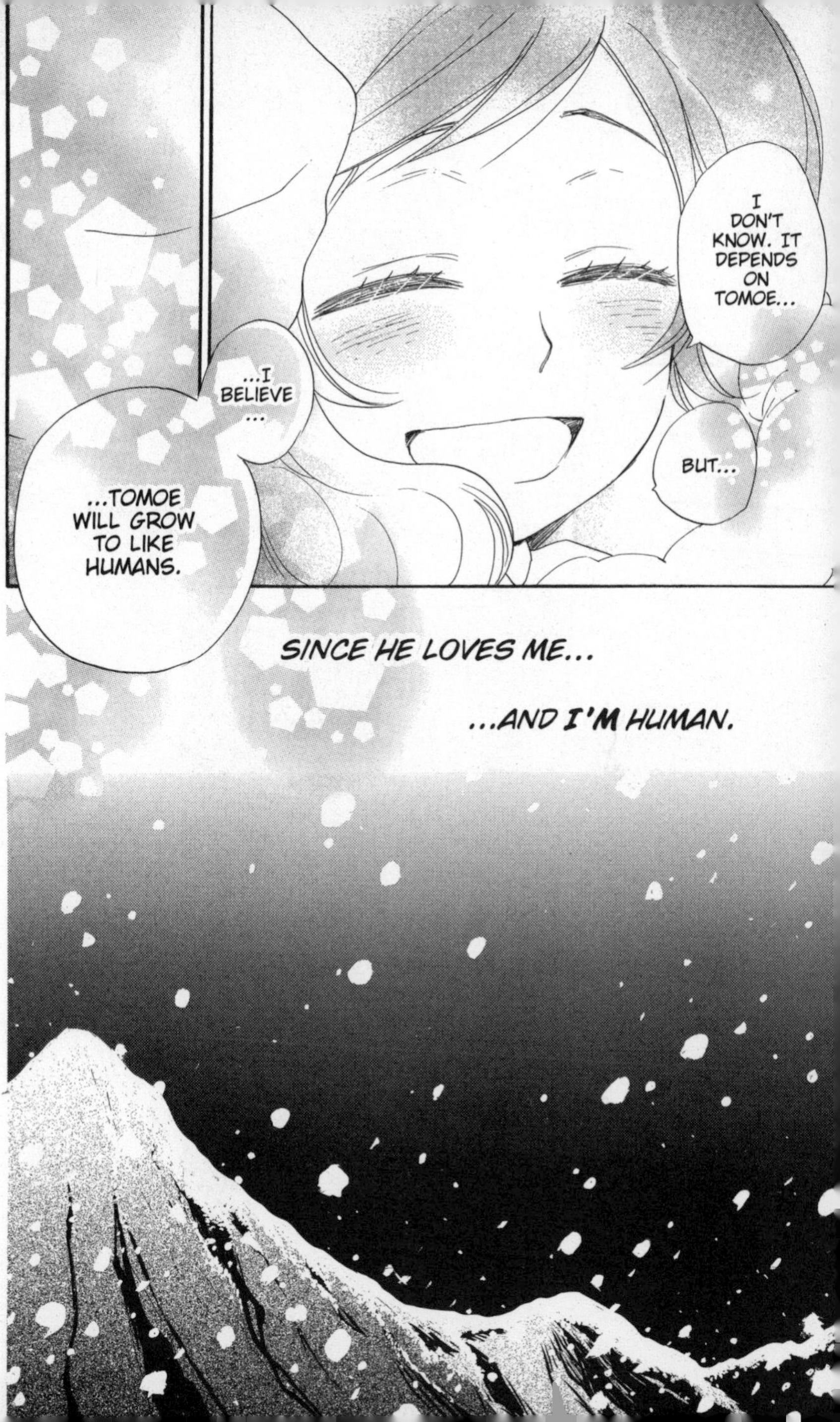
I DON'T KNOW. IT DEPENDS ON TOMOE...
BUT...
...I BELIEVE...
...TOMOE WILL GROW TO LIKE HUMANS.
SINCE HE LOVES ME...
...AND **I'M** HUMAN.

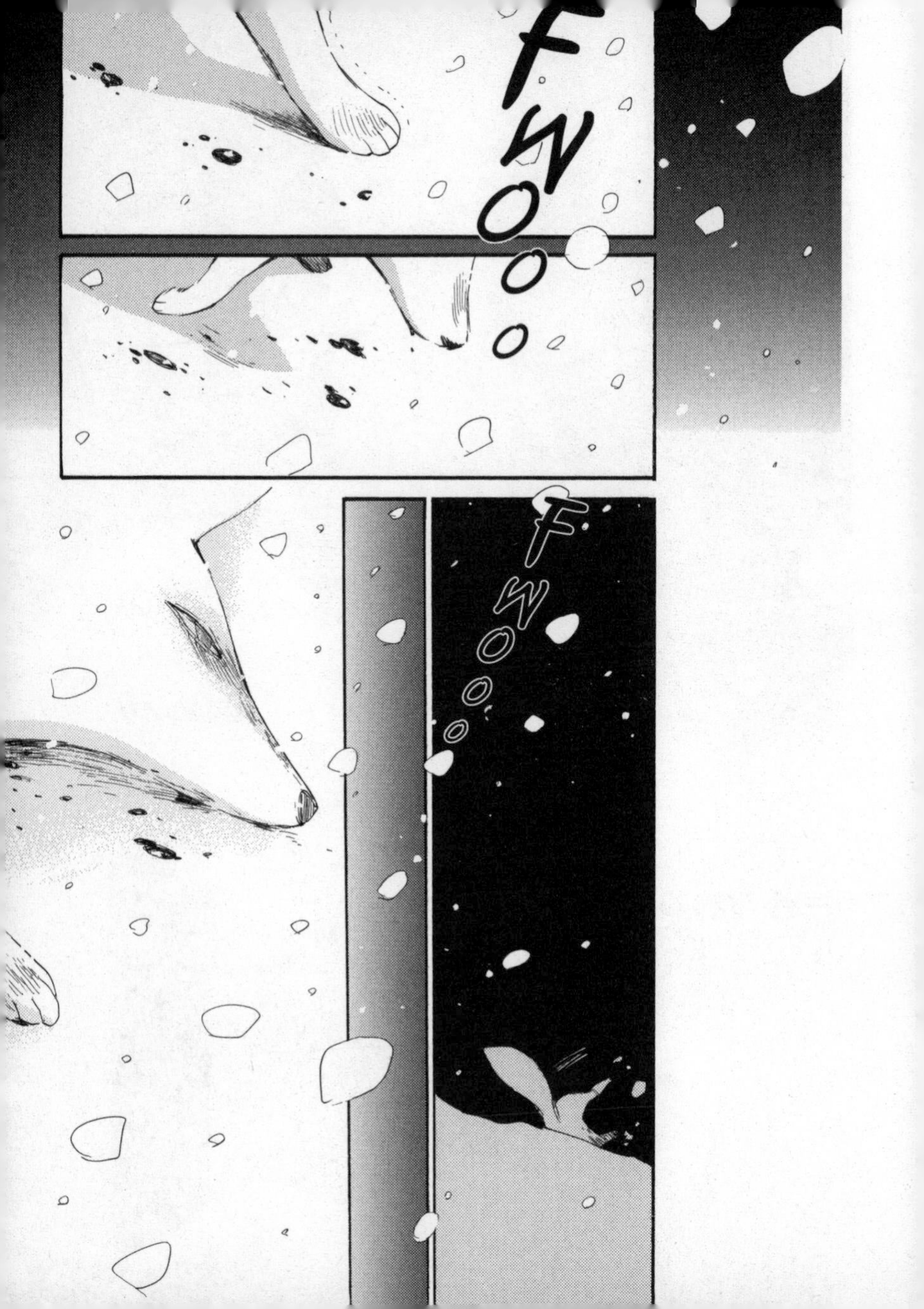
FWOOO
FWOOO

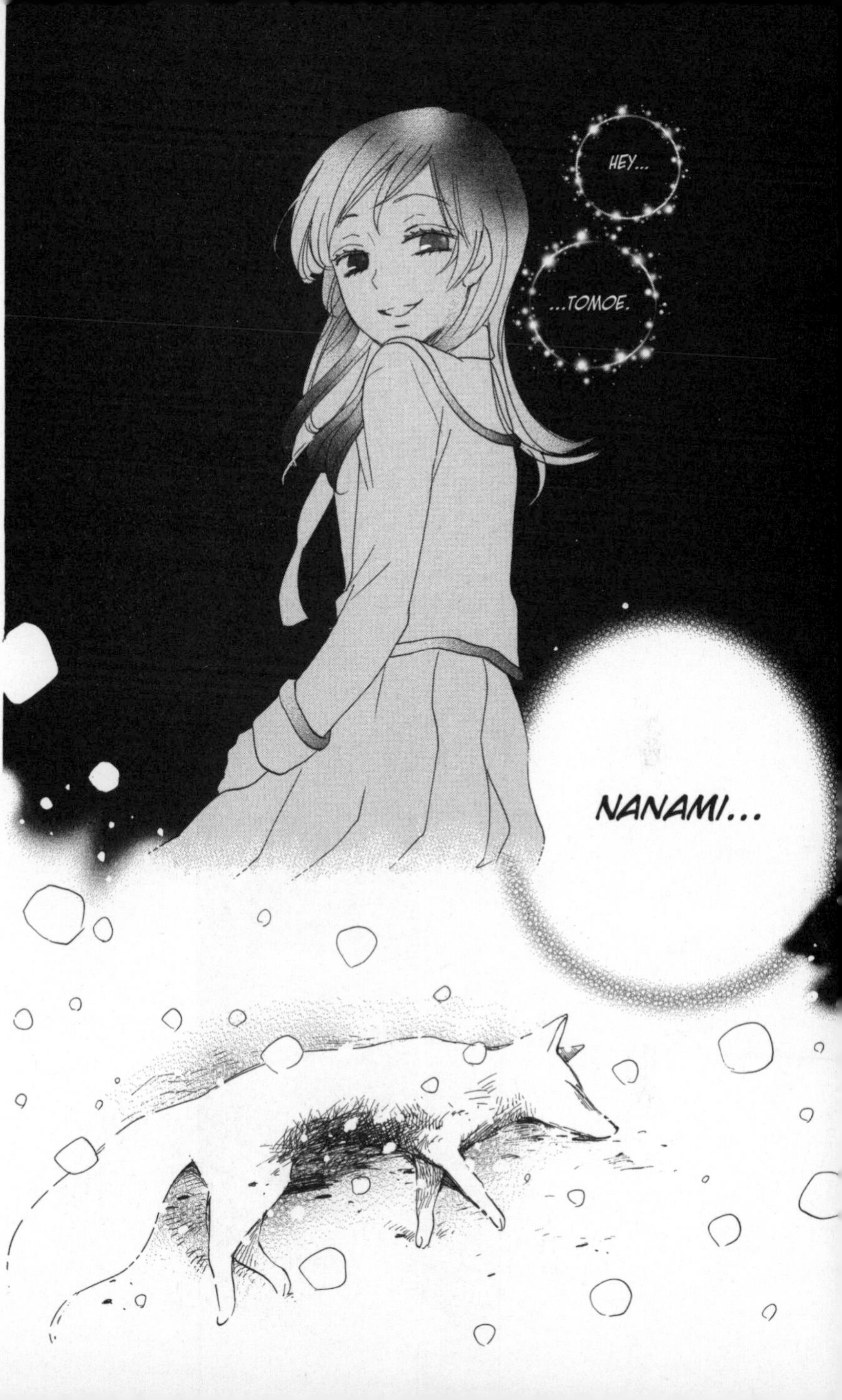
HEY...
...TOMOE.
NANAMI...

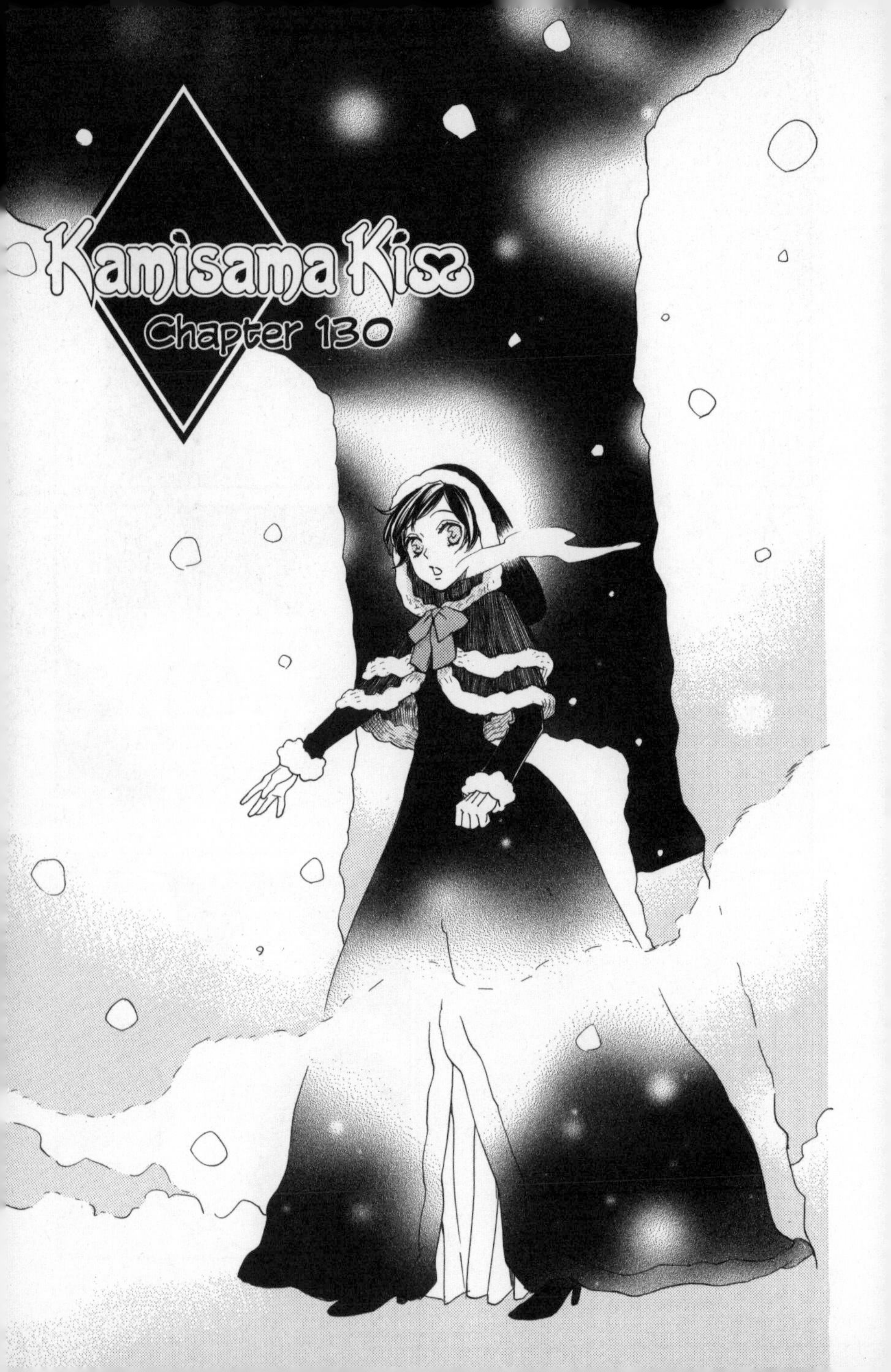
Kamisama Kiss
Chapter 130

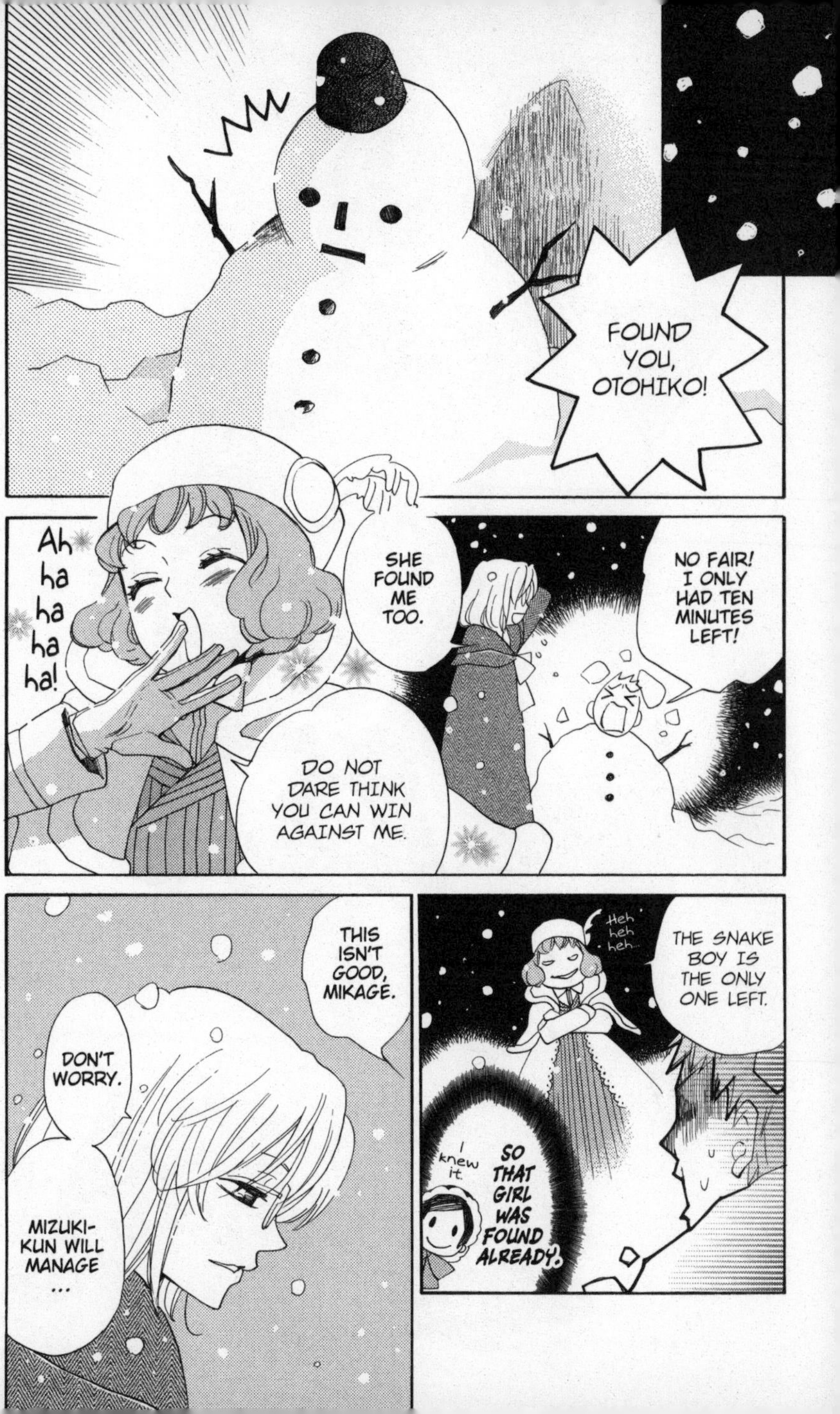
FOUND YOU, OTOHIKO!
NO FAIR! I ONLY HAD TEN MINUTES LEFT!
SHE FOUND ME TOO.
Ah ha ha ha ha!
DO NOT DARE THINK YOU CAN WIN AGAINST ME.
Heh heh heh...
THE SNAKE BOY IS THE ONLY ONE LEFT.
SO THAT GIRL WAS FOUND ALREADY.
I knew it.
THIS ISN'T GOOD, MIKAGE.
DON'T WORRY.
MIZUKI-KUN WILL MANAGE ...

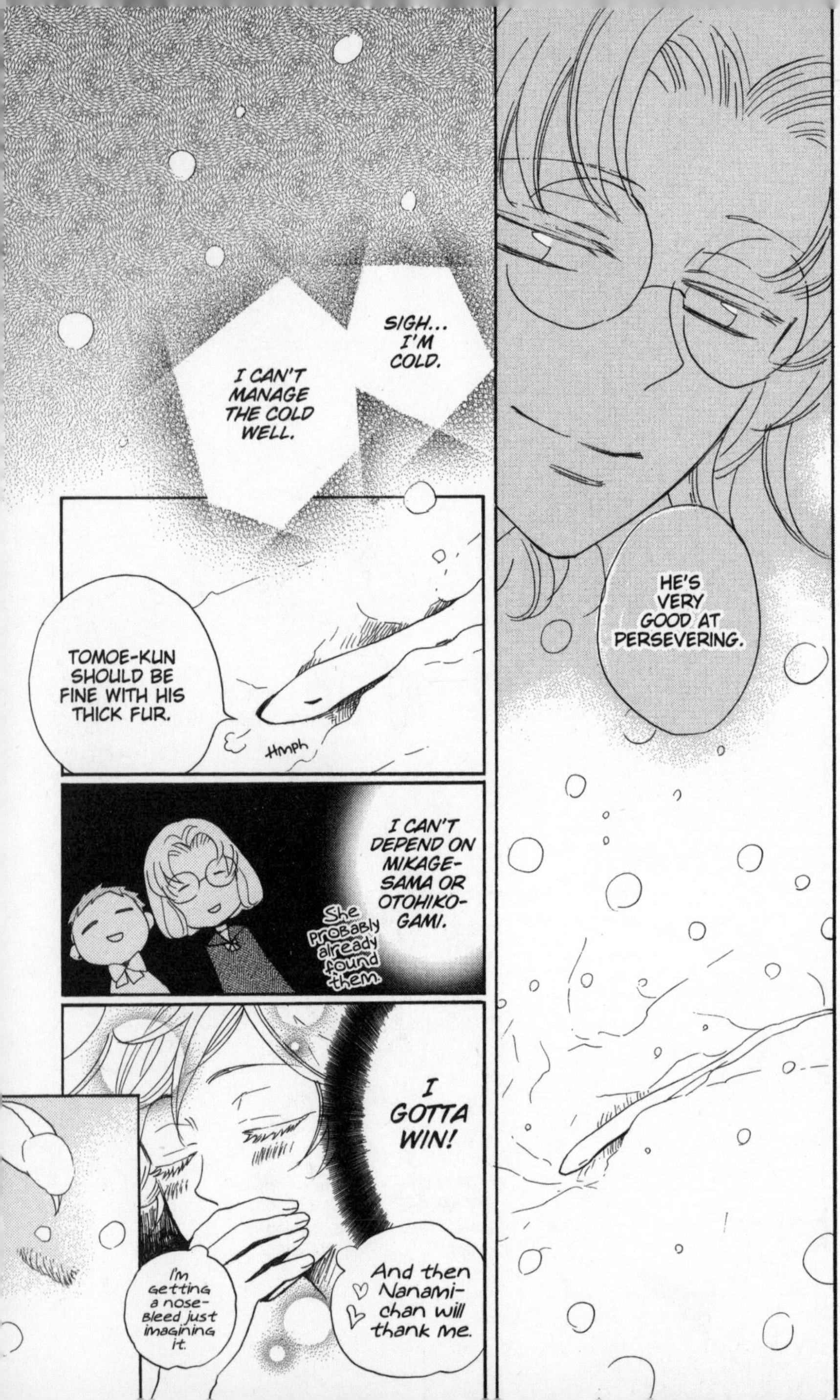
HE'S VERY GOOD AT PERSEVERING.
SIGH... I'M COLD.
I CAN'T MANAGE THE COLD WELL.
TOMOE-KUN SHOULD BE FINE WITH HIS THICK FUR.
Hmph
I CAN'T DEPEND ON MIKAGE-SAMA OR OTOHIKO-GAMI.
She probably already found them.
I GOTTA WIN!
And then Nanami-chan will thank me.
I'm getting a nose-bleed just imagining it.

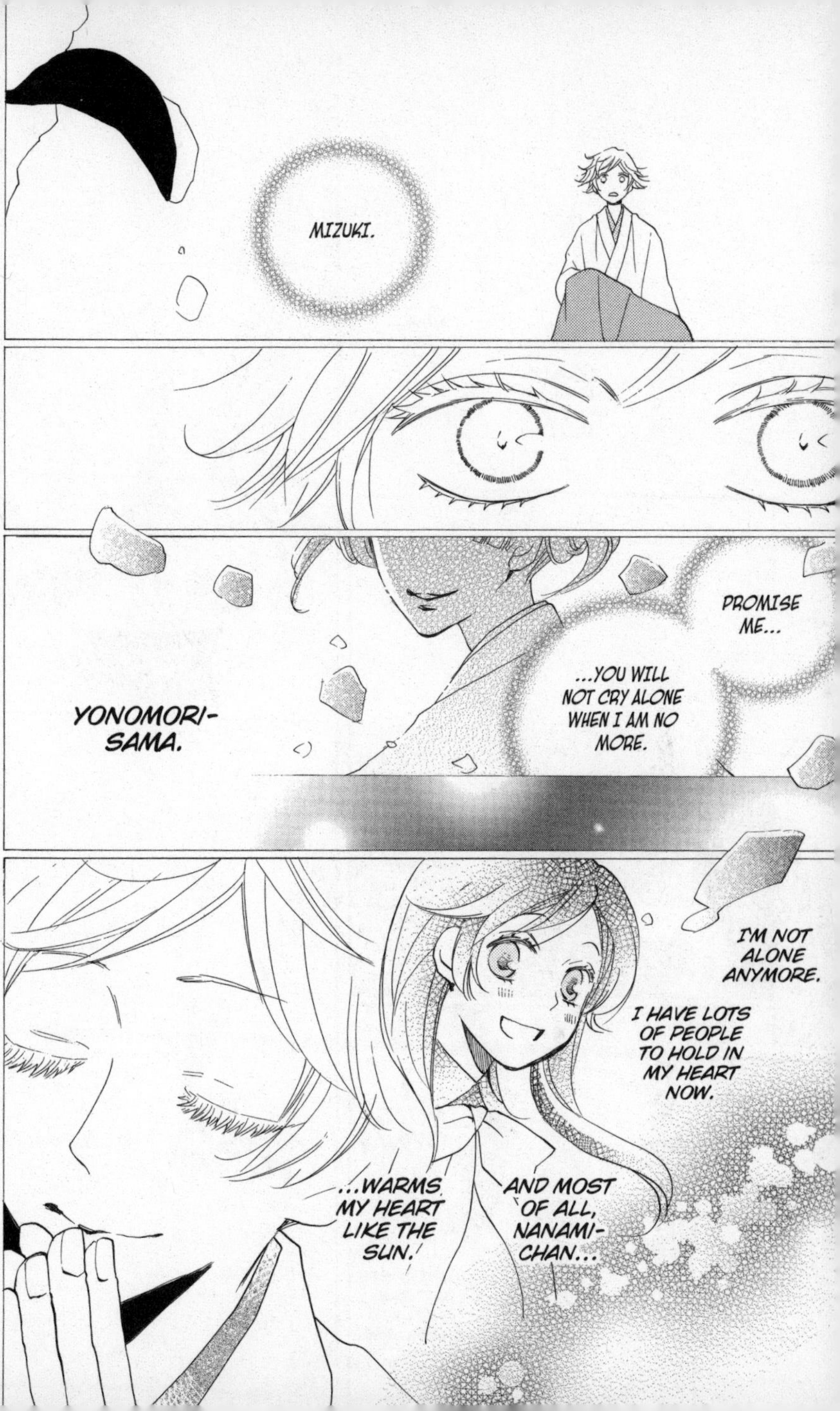
MIZUKI.
PROMISE ME...
...YOU WILL NOT CRY ALONE WHEN I AM NO MORE.
YONOMORI-SAMA.
I'M NOT ALONE ANYMORE.
I HAVE LOTS OF PEOPLE TO HOLD IN MY HEART NOW.
AND MOST OF ALL, NANAMI-CHAN...
...WARMS MY HEART LIKE THE SUN.

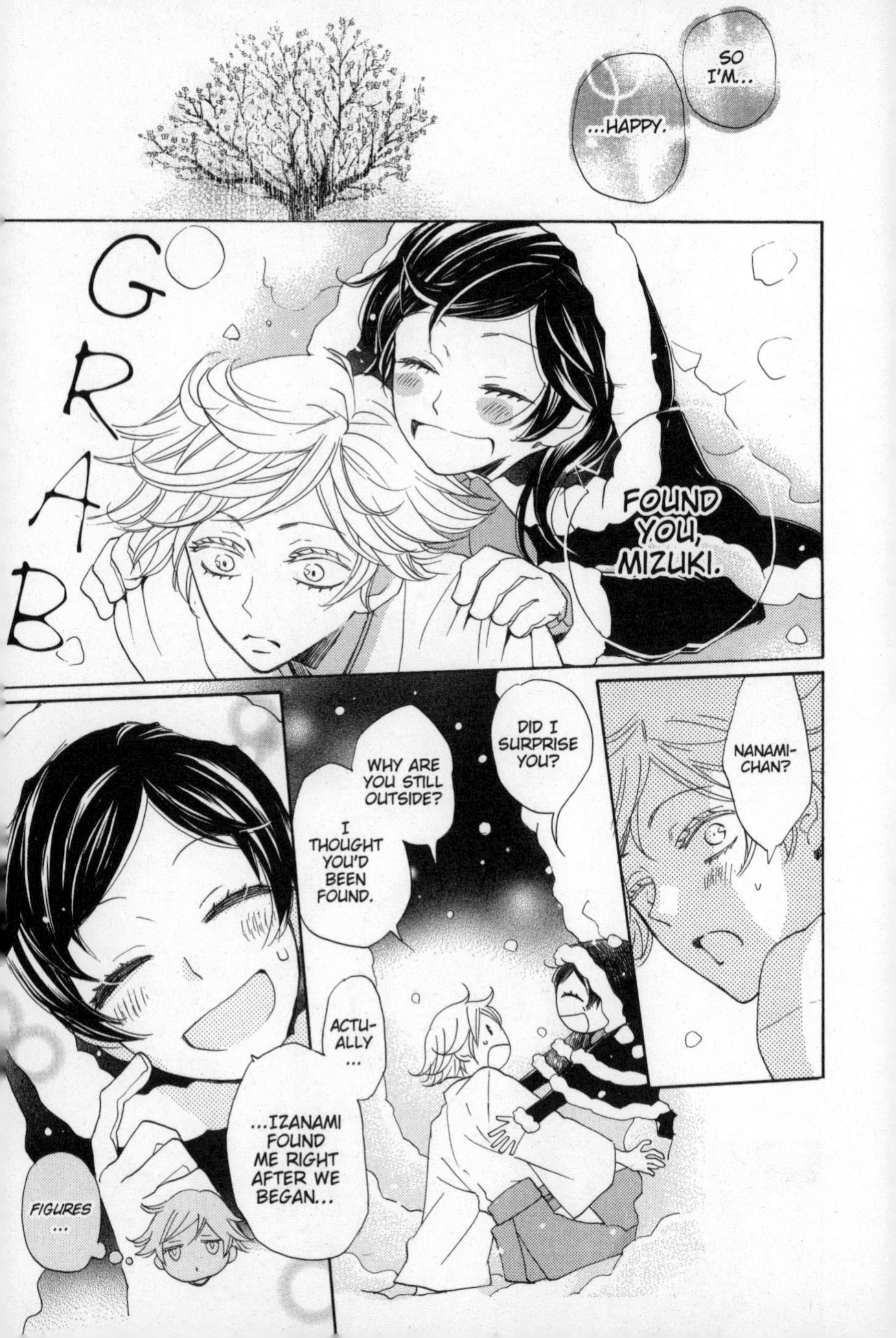
SO I'M...
...HAPPY.
GRAB
FOUND YOU, MIZUKI.
NANAMI-CHAN?
DID I SURPRISE YOU?
WHY ARE YOU STILL OUTSIDE?
I THOUGHT YOU'D BEEN FOUND.
ACTU-ALLY...
...IZANAMI FOUND ME RIGHT AFTER WE BEGAN...
FIGURES...

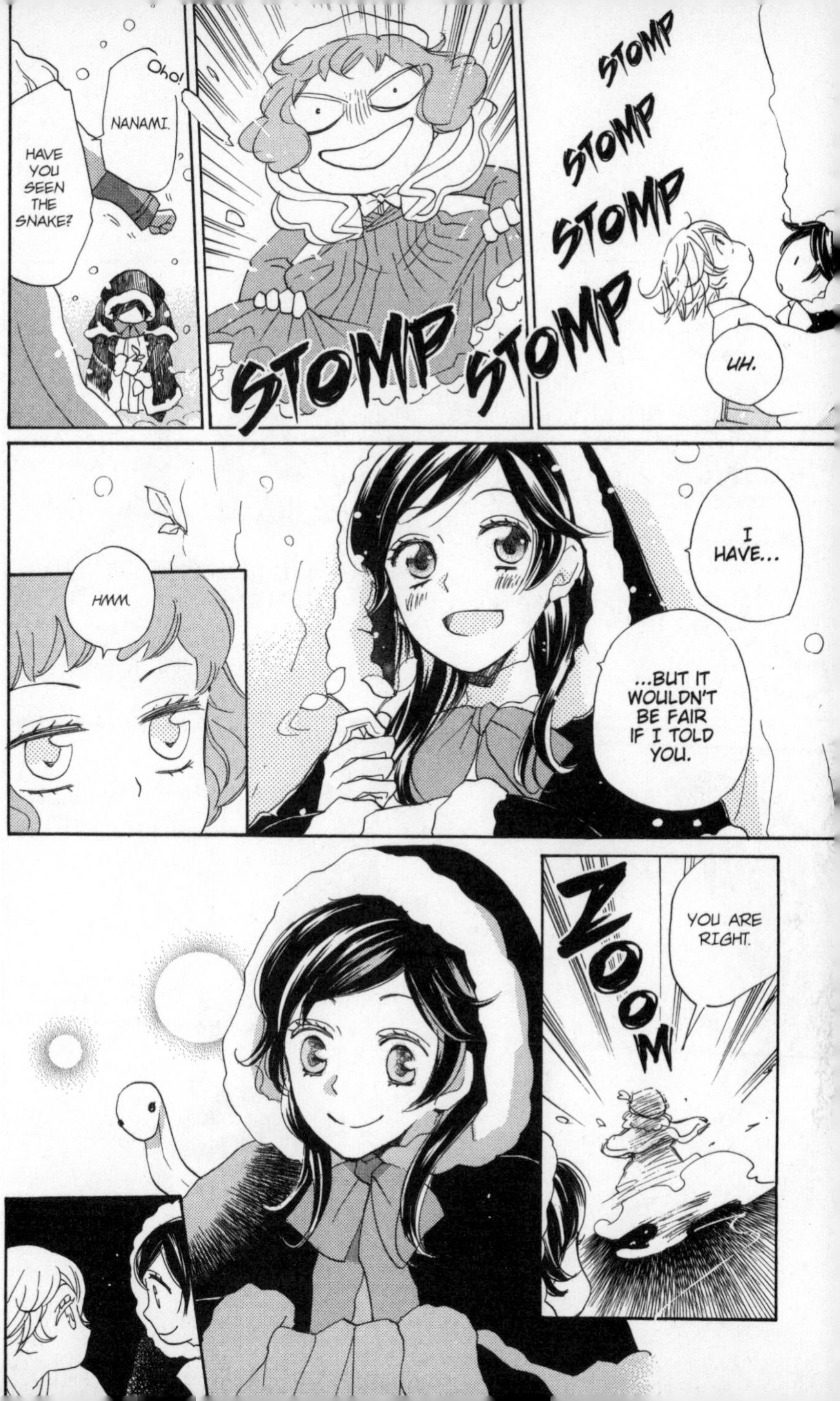
UH.
STOMP
STOMP
STOMP
STOMP
STOMP
STOMP
Oho!
NANAMI.
HAVE YOU SEEN THE SNAKE?
I HAVE...
...BUT IT WOULDN'T BE FAIR IF I TOLD YOU.
HMM.
YOU ARE RIGHT.
ZOOM

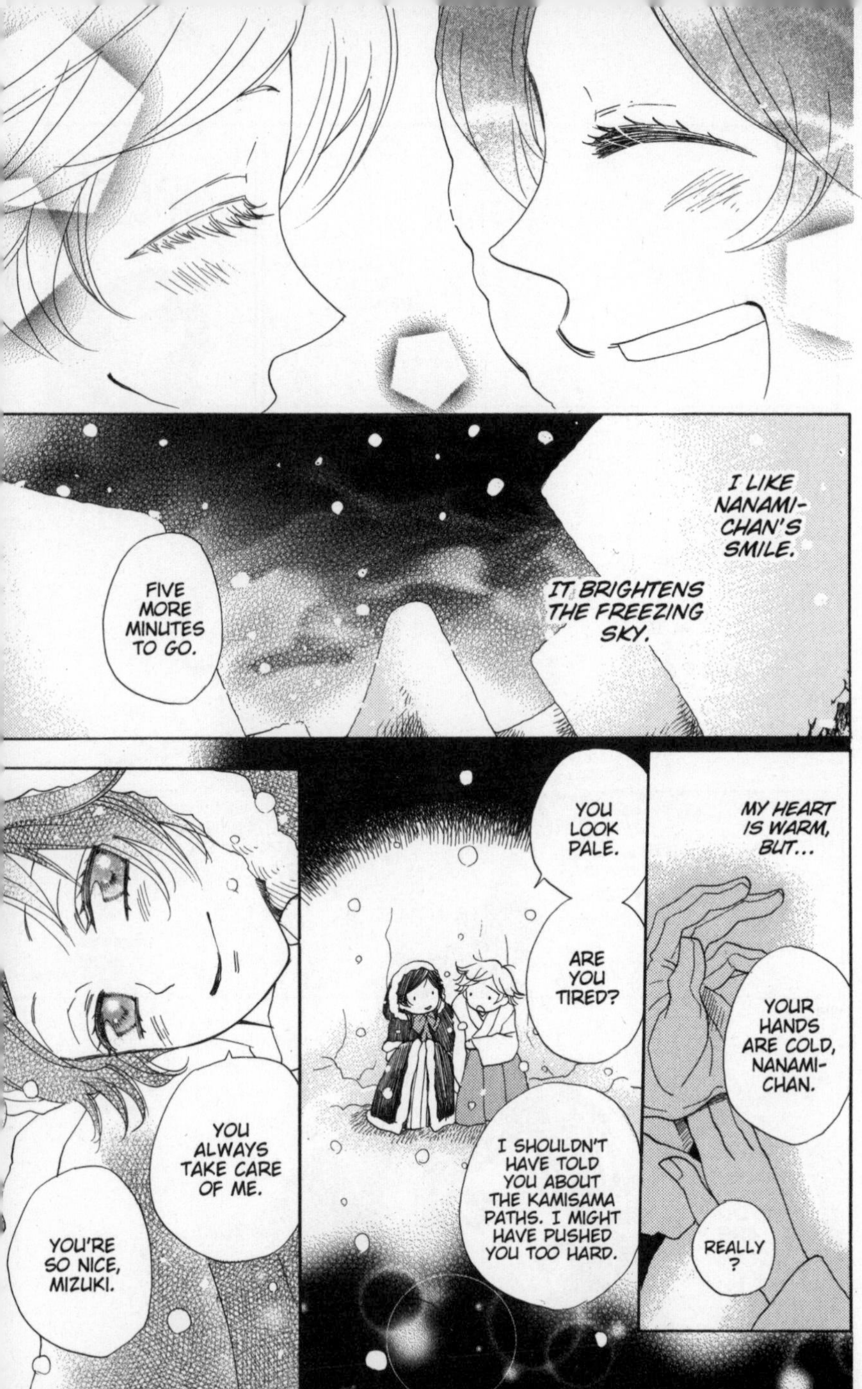
I LIKE NANAMI-CHAN'S SMILE.
IT BRIGHTENS THE FREEZING SKY.
FIVE MORE MINUTES TO GO.
MY HEART IS WARM, BUT...
YOUR HANDS ARE COLD, NANAMI-CHAN.
REALLY?
YOU LOOK PALE.
ARE YOU TIRED?
I SHOULDN'T HAVE TOLD YOU ABOUT THE KAMISAMA PATHS. I MIGHT HAVE PUSHED YOU TOO HARD.
YOU ALWAYS TAKE CARE OF ME.
YOU'RE SO NICE, MIZUKI.

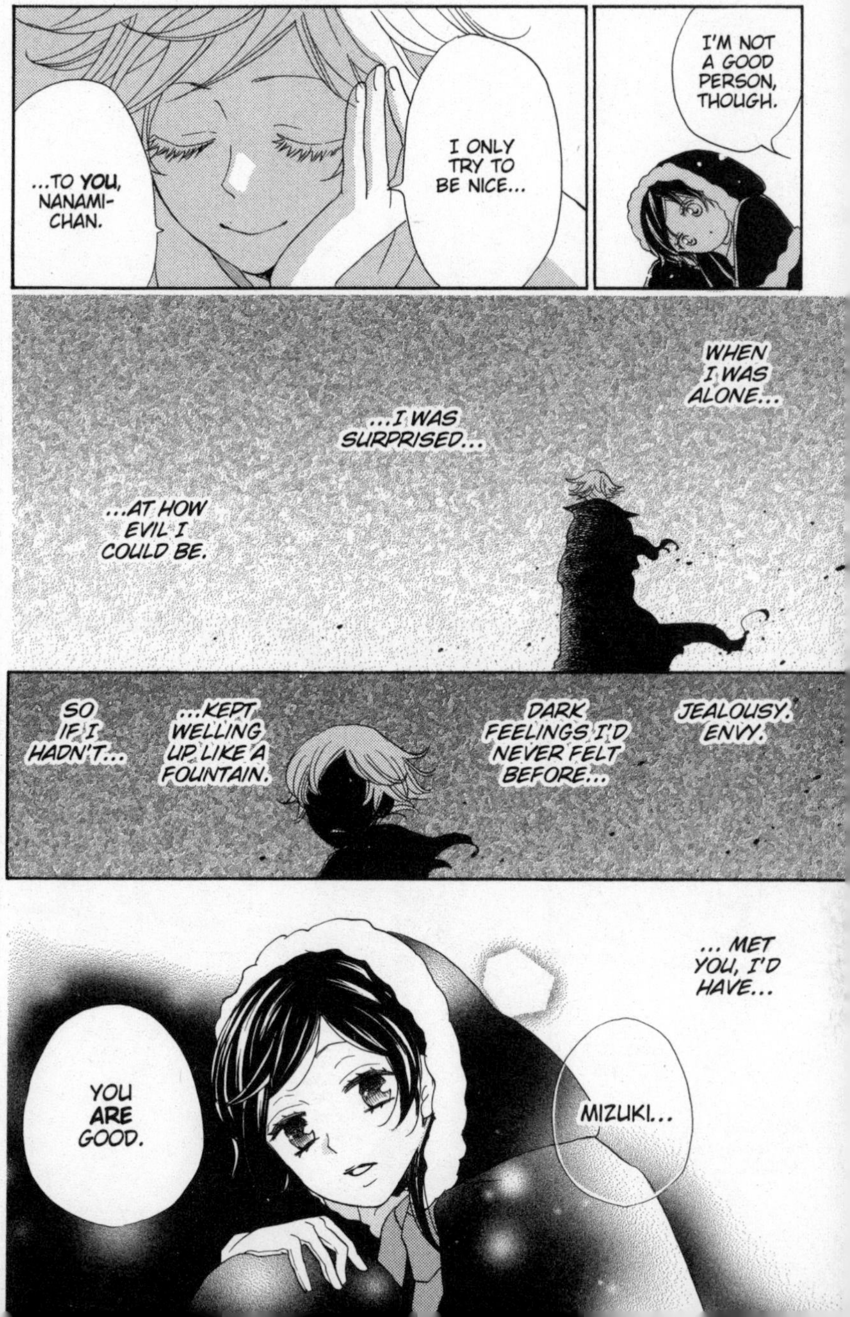
I'M NOT A GOOD PERSON, THOUGH.
I ONLY TRY TO BE NICE...
...TO YOU, NANAMI-CHAN.
WHEN I WAS ALONE...
...I WAS SURPRISED...
...AT HOW EVIL I COULD BE.
JEALOUSY. ENVY.
DARK FEELINGS I'D NEVER FELT BEFORE...
...KEPT WELLING UP LIKE A FOUNTAIN.
SO IF I HADN'T...
... MET YOU, I'D HAVE...
MIZUKI...
YOU ARE GOOD.

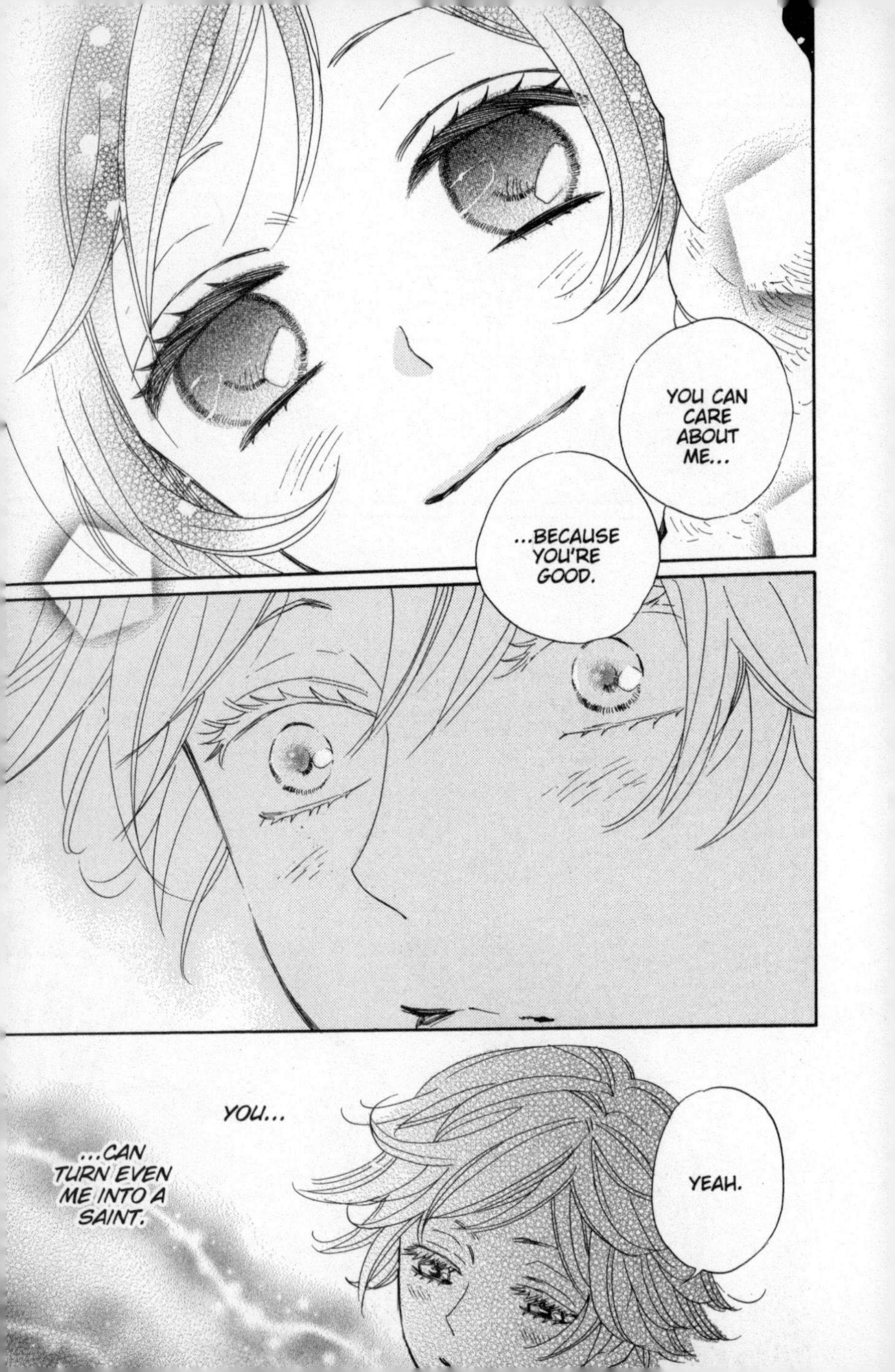
YOU CAN CARE ABOUT ME...
...BECAUSE YOU'RE GOOD.
YEAH.
YOU...
...CAN TURN EVEN ME INTO A SAINT.

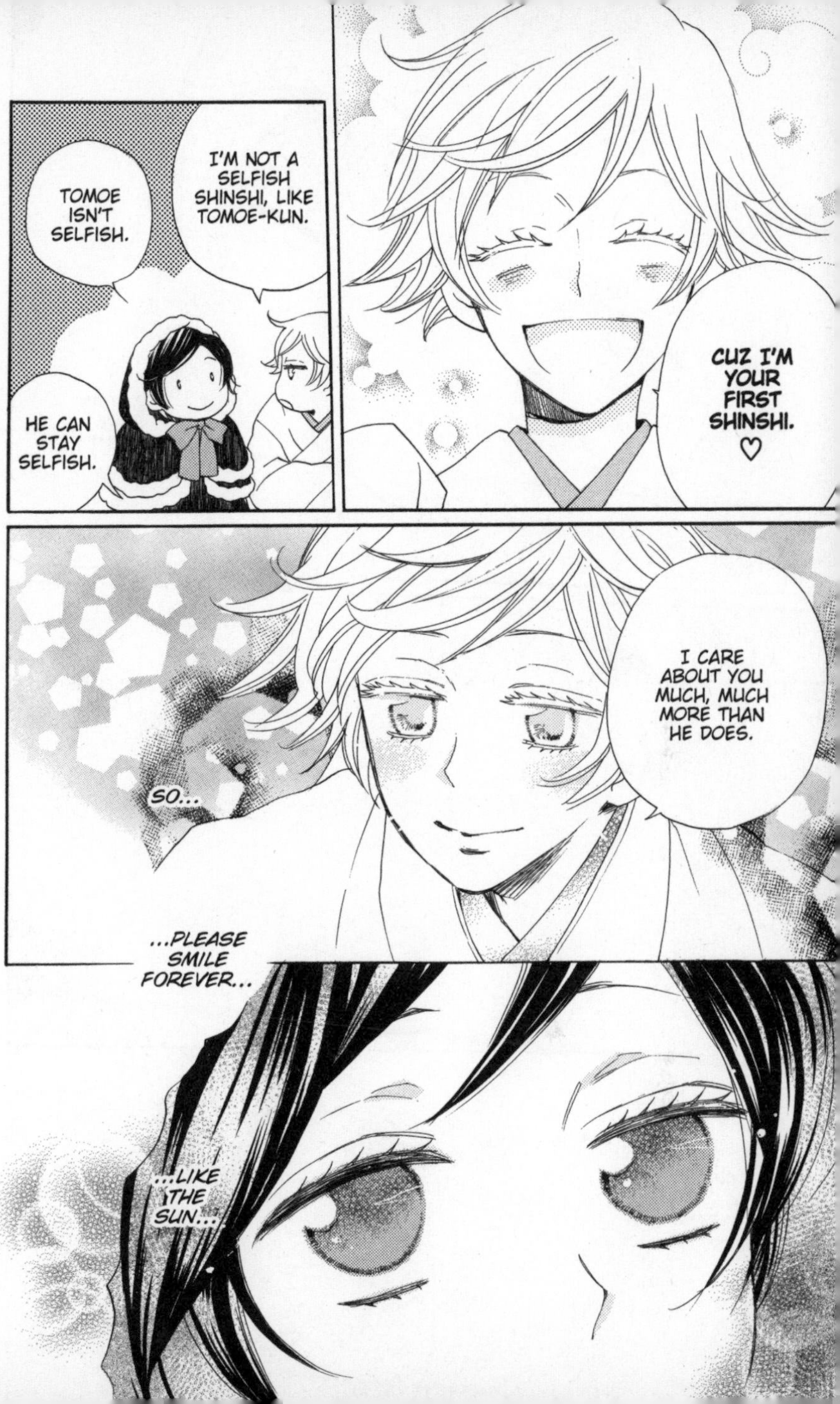
CUZ I'M YOUR FIRST SHINSHI. ♡
I'M NOT A SELFISH SHINSHI, LIKE TOMOE-KUN.
TOMOE ISN'T SELFISH.
HE CAN STAY SELFISH.
I CARE ABOUT YOU MUCH, MUCH MORE THAN HE DOES.
SO...
...PLEASE SMILE FOREVER...
...LIKE THE SUN...

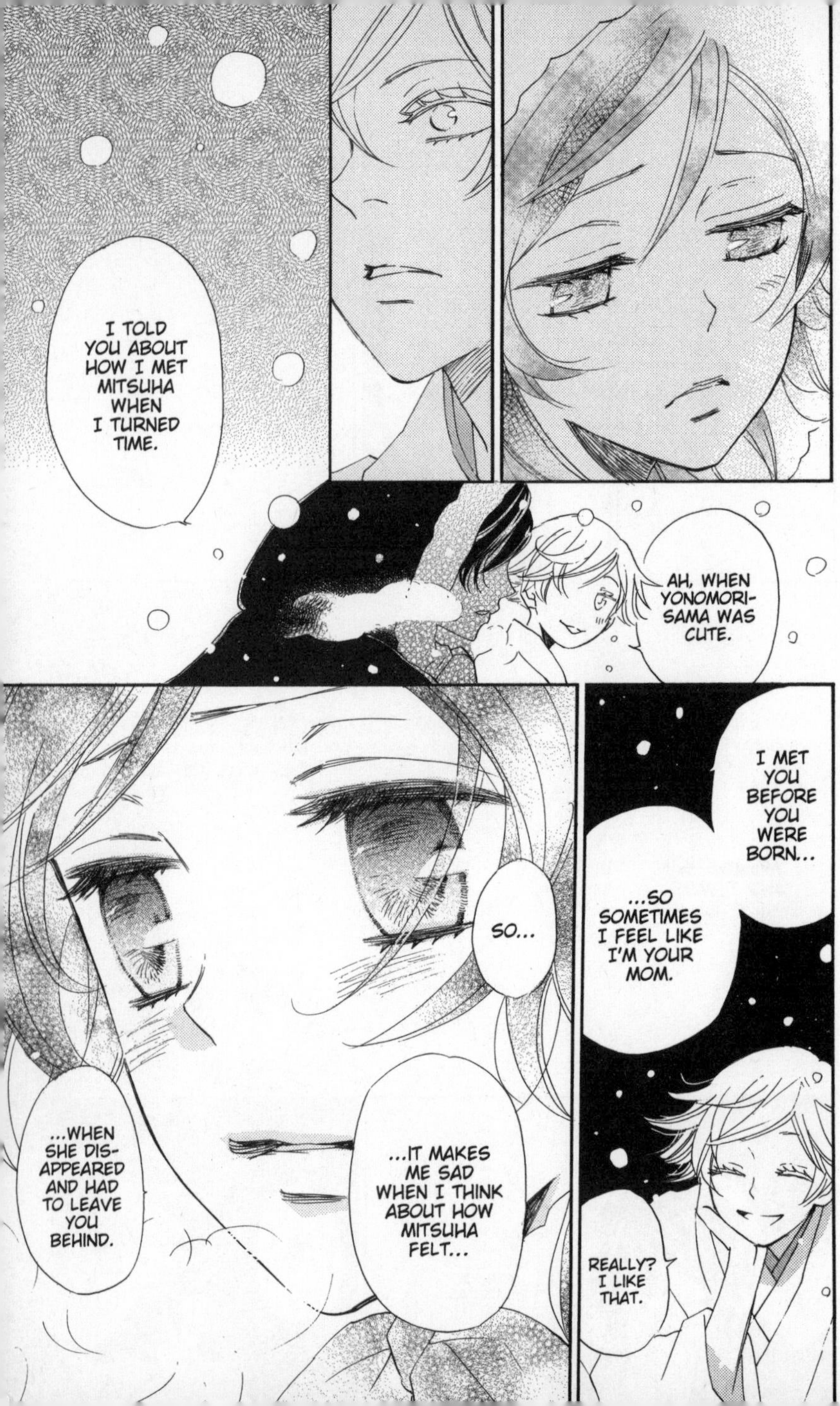
I TOLD YOU ABOUT HOW I MET MITSUHA WHEN I TURNED TIME.
AH, WHEN YONOMORI-SAMA WAS CUTE.
I MET YOU BEFORE YOU WERE BORN...
...SO SOMETIMES I FEEL LIKE I'M YOUR MOM.
REALLY? I LIKE THAT.
SO...
...IT MAKES ME SAD WHEN I THINK ABOUT HOW MITSUHA FELT...
...WHEN SHE DIS-APPEARED AND HAD TO LEAVE YOU BEHIND.

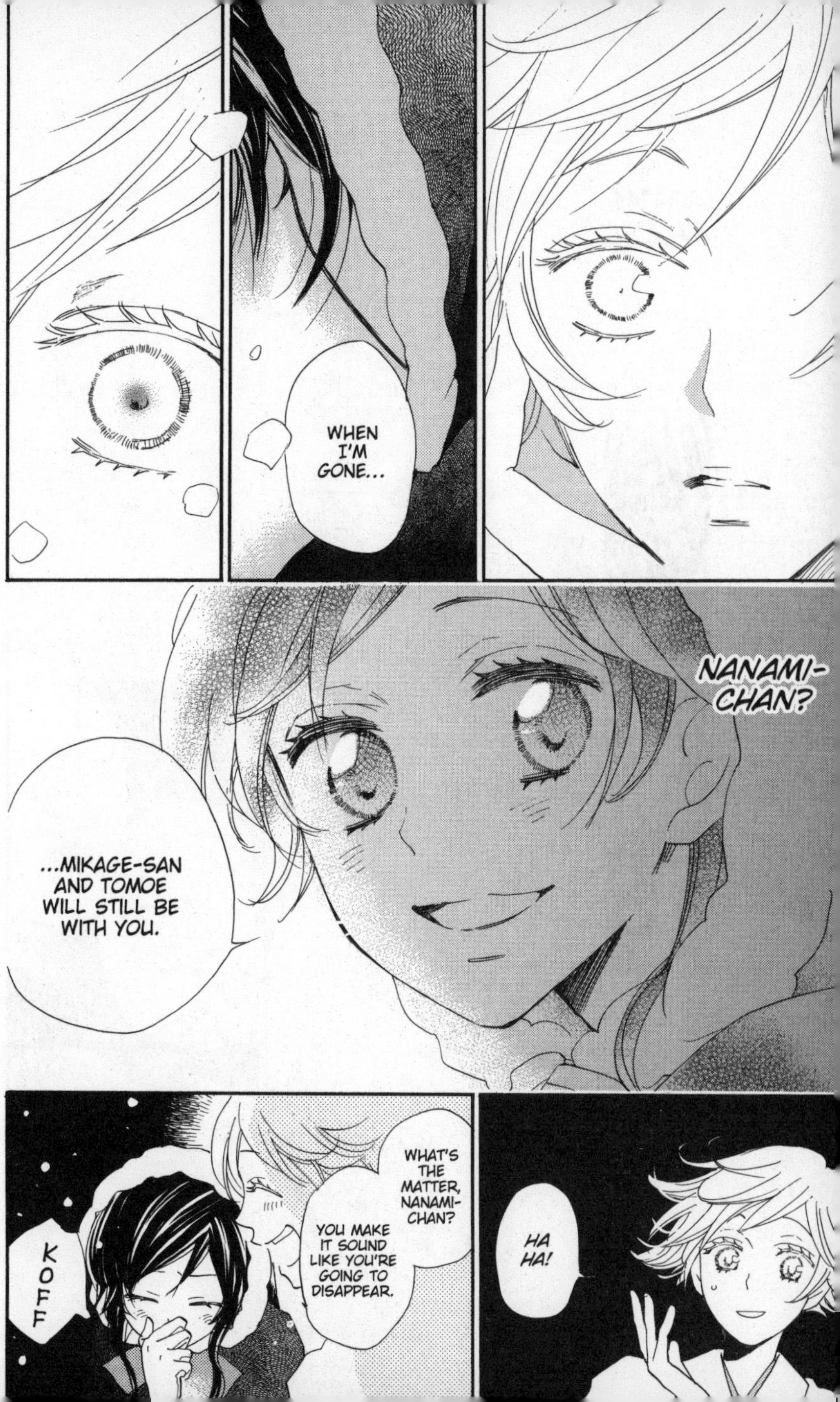
WHEN I'M GONE...
NANAMI-CHAN?
...MIKAGE-SAN AND TOMOE WILL STILL BE WITH YOU.
HA HA!
WHAT'S THE MATTER, NANAMI-CHAN?
YOU MAKE IT SOUND LIKE YOU'RE GOING TO DISAPPEAR.
KOFF

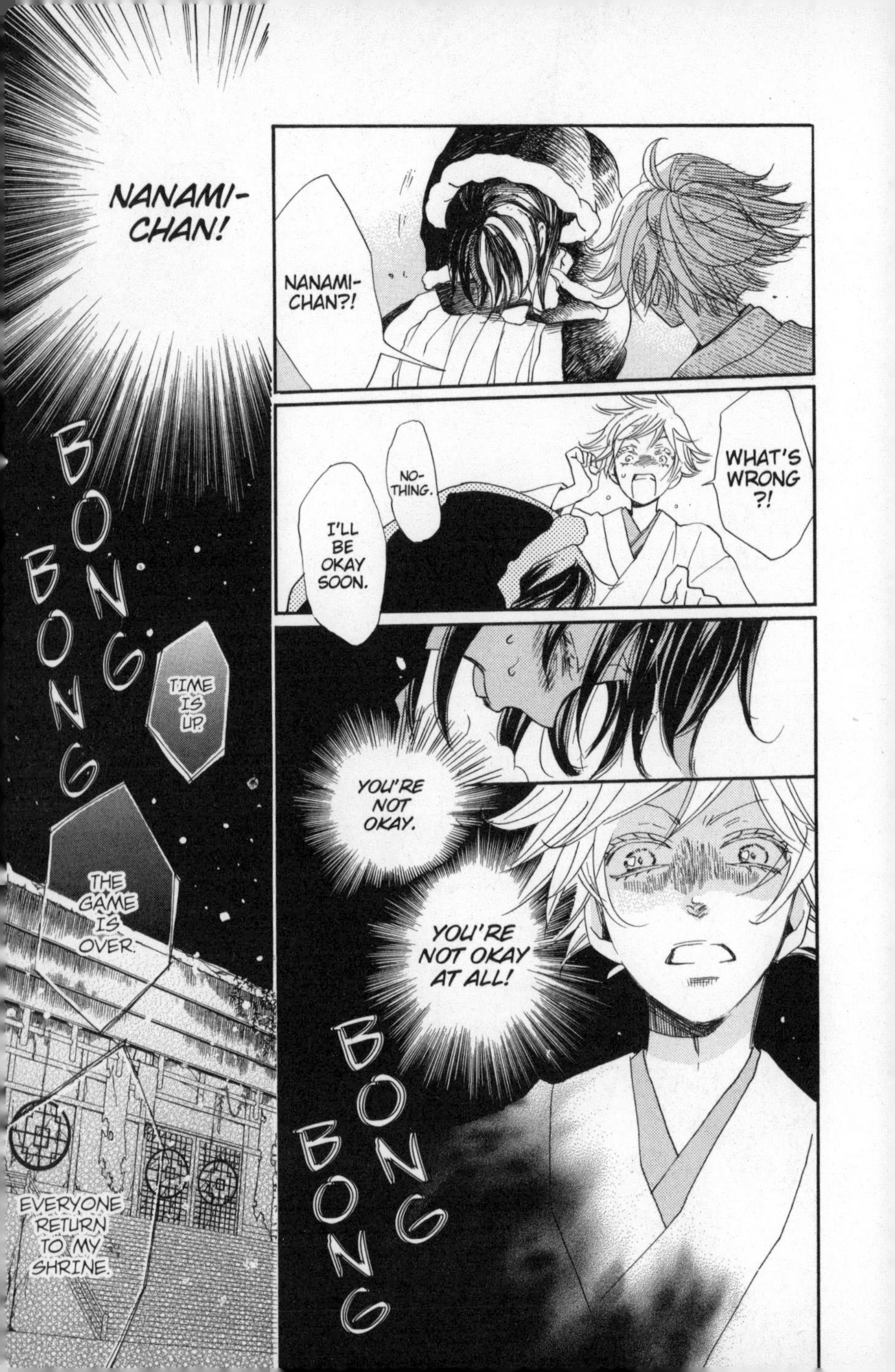
NANAMI-CHAN?!
WHAT'S WRONG?!
NO-THING.
I'LL BE OKAY SOON.
YOU'RE NOT OKAY.
YOU'RE NOT OKAY AT ALL!
BONG BONG
NANAMI-CHAN!
BONG BONG
TIME IS UP.
THE GAME IS OVER.
EVERYONE RETURN TO MY SHRINE.

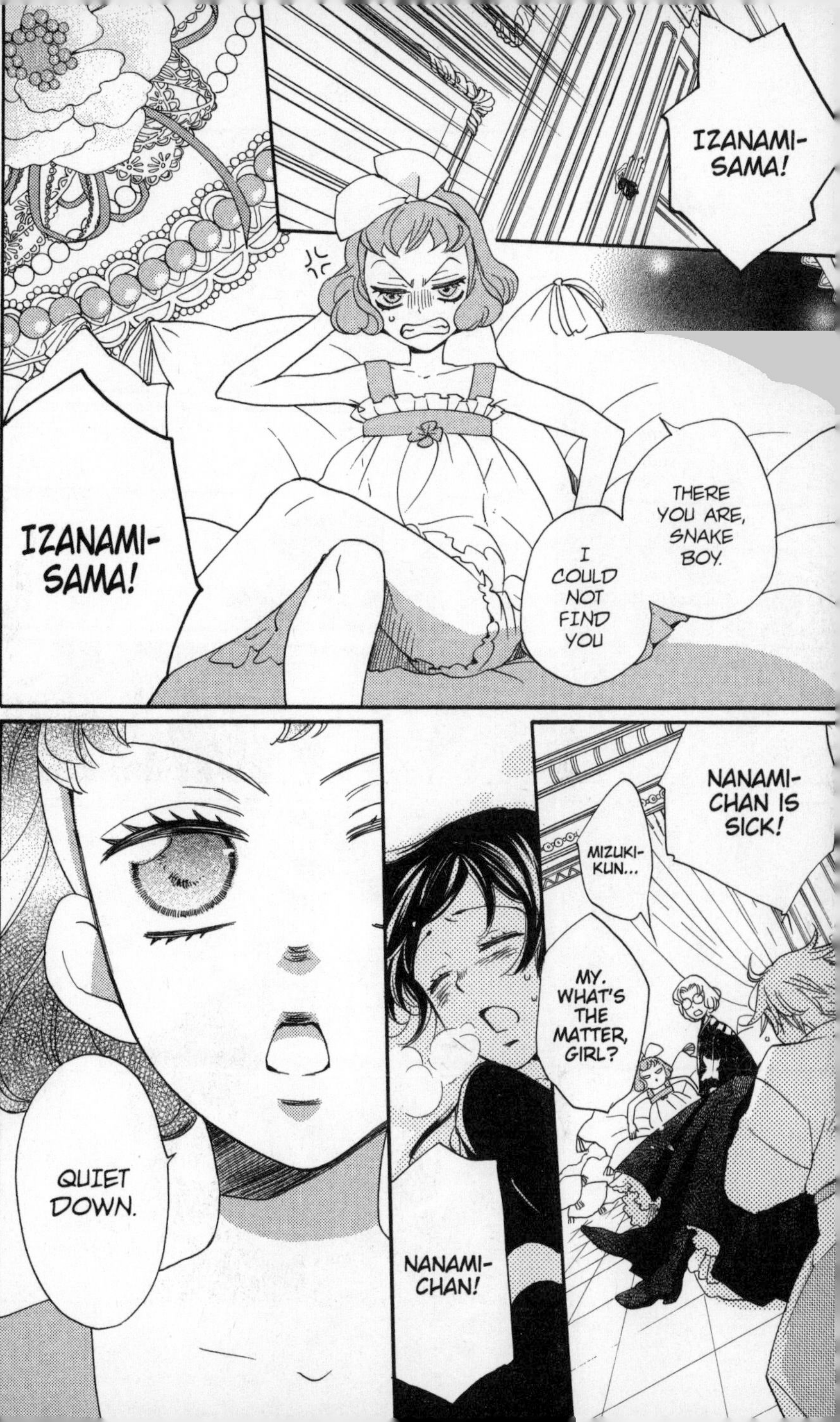
IZANAMI-SAMA!
THERE YOU ARE, SNAKE BOY.
I COULD NOT FIND YOU
IZANAMI-SAMA!
NANAMI-CHAN IS SICK!
MIZUKI-KUN...
MY. WHAT'S THE MATTER, GIRL?
NANAMI-CHAN!
QUIET DOWN.

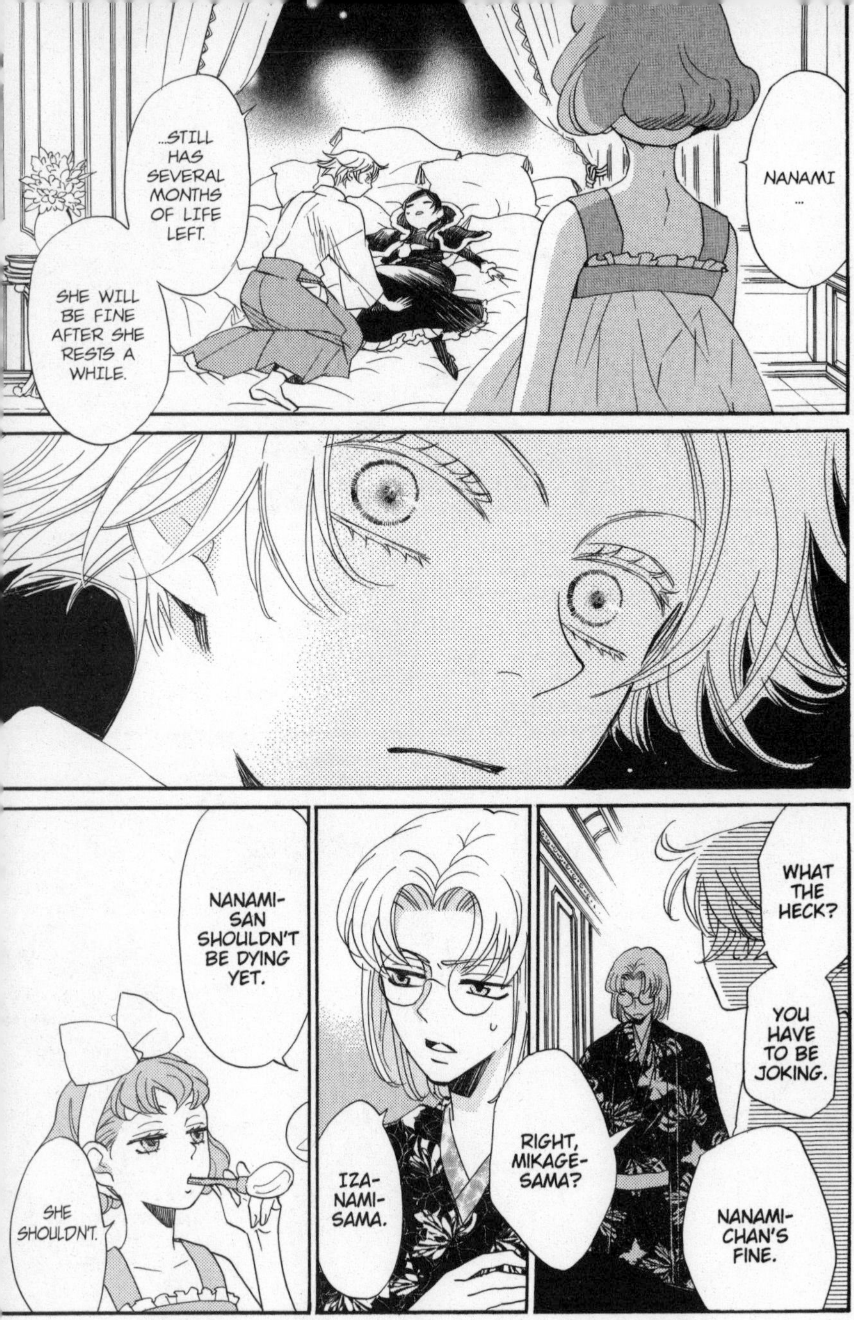
NANAMI ...
...STILL HAS SEVERAL MONTHS OF LIFE LEFT.
SHE WILL BE FINE AFTER SHE RESTS A WHILE.
WHAT THE HECK?
YOU HAVE TO BE JOKING.
NANAMI-CHAN'S FINE.
RIGHT, MIKAGE-SAMA?
IZA-NAMI-SAMA.
NANAMI-SAN SHOULDN'T BE DYING YET.
SHE SHOULDN'T.

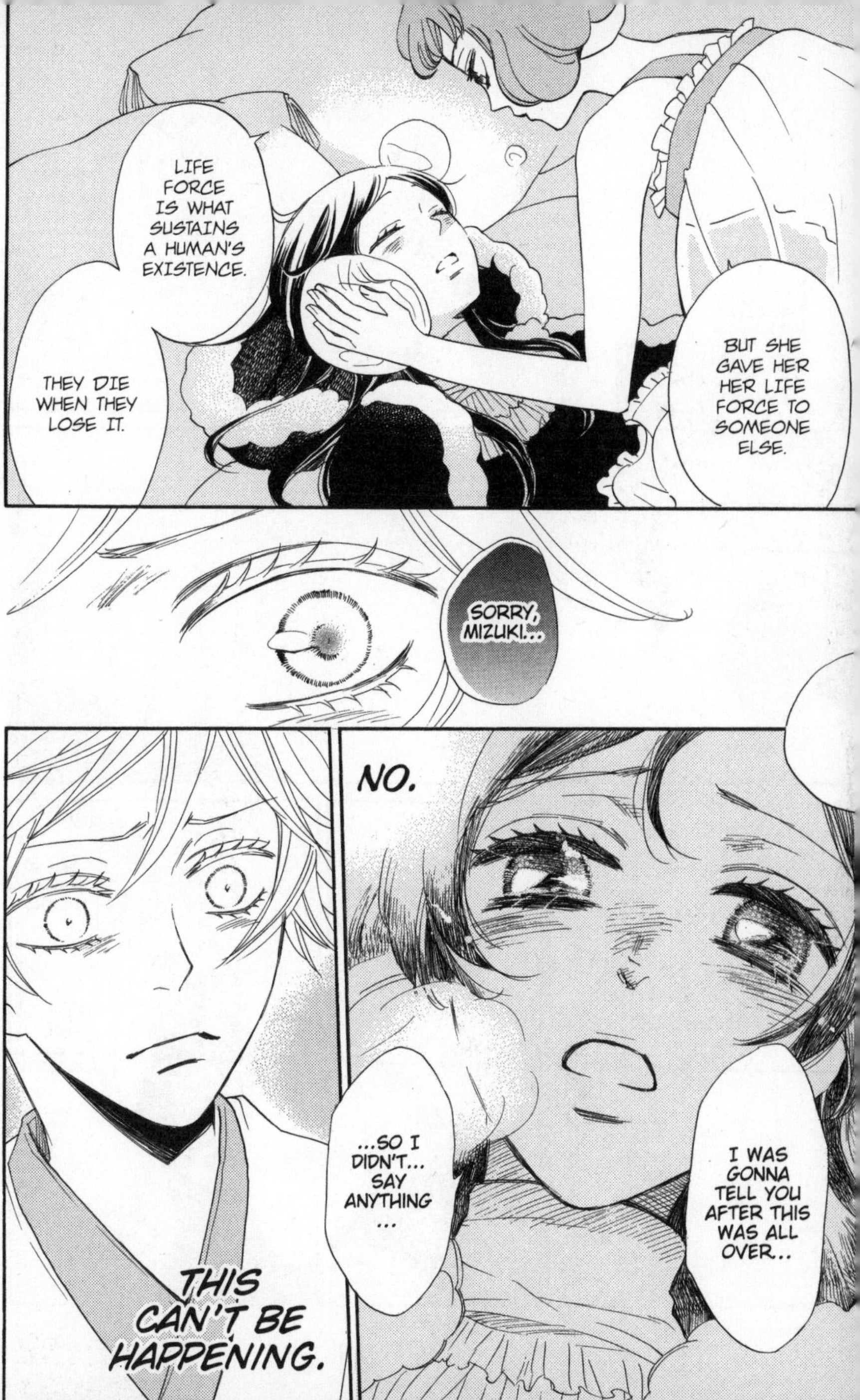
LIFE FORCE IS WHAT SUSTAINS A HUMAN'S EXISTENCE.
THEY DIE WHEN THEY LOSE IT.
BUT SHE GAVE HER HER LIFE FORCE TO SOMEONE ELSE.
SORRY, MIZUKI...
NO.
I WAS GONNA TELL YOU AFTER THIS WAS ALL OVER...
...SO I DIDN'T... SAY ANYTHING...
THIS CAN'T BE HAPPENING.

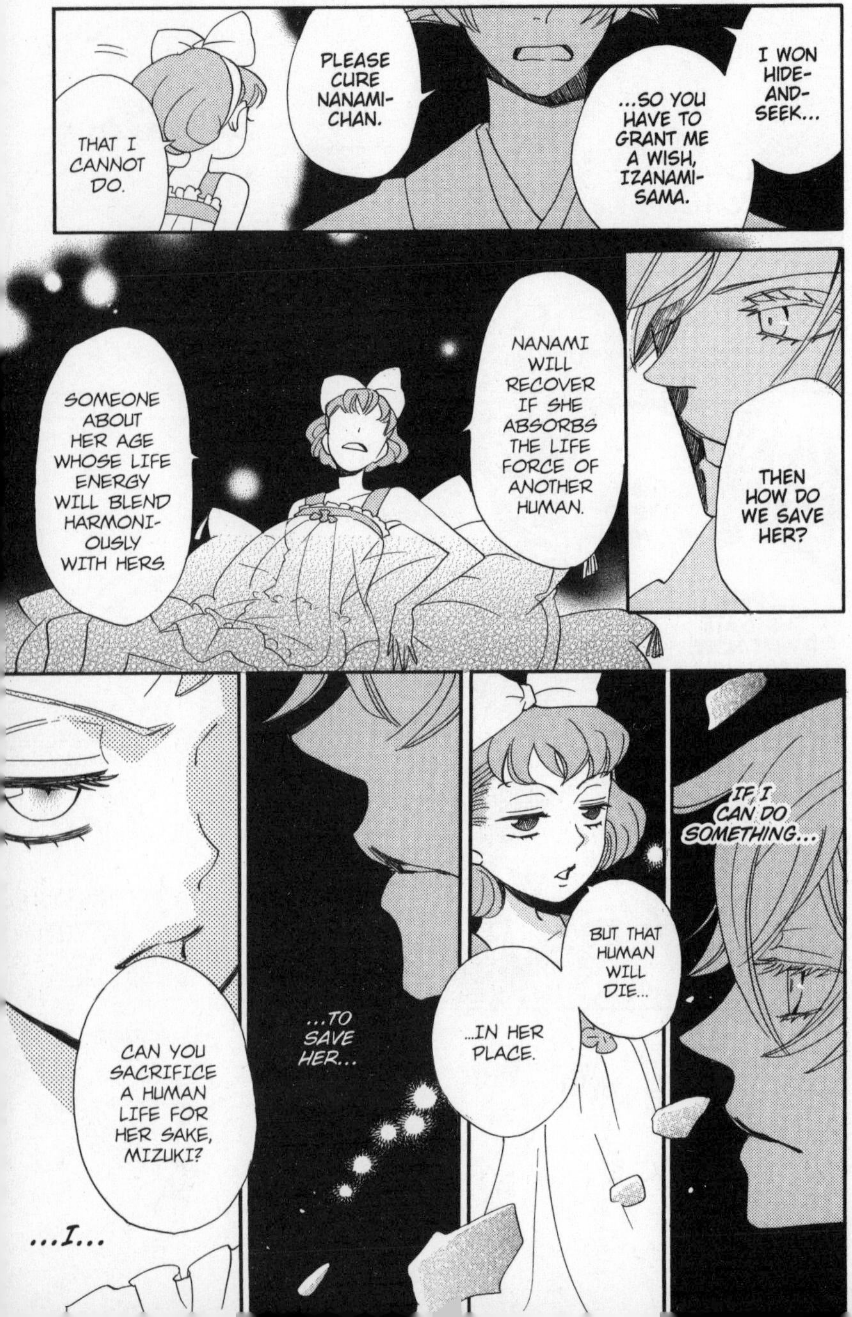
I WON HIDE-AND-SEEK...
...SO YOU HAVE TO GRANT ME A WISH, IZANAMI-SAMA.
PLEASE CURE NANAMI-CHAN.
THAT I CANNOT DO.
THEN HOW DO WE SAVE HER?
NANAMI WILL RECOVER IF SHE ABSORBS THE LIFE FORCE OF ANOTHER HUMAN.
SOMEONE ABOUT HER AGE WHOSE LIFE ENERGY WILL BLEND HARMONIOUSLY WITH HERS.
IF I CAN DO SOMETHING...
BUT THAT HUMAN WILL DIE...
...IN HER PLACE.
...TO SAVE HER...
CAN YOU SACRIFICE A HUMAN LIFE FOR HER SAKE, MIZUKI?
...I...

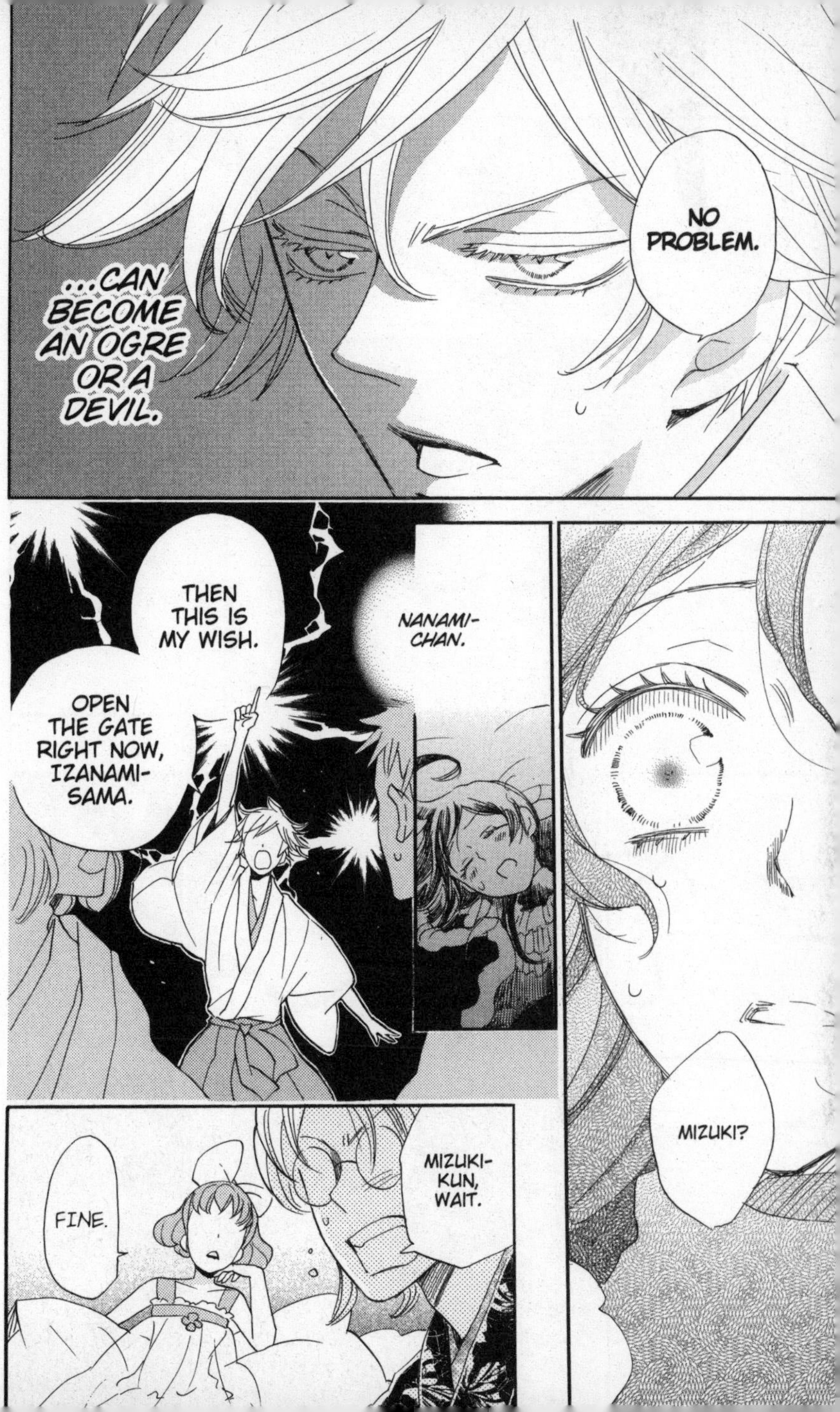
NO PROBLEM.
...CAN BECOME AN OGRE OR A DEVIL.
MIZUKI?
NANAMI-CHAN.
THEN THIS IS MY WISH.
OPEN THE GATE RIGHT NOW, IZANAMI-SAMA.
MIZUKI-KUN, WAIT.
FINE.

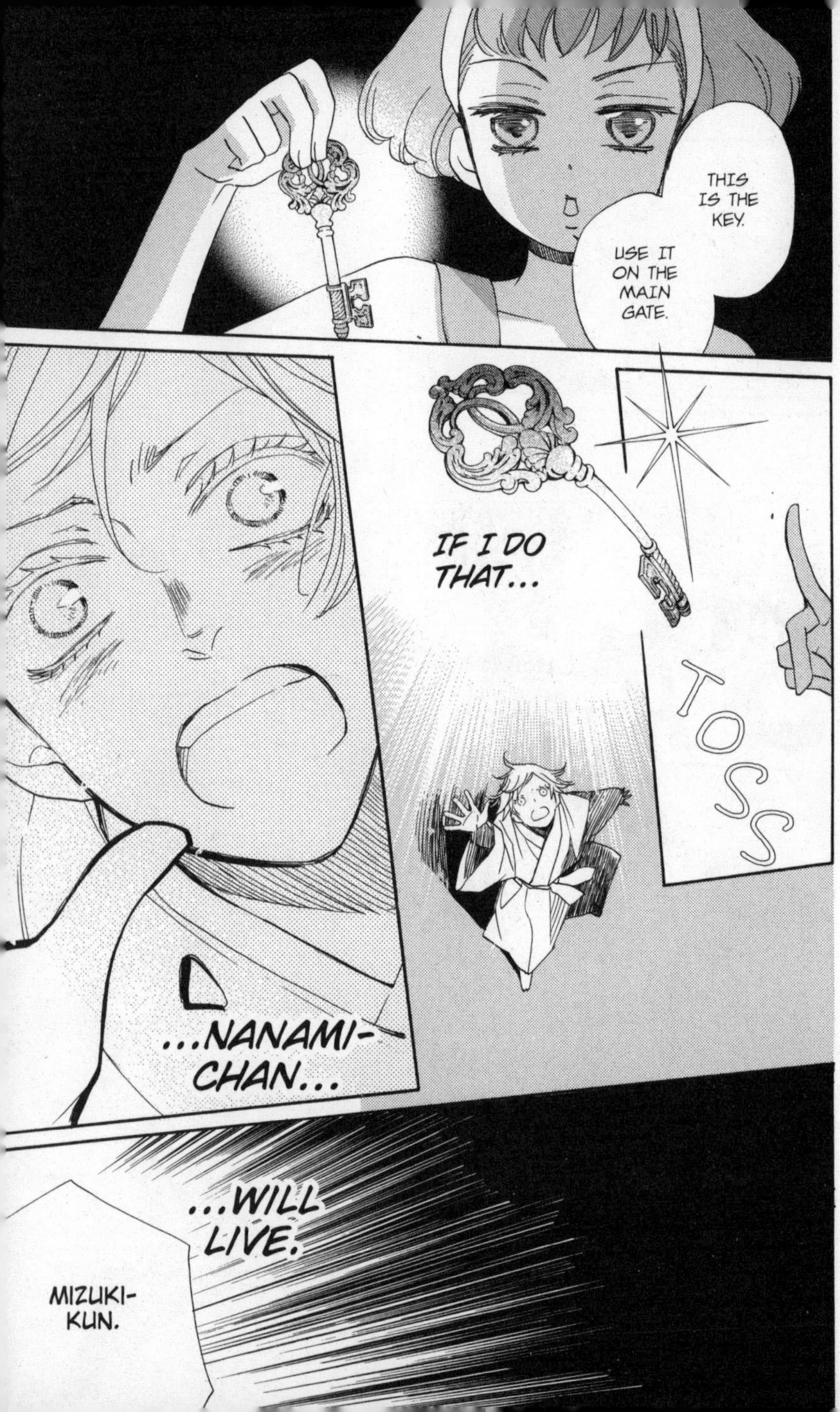
THIS IS THE KEY.
USE IT ON THE MAIN GATE.
TOSS
IF I DO THAT...
...NANAMI-CHAN...
...WILL LIVE.
MIZUKI-KUN.

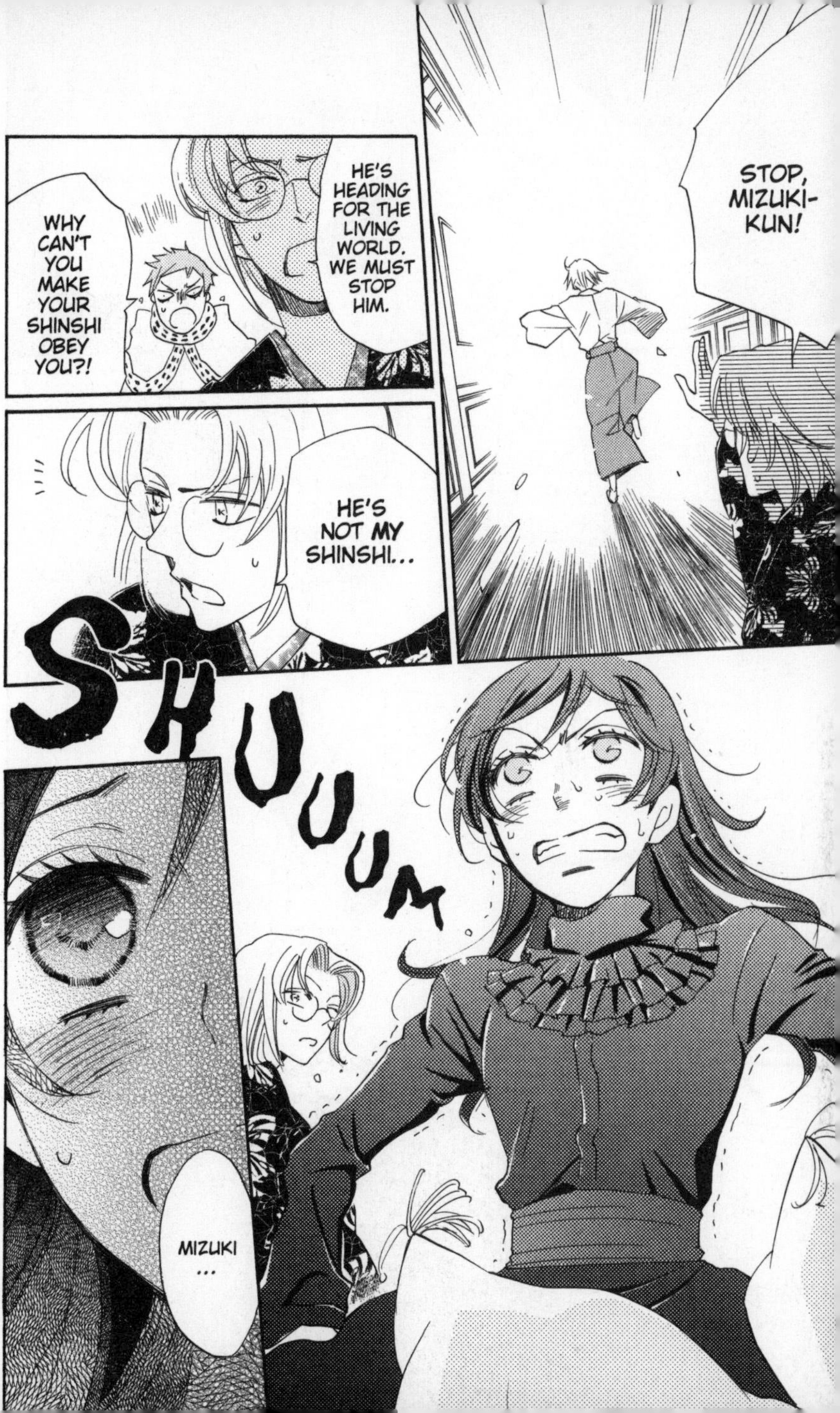
STOP, MIZUKI-KUN!
HE'S HEADING FOR THE LIVING WORLD. WE MUST STOP HIM.
WHY CAN'T YOU MAKE YOUR SHINSHI OBEY YOU?!
HE'S NOT MY SHINSHI...
SHUUUM
MIZUKI ...

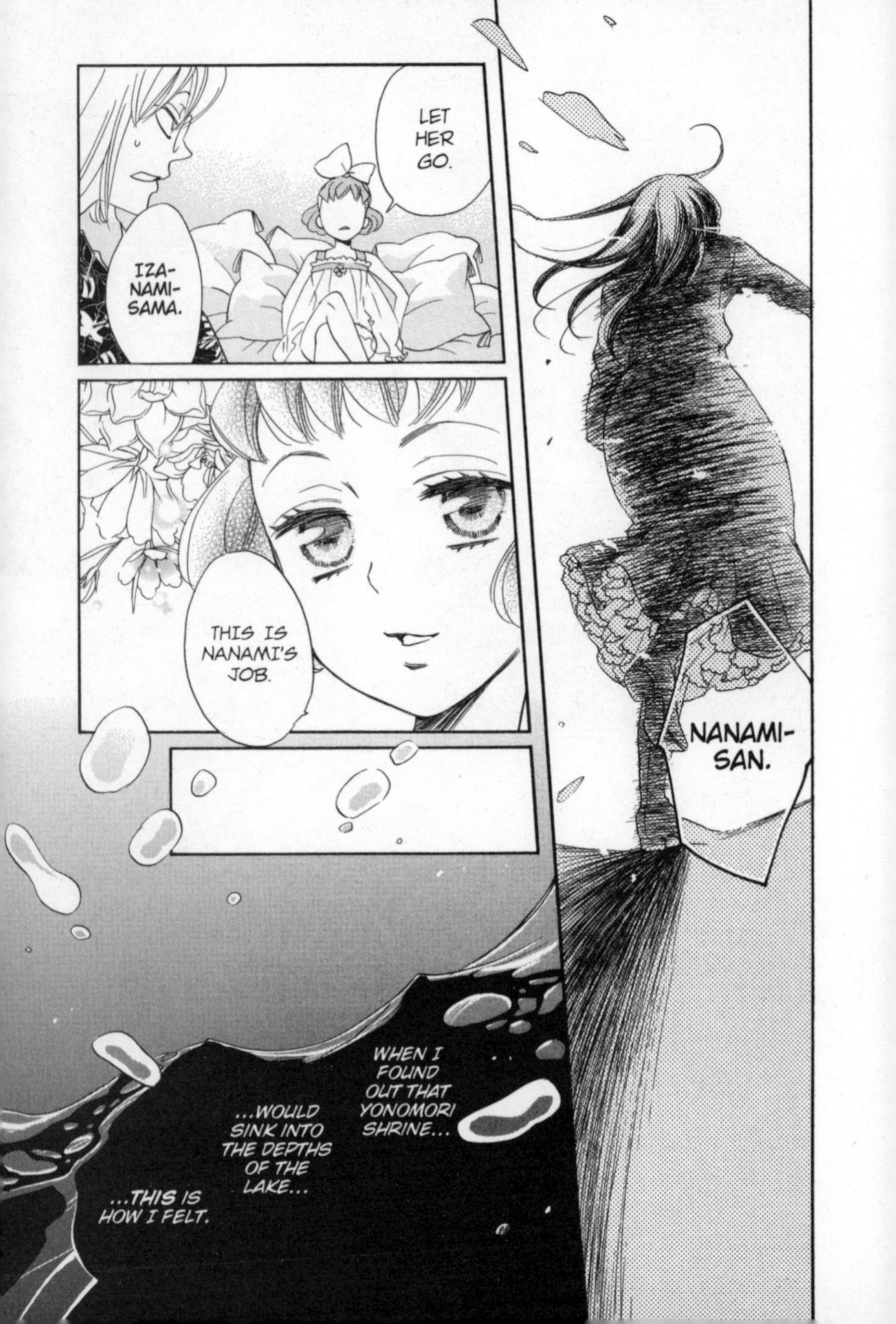
NANAMI-SAN.
LET HER GO.
IZA-NAMI-SAMA.
THIS IS NANAMI'S JOB.
WHEN I FOUND OUT THAT YONOMORI SHRINE...
...WOULD SINK INTO THE DEPTHS OF THE LAKE...
...THIS IS HOW I FELT.

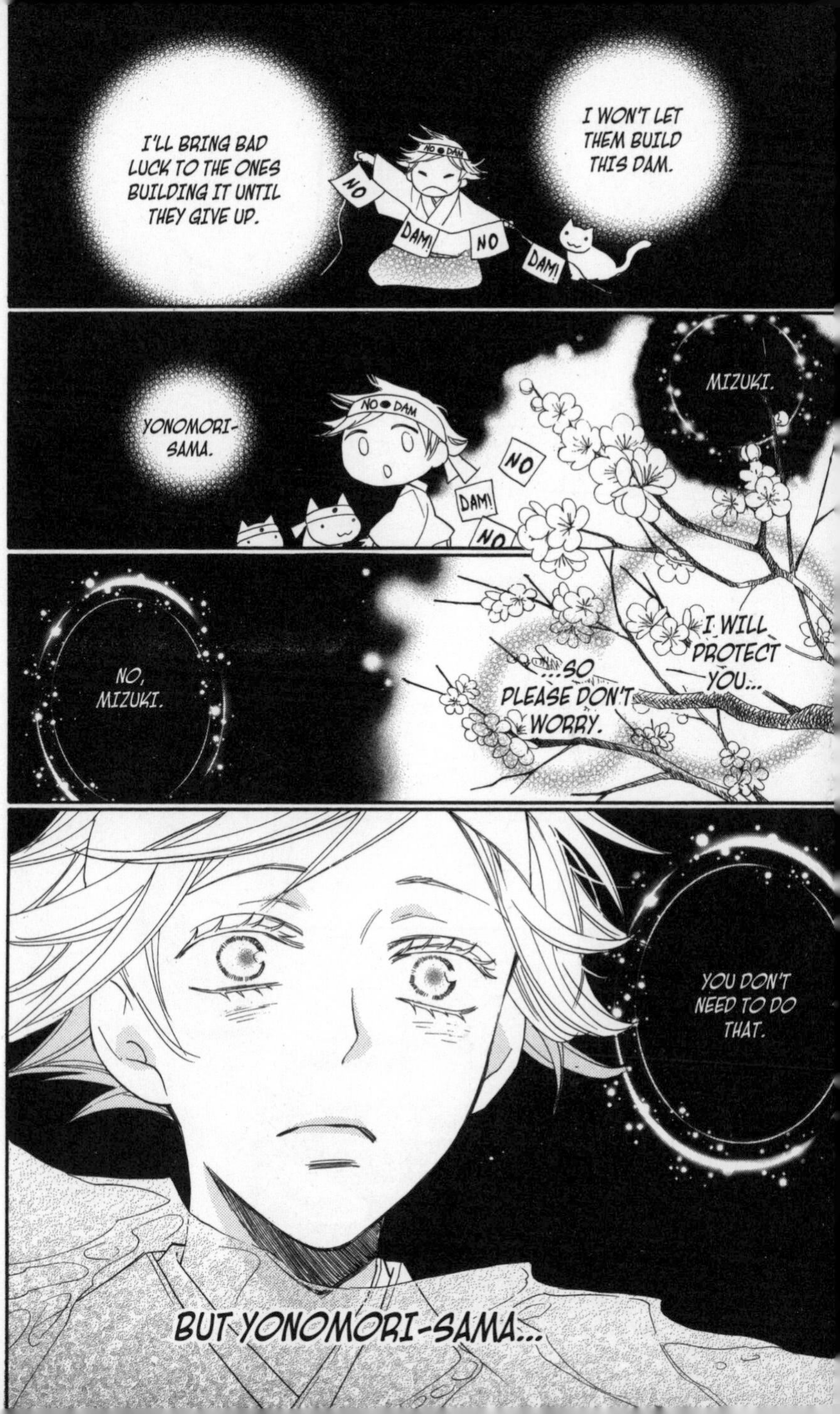
I WON'T LET THEM BUILD THIS DAM.
I'LL BRING BAD LUCK TO THE ONES BUILDING IT UNTIL THEY GIVE UP.
NO DAM
NO DAM! NO DAM!
MIZUKI.
YONOMORI-SAMA.
NO DAM
NO DAM! NO
I WILL PROTECT YOU...
...SO PLEASE DON'T WORRY.
NO, MIZUKI.
YOU DON'T NEED TO DO THAT.
BUT YONOMORI-SAMA...

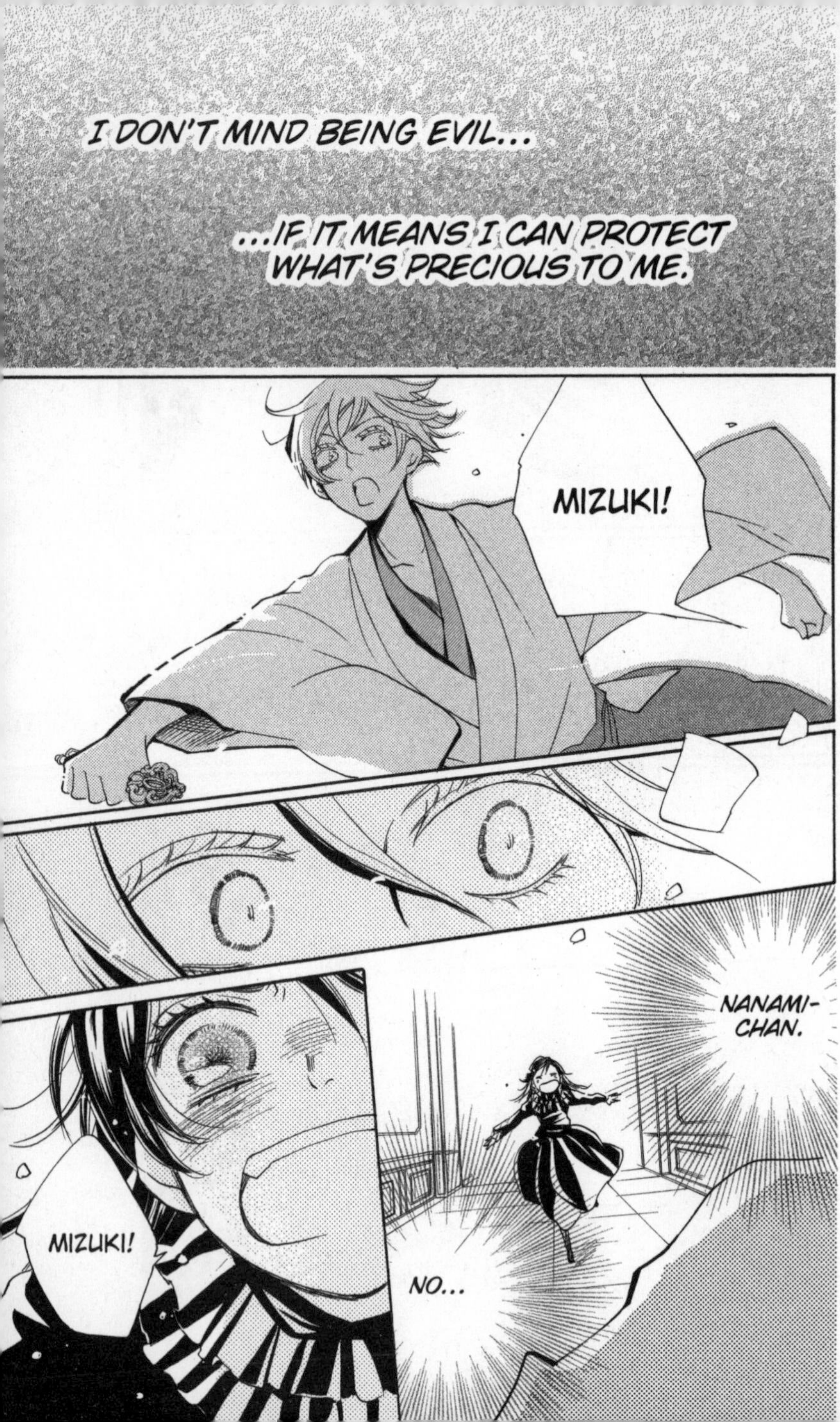
I DON'T MIND BEING EVIL...
...IF IT MEANS I CAN PROTECT WHAT'S PRECIOUS TO ME.
MIZUKI!
NANAMI-CHAN.
NO...
MIZUKI!

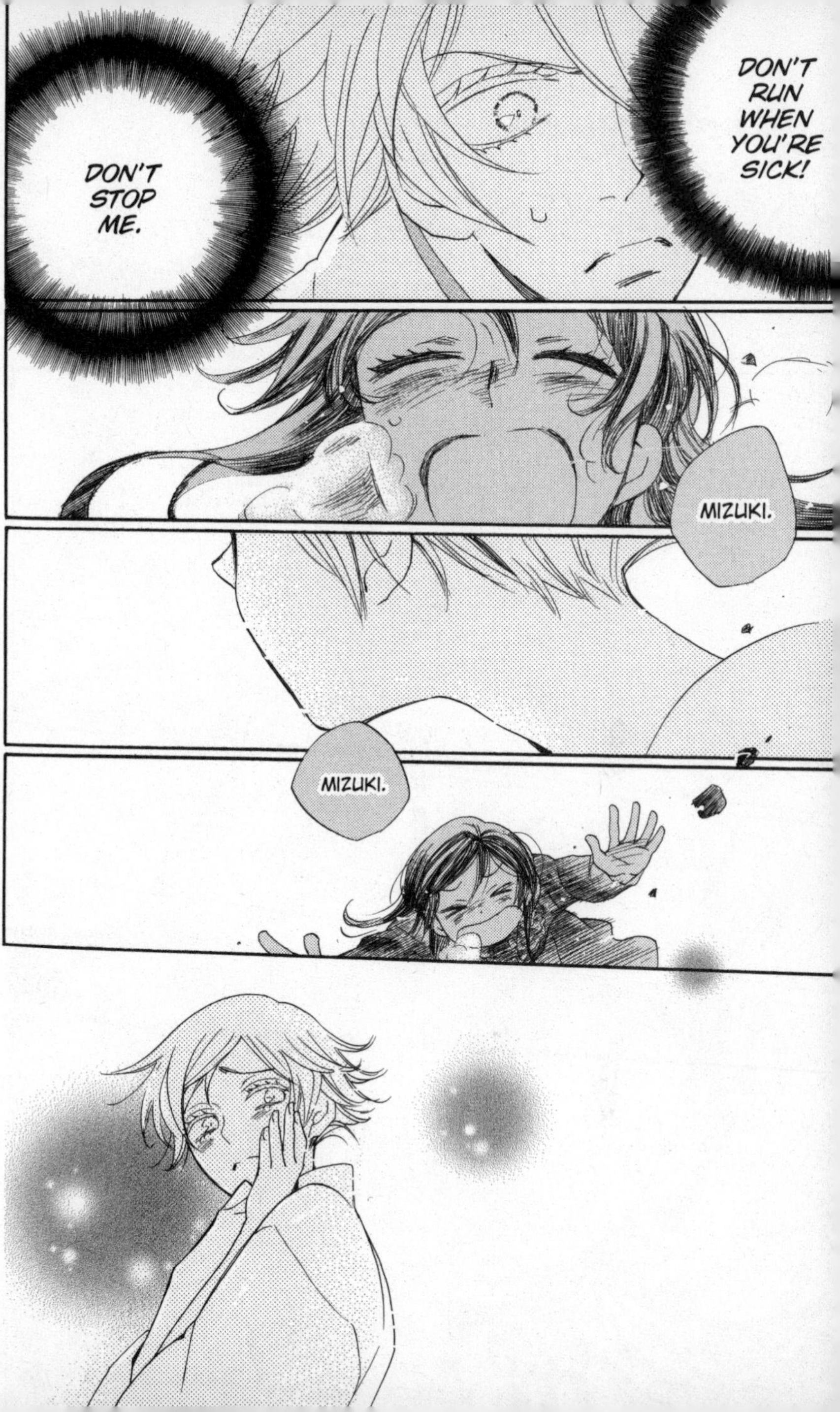

DON'T RUN WHEN YOU'RE SICK!
DON'T STOP ME.
MIZUKI.
MIZUKI.

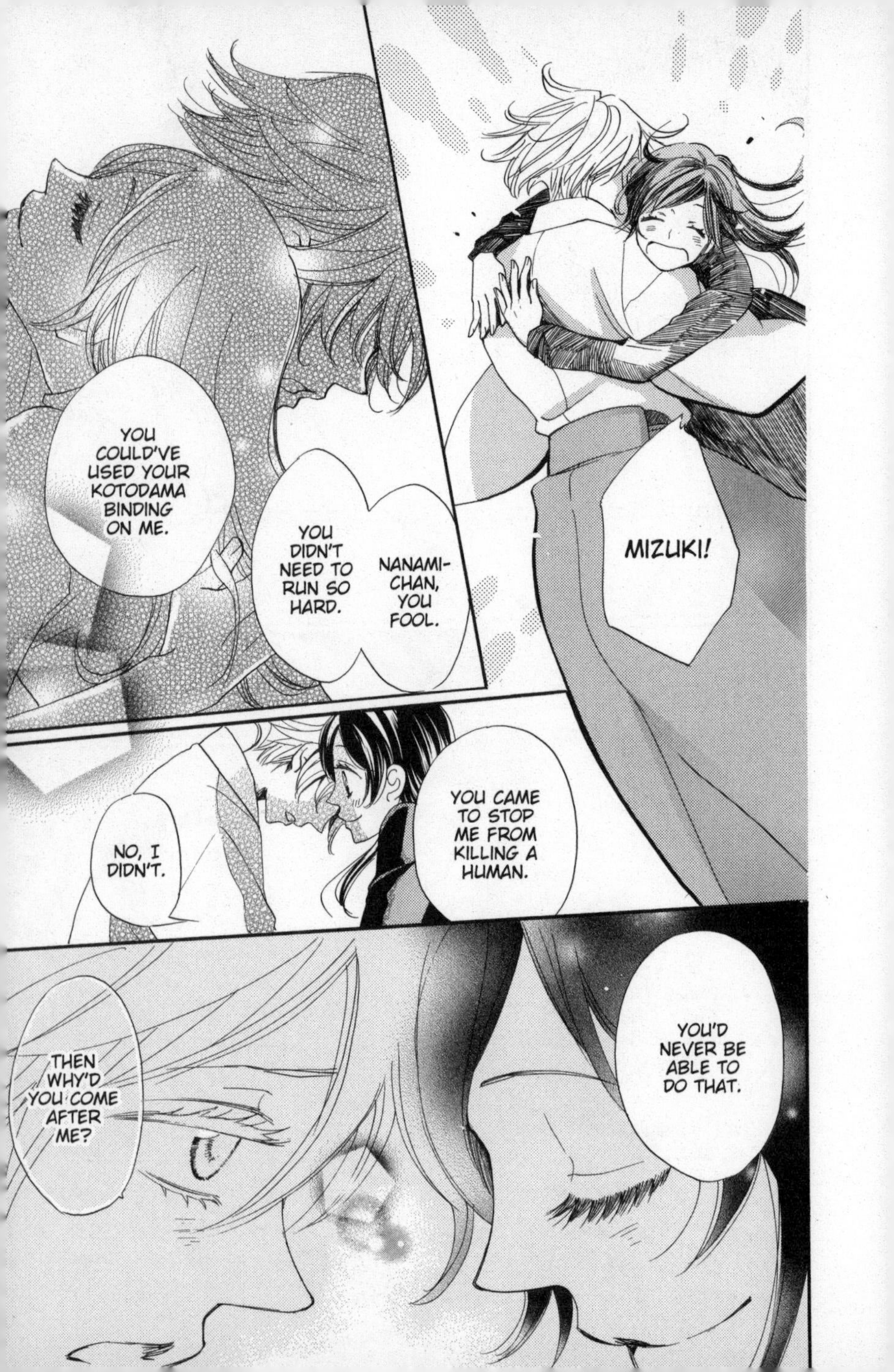
MIZUKI!
NANAMI-CHAN, YOU FOOL.
YOU DIDN'T NEED TO RUN SO HARD.
YOU COULD'VE USED YOUR KOTODAMA BINDING ON ME.
YOU CAME TO STOP ME FROM KILLING A HUMAN.
NO, I DIDN'T.
YOU'D NEVER BE ABLE TO DO THAT.
THEN WHY'D YOU COME AFTER ME?

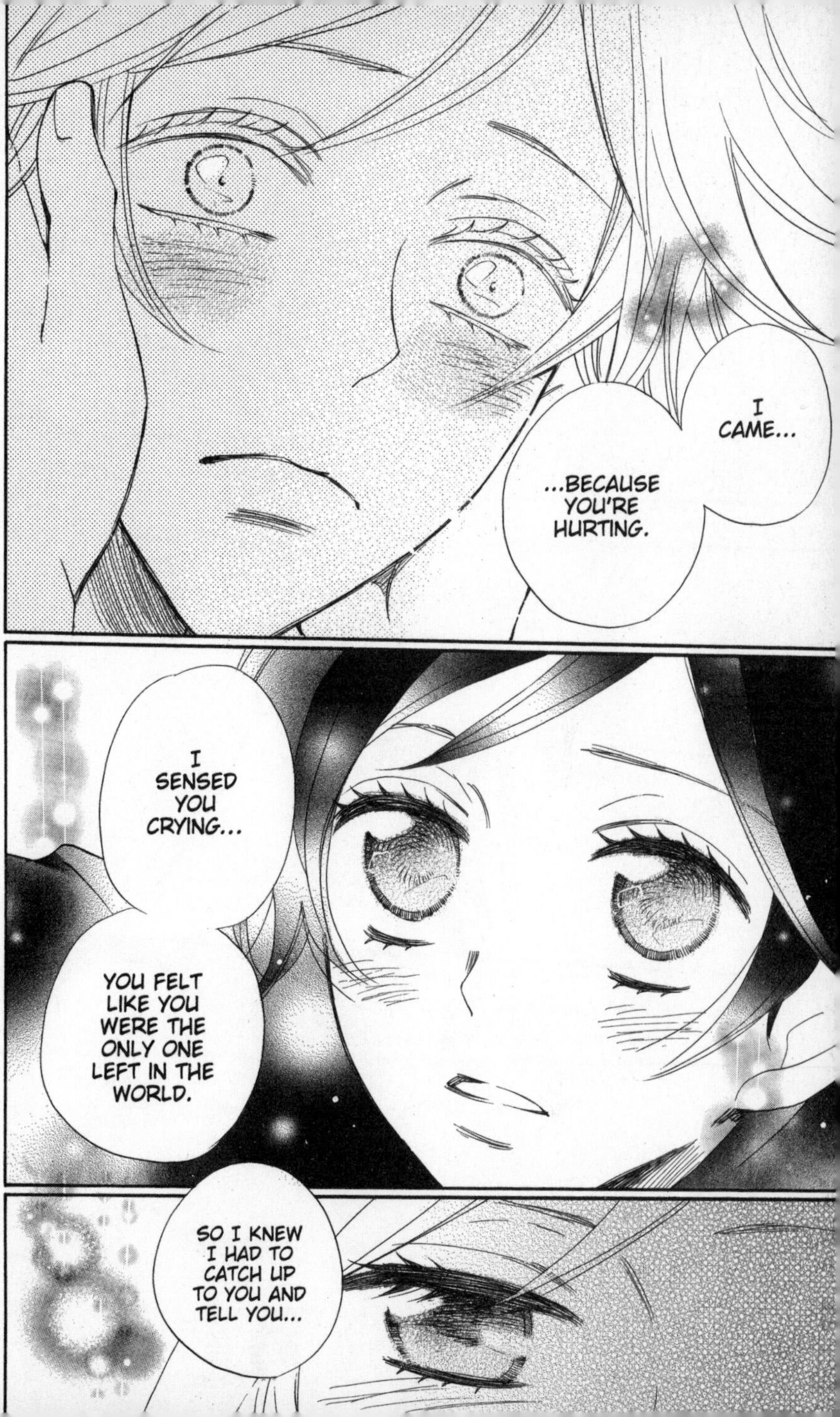
I CAME...
...BECAUSE YOU'RE HURTING.
I SENSED YOU CRYING...
YOU FELT LIKE YOU WERE THE ONLY ONE LEFT IN THE WORLD.
SO I KNEW I HAD TO CATCH UP TO YOU AND TELL YOU...

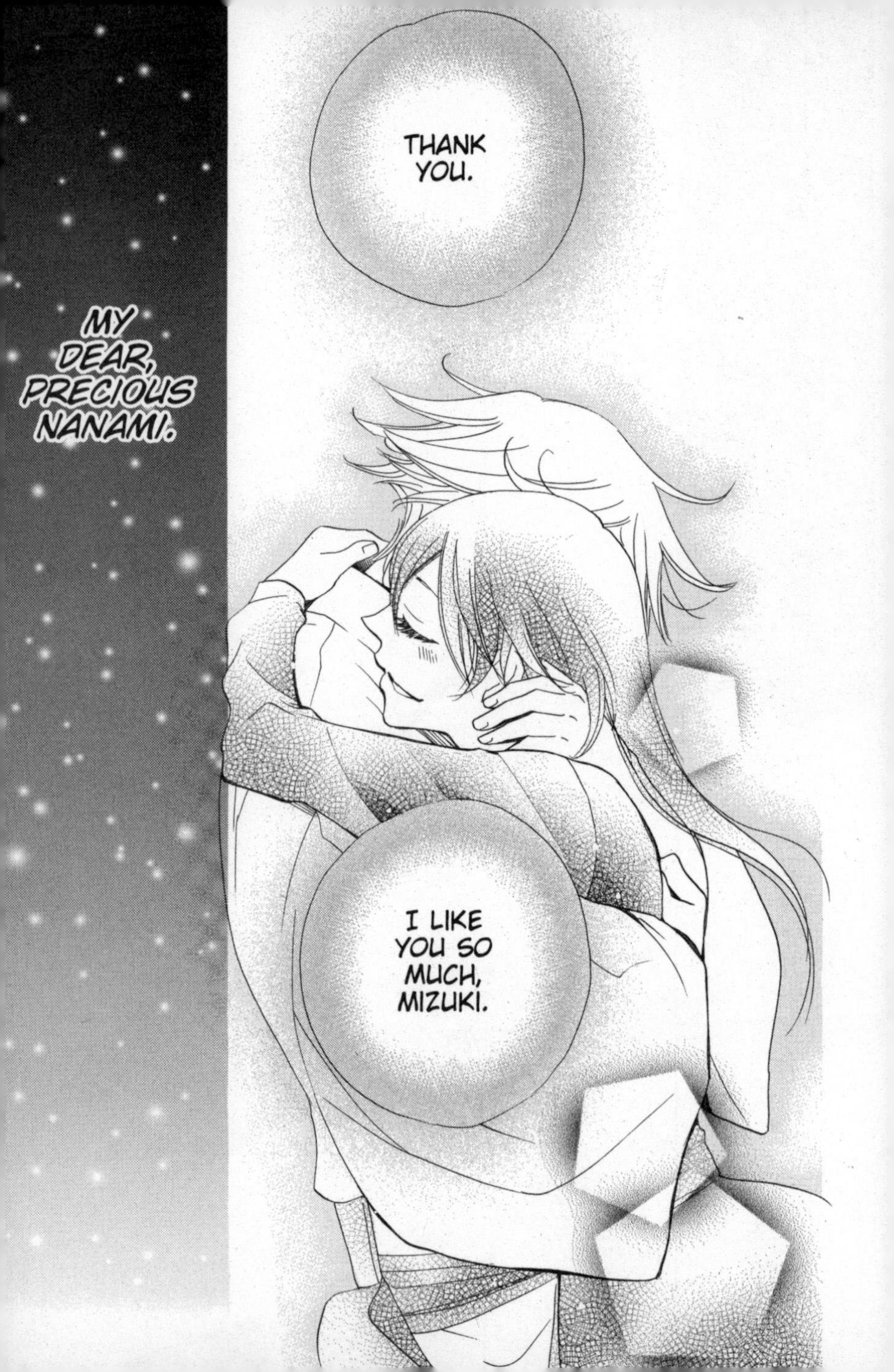
THANK YOU.
I LIKE YOU SO MUCH, MIZUKI.
MY DEAR, PRECIOUS NANAMI.

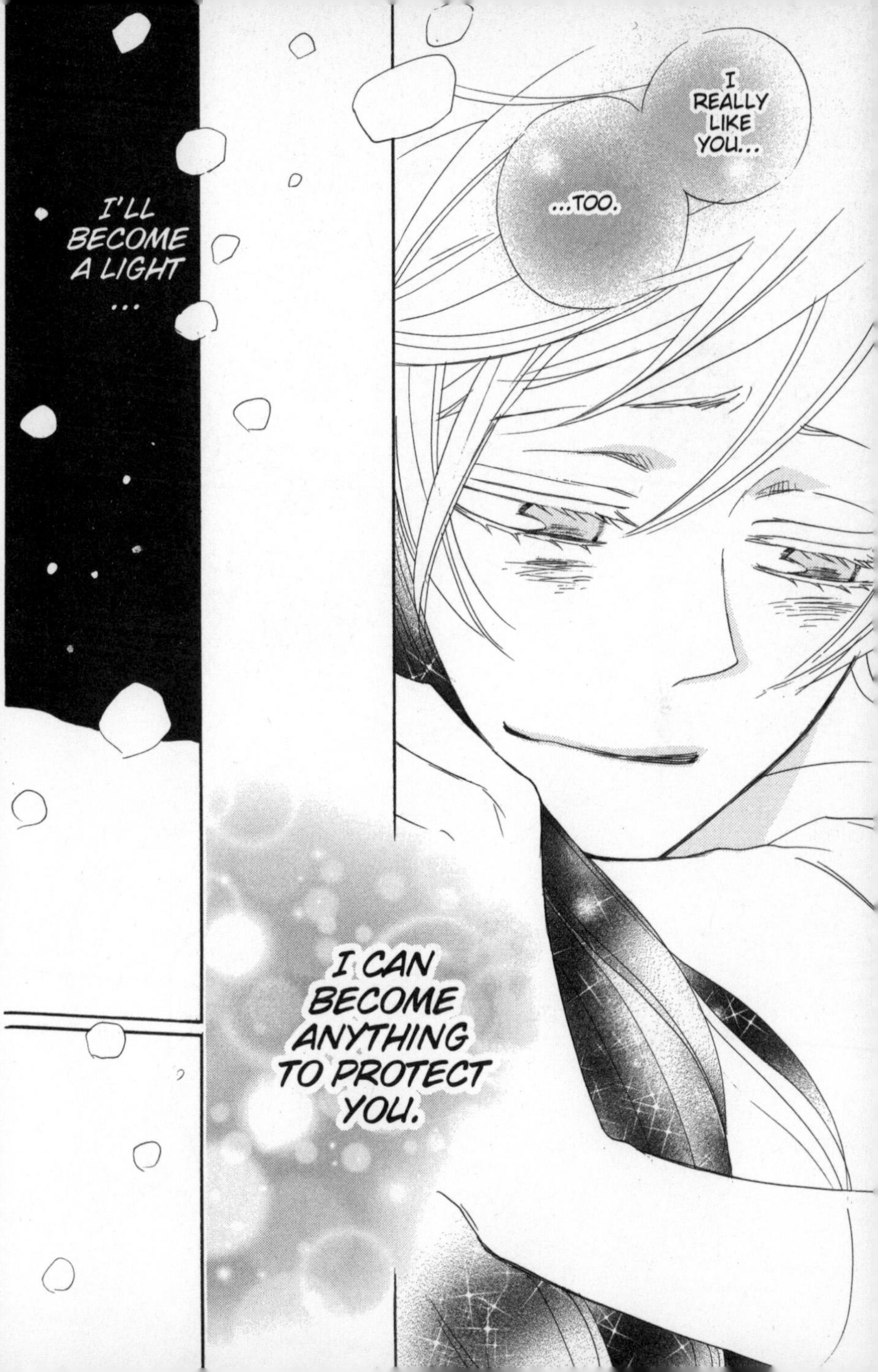
I REALLY LIKE YOU...
...TOO.
I'LL BECOME A LIGHT ...
I CAN BECOME ANYTHING TO PROTECT YOU.

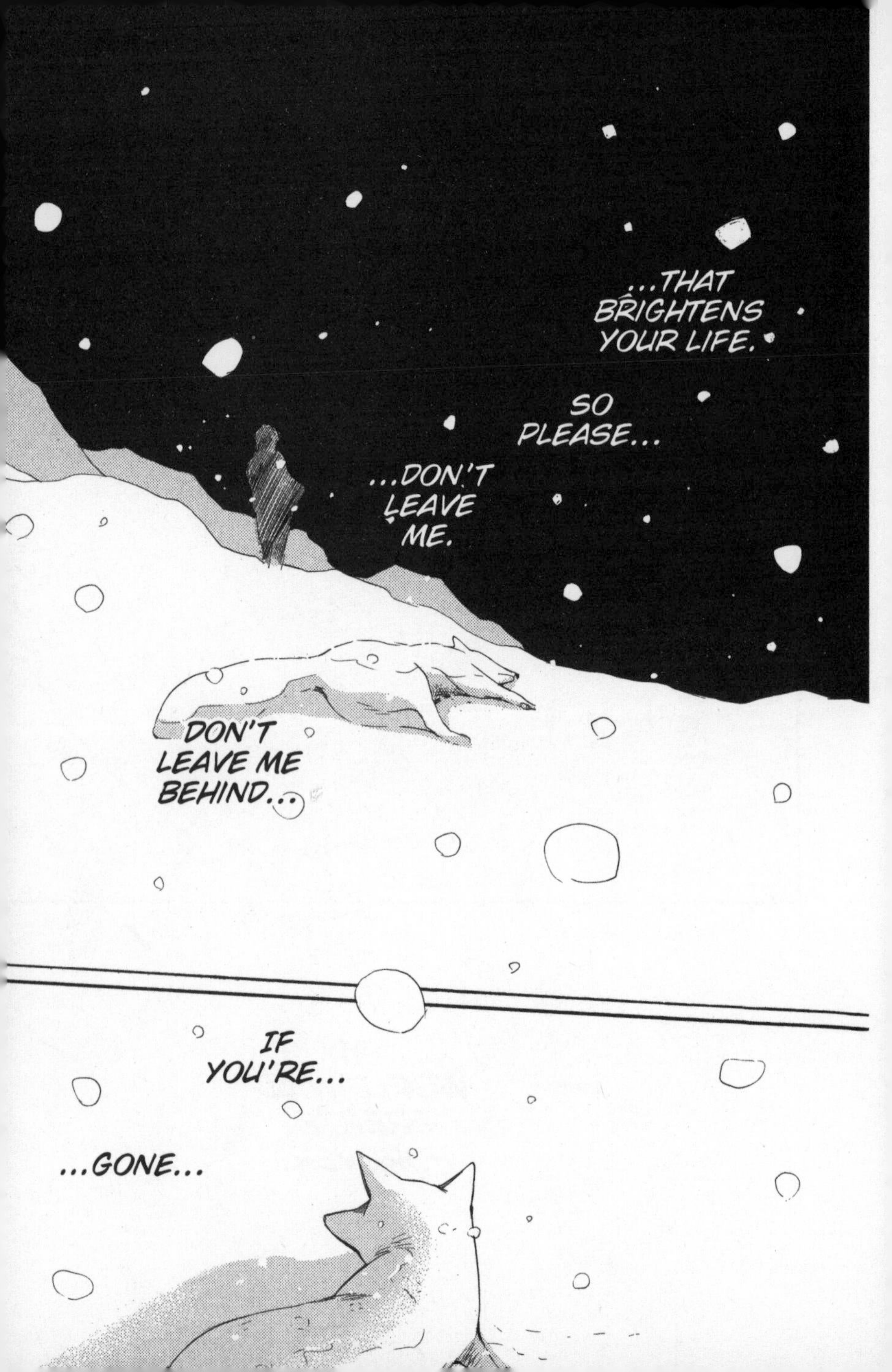
...THAT BRIGHTENS YOUR LIFE.
SO PLEASE...
...DON'T LEAVE ME.
DON'T LEAVE ME BEHIND...
IF YOU'RE...
...GONE...

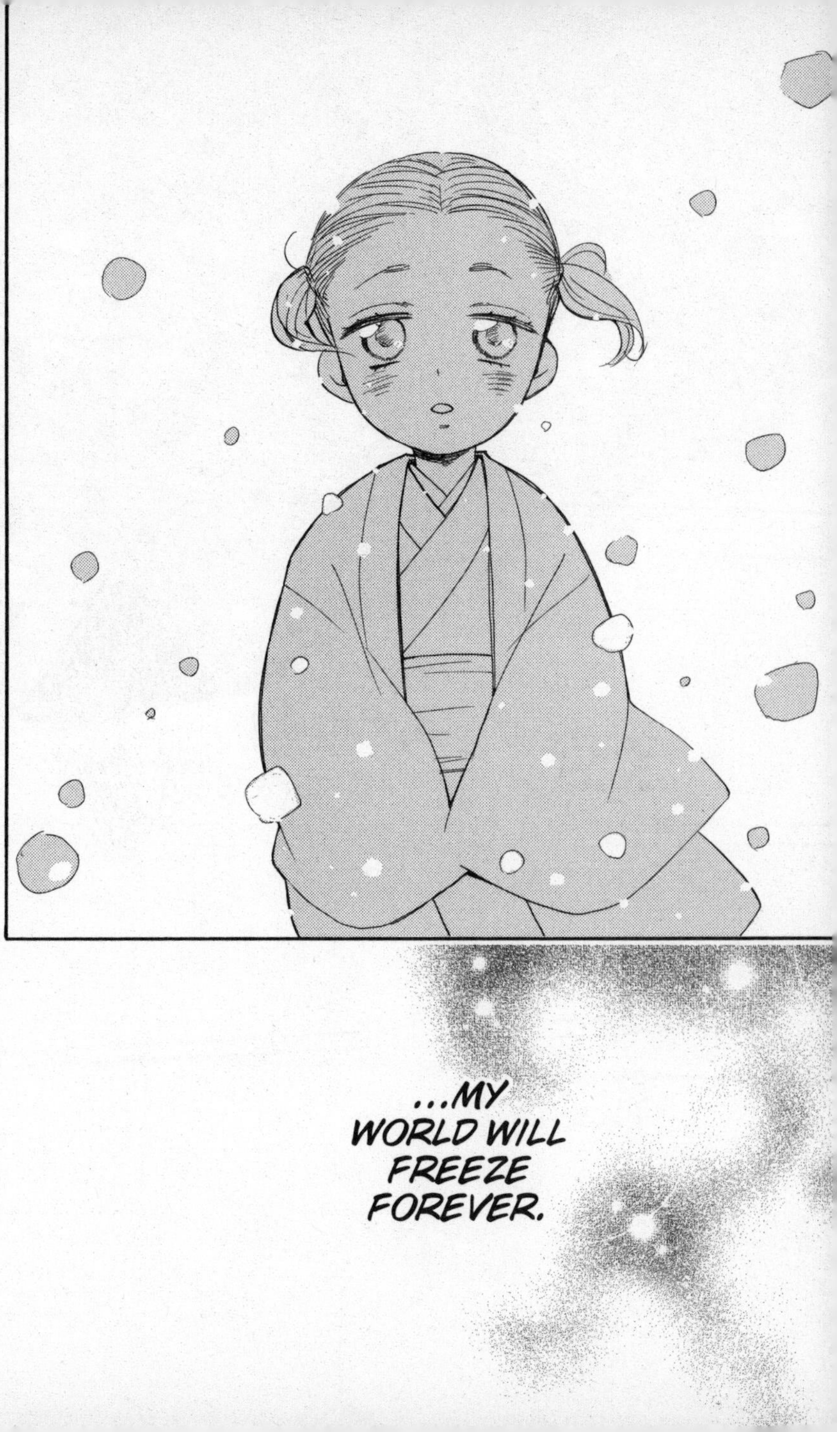
...MY WORLD WILL FREEZE FOREVER.

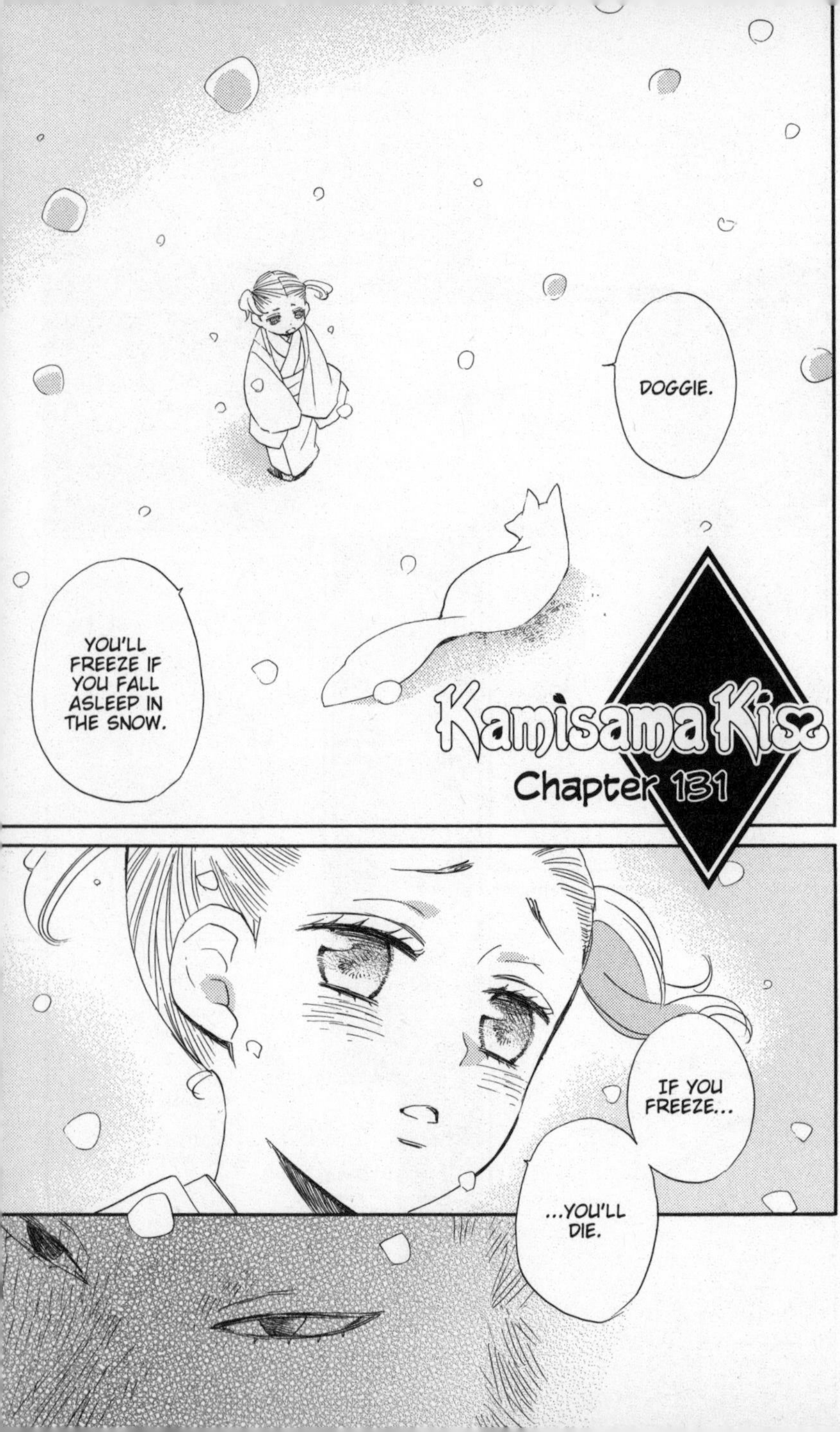
DOGGIE.
Kamisama Kiss
Chapter 131
YOU'LL FREEZE IF YOU FALL ASLEEP IN THE SNOW.
IF YOU FREEZE...
...YOU'LL DIE.

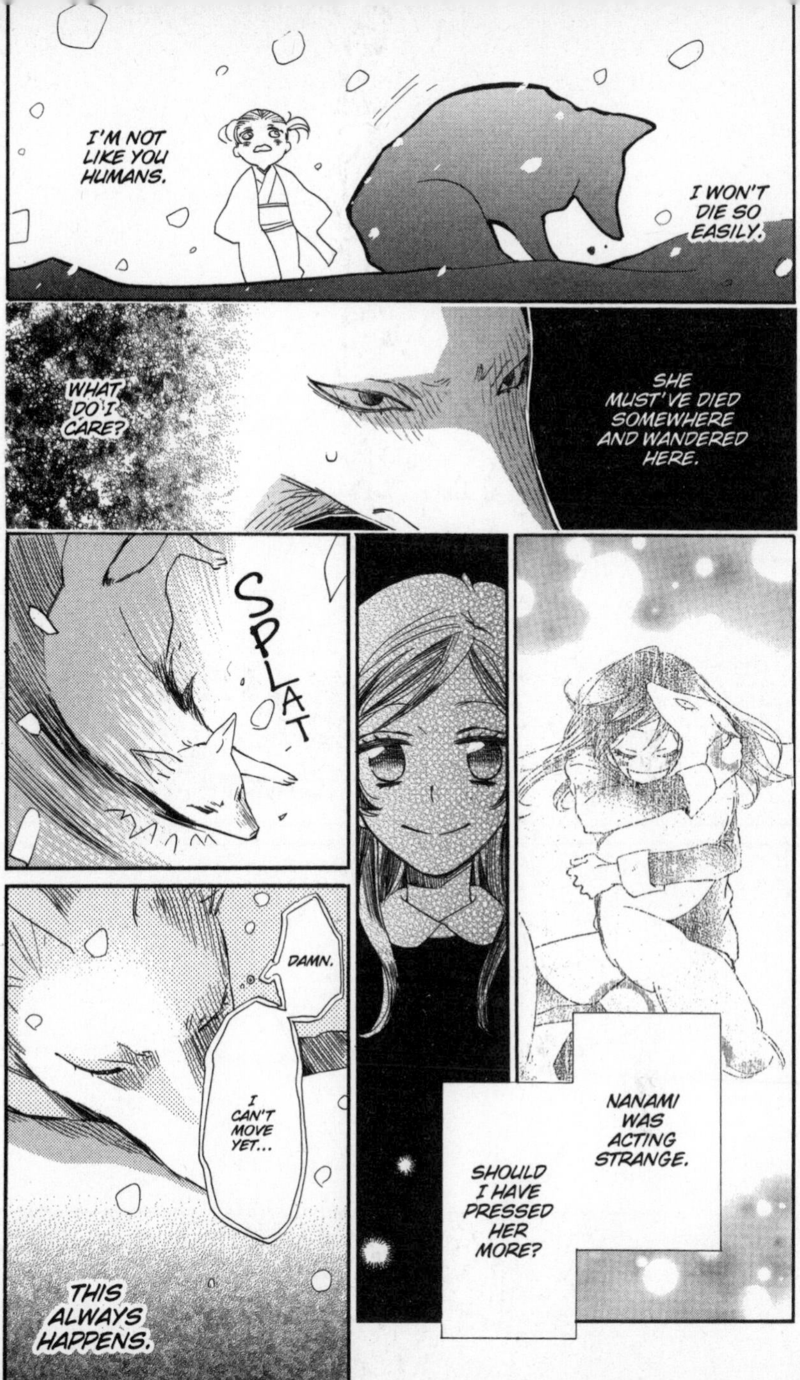
I WON'T DIE SO EASILY.
I'M NOT LIKE YOU HUMANS.
SHE MUST'VE DIED SOMEWHERE AND WANDERED HERE.
WHAT DO I CARE?
NANAMI WAS ACTING STRANGE.
SHOULD I HAVE PRESSED HER MORE?
SPLAT
DAMN.
I CAN'T MOVE YET...
THIS ALWAYS HAPPENS.

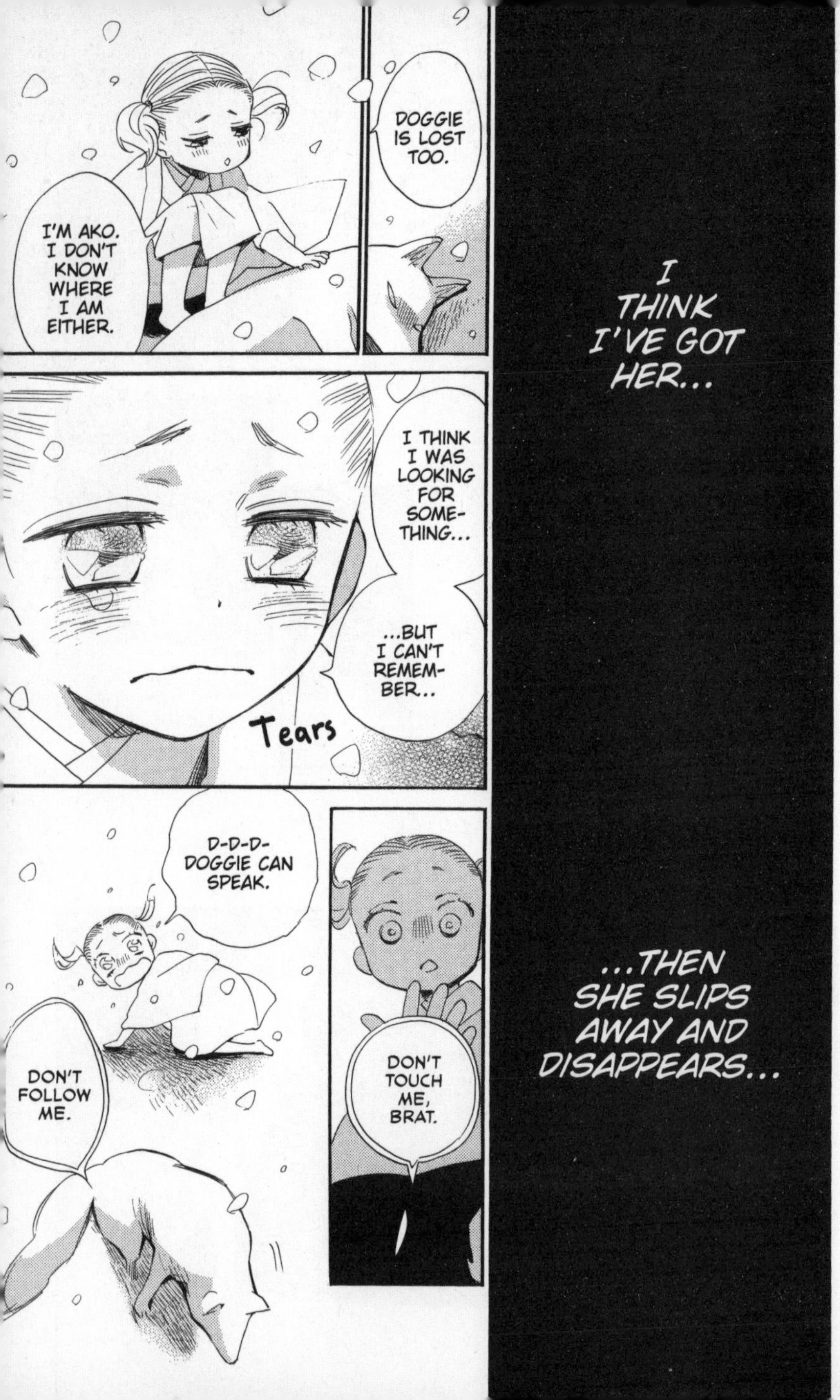

I THINK I'VE GOT HER...
...THEN SHE SLIPS AWAY AND DISAPPEARS...
DOGGIE IS LOST TOO.
I'M AKO. I DON'T KNOW WHERE I AM EITHER.
I THINK I WAS LOOKING FOR SOME-THING...
...BUT I CAN'T REMEM-BER...
Tears
DON'T TOUCH ME, BRAT.
D-D-D-DOGGIE CAN SPEAK.
DON'T FOLLOW ME.

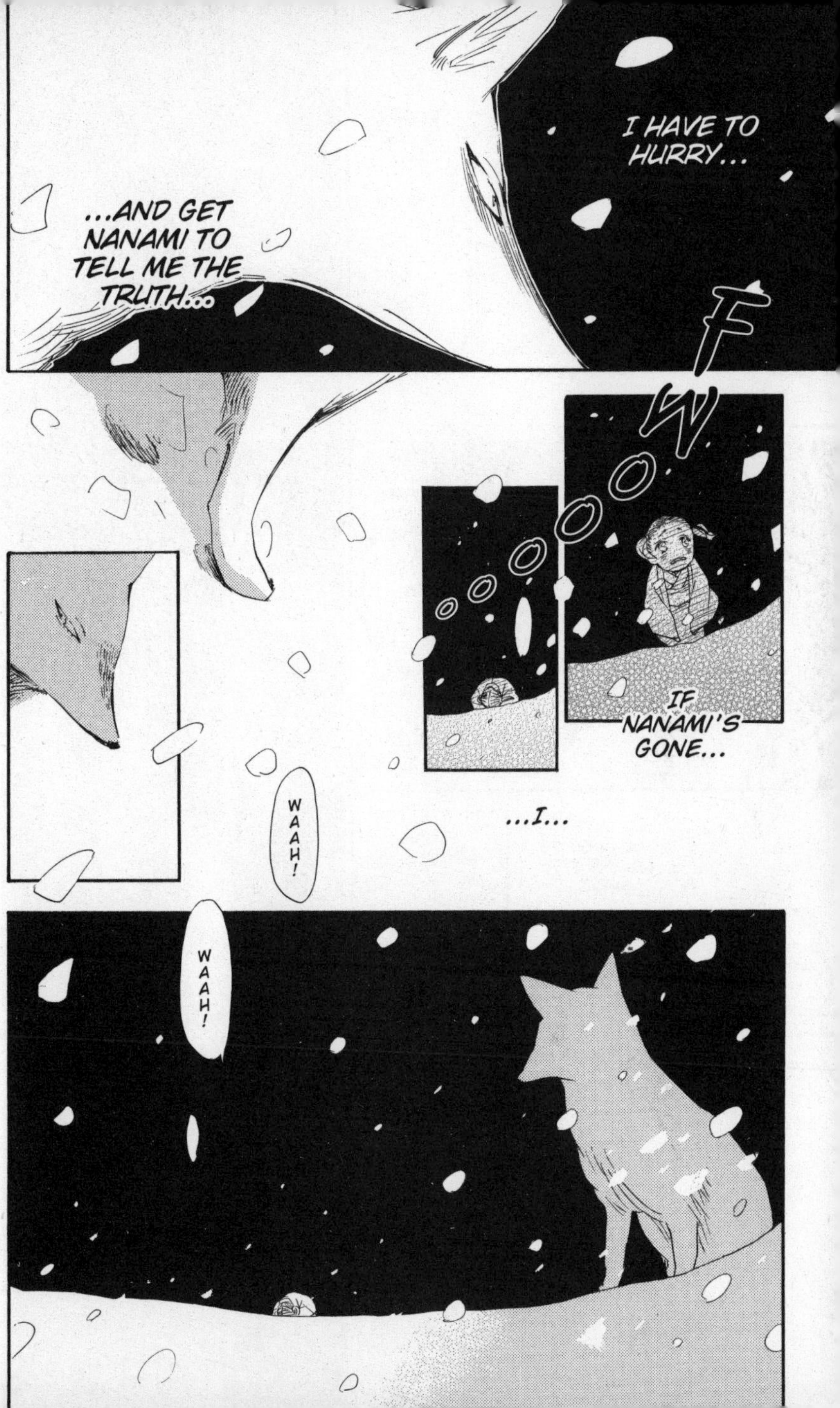
I HAVE TO HURRY...
...AND GET NANAMI TO TELL ME THE TRUTH...
FWOOOOOO
IF NANAMI'S GONE...
...I...
WAAAH!
WAAAH!

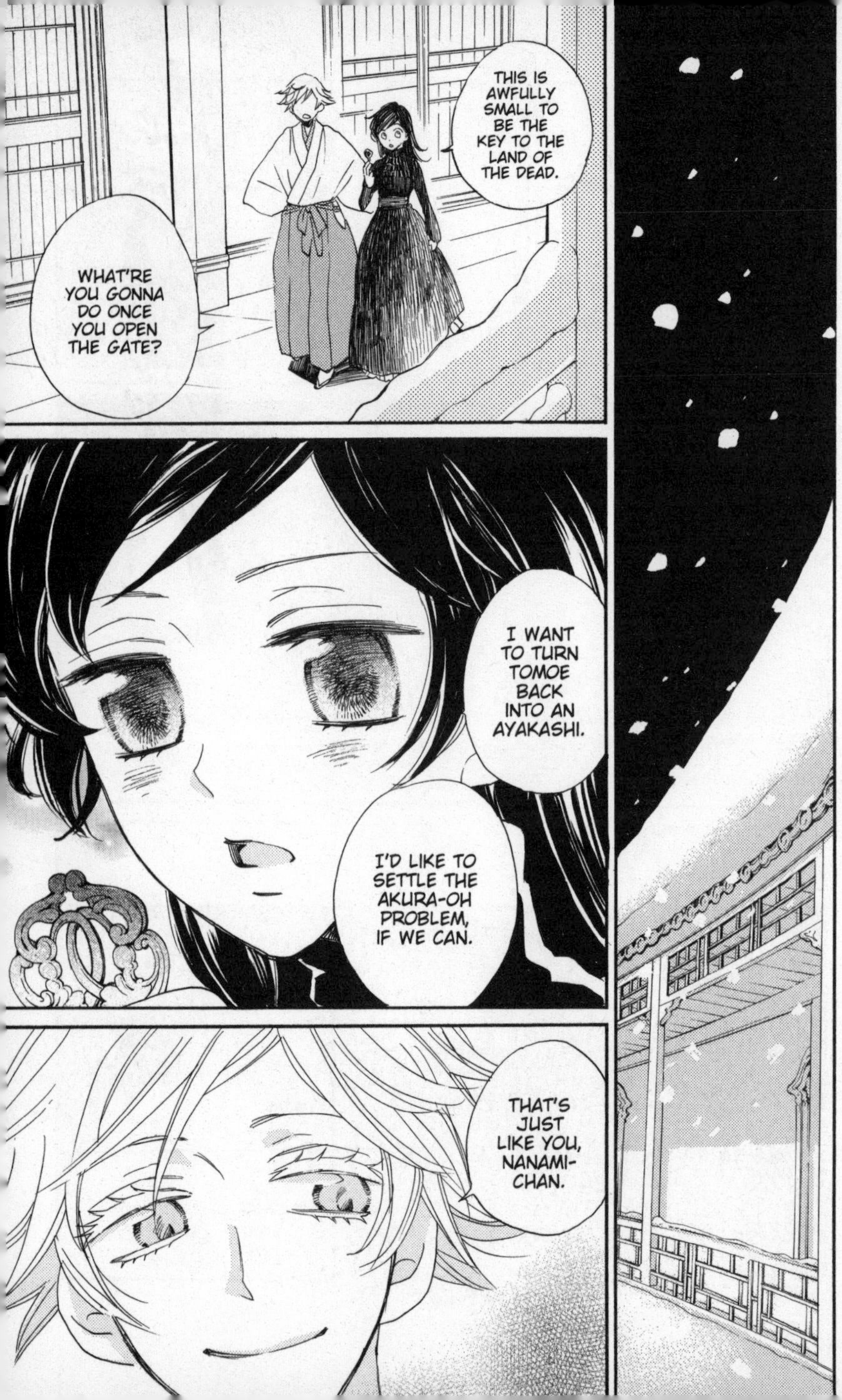
THIS IS AWFULLY SMALL TO BE THE KEY TO THE LAND OF THE DEAD.
WHAT'RE YOU GONNA DO ONCE YOU OPEN THE GATE?
I WANT TO TURN TOMOE BACK INTO AN AYAKASHI.
I'D LIKE TO SETTLE THE AKURA-OH PROBLEM, IF WE CAN.
THAT'S JUST LIKE YOU, NANAMI-CHAN.

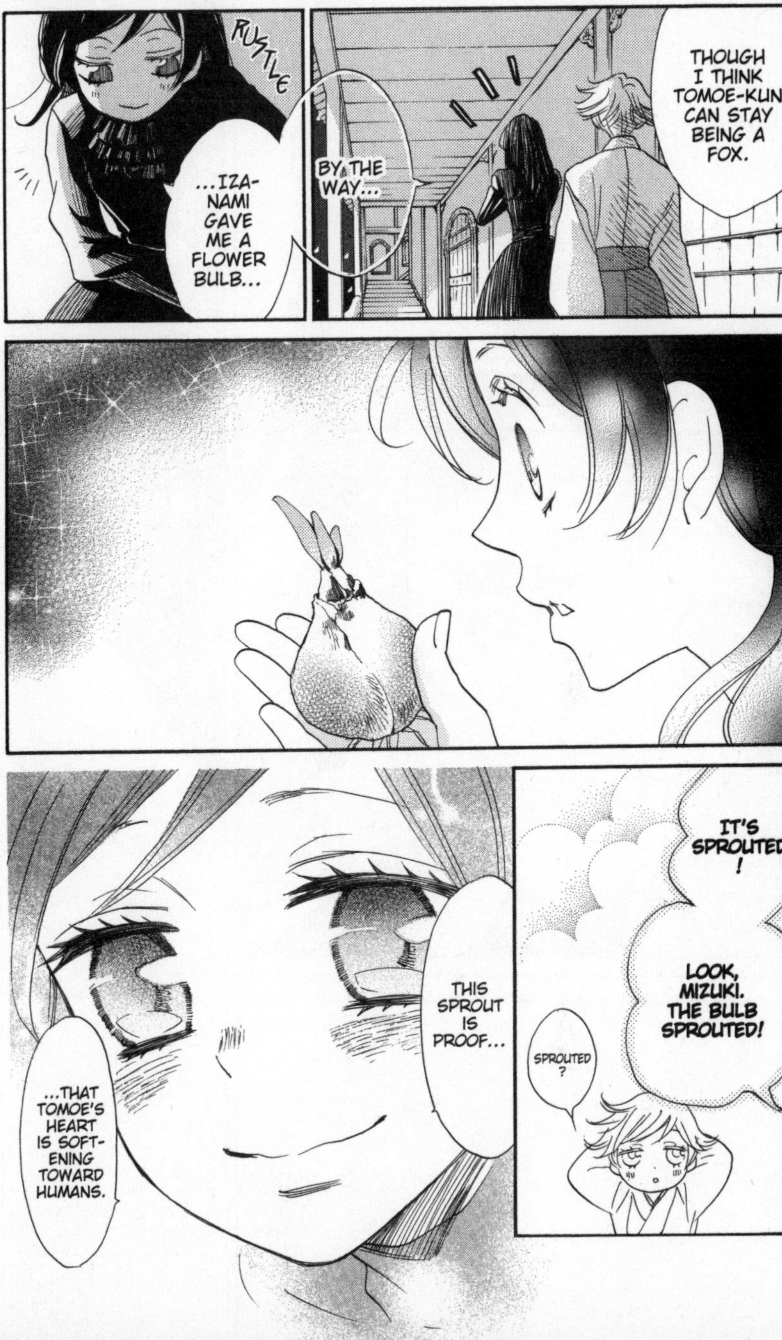
THOUGH I THINK TOMOE-KUN CAN STAY BEING A FOX.
BY THE WAY...
RUSTLE
...IZA-NAMI GAVE ME A FLOWER BULB...
IT'S SPROUTED!
LOOK, MIZUKI. THE BULB SPROUTED!
SPROUTED?
THIS SPROUT IS PROOF...
...THAT TOMOE'S HEART IS SOFT-ENING TOWARD HUMANS.

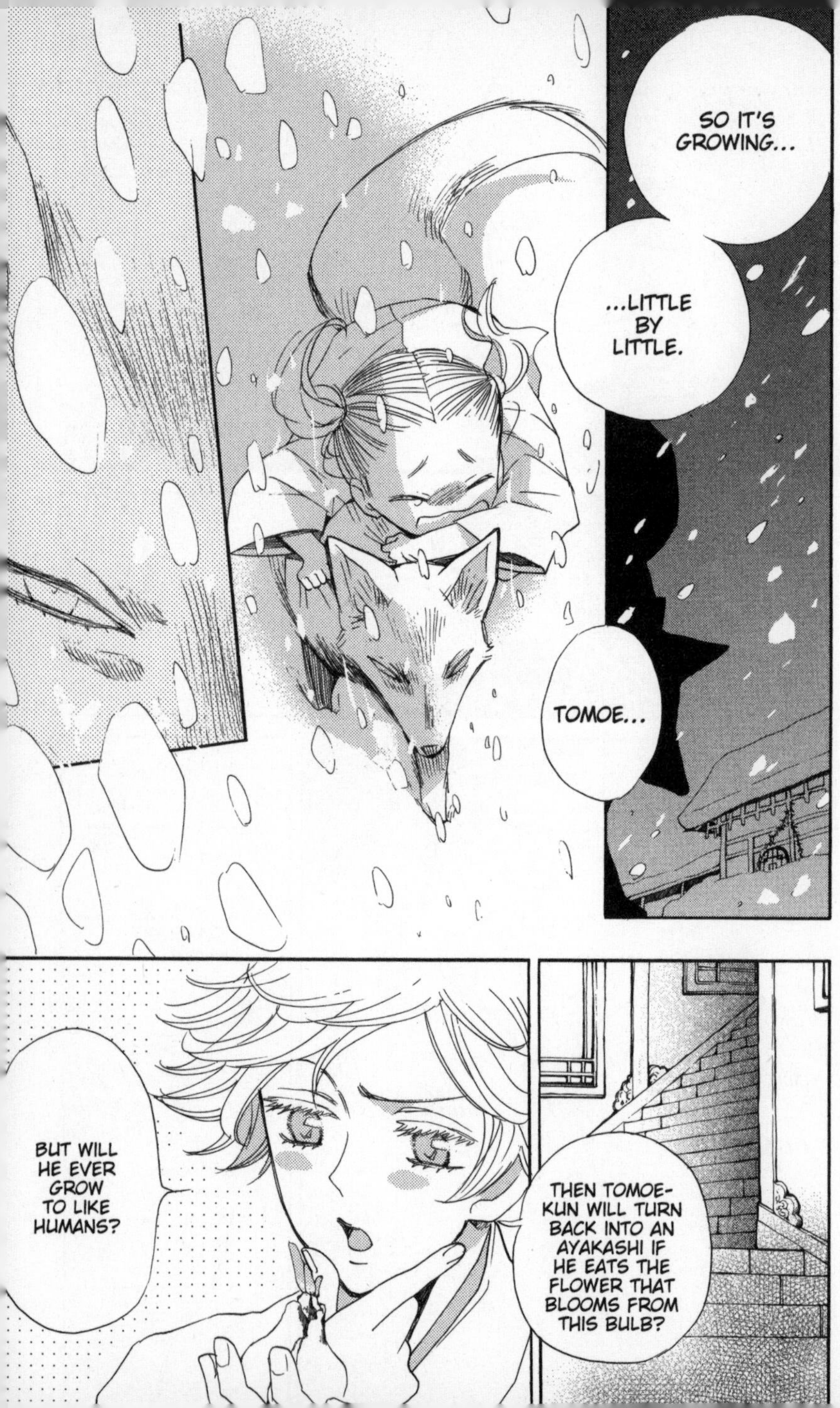
SO IT'S GROWING...
...LITTLE BY LITTLE.
TOMOE...
THEN TOMOE-KUN WILL TURN BACK INTO AN AYAKASHI IF HE EATS THE FLOWER THAT BLOOMS FROM THIS BULB?
BUT WILL HE EVER GROW TO LIKE HUMANS?

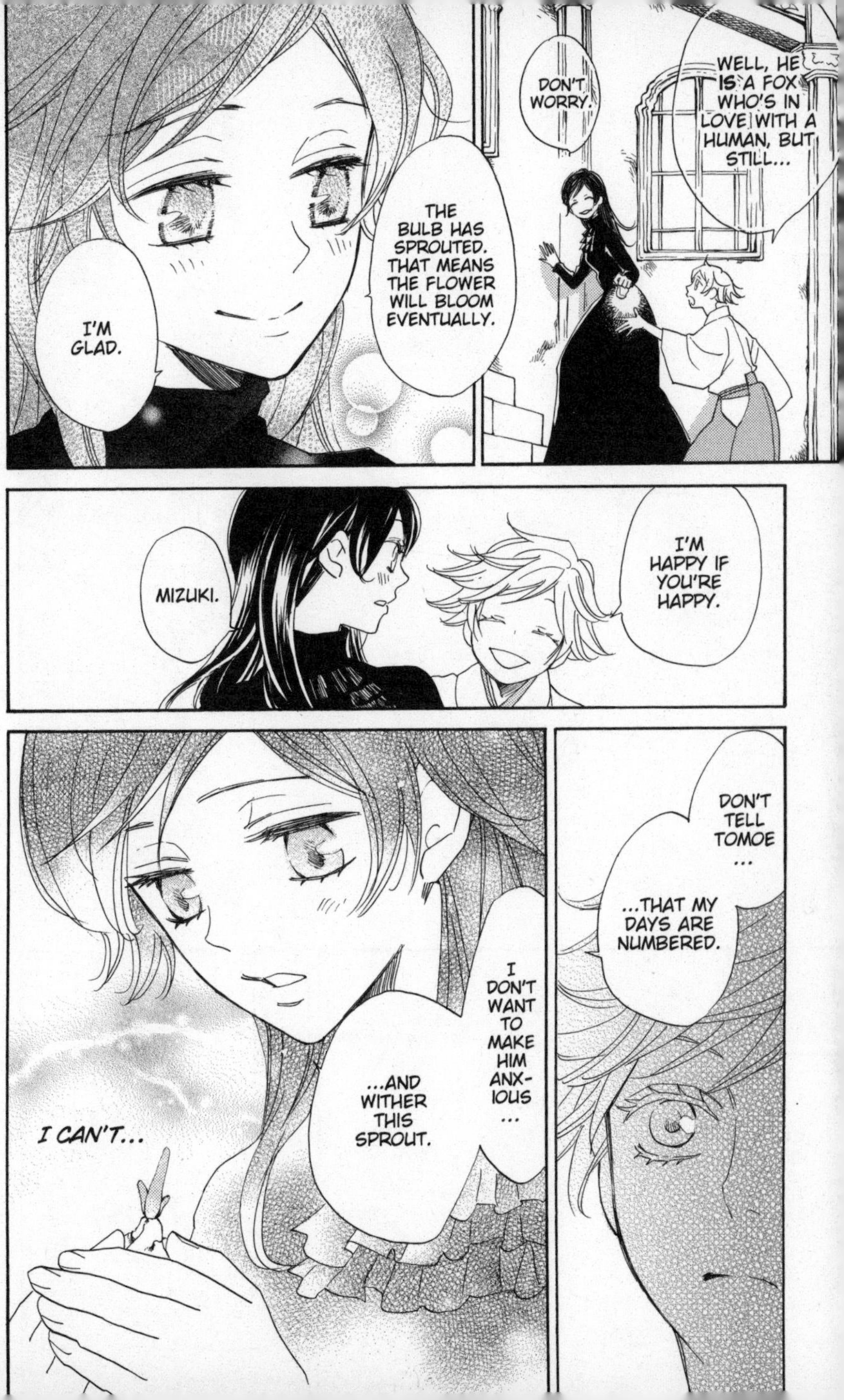
WELL, HE IS A FOX WHO'S IN LOVE WITH A HUMAN, BUT STILL...
DON'T WORRY.
THE BULB HAS SPROUTED. THAT MEANS THE FLOWER WILL BLOOM EVENTUALLY.
I'M GLAD.
I'M HAPPY IF YOU'RE HAPPY.
MIZUKI.
DON'T TELL TOMOE...
...THAT MY DAYS ARE NUMBERED.
I DON'T WANT TO MAKE HIM ANXIOUS...
...AND WITHER THIS SPROUT.
I CAN'T...

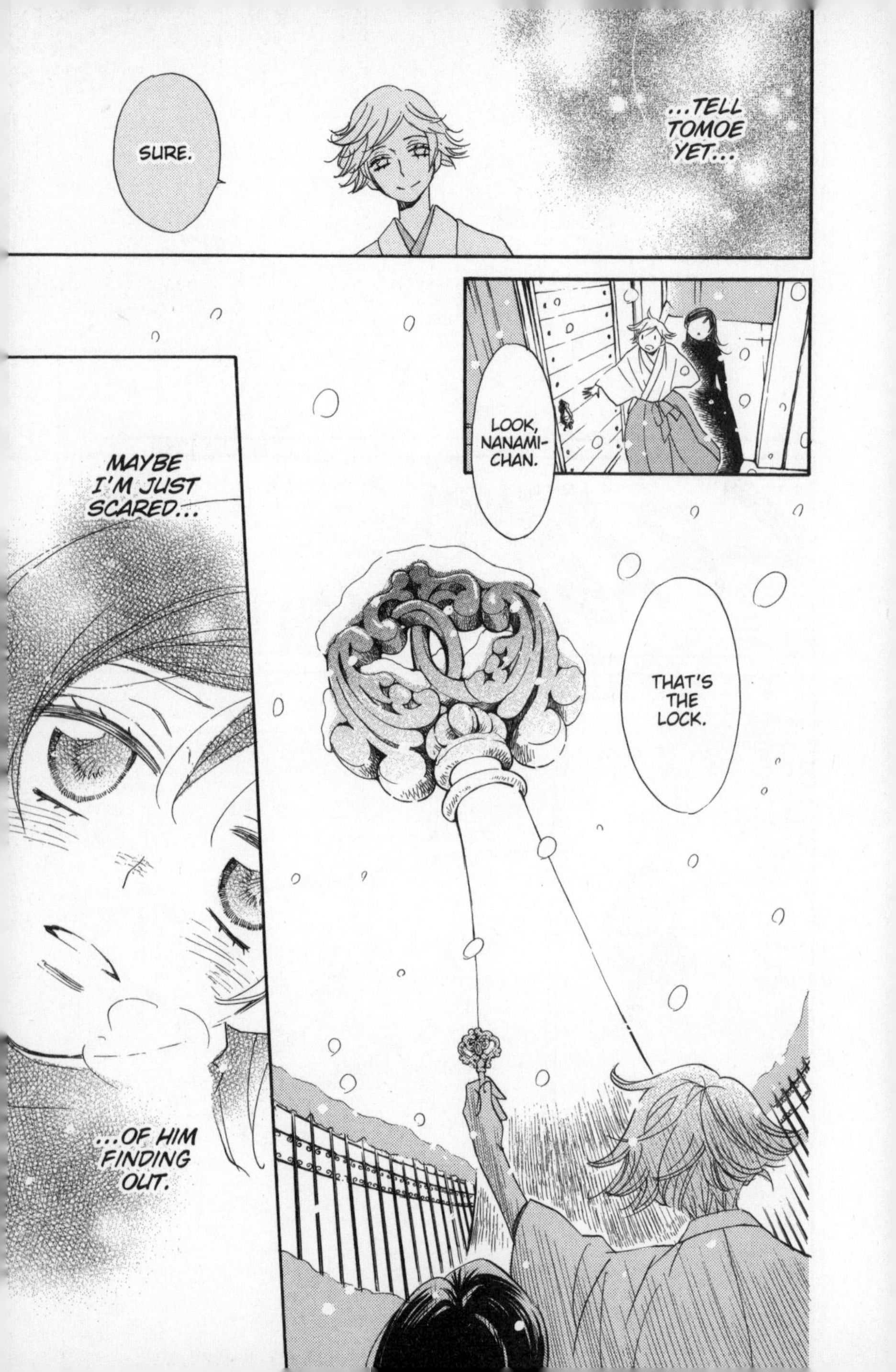
...TELL TOMOE YET...
SURE.
LOOK, NANAMI-CHAN.
THAT'S THE LOCK.
MAYBE I'M JUST SCARED...
...OF HIM FINDING OUT.

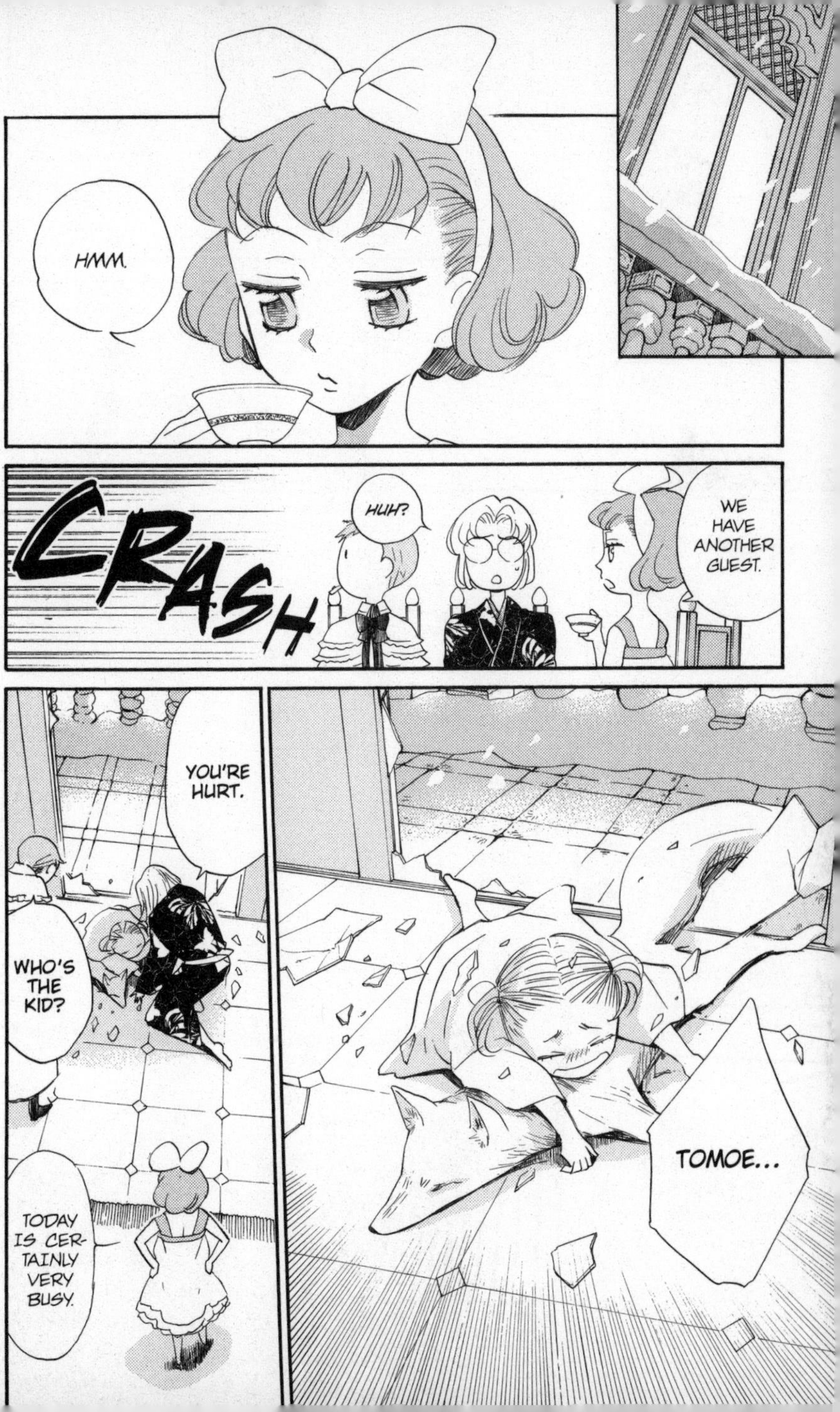
HMM.
WE HAVE ANOTHER GUEST.
HUH?
CRASH
TOMOE...
YOU'RE HURT.
WHO'S THE KID?
TODAY IS CER-TAINLY VERY BUSY.

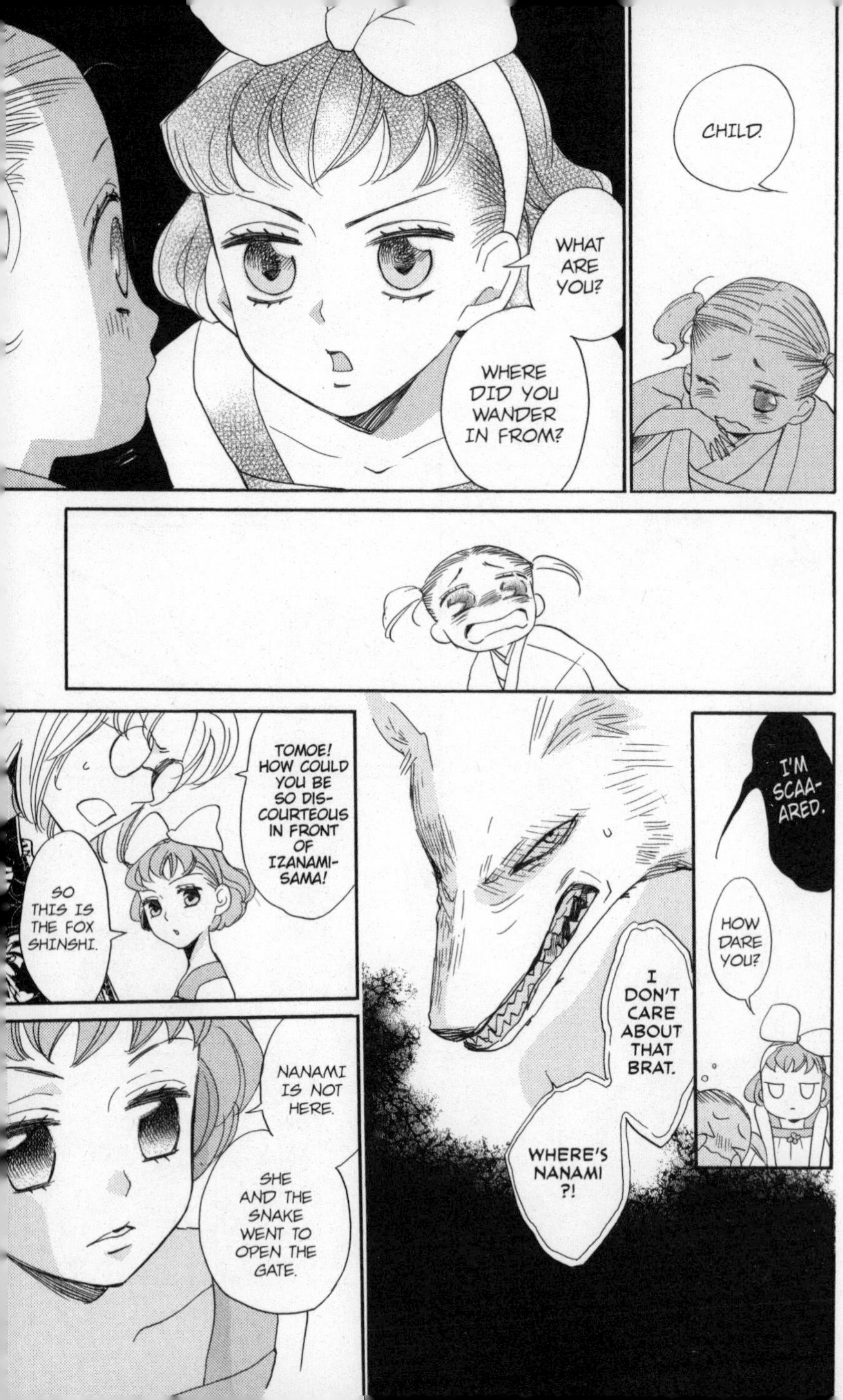
CHILD.
WHAT ARE YOU?
WHERE DID YOU WANDER IN FROM?
I'M SCAA-ARED.
HOW DARE YOU?
I DON'T CARE ABOUT THAT BRAT.
WHERE'S NANAMI ?!
TOMOE! HOW COULD YOU BE SO DIS-COURTEOUS IN FRONT OF IZANAMI-SAMA!
SO THIS IS THE FOX SHINSHI.
NANAMI IS NOT HERE.
SHE AND THE SNAKE WENT TO OPEN THE GATE.

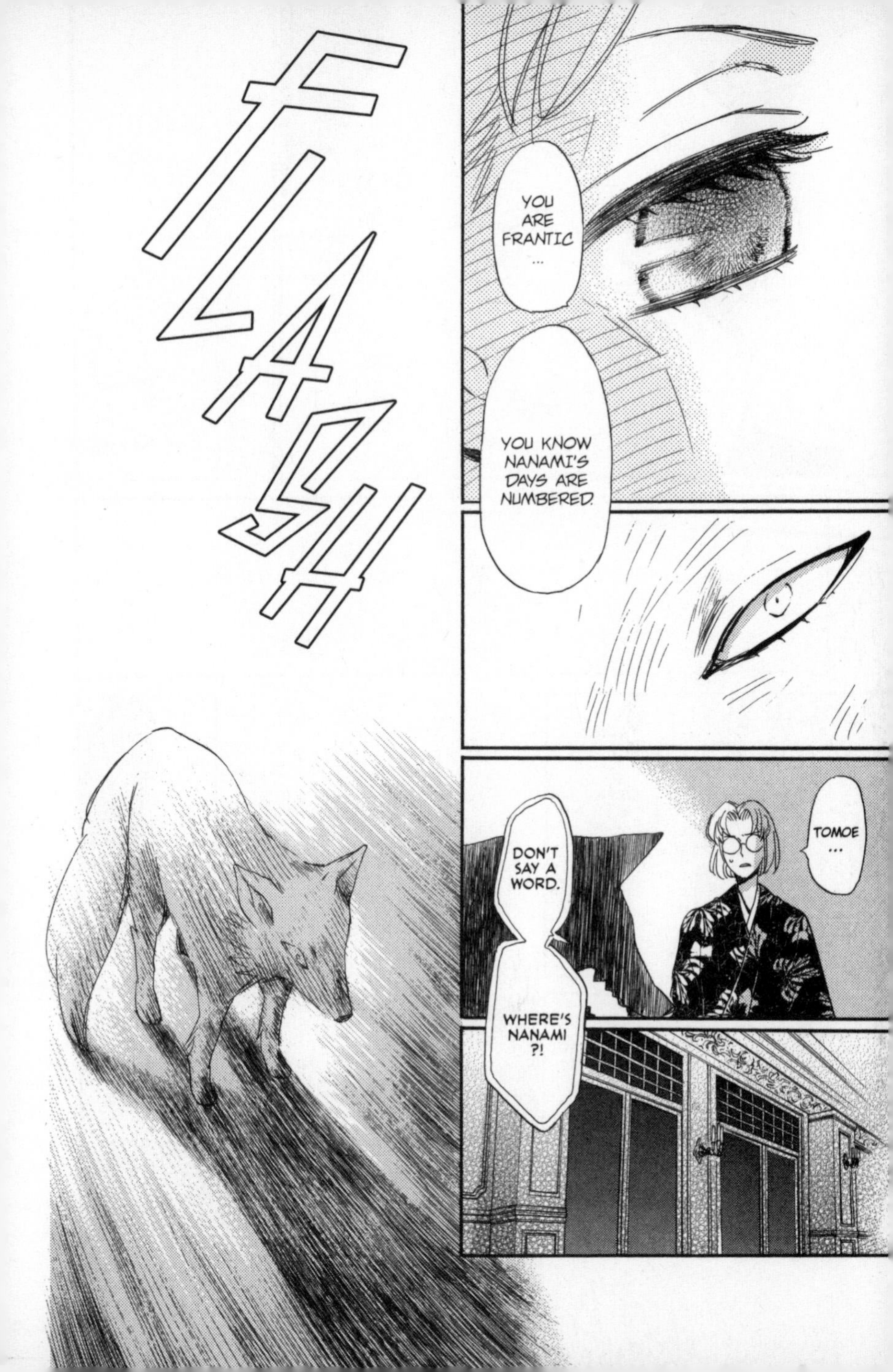
YOU ARE FRANTIC ...
YOU KNOW NANAMI'S DAYS ARE NUMBERED.
TOMOE ...
DON'T SAY A WORD.
WHERE'S NANAMI ?!
FLASH

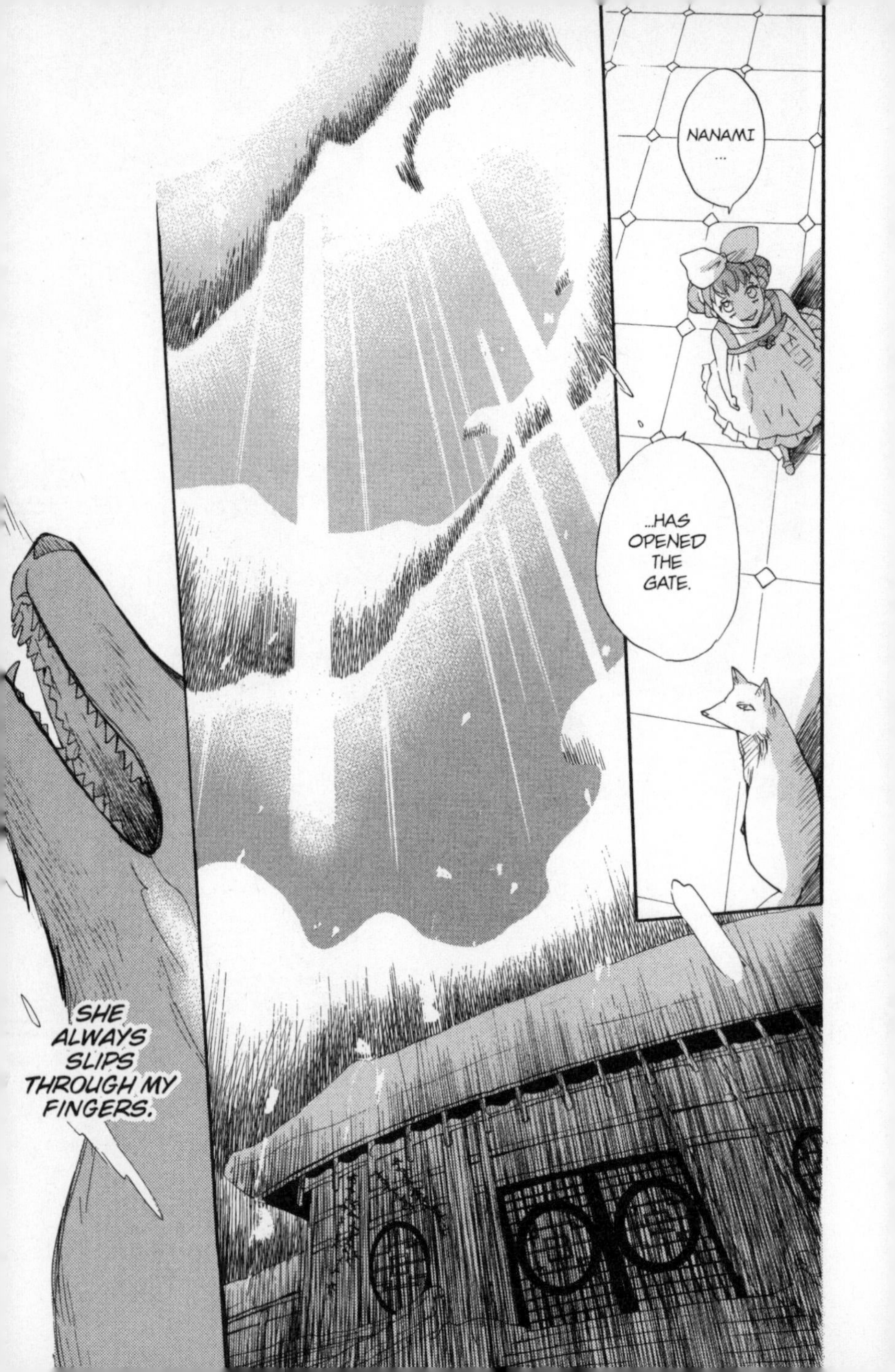
NANAMI ...
...HAS OPENED THE GATE.
SHE ALWAYS SLIPS THROUGH MY FINGERS.

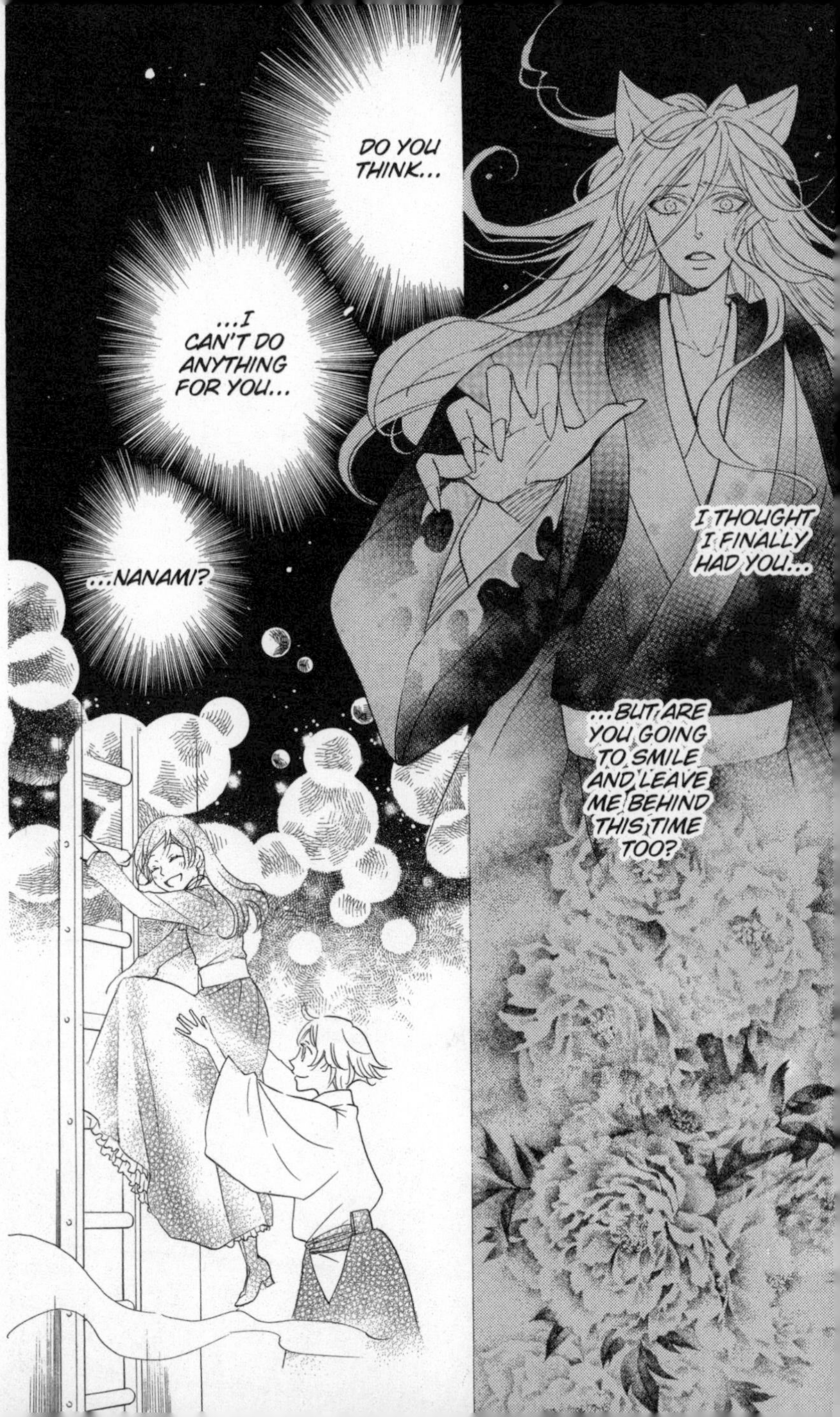
I THOUGHT I FINALLY HAD YOU...
...BUT ARE YOU GOING TO SMILE AND LEAVE ME BEHIND THIS TIME TOO?
DO YOU THINK...
...I CAN'T DO ANYTHING FOR YOU...
...NANAMI?

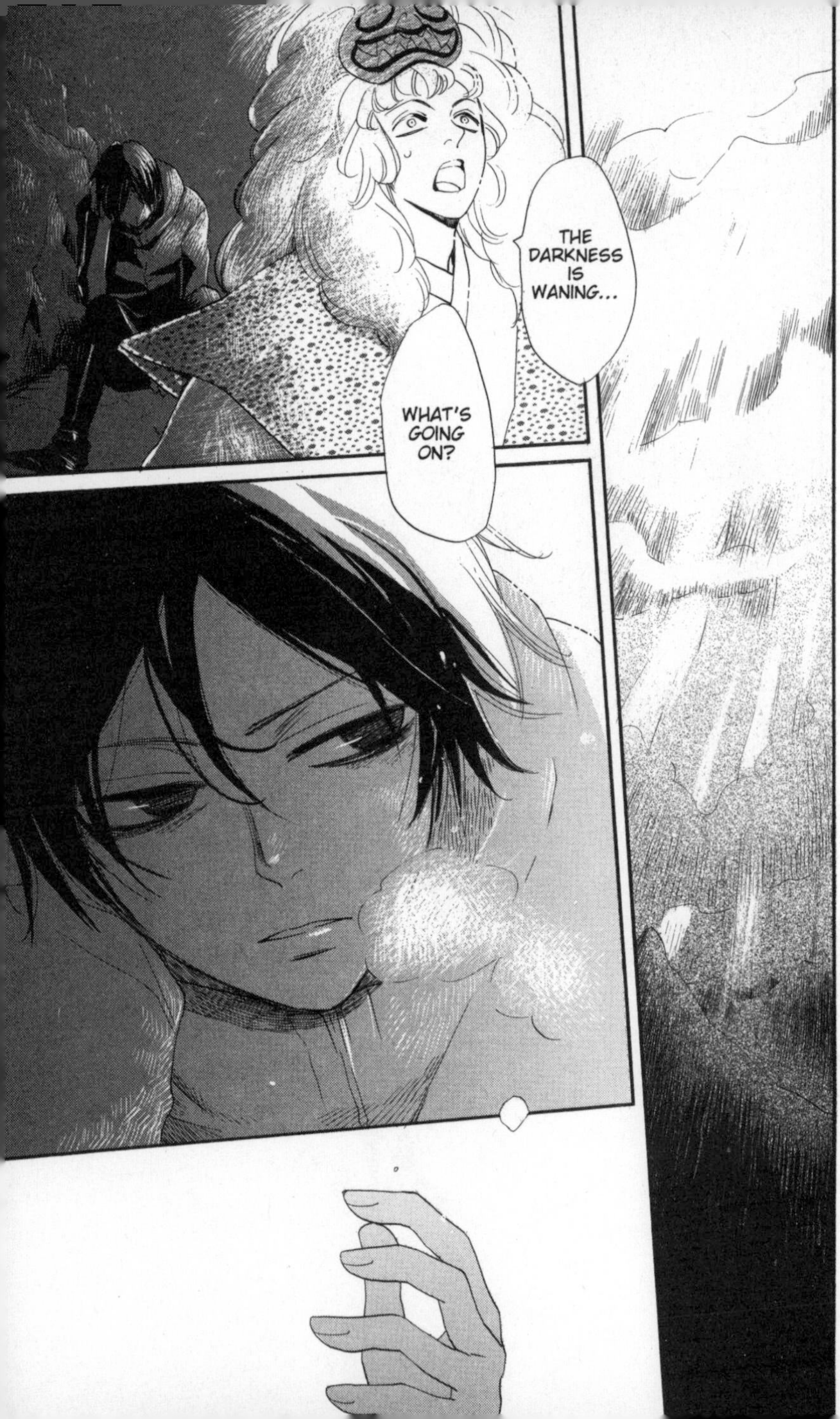
THE DARKNESS IS WANING...
WHAT'S GOING ON?

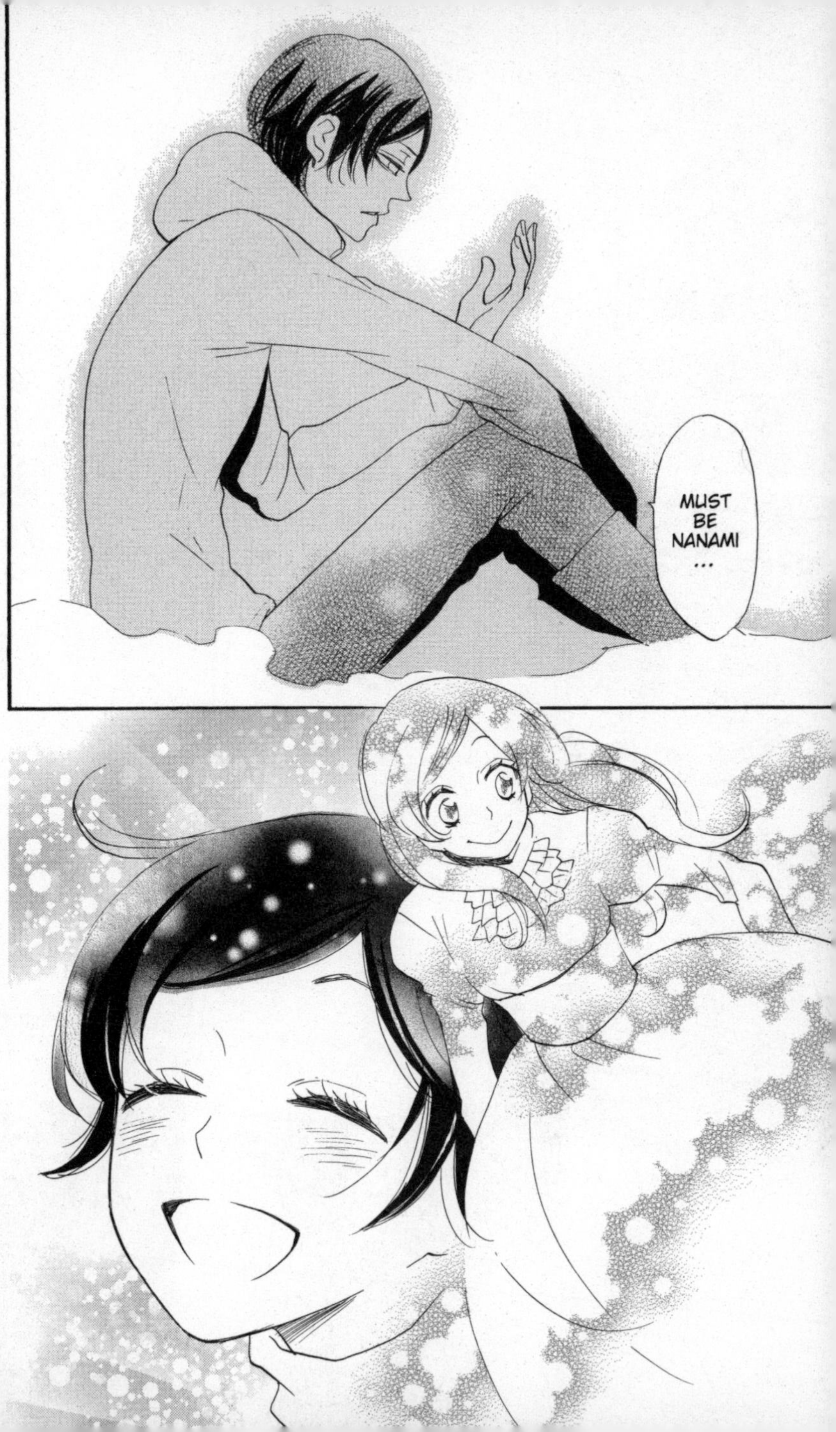
MUST BE NANAMI ...

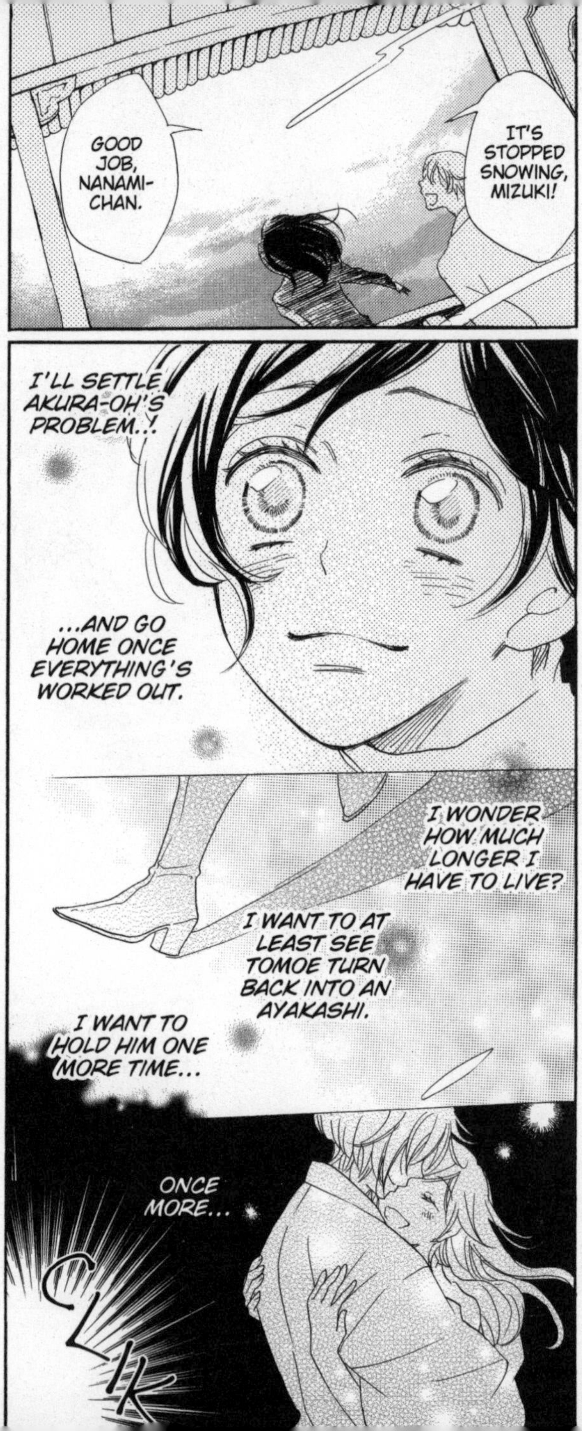
IT'S STOPPED SNOWING, MIZUKI!
GOOD JOB, NANAMI-CHAN.
I'LL SETTLE AKURA-OH'S PROBLEM..!
...AND GO HOME ONCE EVERYTHING'S WORKED OUT.
I WONDER HOW MUCH LONGER I HAVE TO LIVE?
I WANT TO AT LEAST SEE TOMOE TURN BACK INTO AN AYAKASHI.
I WANT TO HOLD HIM ONE MORE TIME...
ONCE MORE...
CLIK

Thank you for reading this far!

If you have any comments and thoughts about volume 22, let me know! ✿

✿ ✿ ✿ ✿ ✿

The address is...

Julietta Suzuki
c/o Shojo Beat
VIZ Media, LLC
P.O. Box 77010
San Francisco, CA
94107

✿ ✿ ✿ ✿ ✿

I'll be waiting ♡

I blog and tweet, so take a look when you have time. ♡

Now then. I hope we'll be able to meet again in the next volume...!

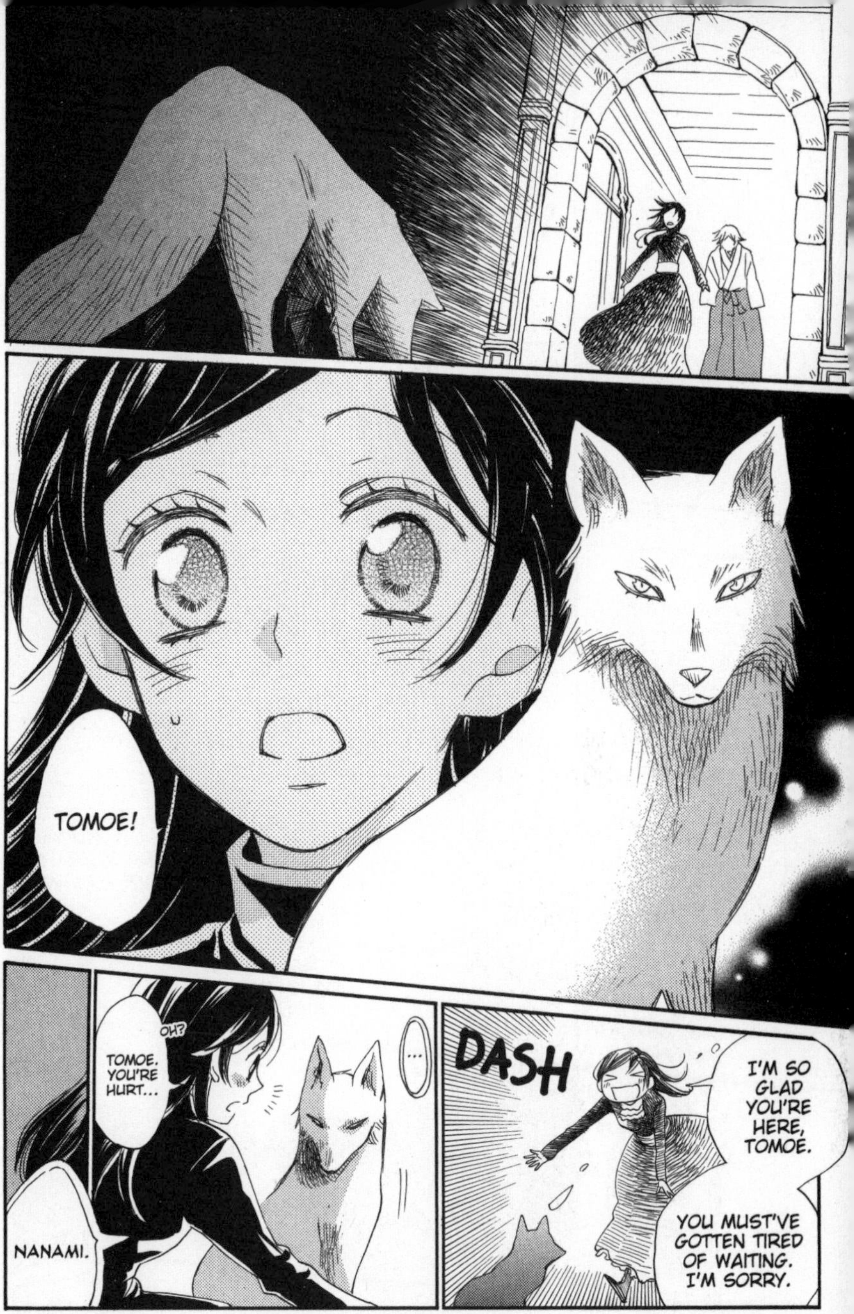
TOMOE!
I'M SO GLAD YOU'RE HERE, TOMOE.
DASH
YOU MUST'VE GOTTEN TIRED OF WAITING. I'M SORRY.
...
OH?
TOMOE. YOU'RE HURT...
NANAMI.

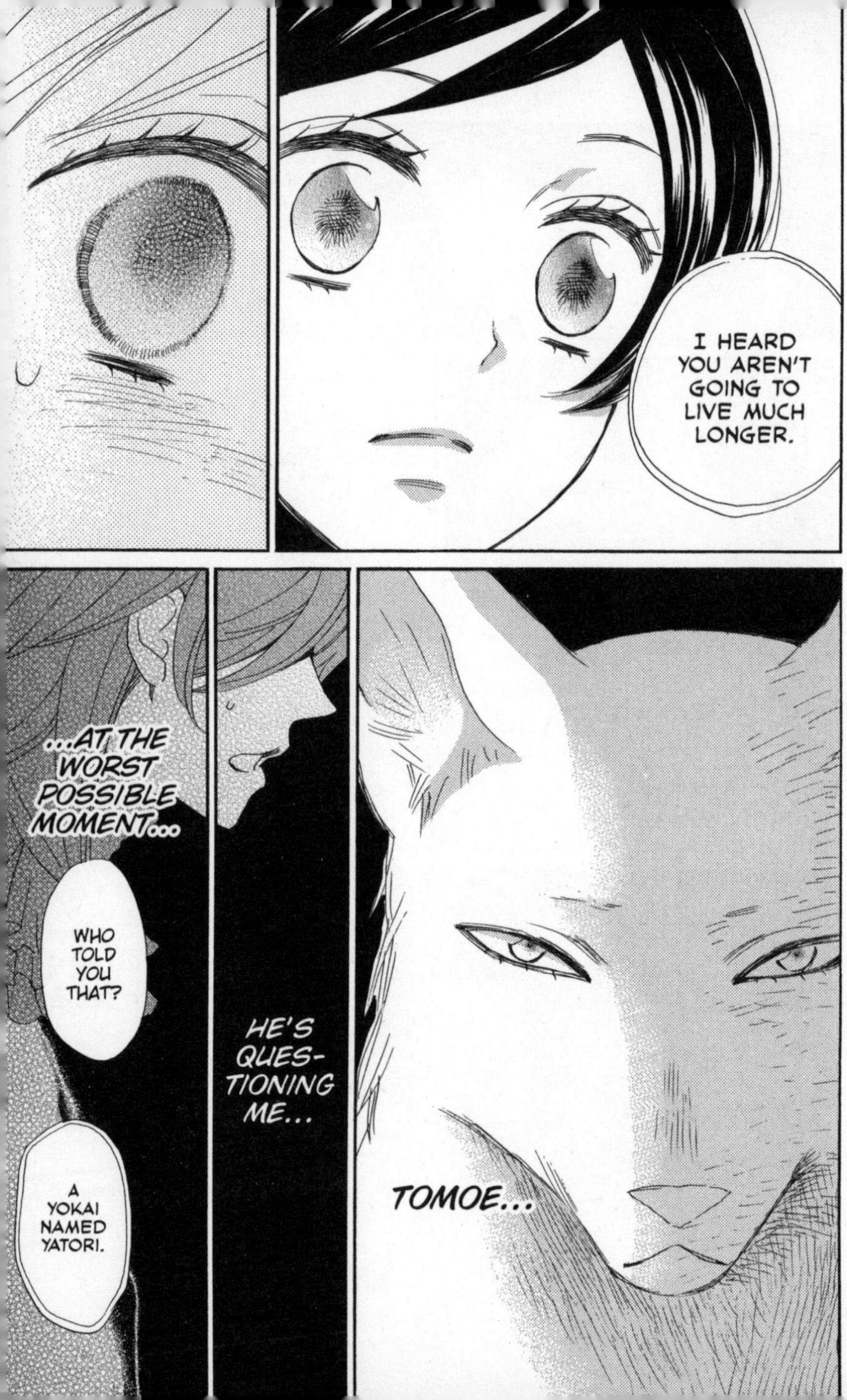
I HEARD YOU AREN'T GOING TO LIVE MUCH LONGER.
TOMOE...
HE'S QUES-TIONING ME...
...AT THE WORST POSSIBLE MOMENT...
WHO TOLD YOU THAT?
A YOKAI NAMED YATORI.

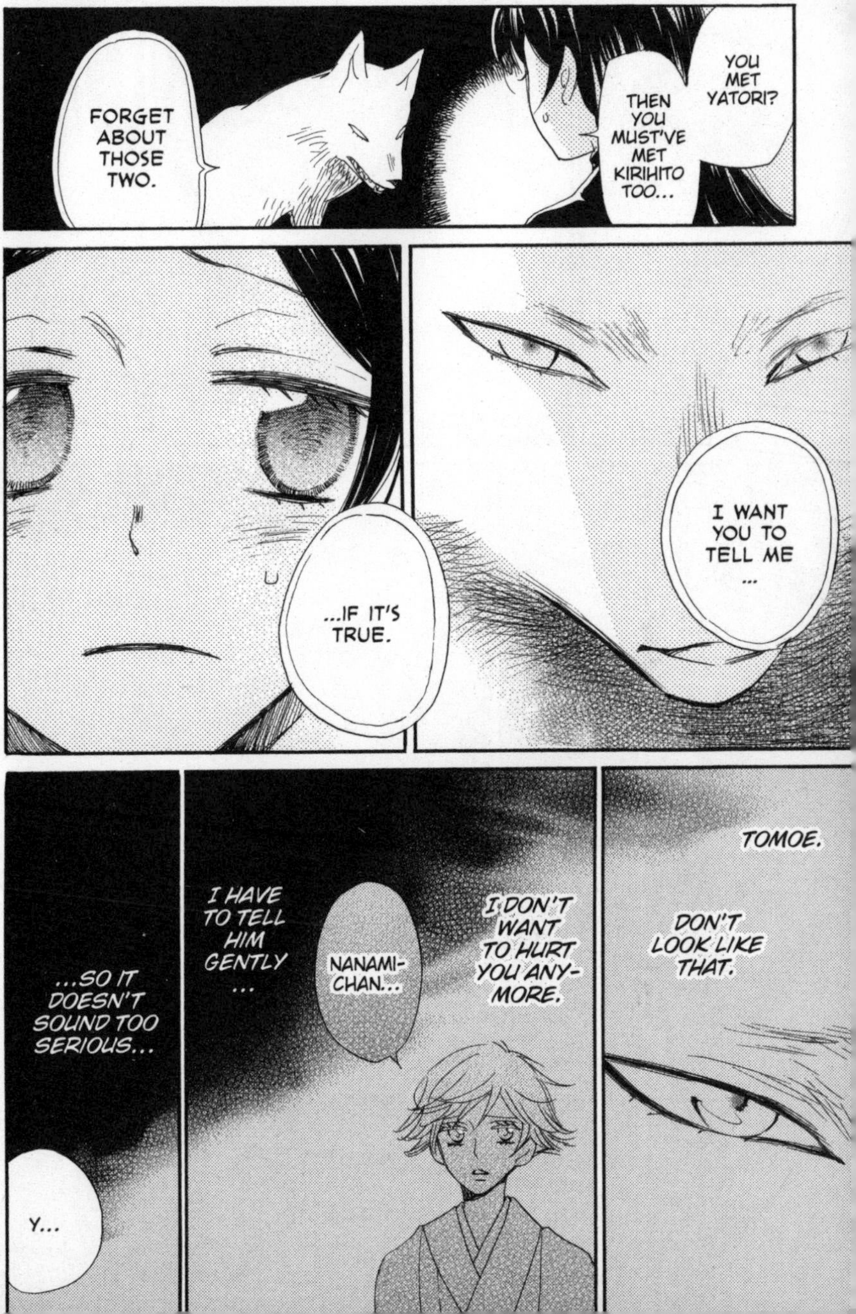
YOU MET YATORI?
THEN YOU MUST'VE MET KIRIHITO TOO...
FORGET ABOUT THOSE TWO.
I WANT YOU TO TELL ME ...
...IF IT'S TRUE.
TOMOE.
DON'T LOOK LIKE THAT.
I DON'T WANT TO HURT YOU ANY-MORE.
NANAMI-CHAN...
I HAVE TO TELL HIM GENTLY ...
...SO IT DOESN'T SOUND TOO SERIOUS...
Y...

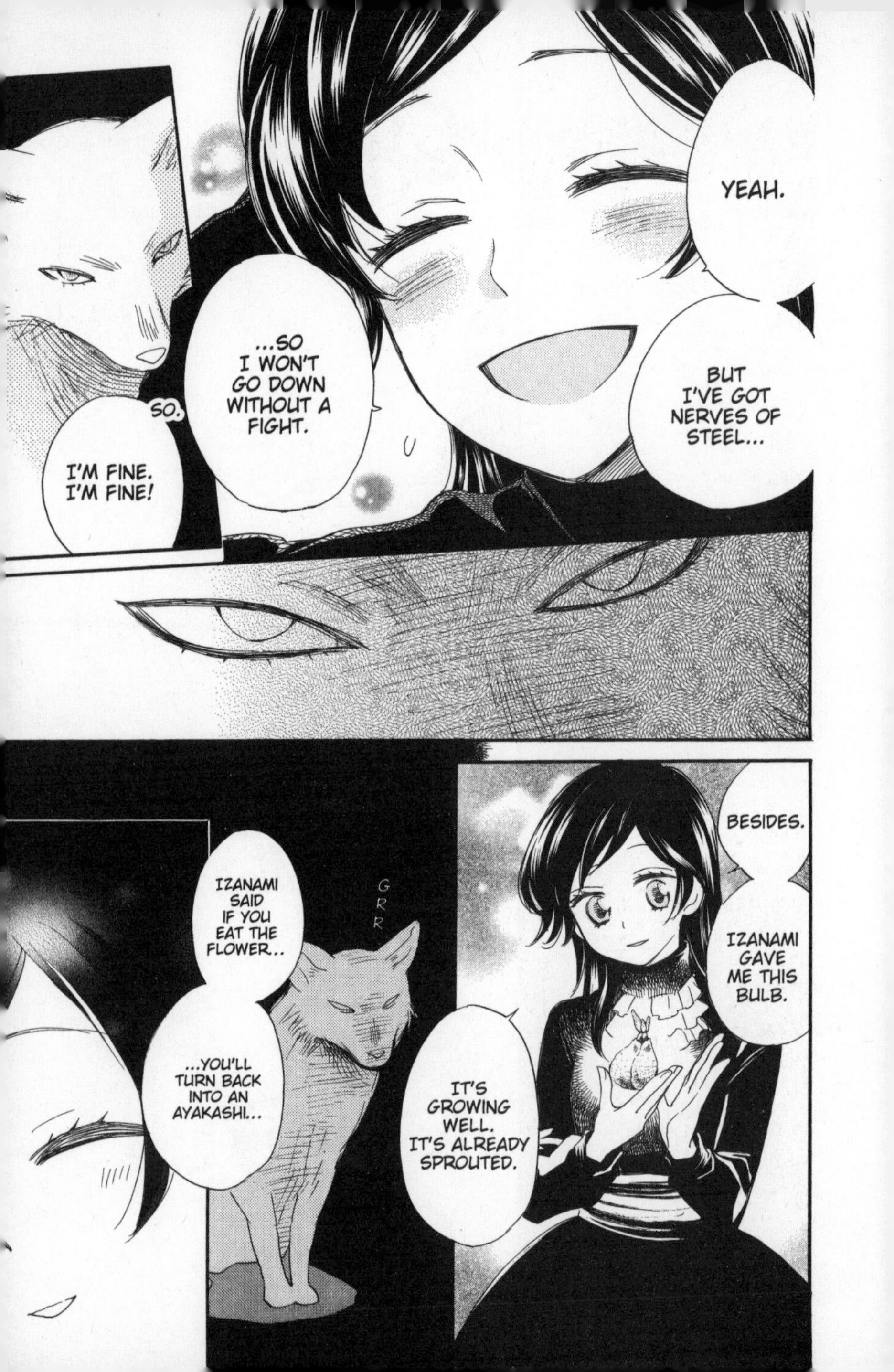
YEAH.
BUT I'VE GOT NERVES OF STEEL...
...SO I WON'T GO DOWN WITHOUT A FIGHT.
SO.
I'M FINE. I'M FINE!
BESIDES.
IZANAMI GAVE ME THIS BULB.
IT'S GROWING WELL. IT'S ALREADY SPROUTED.
GRR
IZANAMI SAID IF YOU EAT THE FLOWER...
...YOU'LL TURN BACK INTO AN AYAKASHI...

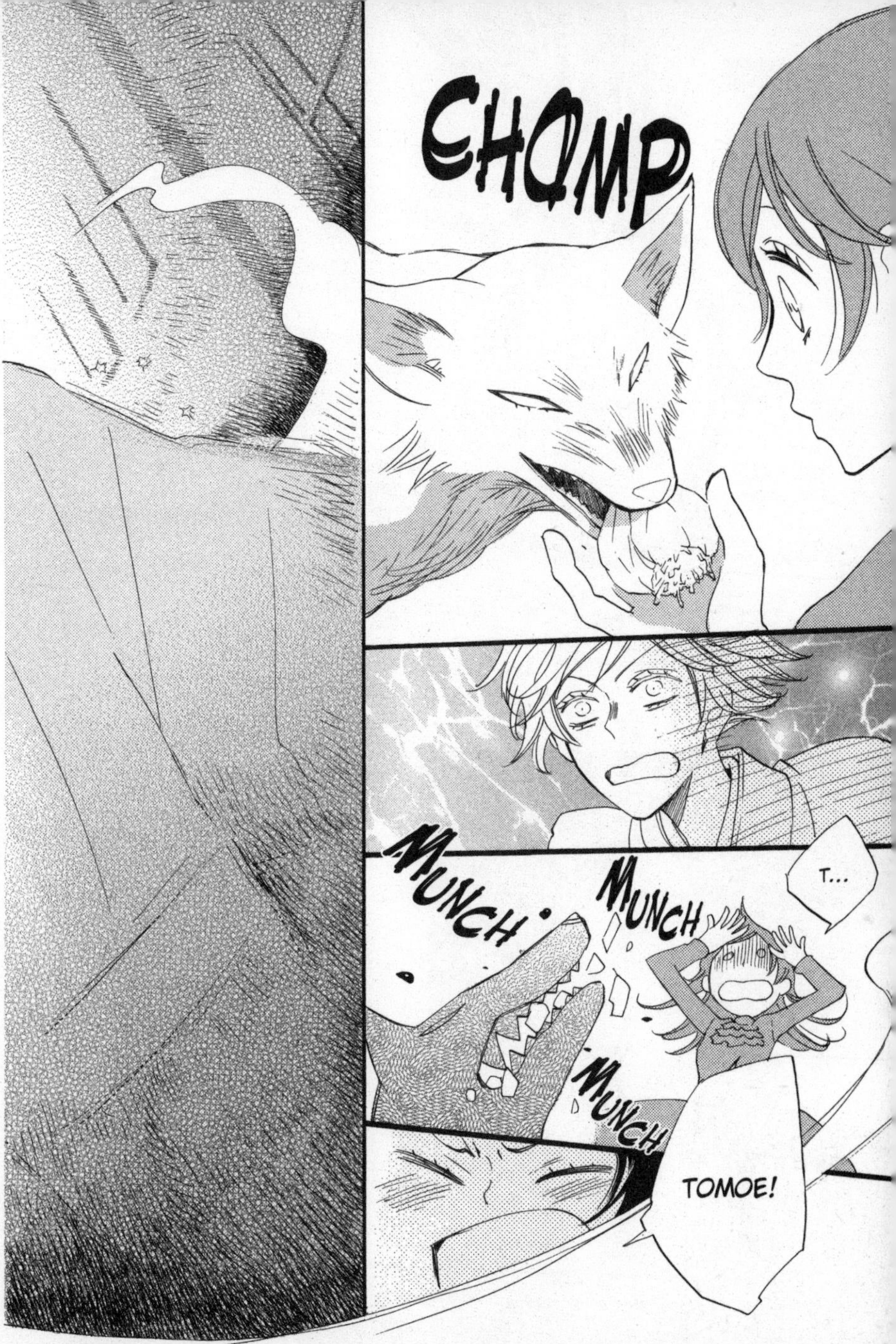
CHOMP
T...
MUNCH
MUNCH
MUNCH
TOMOE!

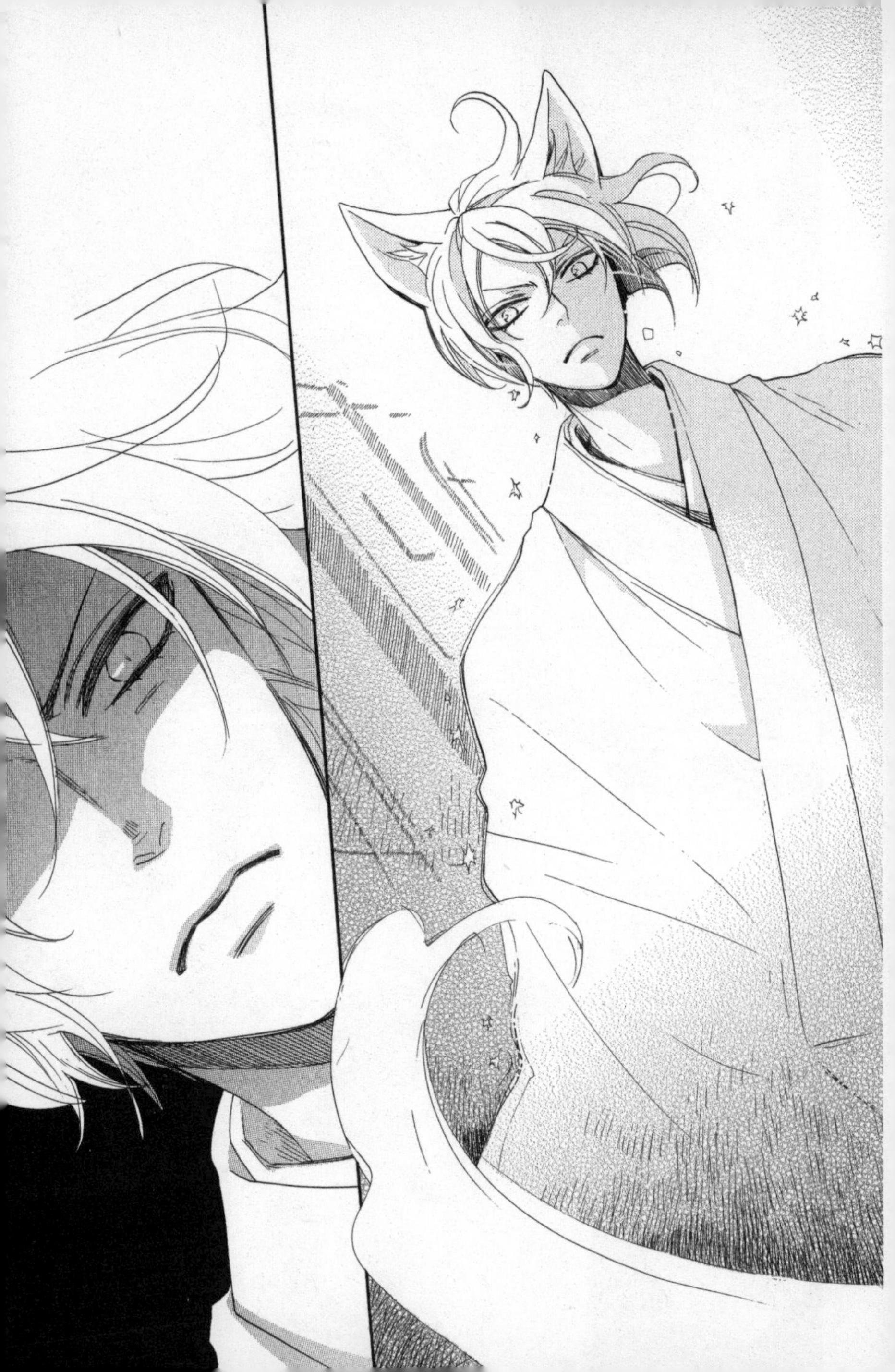

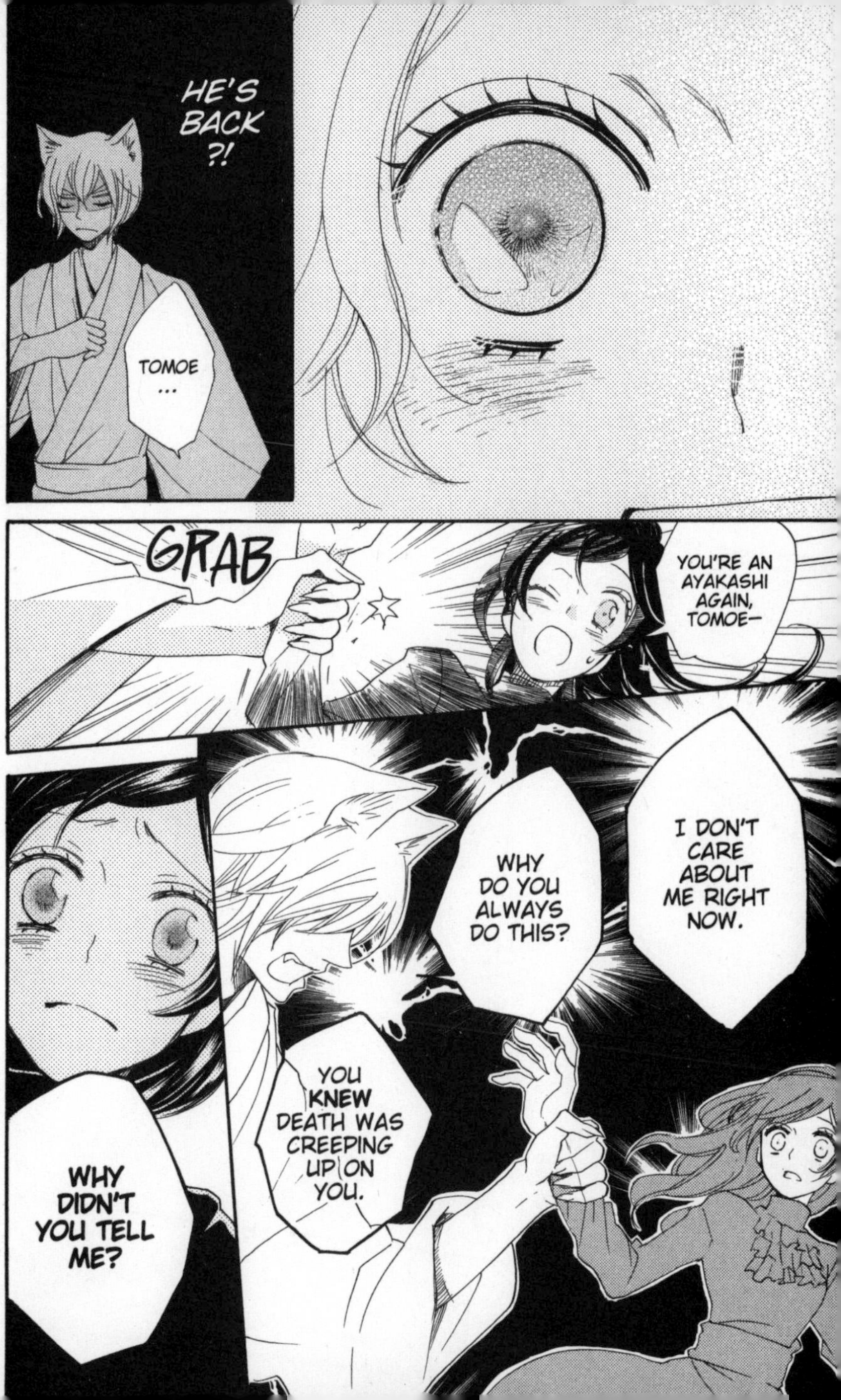
HE'S BACK ?!
TOMOE ...
YOU'RE AN AYAKASHI AGAIN, TOMOE—
GRAB
I DON'T CARE ABOUT ME RIGHT NOW.
WHY DO YOU ALWAYS DO THIS?
YOU KNEW DEATH WAS CREEPING UP ON YOU.
WHY DIDN'T YOU TELL ME?

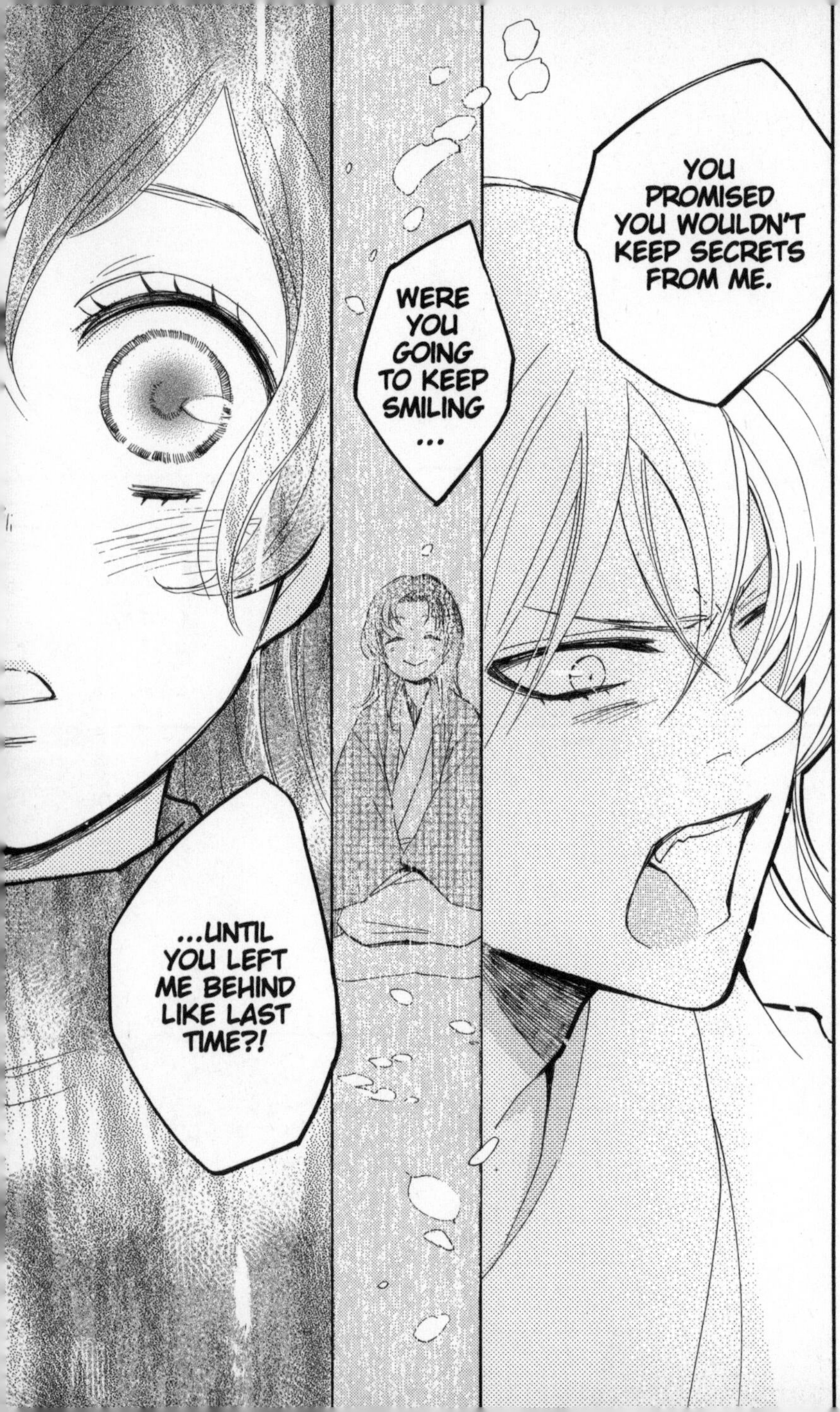
YOU PROMISED YOU WOULDN'T KEEP SECRETS FROM ME.
WERE YOU GOING TO KEEP SMILING ...
...UNTIL YOU LEFT ME BEHIND LIKE LAST TIME?!

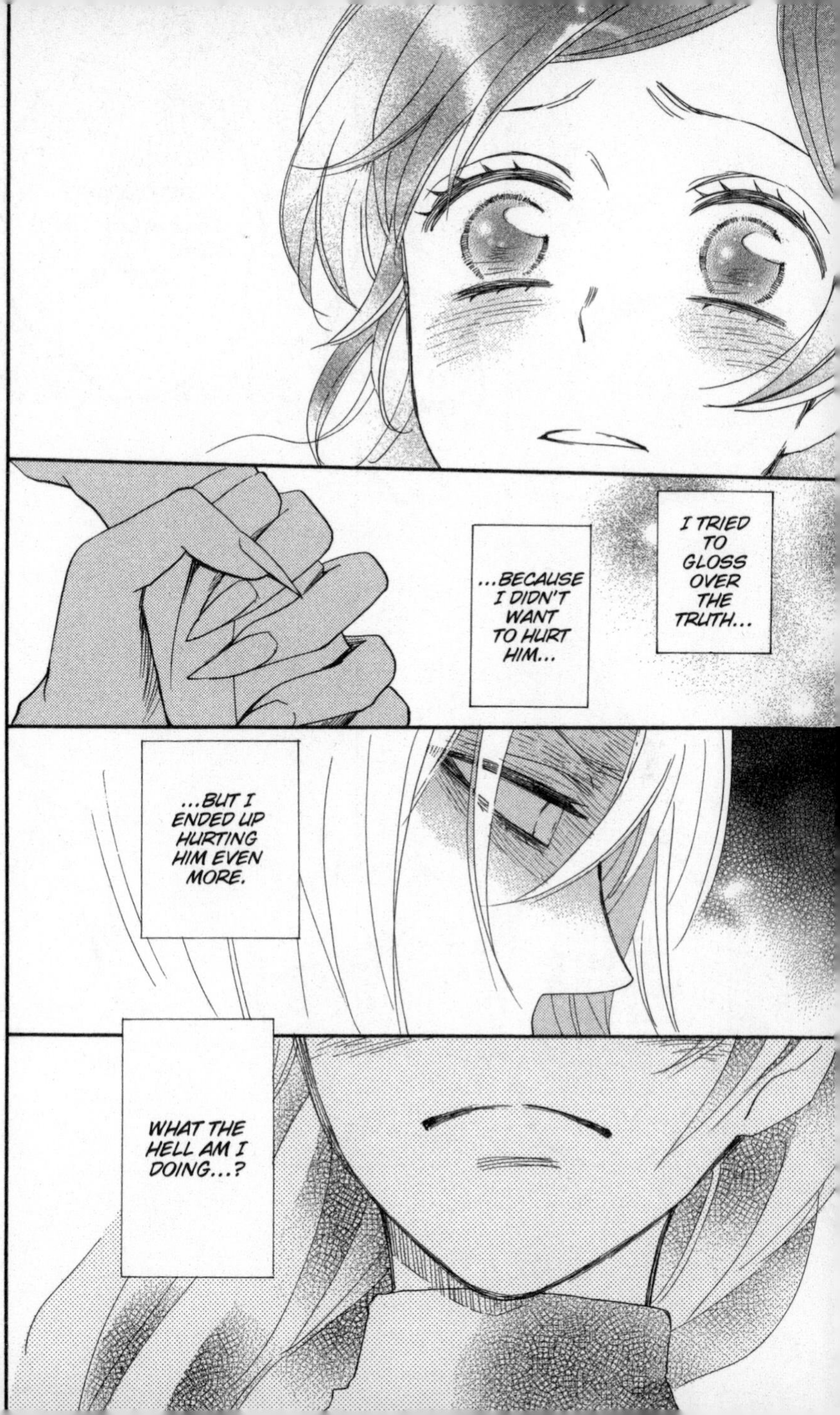
I TRIED TO GLOSS OVER THE TRUTH...
...BECAUSE I DIDN'T WANT TO HURT HIM...
...BUT I ENDED UP HURTING HIM EVEN MORE.
WHAT THE HELL AM I DOING...?

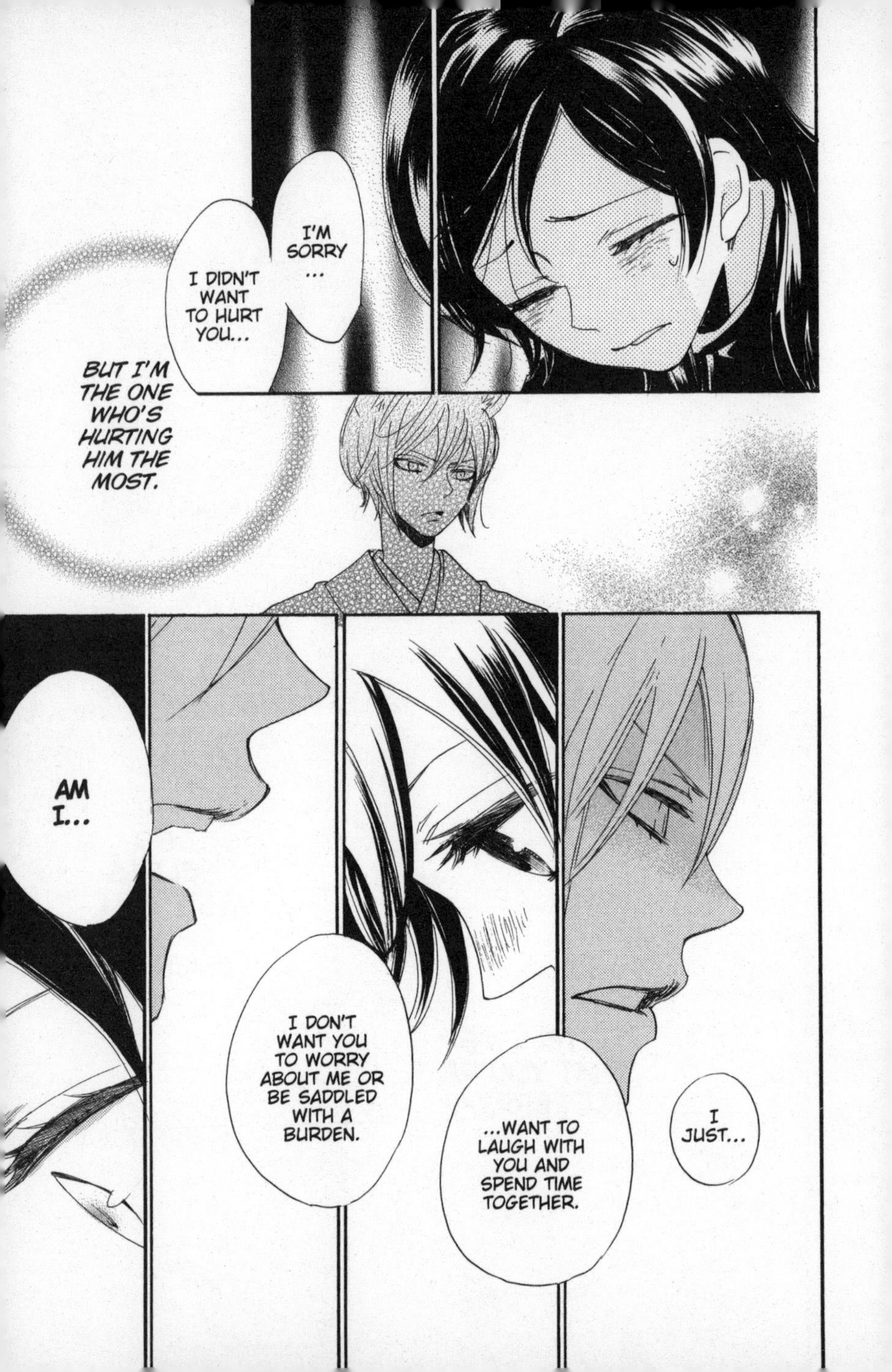
I'M SORRY ...
I DIDN'T WANT TO HURT YOU...
BUT I'M THE ONE WHO'S HURTING HIM THE MOST.
I JUST...
...WANT TO LAUGH WITH YOU AND SPEND TIME TOGETHER.
I DON'T WANT YOU TO WORRY ABOUT ME OR BE SADDLED WITH A BURDEN.
AM I...

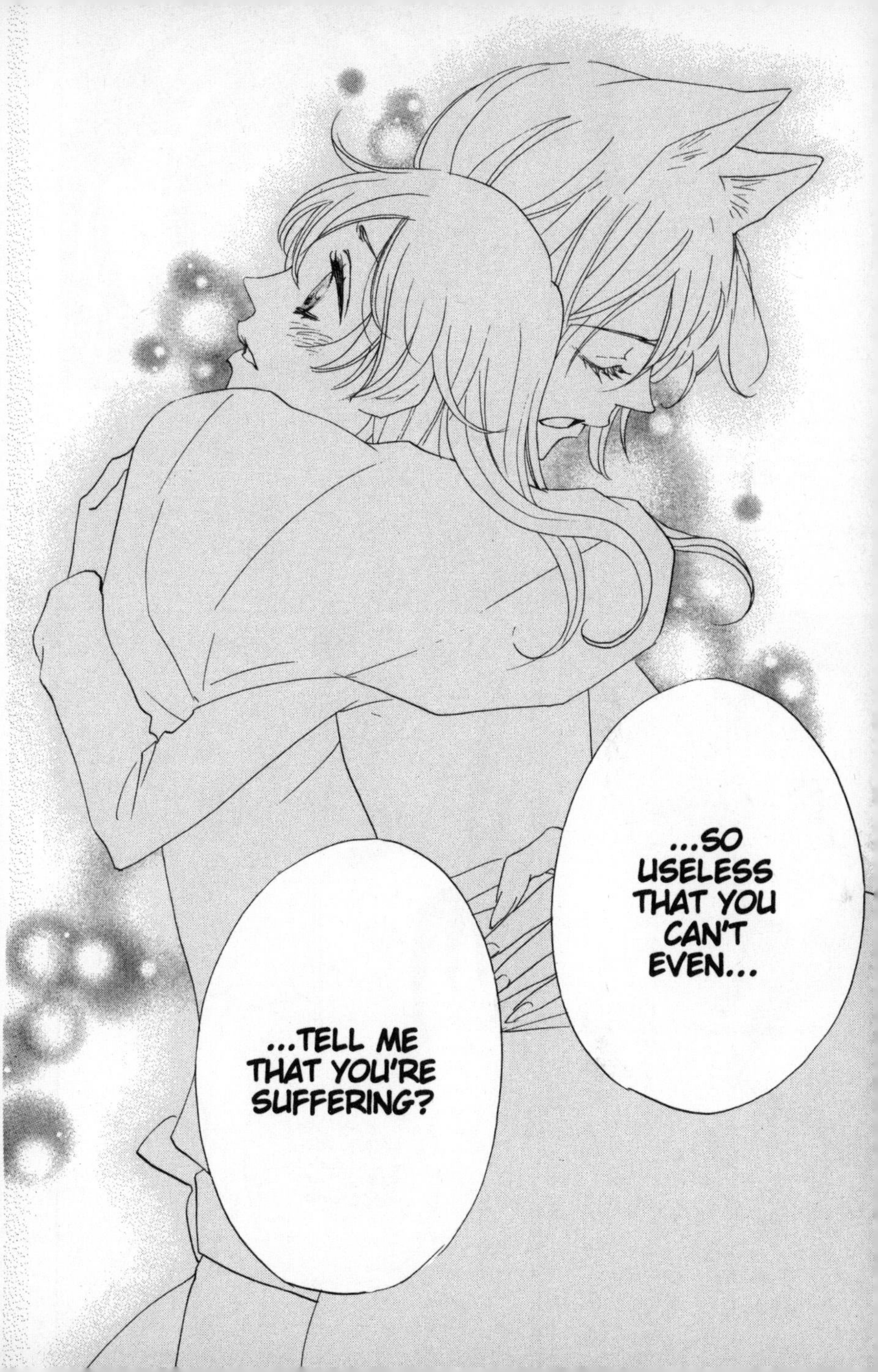
...SO USELESS THAT YOU CAN'T EVEN...
...TELL ME THAT YOU'RE SUFFERING?

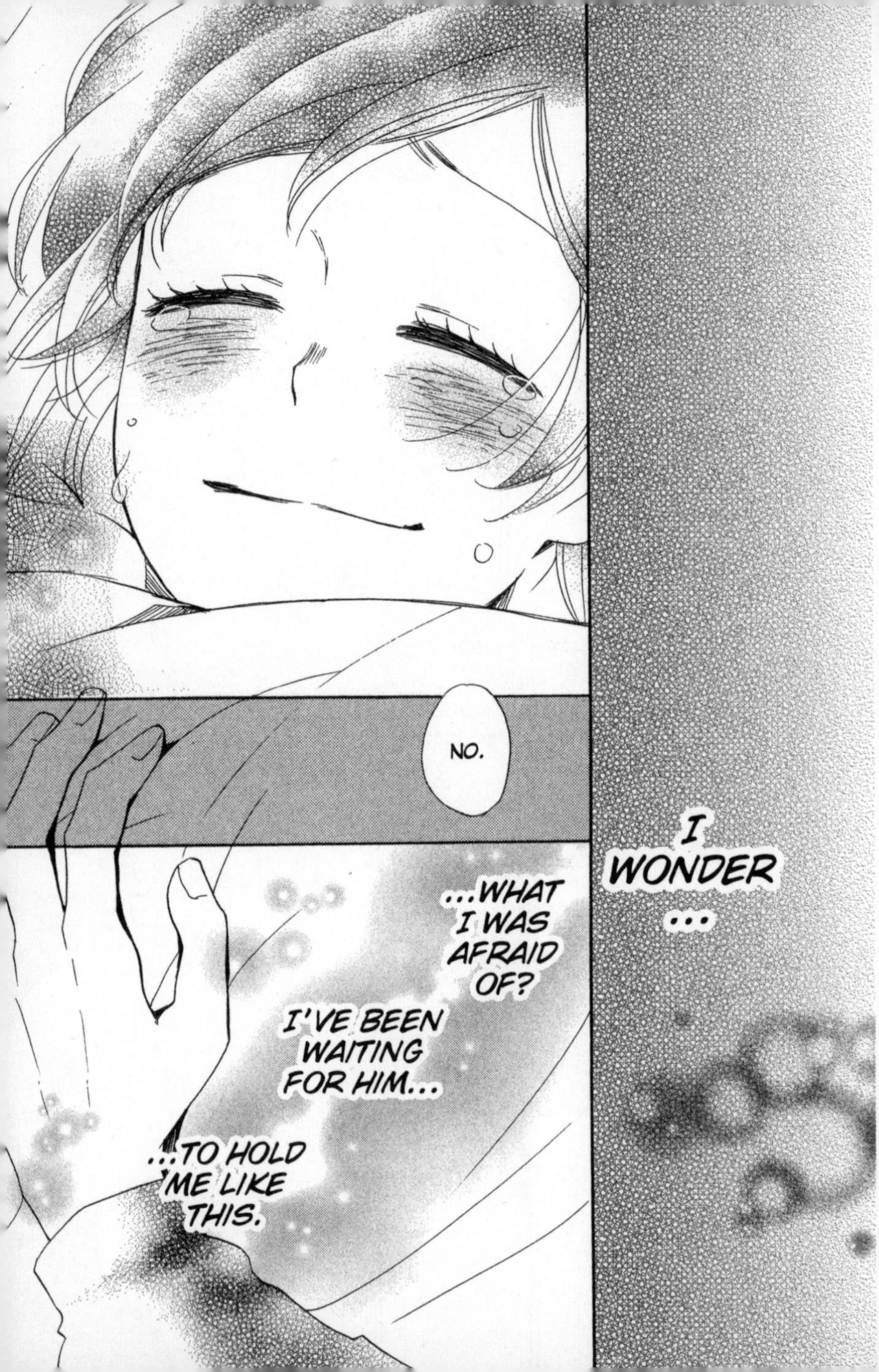
I WONDER...
NO.
...WHAT I WAS AFRAID OF?
I'VE BEEN WAITING FOR HIM...
...TO HOLD ME LIKE THIS.

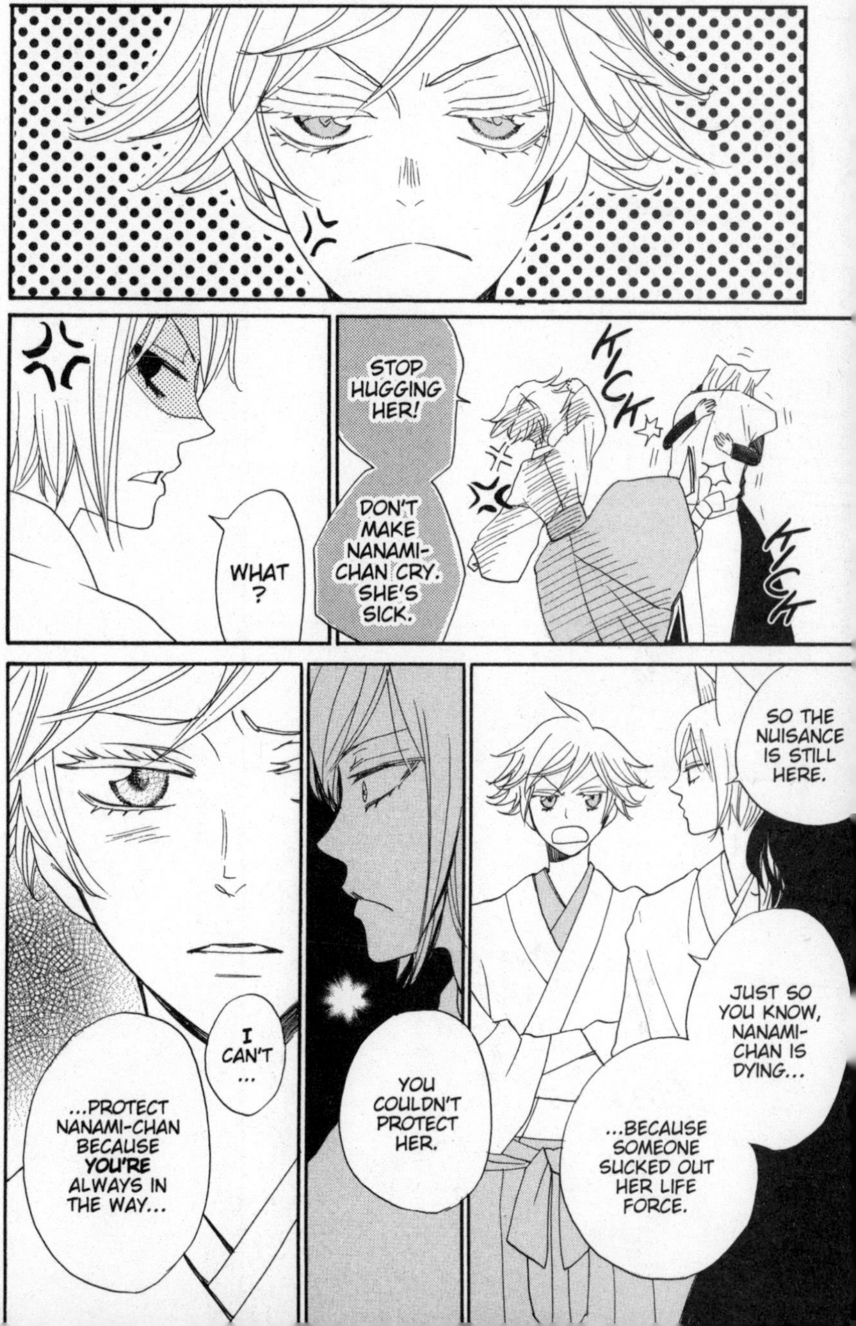
KICK
KICK
STOP HUGGING HER!
DON'T MAKE NANAMI-CHAN CRY. SHE'S SICK.
WHAT?
SO THE NUISANCE IS STILL HERE.
JUST SO YOU KNOW, NANAMI-CHAN IS DYING...
...BECAUSE SOMEONE SUCKED OUT HER LIFE FORCE.
YOU COULDN'T PROTECT HER.
I CAN'T...
...PROTECT NANAMI-CHAN BECAUSE **YOU'RE** ALWAYS IN THE WAY...

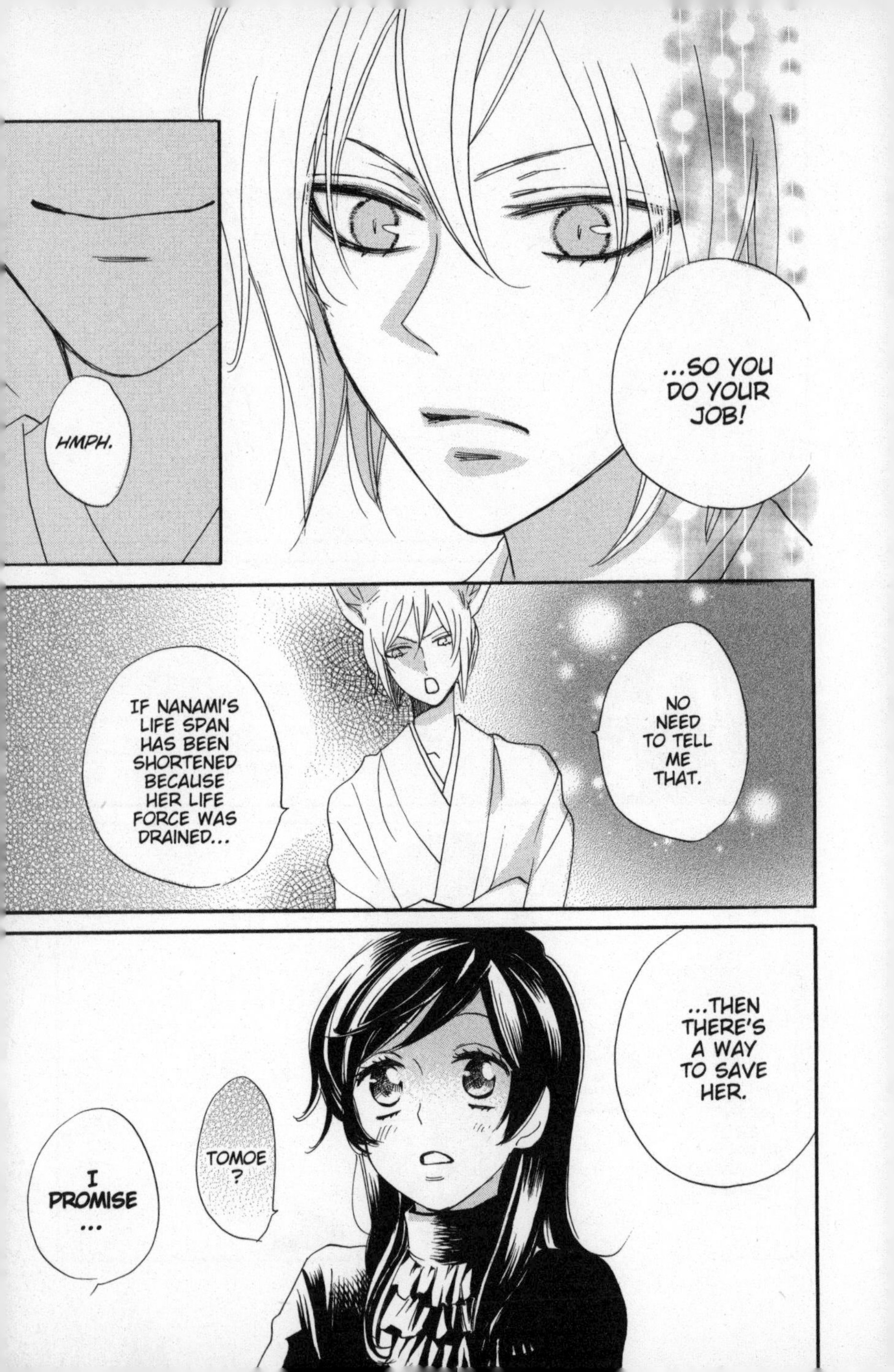
...SO YOU DO YOUR JOB!
HMPH.
NO NEED TO TELL ME THAT.
IF NANAMI'S LIFE SPAN HAS BEEN SHORTENED BECAUSE HER LIFE FORCE WAS DRAINED...
...THEN THERE'S A WAY TO SAVE HER.
TOMOE?
I PROMISE...

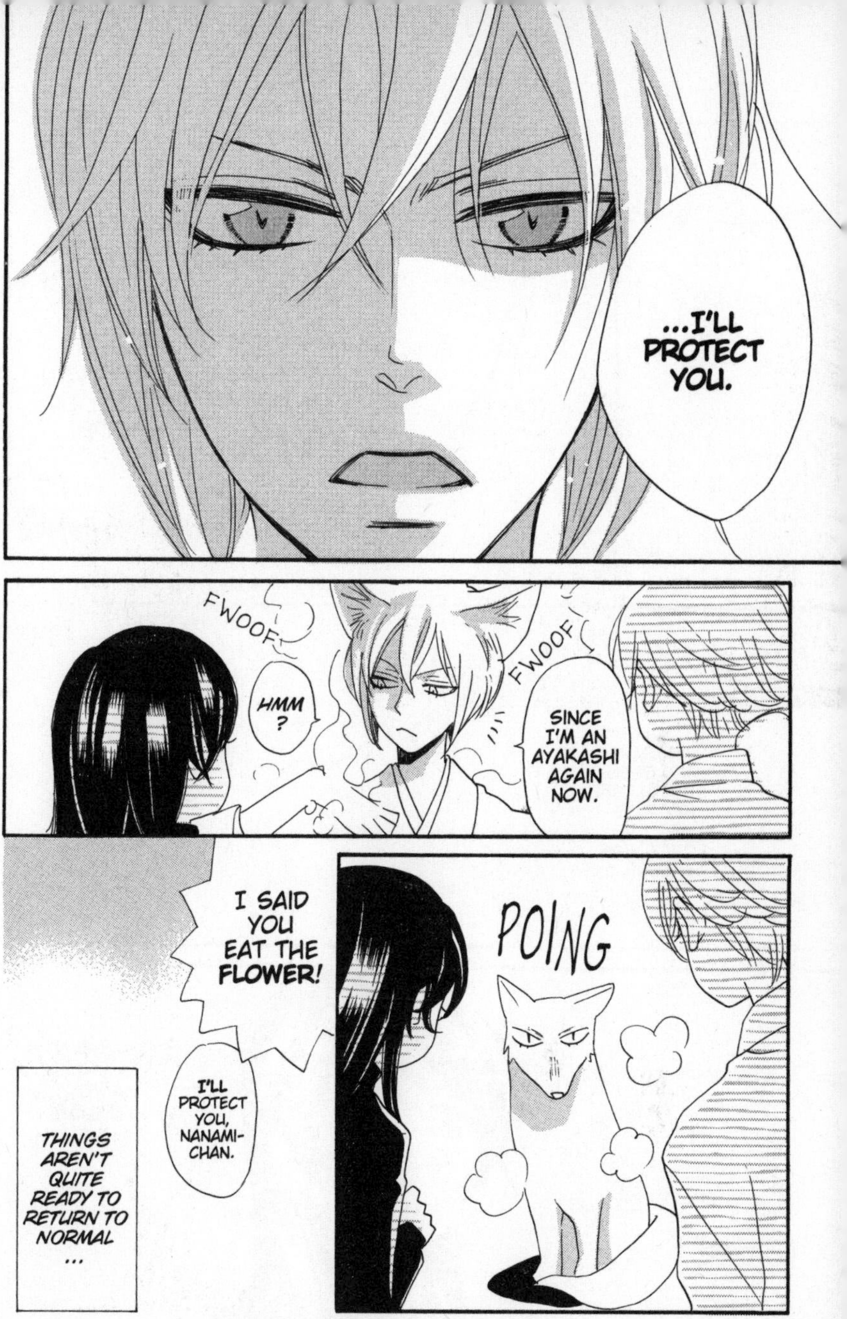
...I'LL PROTECT YOU.
FWOOF
SINCE I'M AN AYAKASHI AGAIN NOW.
FWOOF
HMM?
POING
I SAID YOU EAT THE FLOWER!
I'LL PROTECT YOU, NANAMI-CHAN.
THINGS AREN'T QUITE READY TO RETURN TO NORMAL ...

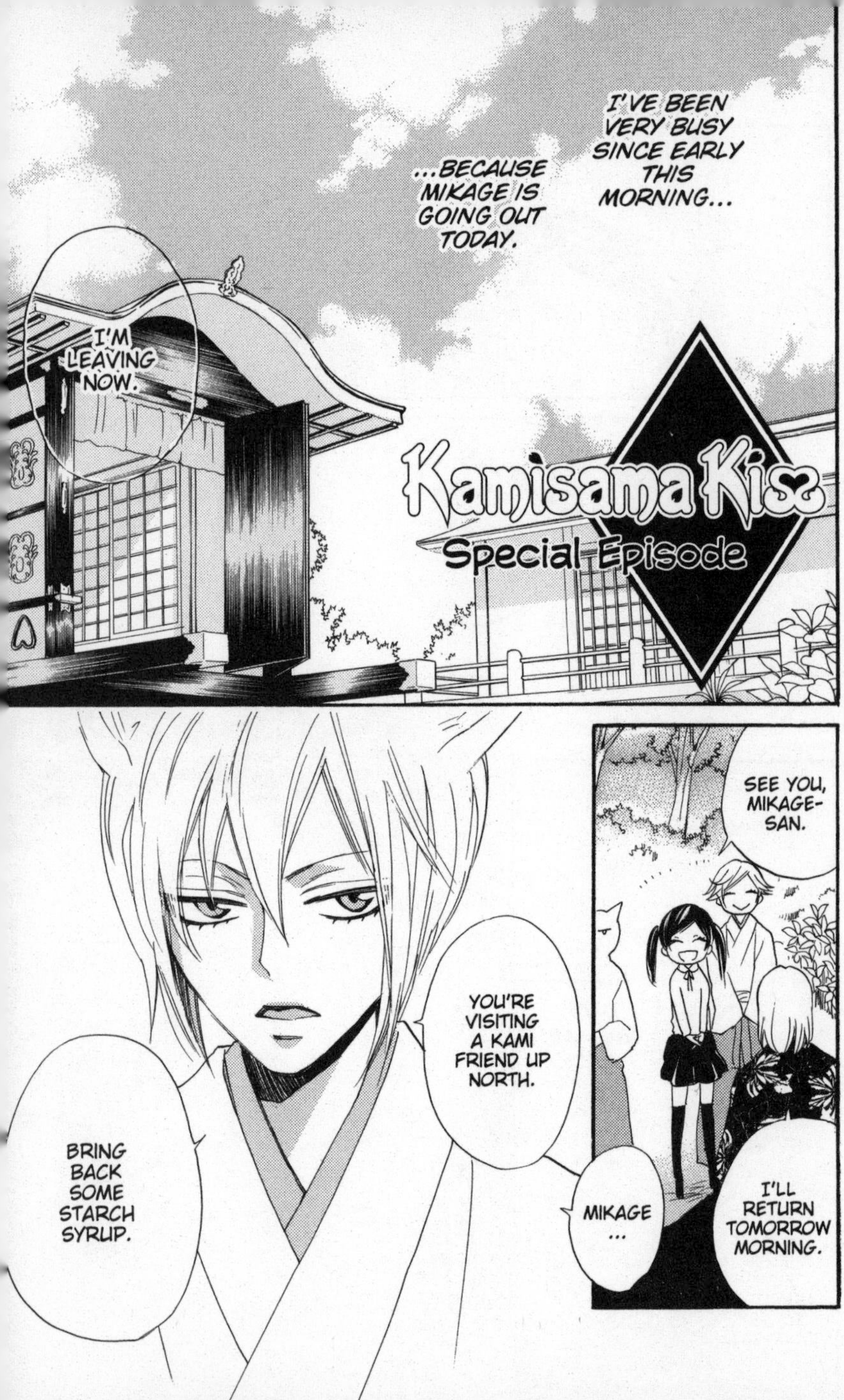
I'VE BEEN VERY BUSY SINCE EARLY THIS MORNING...
...BECAUSE MIKAGE IS GOING OUT TODAY.
Kamisama Kiss
Special Episode
I'M LEAVING NOW.
SEE YOU, MIKAGE-SAN.
I'LL RETURN TOMORROW MORNING.
YOU'RE VISITING A KAMI FRIEND UP NORTH.
MIKAGE ...
BRING BACK SOME STARCH SYRUP.

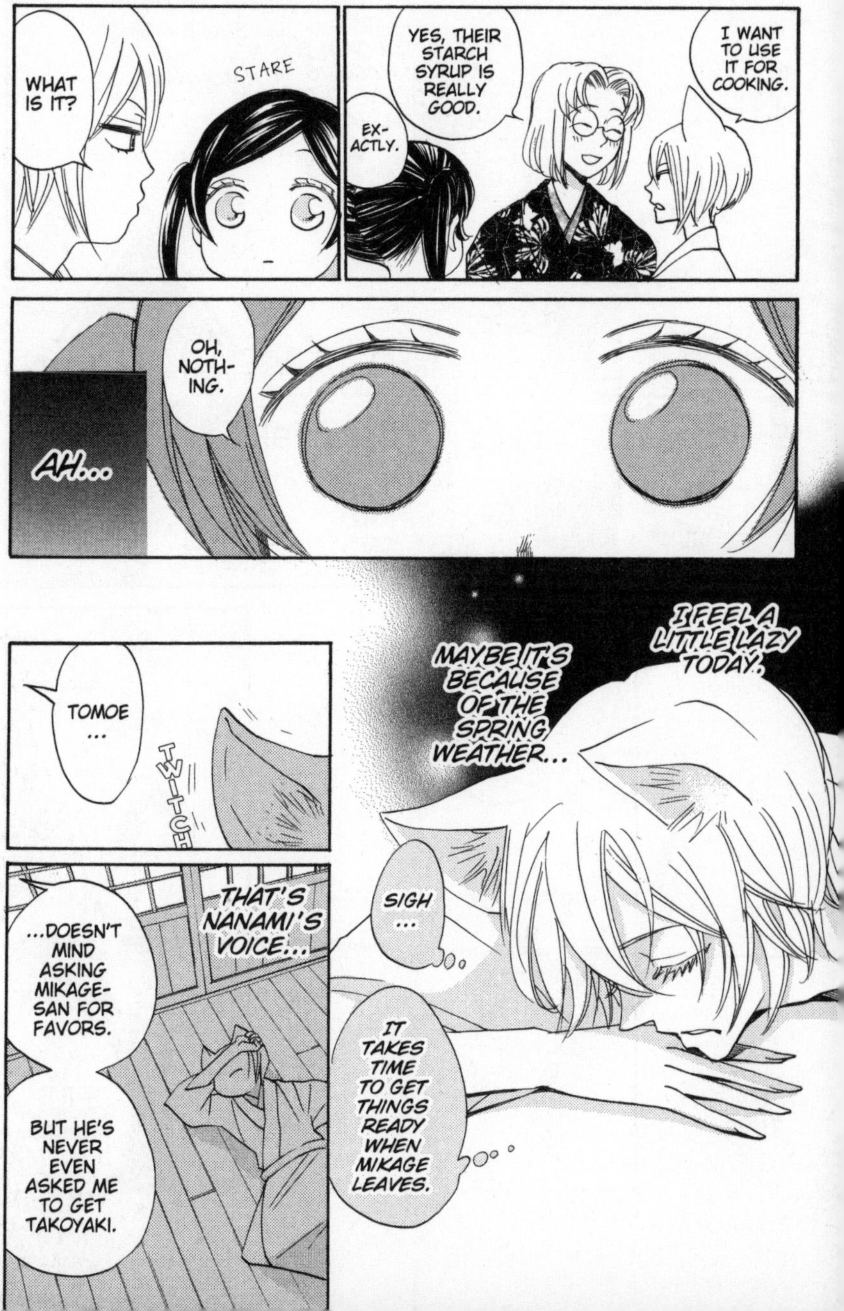
I WANT TO USE IT FOR COOKING.
YES, THEIR STARCH SYRUP IS REALLY GOOD.
EX-ACTLY.
STARE
WHAT IS IT?
OH, NOTH-ING.
AH...
I FEEL A LITTLE LAZY TODAY.
MAYBE IT'S BECAUSE OF THE SPRING WEATHER...
SIGH...
IT TAKES TIME TO GET THINGS READY WHEN MIKAGE LEAVES.
TOMOE...
TWITCH
THAT'S NANAMI'S VOICE...
...DOESN'T MIND ASKING MIKAGE-SAN FOR FAVORS.
BUT HE'S NEVER EVEN ASKED ME TO GET TAKOYAKI.

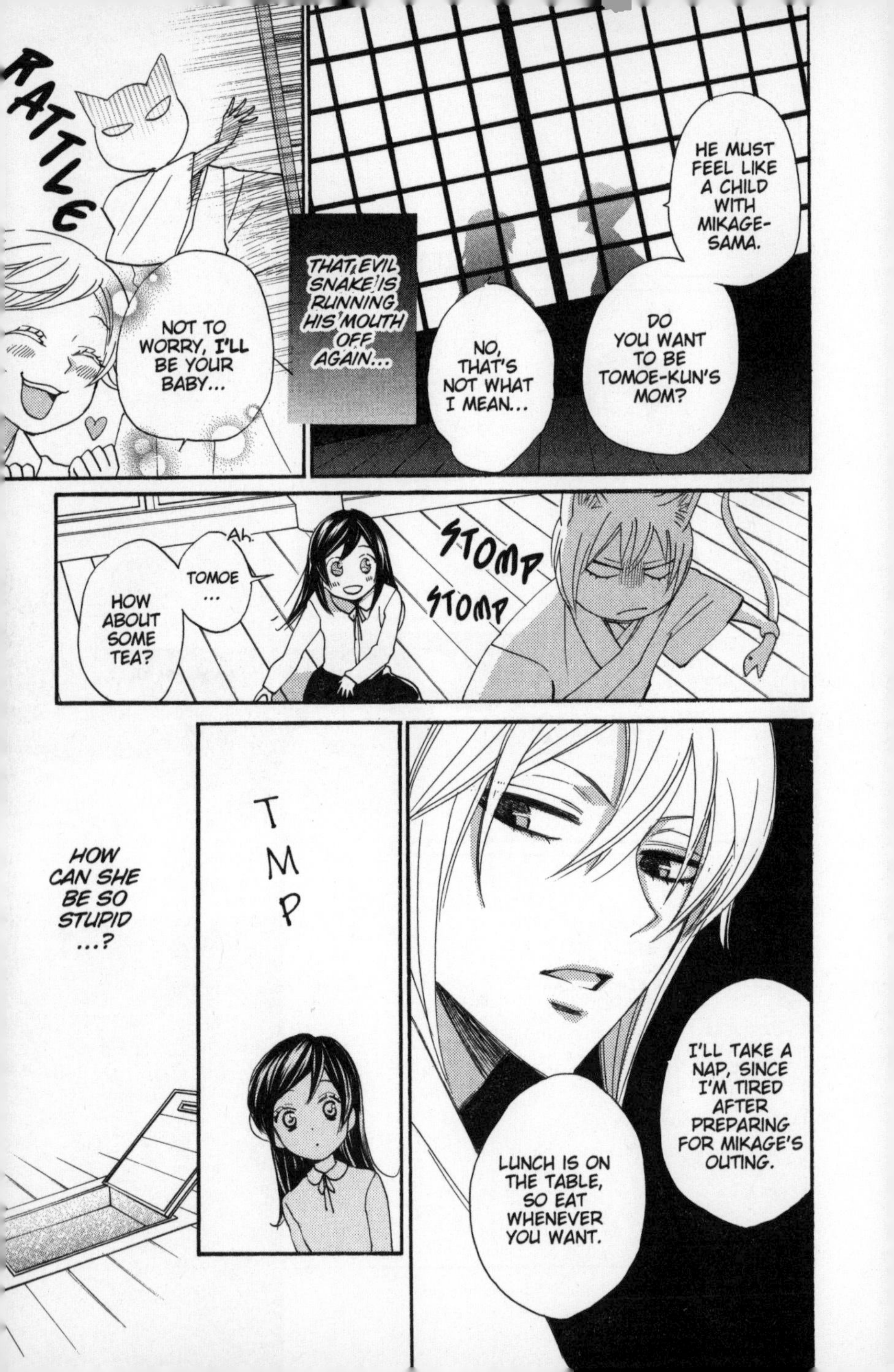
HE MUST FEEL LIKE A CHILD WITH MIKAGE-SAMA.
DO YOU WANT TO BE TOMOE-KUN'S MOM?
NO, THAT'S NOT WHAT I MEAN...
THAT EVIL SNAKE IS RUNNING HIS MOUTH OFF AGAIN...
RATTLE
NOT TO WORRY, I'LL BE YOUR BABY...
STOMP
STOMP
Ah.
TOMOE ...
HOW ABOUT SOME TEA?
I'LL TAKE A NAP, SINCE I'M TIRED AFTER PREPARING FOR MIKAGE'S OUTING.
LUNCH IS ON THE TABLE, SO EAT WHENEVER YOU WANT.
TMP
HOW CAN SHE BE SO STUPID ...?

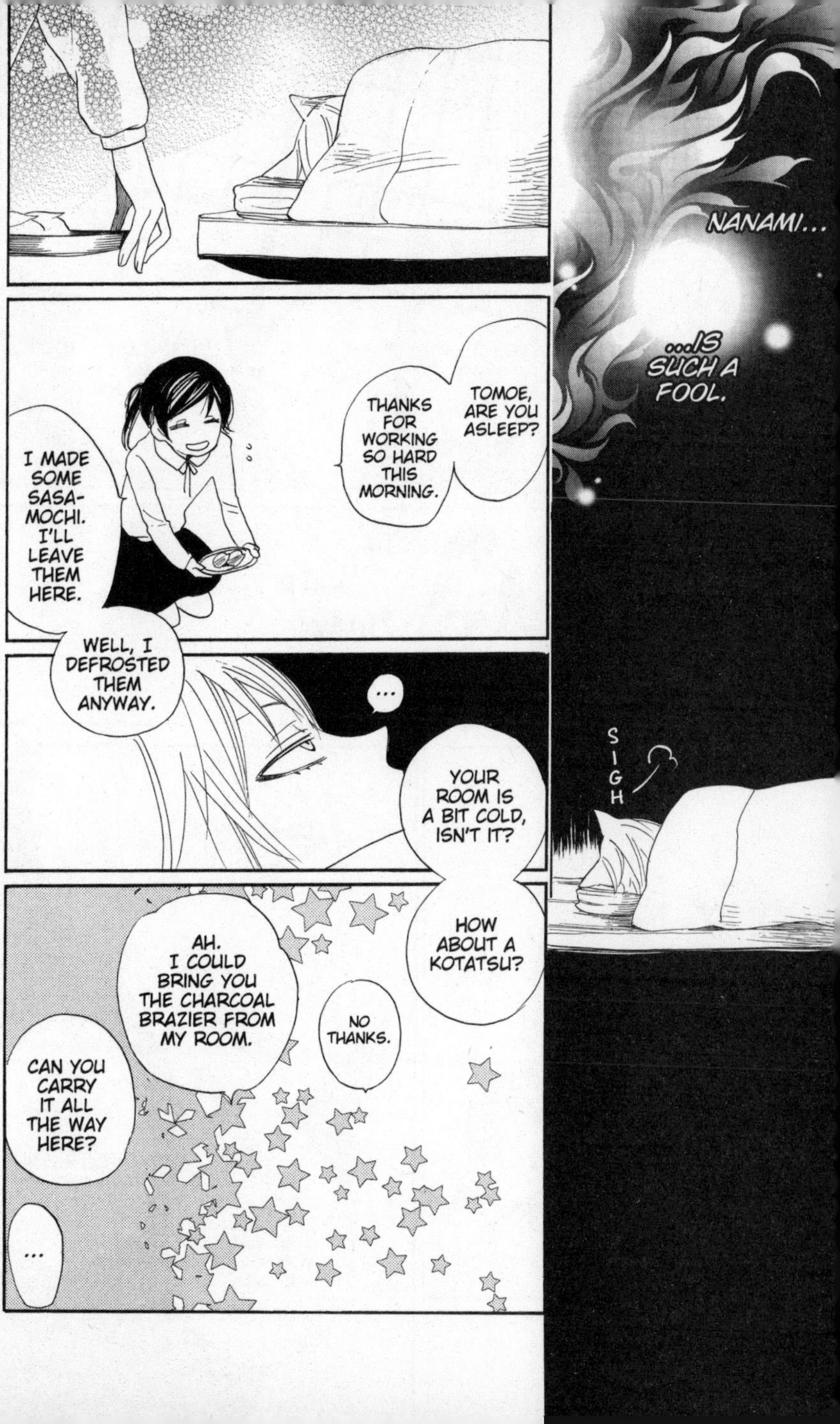
NANAMI...
...IS SUCH A FOOL.
SIGH
TOMOE, ARE YOU ASLEEP?
THANKS FOR WORKING SO HARD THIS MORNING.
I MADE SOME SASA-MOCHI. I'LL LEAVE THEM HERE.
WELL, I DEFROSTED THEM ANYWAY.
...
YOUR ROOM IS A BIT COLD, ISN'T IT?
HOW ABOUT A KOTATSU?
NO THANKS.
AH. I COULD BRING YOU THE CHARCOAL BRAZIER FROM MY ROOM.
CAN YOU CARRY IT ALL THE WAY HERE?
...

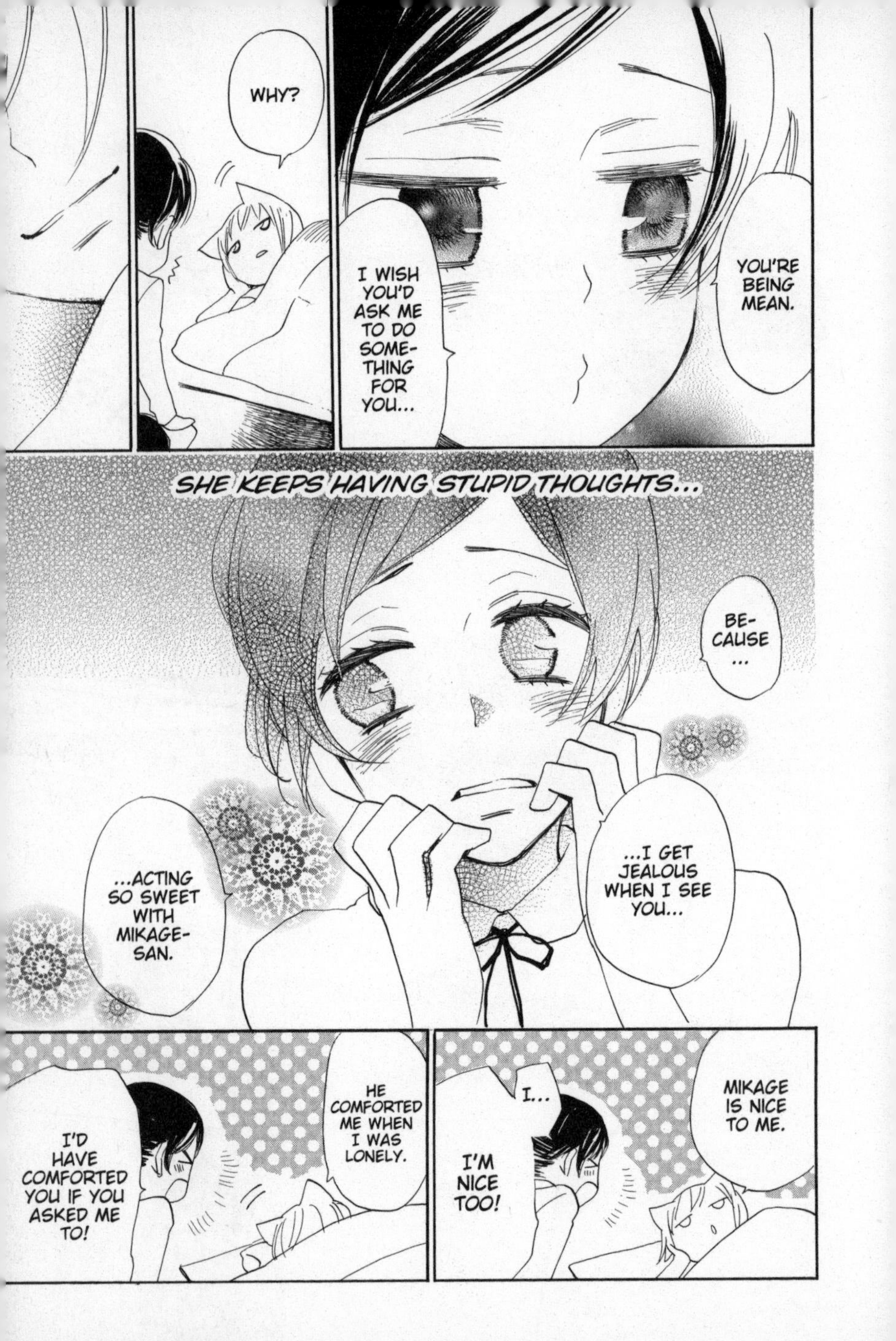
YOU'RE BEING MEAN.
I WISH YOU'D ASK ME TO DO SOME-THING FOR YOU...
WHY?
SHE KEEPS HAVING STUPID THOUGHTS...
BE-CAUSE ...
...I GET JEALOUS WHEN I SEE YOU...
...ACTING SO SWEET WITH MIKAGE-SAN.
MIKAGE IS NICE TO ME.
I...
I'M NICE TOO!
HE COMFORTED ME WHEN I WAS LONELY.
I'D HAVE COMFORTED YOU IF YOU ASKED ME TO!

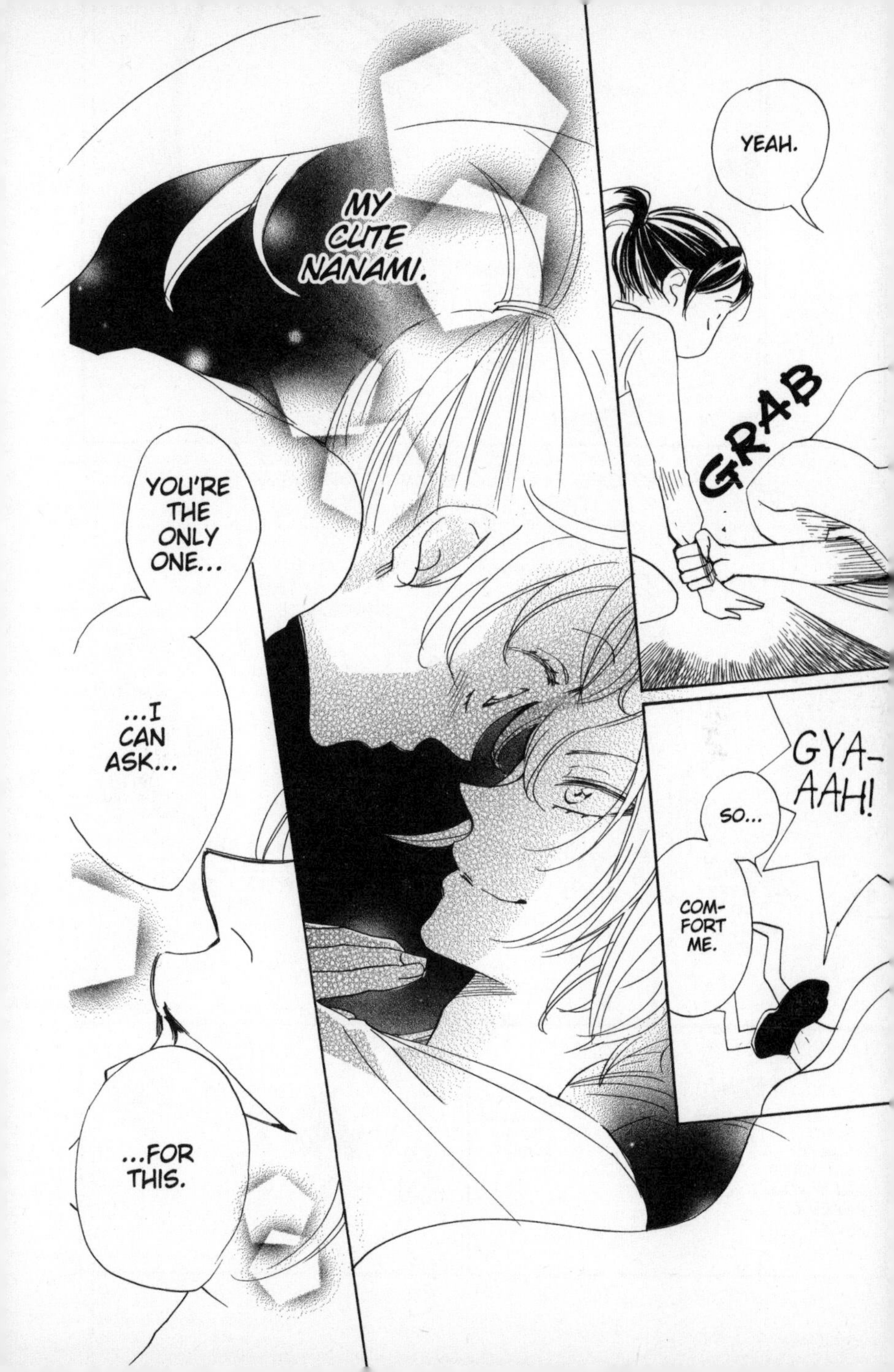
YEAH.
GRAB
GYA-AAH!
SO...
COMFORT ME.
MY CUTE NANAMI.
YOU'RE THE ONLY ONE...
...I CAN ASK...
...FOR THIS.

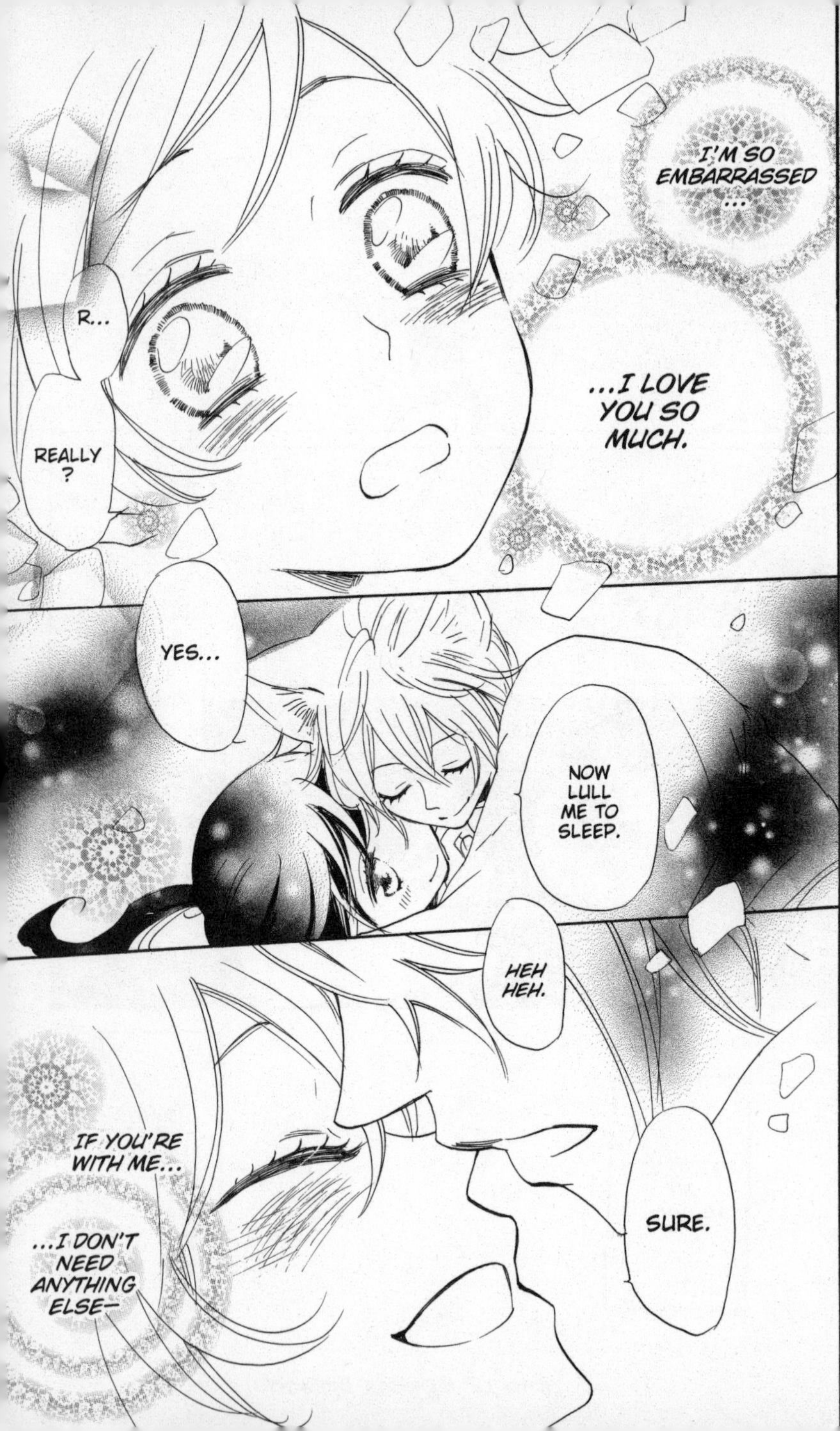
I'M SO EMBARRASSED ...
...I LOVE YOU SO MUCH.
R...
REALLY?
YES...
NOW LULL ME TO SLEEP.
HEH HEH.
SURE.
IF YOU'RE WITH ME...
...I DON'T NEED ANYTHING ELSE—

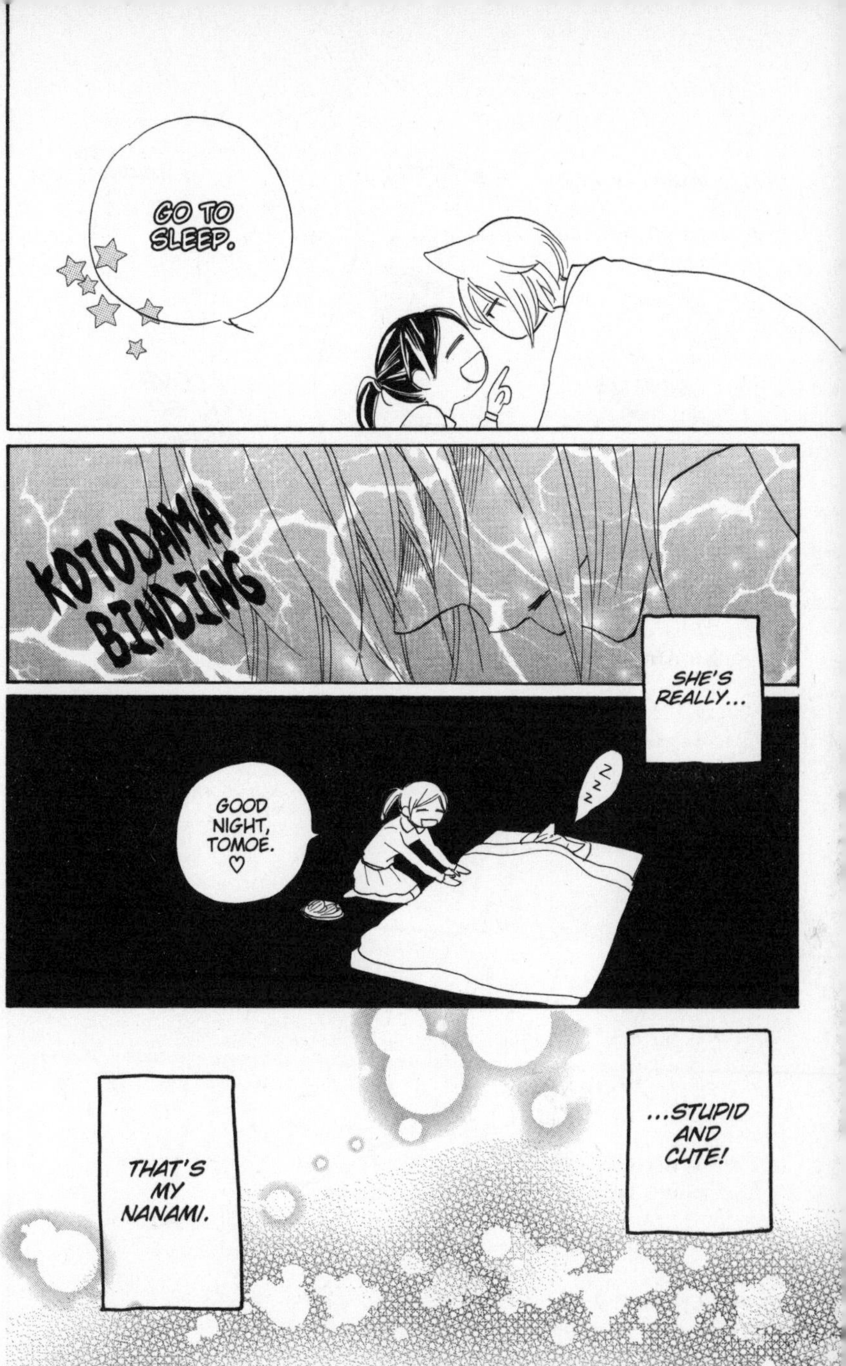
GO TO SLEEP.
KOTODAMA BINDING
SHE'S REALLY...
Z Z Z
GOOD NIGHT, TOMOE. ♡
...STUPID AND CUTE!
THAT'S MY NANAMI.

End of Special Episode

The Otherworld

Ayakashi is an archaic term for yokai.

Kami are Shinto deities or spirits. The word can be used for a range of creatures, from nature spirits to strong and dangerous gods.

Kitsunebi is literally "foxfire" and are the flames controlled by fox yokai.

Kotodama - is literally "word spirit," the spiritual power believed to dwell in words. In Shinto, the words you speak are believed to affect reality.

Onibi-warashi are like will-o'-the-wisps.

Shikigami are spirits that are summoned and employed by onmyoji (yin-yang sorcerers).

Shinshi are birds, beasts, insects or fish that have a special relationship with a kami.

Tengu are a type of yokai. They are sometimes associated with excess pride.

Tochigami (or *jinushigami*) are deities of a specific area of land.

Yokai are demons, monsters or goblins.

Honorifics

-chan is a diminutive most often used with babies, children or teenage girls.

-dono roughly means "my lord," although not in the aristocratic sense.

-kun is used by persons of superior rank to their juniors. It can sometimes have a familiar connotation.

-san is a standard honorific similar to Mr., Mrs., Miss or Ms.

-sama is used with people of much higher rank.

Notes

Page 23, panel 5: Izunami
Japanese goddess of creation and death, and wife of creator god Izanagi. She died giving birth to Kagu-tsuchi (a fire deity) and now rules the land of the dead.

Page 29, panel 2: Ama-no-iwato
The cave where Amaterasu retreated when her brother Susano'o was behaving badly. It literally means "Amaterasu's cave."

Page 51, panel 2: Izumo
A city in Shimane Prefecture and home to Izumo Oyashiro shrine, one of the most sacred sites in Shinto. Ôkuninushi (Daikokuten) is the kami enshrined in Izumo Oyashiro.

Page 191, panel 3: Starch syrup
Called *mizuame* ("water candy") in Japanese, it is a thick liquid sweetener made when starch is converted to sugars.

Page 192, panel 6: Takoyaki
Dough balls with pieces of octopus in them. They are made using a hot plate and are often sold at Japanese festivals. *Tako* means "octopus" in Japanese.

Page 194, panel 3: Sasamochi
Mochi (sticky rice cakes) wrapped in *sasa* (bamboo leaves).

Page 194, panel 5: Kotatsu
A low, wooden table frame with an electric heat source underneath. A futon or quilt is placed on the frame to keep the heat in, and a table is put on top of the futon.